# KUMARI JAYAWARDENA &
# MALATHI DE ALWIS

# Embodied Violence
*Communalising Women's Sexuality in South Asia*

# ZED BOOKS
**London & New Jersey**

*Embodied Violence: Communalising Women's Sexuality in South Asia*
is published in South Asia by Kali for Women,
B1/8 Hauz Khas, New Delhi 110 016,
and in the rest of the world by
Zed Books Ltd, 7 Cynthia St, London NI 9JF, UK and
165 First Avenue, Atlantic Highlands, New Jersey, 07716, USA, in 1996

Cover designed by Andrew Corbett

Typeset by Kali for Women
Printed and bound in the United Kingdom by
Biddles Ltd, Guildford and King's Lynn

A catalogue record for this available from the Library of Congress.

Zed Books
ISBN 1 85649 447 0 hb
ISBN 1 85649 448 9 pb

# Contents

vi   Contents

# Preface

The majority of papers in this collection were first presented at the conference on "Women: The State, Fundamentalism, and Cultural Identity in South Asia" which was held in Sri Lanka in March 1992 under the auspices of the Social Scientists' Association of Sri Lanka, with funding from the Canadian International Development Agency (CIDA).

The delay in publishing this volume was due to several reasons, both political and personal, and is a telling indictment on how challenged and over-stretched the feminist academic-activist is in South Asia. The ensuing years between the conference and this volume have witnessed a change of governments in Pakistan and Sri Lanka, communal riots in India and mass unrest in Bangladesh while at the same time, much energy has been expended in the various preparations leading upto the NGO Forum on Women in Beijing attended by around 40,000 women from across the globe.

We especially regret the fact that many who presented papers at the conference and participated in the lively discussions that often extended to the early hours of the morning were unable to re-work their papers in time due to their involvement in various other feminist projects. To Kamala Bhasin, Amrita Chhachhi, Nighat Said Khan and Ritu Menon, who were involved in planning this conference from its inception, we extend a special thank you. We are also indebted to Sepali Kottegoda, Shani Jayawardene and the staff at the Social Scientists' Association for the efficient coordination of the conference, as well as to the editorial staff at Kali for Women for their skilled input. Our sincere gratitude finally to our publisher Ritu Menon whose infinite patience and generosity of spirit—the quintessential attributes of a 'long-suffering' friend, propelled us to at least provide some kind of closure to this project.

This volume was conceived and gestated in troubled times; times in which fanaticism has a strangle-hold on the sub-continent; times in which the everyday lives of innocent citizens have become fraught with fear and suspicion, hatred and violence. While a significant percentage of South Asian women now actively participate as instruments of destruction in the military, in militant movements and as part of the strident forces of communalism, an even larger percentage of women continue to be at the receiving end of communalised rage and aggression. It is they who nurse their wounded, weep for their murdered and seek their 'disappeared', who watch their houses burn, languish in refugee camps, support their households and yet go on protest marches. It is they who are abducted, raped and tortured, their scarred minds and bodies embodiments of one community's shame and another's rage. Yet they go on living and resisting. It is to these women, courageous dissenters, survivors against all odds, that we dedicate this book.

Kumari Jayawardena & Malathi de Alwis

Colombo, September 1995

# Introduction

## Communalising women's sexuality in South Asia

KUMARI JAYAWARDENA
MALATHI DE ALWIS

Today we watch with horror as wave upon wave of right wing fanaticism, fundamentalism, bigotry and misogyny engulf South Asia, and chauvinist forces make deep inroads into politics. One of the most recurrent concerns articulated by the feminist movement in the 1990s is the alarming spread of fundamentalism. In South Asia, fundamentalist agendas are increasingly manipulating religious as well as ethnic and nationalist loyalties as a source of cultural legitimacy. The demolition of the Babri Masjid in India on December 6, 1992, and the ensuing massacre of Muslims in several states in India, as well as atrocities on Hindus in Bangladesh and Pakistan reflect the contemporary crisis of identity. In Sri Lanka, the fifteen year conflict between Tamils and Sinhala Buddhists has riven the country as the feud gets more bitter and violent with each passing day.

As we well know, such spectacular 'moments' of violence are merely the tip of the iceberg; what lies submerged is a long history of complex human relationships imbricated in constantly shifting nexuses of power. This history is of pressing concern for feminists since fundamentalism naturalises and sacralises the family and sexuality and secludes women from the public sphere. Fundamentalism uses women's bodies as a battlefield in its struggle to appropriate institutional power, and is therefore a political phenomenon.

The ideological base of identity politics and exclusivism is not new; it goes back a hundred years or so to a period of nationalist upsurge against both British rule and the foreign religion (Christianity). During colonialism, religious revivalism was a powerful opposition movement. This revivalism involved an assertion of a national identity and a cultural/linguistic consciousness that was constructed in opposition to the identity/culture imposed on colonised peoples by their European rulers. The revivalism of the majority communities had adverse effects on minorities and women. Women's biological role — motherhood — was important for carrying out the revivalist national project. Revivalism, with its logic of totalizing the nation with a view to levelling out internal social differentiation and suppressing class/ caste differences, always targets women first. As many feminists have pointed out, women were constructed as 'Mothers of the Nation' and their biological role as reproducers of the nation was highlighted. This instrumentalizes women's reproductive functions and their bodies in the interests of the State. The nationalist project, while drawing women out into the anti-imperialist struggle (addressing public meetings, running schools for girls, fighting for the right to vote, etc.), simultaneously imposed a new agenda for women as cultural carriers of tradition.

While the basis for identity has shifted within each country, each ethnic group still has its myths of origin (Aryan, Dravidian, Semitic) and its Golden Age in which women were 'free'. They were situated and idealised within a broader framework of a 'glorious' mythical past in which social divisions were absent. The inheritors of this past were 'sons of the soil' with claims to prior possession of the land. In such a context, the minorities were represented as invaders, outsiders or aliens who corrupted the pristine purity of the majority. They were accused of destroying ancient traditions and the old idyllic way of life and disrupting the political hegemony of a 'united' polity; most of all, they represented the threat of rape and thereby the possible 'pollution' of the 'daughters of the soil'. Again, women are reduced to their bodies, for as 'women-mother' they become (sex) objects in the possession of a male national collectivity. This is why the issue of rape takes on such a charged emotional aspect. As property of the national collective, the woman-mother symbolises the sacred, inviolable borders of the nation.

Nationalism in South Asia was not solely oppressive, it also produced a liberal reformist agenda to 'cleanse' some of the social evils of society. While certain women played an important role in the early stages of the nationalist projects, it was often men who shaped the agenda of social reform. It is also interesting to note that the emphasis fell on the family as the key social institution and on motherhood as women's primary role. Attempts were made to educate women, abolish sati and other evils and discourage female seclusion. But the ultra nationalists resisted legislative and reformist changes as an unwanted intrusion by the colonial government and local reformers into the 'sacred' space of domestic life.

Many of the social reformers who were active in the revivalist/ nationalist period focused on issues which would 'protect' women, rather than on their rights which would enable them to be more active subjects in the public domain. B. G. Tilak, who was ironically called Lokmanya (Revered by the World) led a social crusade in India in the 1890s, a period when the site of struggle between reformists and traditionalists was the issue of raising the 'age of consent' for females from 10 to 12. In Sri Lanka, Buddhist ideo- logues of the turn of the century such as the Anagarika Dharmapala, advocated a "Return to Righteousness", denouncing the decline of Sinhala Buddhists and the creation of a nation of 'bastards' and 'hybrids', through western influence.

The issue of symbolic and cultural representation was useful in opposing western political hegemony. Religious nationalism referred back to a better past in which women were a symbol of cultural purity. Women as a category were central in the recre- ation of community. This aspect of how they were viewed helps us to understand why constructions of the 'ideal woman' by revival- ists from the early twentieth century onwards, were so frequent.

In Sri Lanka, the ideal Sinhala-Buddhist woman was a 'pancha kalyani' (complete with fair skin, long black hair, attractive body, youthful appearance and beautiful teeth). The limits of her education were carefully stipulated, and the 'wife and mother' model promoted among the elite and lower middle classes in South Asia. Class became an important variable in the revivalist and nationalist movements. Educated middle class men sought "civilized (house) wives" and elaborated rules for the women of their ethnic group. Working class and peasant women of the same ethnic group were not their concern and the exploitation of poor women as cheap labour in agriculture, factories and plantations, continued. Constructions of 'ideal' women as representative of culture conform to this erasure of certain classes of women and certain types of labour performed by them.

## Constructions of femininity

In South Asia, during colonial times, there was a particular notion of 'respectability;' rules for 'respectable' women were laid down, traditions were invented, and the reconstructed ideal woman of the ethnic/ religious middle class group was represented as a symbol of its purity. It is for this reason that gender and class become central to understanding ethnic and social exclusivism, religious fanaticism and identity politics. Religious nationalism conflated class differences in the appeal to a better past — shifting the struggle of different social groups to 'imagined' areas of conflict such as women's dress. One of the targets of nationalist discourse was practices representing westernisation, considered a trespass on cultural integrity. Religious nationalism offered an alternative to the supposed 'ills' of 'modern' society. While religious revivalism treats women as passive subjects, women themselves may resist this and assert themselves as active subjects.

The liberal–left reformist tendencies of the anti-imperialist movement with its agenda of gender equity, secularism and democracy, were not vigorously pursued in the post-independence era. National liberation,—which upheld the vision of a new age, free from foreign rule, with full rights for minorities and women,— once achieved, was followed by disruptions of the nation-state. Based on ultra nationalism and religious fanaticism, this fissuring resulted in challenges to some of women's earlier won rights. Thus, whereas national liberation struggles were often positive for women, post-colonial nationalism in South Asia took on a chauvinist hue, tinged with misogyny. Today, the struggles against both national chauvinism and male chauvinism are led by the women's movements of South Asia. They highlight atrocities like sati, dowry deaths and all forms of violence against women, as well as patriarchal religious fanaticism that tries to manipulate and control them. This is done through religious laws and codes of conduct that enforce subservience and subordination and even extend to the invention of rules on women's dress and behaviour. It is significant that a Bangladeshi woman, Taslima Nasrin came to fame and notoriety with her novel *Lajja*, symbolising the two oppressions in South Asian society today: the oppression of minorities and women.

In South Asia, once a forced hegemonic identity was established, of Islam, Hinduism or Buddhism, any deviation from this straight and narrow path became 'unpatriotic' and, therefore, subversive. Women who converted from or denied the religion of their birth, or married into another race or ethnic group were specially marked out as threats to the existing order. One of the reigning demons has been Christianity, and Christians have been regarded by those of other religions as traitors to the nation. Christians became 'the Other' within. Women who converted were the worst culprits since they had abandoned their sacred role of 'reproducing the nation'. Christianity has been deemed the outside 'polluting' religion; the conversion of Pandita Ramabai in India, who as early as the 1880s, publicly denounced Hindu patriarchy and converted to Christianity, caused a sensation. These characteristics of religious nationalist discourse must be seen in the light of their broader implications for issues of national identity.

Just as early liberal nationalists understood the importance of drawing women into the anti-imperialist struggle and the modernising process, post-colonial purveyors of fanaticism of various kinds are trying to incorporate women into their retrograde movements, based on a mythic religious and ethnic identity. All over South Asia we see the phenomenon of right-wing fanaticism highlighting women 'leaders' and giving them roles to propagate religious and social messages. They are the new 'mothers in the fatherland' and it would be unrealistic to discount the use made of women for such political agendas, and the appeal of such right wing charismatic movements for women. Perhaps this is a new version of "the heart of the heartless world". Thus ultra-nationalist movements have used women as cultural representatives and constructed them in relation to western domination. Women are the carriers of 'authenticity'; this puts them in a difficult position vis-a-vis their gender and religious identities. This dilemma needs to be recognised as it helps us understand why some women accept their 'construction' in order to defend their culture.

The pressures of belonging to a minority discriminated community, for example, forced two Muslim women in India, Shehnaaz Sheikh and Shah Bano to temporarily suspend taking up the issues of divorce and maintenance on secular grounds, since the challenge to Muslim personal law was perceived as a threat to the identity of the Muslim community as a whole. This means that we need to locate identities within power relations and recognise that people have multiple identities. (Asserting one's gender identity loses its appeal if it is located within a struggle for one's ethnic identity.)

Not all women accept the manipulation of their gender identity, however. Repression produces resistance, and in South Asia women's consciousness of the dangers of religious fundamentalism and fanaticism has also increased. One hopeful sign in the region has been the growing resistance of women to these dangerous trends and the emergence of individual women who have spoken up in spite of death threats and harassment. In the 1970s and 1980s women in Pakistan were on the frontline of opposition to retrograde laws affecting women, such as the Hudood Ordinance. Inspite of organised mass hysteria women lawyers in Bangladesh and Pakistan have very bravely taken up the dangerous causes of Taslima Nasrin and Christian minorities, respectively. Feminists in Sri Lanka have, from the late 1970s, exposed the politics of Sinhala Buddhist chauvinists and their double standards in respect of women, and in India, vociferous women's groups have agitated on the Shah Bano case, sati, dowry deaths and the continuance of personal laws.

Despite the active role that women have played in challenging oppressive structures it is they who are the first to be marginalised, whether in the political or social sphere. Linked to ultra-nationalist and revivalist ideologies has been the tendency, over the past hundred years, to demonise the emergent 'new woman' of South Asia. For example, Hindu, Islamic and Buddhist 'revivals' of the late nineteenth century — which were part of the nationalist project — spoke of the Aryan woman of Vedic times, the women in early Buddhism and women in the Koran as 'liberated' women. Women's decline was attributed to outside invasions in historical epochs, or to colonial rule and missionary influence. The spread of modern education, talk of 'women's rights' and the entry of women into professions in South Asia led ideologues of various religious traditions to denounce these women as foreign influenced, corrupt and immoral. Women were viewed as potential disruptors and it is their behaviour which became/becomes targetted for control.

Women's experience has been influenced by the rise of religious nationalist discourse. Nationalism attempts to legitimate the collective in time and space. Part of the appeal of nationalism is that it emerges in relation to an external threat to the collective.

Activists in the nationalist project gain energy from an appeal to ethical resistance. Women are seen to be the repository of tradition and their 'inviolability' has been a powerful tool of cultural defence against modernisation and westernisation. Nonetheless the control of women's bodies as the symbolic space of the nation has often involved women's oppression. They have resisted this 'construction' as it has often been accompanied by their subordination.

The political implications of the gender/ethnicity divide relate to whether a unified women's movement is possible. Women's organisations may limit themselves to organising on the basis of ethnicity; this means that gender subordination takes second place in the context of an appeal to ethnic identity. This needs to be challenged since ethnic identification can lead to increasing conflict. As to the idealisation of women, the problem with the reification of the role of women is that it has conflated class/ caste issues. This is one of the problems with nationalism — it seeks to homogenise. This may be possible in response to an external threat, but once the threat recedes, social and economic difference will reappear and expose the illusory nature of the homogeneous national self. Plurality within society dislodges the myths of nationalists. This may be one reason why nationalists spend so much energy recreating the religious/ ethnic enemy within, whether it is Christian, Muslim, Hindu, Sinhala or Tamil. Creating an internal disruptor is the way nationalists try to transcend internal differentiation. For a nation-state with different ethnic groups this poses problems for continuity and peaceful co-existence. That is why it is important to deconstruct national/ethnic identity. Challenging sexism may help to expose the illusory promises of nationalism. If women can understand their own oppression they will be better placed to understand other oppressions since they are linked and supported by similar social structures.

This collection of essays is centrally concerned with exploring the articulation of communal violence within particular nexuses of power. Rather than concentrate on the event of violence per se we wish to focus on how such violence reconfigures women's experiences, how it 'facilitates' the formation of particular identities and the dissemination of specific ideologies, and how it positions women vis a vis their communities as well as the State. Our intellectual labour follows the trajectory of inquiry charted by recent feminist texts such as *Recasting Women: Essays in Colonial History* and *Forging Identities: Gender, Communities and the State*. Through its project to interrogate the historical, economic and political processes that reconstituted patriarchy in colonial India, *Recasting Women* provided a critical contribution to the field of feminist historiography as well as to debates on nationalism, by extending the feminist problematic beyond the constricting paradigms of reform and reawakening, delineating how "the underbelly of every attempt towards identity has been a redescription of women of different classes".[1] *Forging Identities*, compiled in the aftermath of recent anti-Muslim pogroms and the ascendance of Hindu right-wing organisations in India, attempts to fracture stereotyped notions of a monolithic religion — Islam — and a homogeneous community — the Muslims — by producing nuanced readings of Muslim women's positioning within their own community as well as their relationship to broader processes such as the law, the economy, the State, etc. The reaffirmation of religio-cultural distinctions and identities in the face of heightening Hindu consciousness is questioned in the light of strictures placed upon Muslim women's rights and interests by community/ religious leaders who, thus, not only legitimise repressive patriarchal regimes but often collude with the State in the socialisation and creation of such a Muslim identity, "so that community and State legitimise and reproduce each other".[2]

In the face of these texts' sustained and rigorous interrogation of the formation of communalised and gendered identities in (largely) north India, we have been somewhat ambitious by attempting to extend our analysis of similar processes to Pakistan, Sri Lanka and Bangladesh. While we make no claims to be representative, we hope that such an exercise will at least enable useful comparisons and provocative juxtapositions for what it might lose in terms of representativeness or range. By giving exposure to the work of younger feminist scholars/activists along with that of their more seasoned and experienced colleagues, we also hope to encourage a dialogue not merely across regions, but across generations as well.

I

" 'Communalism' today means the advocacy of violence," noted

Gyan Pandey.[3] We are interested here in pursuing the question of how communalism, operating within patriarchal structures of power, implies the advocacy of violence, often sexual violence, towards women. Communal violence frequently resorts to the violation of the 'Other's' woman for, as Kamala Visweswaran reminds us, a woman's modesty signifies the masculinity of her community. She becomes "the symbol of violence as the shame and subjection of her community is represented in her".[4] Ironically, the common denominator that cuts across all communities, and often classes as well in South Asia, remains notions of female modesty. The sexual and moral codes imposed on women, codified and disseminated through hegemonic patriarchal institutions and instruments such as the State, law, religious tenets and their interpreters, the school, the family, etc., share many similarities, despite their being categorised as Muslim, Christian, Hindu, Buddhist and so on.

As several feminists have noted over the years, patriarchal discourses on the modesty of women are really about sexuality. Sexuality, which Michel Foucault posits as a "dense transfer point for relations of power. . . one of those endowed with the greatest instrumentality"[5] is even more boldly defined as a "vector of oppression" by feminist Gayle Rubin who asserts that much of the oppression of women is "borne by, mediated through, and constricted within sexuality".[6] While many Euro-American feminists, from the Sixties onwards, have attempted to deconstruct the patriarchal equation of sexuality with danger as well as to rediscover the pleasures of female sexuality (a project which has been embraced by contemporary South Asian feminists as well), one cannot ignore the present escalation of sexually repressive practices and rhetoric in collocation with the heightening of communal consciousness. Such changes are frequently marked upon or through the woman's body, as an increasing number of young Muslim women adopt the veil in South Asia, or widow immolation is revived in north India, for example.

The centrality of the woman's body in communalised discourses and practices is particularly well articulated in our opening essay by Ritu Menon and Kamla Bhasin, on the 'recovery' of abducted women from India and Pakistan, post-Partition. In the same way that Hindu sacred sites are forcibly reclaimed from the grasp of 'usurping' Muslims today, Hindu women were forcibly recovered form the 'polluting' embrace of Muslim men several decades ago. The Indian State was not merely concerned with the physical recovery of converted women; their grasp extended to the products of these women's bodies, i.e., their offspring, especially "any male child below the age of 16". This dismembering of 'illegal' families and communities and the violent negation of women's agency and rights was conducted in the interests of a secure Hindu nation by a seemingly secular State. As Menon and Bhasin point out, this proposed 'amicable' exchange of women's bodies between the two nations was a much more charged issue for India than Pakistan possibly because it was India that had to reconcile itself to its own dismemberment and diminution and thus needed to reassure itself that it could still fulfil its duties towards its citizens "both in the matter of securing what was their due, and in confirming itself as their protector". Originally abducted as war booty, these women were once again reduced to the status of goods and chattel, their reclaimed bodies and their products providing a crucial statistic through which a nation's masculinity could be gauged; their 'recovery' thus, was not a project of salvation but a battle for virility.

Menon and Bhasin, who have sensitively attempted to put faces to these now nameless statistics of 'recovered' women, also endeavour to disrupt the 'official' narratives of Partition through the voices as well as the silences of these raped, humiliated, murdered, abducted, reclaimed, rejected women who, despite their seeming helplessness in the face of multiple patriarchies of the State, the police, the community and the family, resisted at every turn. Similarly, Kalpana Kannabiran's essay on the rape of Rameeza Bee—another unremembered name added to the escalating statistic of sexual violence in India—argues against the patriarchy of the legal system, the State and the community which attempts to displace and even legitimise the violence that was done to Rameeza by communalising and sexualising her. By forcing Rameeza to prove that she was a 'good' Muslim and a 'moral' woman, the Commission of Enquiry—an instrument of the Indian State—initiates a particular reconstitution of her identity that is more in keeping with hegemonic patriarchal and nationalist notions that the woman's place is within her family and community; any woman who refuses such a definition warrants punishments such as rape which the representatives of the State and the upholders of the law (the police) are so assiduous in meting out. The more marginalised women are in terms of ethnicity, class and status, the less access they have to justice and redress for such 'punishments'.

## II

Patriarchal hegemony is such that it does not rely on sexual violence alone to keep women in check. As feminists across the globe have demonstrated, one of the most successful ways in which women's sexuality was controlled and disciplined was by confining them within the home and interpellating them into predominantly subordinate and familial subject positions such as daughter, sister, wife and mother. Such interpellations were facilitated through 'ideological state apparatuses' such as the family, the school, media, religious institutions, etc.[7] Our next essay by Shahnaz Rouse discusses why Muslim reformers of various ideological orientations in colonial north India, concurred on the centrality of (segregated) women's education in preparing Muslim women to participate in the construction of the future Muslim Nation and the establishment of a middle class hegemony; it would better equip them "to preserve and protect their cultural heritage and pass it onto their children in their role as mothers and caretakers". While Rouse stresses the fact that Muslim male reformers would not have been able to reach their goal of 'emancipating women' without the consent and agency of women themselves, she also acknowledges the fact that such a cultural and national assertion could only be achieved at the expense of women. The structures of power within which nineteenth century Muslim men often quelled women's voices continues under different formulations within the contemporary nation of Pakistan. One of the best kept secrets, Rouse points out, has been the contribution of Pakistani women to the economy.

Pursuing a similar trajectory as Rouse, Sonia Amin concentrates on giving voice to the everyday lives of Muslim women in late nineteenth century Bengal. Through their reminiscences and writings, Amin recreates for the reader how the sexuality of upper and middle class Muslim women was both literally and metaphorically confined and controlled within the spatial configurations of the *andar mahal* (inner domain). However, as modernity and urbanisation encroached upon these 'traditional' elite families, it was no longer necessary to exercise such overt control on women. Modernity's valorisation of the educated woman provided new avenues for the interpellation of Muslim women into 'ideal woamanhood' and citizenship. The difference now was that the proliferation of cheaply-printed didactic manuals for the "pious but practical Muslim girl" (to take one example), insisted upon agency; "they were meant to be read by the girls themselves, comprehended intellectually, emotionally, and acted upon". Yet, hegemonies are constantly contested and resisted and along with the stereotyped, patriarchal role models of Muslim women, there also flourished role models such as Rokeya Sakhawat Hussein, the pioneer of Muslim women's awakening in Bengal, whose biography was included as a school text in the 1930s.

Sonia Amin's discussion of the interiorisation and domestication of women's bodies is continued, albeit in a different register, by Malathi de Alwis through her analysis of scholarly discourses that sought to displace or deny the sensuality of female bodies represented at Sigiriya, an archaeological site in Sri Lanka. The scholar's valiant efforts to discursively clothe these female bodies as well as locate them within the 'protective' custody of community, religion and patriarchy provides an illuminating entre into the ideological underpinnings of Sinhala Buddhist nationalism in post-independence Sri Lanka; it had to be conclusively established that the female figure "has always been treated with restraint and dignity" in the 'spiritual' East. Yet, the scholars' endeavours to 'de-sexualize' one of the most famous national treasures and crucial links with the 'golden past' of the Sinhalese was contested from within this past and complicated by the dictates of capitalism that pushed an impoverished Third World nation to entice foreign tourists by advertising the very eroticism of its archaic beauties that it had so assiduously tried to 'cover up'.

Jasodhara Bagchi's essay speaks to similar concerns that animate de Alwis, especially in her interrogation of Hindu nationalist and fundamentalist attempts to sacralise the sexuality of Hindu women. As Bagchi points out, Hindu nationalists' efforts to overthrow colonialism and re-invent their 'golden past' hinged upon the "increasing identification of the woman question with the purity of the Shastric injunctions"; in the same way that the religious scriptures were purified and re-interpreted, so were their women reformed and recast in accordance with these sanitised, textual injunctions. While the imagined glorious past of the Hindus bore testimony to their superiority over the polluted usurpers of their land, in the nationalists' reckoning, the purity and morality of elite Hindu women was essential for the rejuvenation of a subjugated nation. This differentiation of a pure Hindu culture and womanhood from those of the 'Other' was further cemented through the employment of mythological and religious role models. These are the very same archetypes that are mobilised by contemporary Hindu fundamentalists under the guise of 'empowering' mass movements of women, while ensuring that they do so for limited and patriarchal ends.

Paola Bacchetta, who has spent several years studying the rhetoric and practices of one such fundamentalist organisation, the Rashtriya Swayamsevak Sangh, discusses in depth the notion of women's 'empowerment' when articulated in the cadences of racism and violence, and its wider implications of making female subordination tolerable and more durable. By allowing the female wing of the RSS, the Samiti, relative autonomy to formulate its "feminine affirming" discourses within its male wing, the Sangh (the RSS) cleverly ensures the complicity of its women members in remaining the "obligatory exclusive communal property" of their men and of the Hindu community at large. Thus, "the borders between communities are policed at the most intimate levels: that of women's consciousness and of their emotions". Such policing of borders, by the Sangh, extends to the geographical and feminised ones of Bharatmata (Mother India) as well as with militant calls for its cleansing through the demolition of mosques — metonyms of what is represented as Muslim male sexual and communal aggression.

We move to yet other metaphors of woman in Neloufer de Mel's essay which focusses on contemporary Sri Lankan war poetry written by women from different class and ethnic backgrounds. These women's writings, which spiritedly confront their marginalisation in an increasingly militarized society riven with ethnic and class hostilities, nevertheless cannot escape "investing in the persona of the Mother, the totality of a woman's identity". Yet, such internalisations by those at the margins continue to be fraught with contradictions and ambiguities; while one poet's exploration of female passions impels her "to write of the topogra-

phy of the female body, positing it as a locus of sexuality and pain",
another's strategy would be a rejection of sexual pleasure in the
hope of seeking from her political comrades, a love that is of 'the
purest kind'. The recognition of such contradictions in the making of women's identities, notes de Mel, is a crucial step towards
confronting the contradictions at the centre which are made
invisible through the hegemony of patriarchy.

## III

Our final two essays are centrally concerned with the bodies and
minds of a particular group of women who have been marginalised,
exploited, violated and persecuted through the ages—widows. As
Uma Chakravarti cogently argues in her extensive essay on the
intersection of gender, Brahmanical patriarchy and nationalism,
debates around landmark legal 'events' such as the Widow
Remarriage Act and the Age of Consent Bill in nineteenth century
India centred on the status of the widow in society and the ownership
and regulation of her sexuality; men wrote about the 'unspeakable';
'delicacy of speech' was thrown to the winds, and the Indian
woman's body was subjected to unprecedented scrutiny. While
providing an invaluable history of how such 'events' enable
opportunists like Tilak to consolidate a Brahmanical Hindu
hegemony, Chakravarti also foregrounds the struggles of an
extraordinary widow, Ramabai, who fought almost single-handedly
to resist the Brahmanical patriarchal control imposed on widows
by integrating these hitherto marginalised women into society and
thus "reconceptualising widowhood and womanhood in a way that
most male reformers could never conceive". However, the critique
of Brahmanical patriarchy that she launched was deflected (for
the moment, successfully) by branding Ramabai a betrayer.
Brahmanical Hindu patriarchal hegemony sought to defuse a
critique of religion and patriarchy, thus ensuring that consent to
patriarchal practice was not withdrawn.
     From the failure of the struggles of widows under colonialism,
we move to an even more insidious practice that is gaining
ascendance today — widow immolation — which as Kumkum
Sangari and Sudesh Vaid note, "is one of the most violent of
patriarchal practices" both in the degree of consent it has received
and the supportive institutions and ideological formations that

rationalise and mythologise it. Providing a crucial analytical distinction between sati and widow immolation, Sangari and Vaid point out that belief in sati "can transform everyday consent to patriarchy into a menacing form of social agency during an immolation"; simultaneous with the representation of consent also occurs a wresting of consent, from the widow, her family, her community. At the same time, the exceptional and spectacular event of widow immolation which is fetishised "is made to do ideological work in the everyday sphere". It is made to ensure the continued subjugation and control of women within the patriarchal structures of family, community and religion in the face of 'evils' such as urbanisation, modernity and westernisation.

In this brief introduction we have sought to locate particular convergences that link these essays together. Our concern with communalism, operating within and through patriarchal structures of power, has particularly foregrounded its varied impositions on women's bodies, as it has legitimised the regulation of their sexuality, their interiorisation and silencing, and rationalised their commodification, their rape and immolation. Such embodied violence, be it overt or subtle, consensual or coercive, has nevertheless been continuously and spiritedly contested both by individual women as well as the women's movements in South Asia. While Pandita Ramabai denounced Hindu patriarchy in India in the 1880s, Taslima Nasrin received a death sentence for her outspoken comments about the persecution of Hindus and women in Bangladesh in the 1990s. In the face of much slander and vituperation, the Women's Franchise Union in Ceylon championed the right of women from all classes and communities to be given the right to vote in 1927, while the Women's Action Forum in Pakistan has been at the forefront of challenges to the authority reposed in the repressive Hudood Ordinance, from the 1980s. Yet, what remains to be seen is whether the women's movement will be strong enough to counter the increasing hegemony of fundamentalist and militant organisation's/parties over masses of women. How much longer will this Women's Action Forum song hold true?

No longer friendless in the world around us
No longer helpless, no longer weak
It is only your fancy
That we sleep, yet unconscious.[8]

## Notes

1. Kumkum Sangari and Sudesh Vaid, "Introduction" in Kumkum Sangari Sudesh Vaid (eds.) *Recasting Women: Essays in Colonial History*. (Delhi: Kali for Women, 1989), p.9.

2. Zoya Hasan, "Introduction" in Zoya Hasan (ed.) *Forging Identities: Gender, Communities and the State*. (Delhi: Kali for Women, 1994), p.ix.

3. Gyanendra Pandey, "Introduction" in Gyanendra Pandey (ed.), *Hindus and Others: The Question of Identity in India Today* (Delhi: Viking/Penguin, 1993), p.2.

4. Kamala Visweswaran, "Family Subjects: An Ethnography of the Women's Question in Indian Nationalism" (PhD thesis, Stanford University, 1990), p.68.

5. Michel Foucault, *History of Sexuality*, Vol.I. trans. Robert Hurley (Penguin Books, 1981), p.103.

6. Gayle Rubin, "Thinking Sex: Notes for a Radical Theory of the Politics of Sexuality" in Carole S Vance, *Pleasure and Danger: Exploring Female Sexuality* (ed.) (London: Routledge & Kegan Paul, 1984), pp.293 & 300-01.

7. cf. Louis Althusser, "Ideology and the Ideological State Apparatus," in *Lenin and Philosophy and Other Essays* (London: New Left Books, 1971), especially pp.162-63.

8. Quoted in Khawar Mumtaz and Farida Shaheed, *Women of Pakistan: Two Steps Forward, One Step Back?* (Karachi: Vanguard Books, 1987), p.123.

# Abducted Women, the State and Questions of Honour

## Three perspectives on the recovery operation in post-Partition India

RITU MENON
KAMLA BHASIN

The substance of this paper is set against the background of the partition of India in 1947, the creation of Pakistan, and the ensuing turmoil as both countries struggled to cope with the aftermath of division. As an event of shattering consequence, Partition retains its pre-eminence even today, despite a couple of wars on our borders and wave after wave of communal violence. It marks a watershed as much in people's consciousness as in the lives of those who were uprooted and had to find themselves again, elsewhere. Chronologies are still qualified with 'before Partition' or 'after Partition'; personal histories are punctuated with references to it, so much so that it sometimes seems as if two quite distinct, rather than concurrent, events took place at independence, and that Partition and its effects are what have lingered in collective memory. Each new eruption of hostility or expression of difference swiftly recalls that bitter and divisive erosion of social relations between Hindus, Muslims and Sikhs, and each episode of brutality is measured against what was experienced then. The rending of the social and emotional fabric that took place in 1947 is still far from mended.

Official and even historical accounts of Partition see it as the unfortunate outcome of sectarian and separatist politics, and as a tragic accompaniment to the exhilaration and promise of a freedom fought for with courage and valour. They have looked at the causes and consequences of the division of the country, analysed the details of the many 'mistakes' and 'miscalculations' made, examined the genesis of the call for a Muslim Homeland, and so on. But when we start looking for social histories or for accounts that try to piece together the fractured reality of the time and of the event itself from a non-official perspective — a perspective from the margins, as it were — we encounter a curious void. Perhaps it has·been too painful, too difficult to separate personal experience from corroborated fact, too hazardous, at least for those who tried to record it, to claim 'objectivity'. Indeed, so far only some 'fiction' seems to have tried to assimilate the enormity of the experience.

For those of us who may or may not have lived through Partition but who did witness the massacre of Sikhs in 1984 and heard the survivors, especially the widows, recall the violence and brutality of 1948, the question of how such events are recorded, and by whom, returns to haunt us and acquires greater urgency with each subsequent episode. Recent considerations of how such accounts are to be written, of the place of personal testimony and of bearing witness, of the desirability of reconstructing biographies or trusting memory or the collective re-telling of tragedy, have highlighted the importance of each of these aspects in presenting an alternative construction of what took place.[1] They have raised the question of the authenticity of such recording—individual bias, political stance, ideology, class and gender, all become factors that are critical to any analysis or representation. When one is trying to unravel the complexity of an event that took place forty-five years ago but still reverberates in the general consciousness, the enterprise becomes even more treacherous. But without such an attempt, the myriad individual and collective histories that simultaneously run parallel to official accounts of historic moments, and are their sequel, almost inevitably get submerged; with them may also be submerged the countering of accepted—and acceptable—versions, to be buried eventually in the rubble of what Gyan Pandey has called the "aberrations" of history.[2]

What is presented here is in the nature of an exploration, an attempt to communicate an experience of Partition through those whose voices have hitherto been absent in any re-telling of it: women who were destituted in one way or another by the event, as forced mass migrations led to an extreme disruption of life at all levels and exposed them to a kind of upheaval that could only proclaim the dark side of freedom. In their recall, the predominant memory is of confusion, dislocation and a severing of roots as they were forced to reckon with the twin aspect of freedom— disintegration and bewildering loss: of place and property, no doubt, but more significantly, of community, of a network of more or less stable relationships, and of a coherent identity. Overriding all these was a violence that was horrifying in its intensity, and one which knew no boundaries; for many women, it was not only 'miscreants', 'outsiders' or 'marauding mobs' that they needed to fear—husbands, fathers, brothers and even sons, could turn killers.[3] That terrible stunning violence and then the silencing pall that descended like a shroud around it have always just hovered at the edges of history; the story of 1947, while one of the attainment of independence, is also a gendered narrative of displacement and dispossession, of large-scale and widespread communal violence, and of the realignment of family, community and national identities as a people were forced to accomodate the dramatically altered reality that now prevailed.

The location of women at the intersection of all these forces, rather than at their periphery, casts an entirely new light on the apparent fixity of defining features of identity like community, religion, nationality. We propose to do this through an examination of the Central Recovery Operation of the Government of India, carried out between 1948–56, which sought to recover those women who had been abducted and forcibly converted during the upheaval, and restore them to their respective families and countries, where they 'rightfully belonged'.

The material is presented in three voices: the voice of the government, bureaucrats and Members of Parliament; the voices of women themselves; and lastly, those of the social workers to whom the work of rehabilitation and resettlement of recovered women was entrusted. Through these three perspectives we hope to demonstrate how ambiguous and conflictual the relationship was between the governments of India and Pakistan; between government officers, social workers and the women to be recovered; between the State and its citizens; between Hindus, Muslims and Sikhs; and finally between the women and their families and society. We argue that it was a particular construction of the identity of the abducted woman that determined the entire recovery operation, one that raises serious questions regarding the Indian State's definition of itself as secular and democratic. We further argue that the State, in its articulation of gender identity and public policy, underlined the primacy of community identity and, implicitly and explicitly, departed from its neutrality in assigning values to the 'legitimate' family and community 'honour', and that it did so through a regulation of women's sexuality. Indeed, through legislation and executive and police action; it effectively reconstituted the multiple patriarchies at work in women's lives within the family and community, and as embedded in institutions and social mores. Finally, it is our contention that it is only when this shift of perspective takes place that the discourse of the State can be interrogated and its assumed secularity challenged.

Our archive is constituted of extensive and intensive interviews with women who survived the trauma of dislocation, of whom many are to be found in homes, rehabilitation centres and shelters even today, in Punjab and Haryana; in-depth interviews with women social workers who were entrusted with the work of rescue, recovery and rehabilitation; interviews with those government officials who were in charge of the various agencies that were set up to co-ordinate relief and rehabilitation; private papers, diaries and autobiographical accounts of those who were engaged in this activity; government documents, and reports of fact-finding committees, private and public; and the Constituent Assembly of India (Legislative) Debates, 1949.[4]

## I

The Hindustan-Pakistan Plan was announced on 3 June 1947 whereby a new political entity, Pakistan, was created, of which West Pakistan was to comprise the Muslim-majority provinces of Sind, the NWFP and 16 districts of Punjab; the remaining 13 districts of undivided Punjab were to be part of India. Although the exact boundary line between the two countries had still to be determined by the Boundary Commission, the exchange of populations had started taking place even before 15 August. Within a week of independence about 11 lakh Hindus and Sikhs had crossed over from West to East Punjab, and in the week following, another 25 lakhs had collected in the refugee camps in West Punjab.[5] By 6 November, 1947 nearly 29,000 refugees had been flown in both directions; about 673 refugee trains were run between 27 August and 6 November, transporting 23 lakh refugees inside India and across the border—of these 13,62,000 were non-Muslim, and 9,39,000 were Muslim. Huge foot convoys, each 30–40,000 strong were organised by the Military Evacuation Organisation and Liaison Agency to move the bulk of the rural population, especially those who still had their cattle and bullock-carts with them. The estimate is that in 42 days (18 September to 29 October) 24 non-Muslim foot columns, 8,49,000 strong, had crossed into India.[6] By the time the migrations were finally over, about eight million people had crossed the newly created boundaries of Punjab and Bengal, carrying with them memories of a kind of violence that the three communities had visited upon each other, unmatched in scale, brutality and intensity.

No-one, they say, foresaw either the rivers of people that would flow from one part of Punjab to the other or the blood that would be shed as they were ambushed and killed in the tens of thousands. The official estimate of lives lost during Partition is placed at half a million, but the number of those destituted would have been much higher. The movement of refugees, though undertaken with military escort as far as possible, was both hazardous and traumatic; convoys were ambushed, families separated, children orphaned, and women abducted, left as hostages or killed by their own families in large numbers. Elsewhere, we have discussed the specific kinds of violence that women experienced at this time both within the family and at the hands of the 'other'; our focus here is on abducted women, and their recovery by both India and Pakistan over almost a decade after Partition.

The material, symbolic and political significance of the abduction of women was not lost either on the women themselves and their families, on their communities, or on leaders and governments. As a retaliatory measure, it was simultaneously an assertion of identity and a humiliation of the rival community through the appropriation of its women. When accompanied by forcible conversion and marriage it could be counted upon to outrage both family and community honour and religious sentiment. The fear of abduction, or of falling into the hands of the enemy compelled hundreds of women to take their own lives, equal numbers to be killed by their own families, and literally thousands of others to carry packets of poison on their persons in the eventuality that they might be captured. And many committed suicide after they were released by their captors for having been thus 'used' and polluted.

Leaders expressed their concern and anger at the "moral depravity" that characterised this "shameful chapter" in the history of both countries; the fact that "our innocent sisters" had been dishonoured was an issue that could not be looked upon with equanimity. "If there is any sore point or distressful fact to which we cannot be reconciled under any circumstances, it is the question of abduction and non-restoration of Hindu women. We all know our history," said one MP in Parliament, "of what happened in the time of Shri Ram when Sita was abducted. Here, where thousands of girls are concerned, we cannot forget this. We can forget all the properties, we can forget every other thing but this cannot be forgotten." And again, "As descendants of Ram we have to bring back every Sita that is alive."[7] A letter dated 4 April, 1947 from Nehru to Evan Jenkins, Governor of Punjab, says: "There is one point, however, to which I should like to draw your attention, and this is the question of rescuing women who have been abducted or forcibly converted. You will realise that nothing adds to popular passions more than stories of abduction of women and so long as these. . . women are not rescued, trouble will simmer and might blaze out."[8] Malik Feroze Khan Noon, on a visit to Bihar, made a public announcement that if women were returned within a week it would be assumed that those returning them had been protecting them and had not committed any offence.[9]

At the level of policy, the first initiative was taken at the 23–25 November, 1946 session of the Indian National Congress at Meerut, at which a resolution was adopted, which stated:

> The Congress views with pain, horror and anxiety the tragedies of Calcutta, East Bengal, Bihar and some parts of Meerut district. . . . These new developments in communal strife are different from any previous disturbances and have involved murders on a mass scale, as also mass conversions. . . abduction and violation of women, and forcible marriage.
>
> Women who have been abducted and forcibly married must be restored to their houses; mass conversions have no significance or validity and people must be given every opportunity to return to the life of their choice.[10]

Communal tension and the ensuing violence escalated at such a rapid pace, however, especially after March 1947, that on 3 September, 1947 leaders and representatives of the governments of India and Pakistan met and resolved that steps be taken to recover and restore abducted persons. Thus, on 17 November, 1947 the All India Congress Committee passed a resolution which stated:

> During these disorders, large numbers of women have been abducted on either side and there have been forcible conversions on a large scale. No

civilised people can recognise such conversions and there is nothing more heinous than the abduction of women. Every effort must be made to restore women to their original homes with the co-operation of the governments concerned.[11]

On 6 December 1947, an Inter-Dominion Conference was held in Lahore at which the two countries agreed upon steps to be taken for the implementation of recovery and restoration, with the appointment of Mridula Sarabhai as chief social worker. The primary responsibility of recovery was that of the local police, assisted by a staff of one AIG, (Assistant Inspector General) two DSPS (Deputy Sub-Inspector of Police), 15 inspectors, 10 sub-inspectors, and 6 ASIS (Assistant Sub-Inspector).[12] Between December 1947 and July 1948 the number of women recovered in both countries was 9,362 in India and 5,510 in Pakistan. Recoveries dropped rather drastically after this date—one reason put forward being the withdrawal of the MEO (Military Evacuation Organisation) from both territories—and it was felt that a more binding arrangement was necessary for satisfactory progress. Accordingly, an agreement was reached between India and Pakistan on 11 November, 1948, that set out the terms for recovery in each dominion. Ordinances were issued in both countries, in January 1949 for India, and May 1949 for Pakistan; in the case of India it was to remain in force till January 1950, in Pakistan till it was abrogated.

The official estimate of the number of abducted women was placed at 50,000 Muslim women in India and 33,000 non-Muslim women in Pakistan. Although Gopalaswami Ayyangar (Minister of Transport, in charge of Recovery) called these figures "rather wild", Mridula Sarabhai believed that the number of abducted women in Pakistan was ten times the 1948 official figure of 12,500.[13] Till December 1949 the number of recoveries in both countries was 12,000 for India, and 6,000 for Pakistan, and the age-wise break-up was as follows:[14]

|  | In Pakistan | In India |
|---|---|---|
|  | [in percentages] | |
| > 12 yrs | 45 | 35 |
| 12 > 35 yrs | 44 | 59 |
| 35 > 50 yrs | 6 | 4 |
| 50 and above | 5 | 2 |

At the Constituent Assembly (Legislative) session held in December 1949, considerable dissatisfaction was expressed at the low rate and slow pace of recovery in Pakistan, especially from Sind, Baluchistan, Azad Kashmir, and the 'closed' districts of Gujrat, Jhelum, Rawalpindi and Campbellpur. Additionally, there was extreme disquiet at the mention of 2000 non-Muslim women being held by government servants in Pakistan and at a Cease Fire being agreed to in Kashmir without negotiating the return of Hindu women abducted there. Some members even went so far as to call for "open war to recover our sisters and daughters lying helpless in Pakistan", or at the very least for retaliatory measures, suggesting that only an exchange of women be considered—what they give is what they will get.

To facilitate recovery and because the ordinance in India expired on 31 December, 1949, Gopalaswami Ayyangar moved a Bill in Parliament on December 15, called The Abducted Persons (Recovery and Restoration) Bill, for the consideration of the house. It extended to the United Provinces of East Punjab and Delhi, the Patiala and East Punjab States Union [PEPSU] and the United State of Rajasthan, and consisted of 10 operative clauses, which the Minister termed "short, simple, straightforward. . . and innocent"; relevant clauses are reproduced below.

### 2. Interpretation

(1) In this Act, unless there is anything repugnant in the subject or context,

(a) 'abducted person' means a male child under the age of sixteen years or a female of whatever age who is, or immediately before the 1st day of March, 1947, was, a Muslim and who, on or after that day and before the 1st day of January, 1949, had become separated from his or her family and is found to be living with or under the control of any other individual or family, and in the latter case includes a child born to any such female after the said date;

...

### 4. Powers of police officers to recover abducted persons

(1) If any police officer, not below the rank of an Assistant Sub-Inspector or any other police officer specially authorised by the Provincial Government in this behalf, has reason to believe that an abducted person resides or is to be found in any place, he may, after recording the reasons for his belief, without warrant, enter and search the place and take into custody any person found therein who, in his opinion, is an abducted person, and deliver or cause such person to be delivered to the custody of the officer in charge of the nearest camp with the least possible delay.

(2) In exercising any powers conferred by sub-section (1) any such police officer may take such steps and may require the assistance of such female persons as may, in his opinion, be necessary for the effective exercise of such power.

. . .

6. *Determination of question whether any person detained is an abducted person*

(1) If any question arises whether a person detained in a camp is or is not an abducted person or whether such person should be restored to his or her relatives or handed over to any other person or conveyed out of India or allowed to leave the camp, it shall be referred to, and decided by, a tribunal constituted for the purpose by the Central Government.

(2) The decision of the tribunal constituted under sub-section (1) shall be final: Provided that the Central Government may, either of its own motion or on the application of any party interested in the matter, review or revise any such decision.

7. *Handing over of abducted persons to persons authorised.*

(1) Any officer in charge of a camp may deliver any abducted person detained in the camp to the custody of such officer or authority as the Provincial Government may, by general or special order, specify in this behalf.

(2) Any officer or authority to whom the custody of any abducted person has been delivered under the provisions of sub-section (1) shall be entitled to receive and hold the person in custody and either restore such person to his or her relatives or convey such person out of India.

8. *Detention in camp not to be questioned by Court*

Notwithstanding anything contained in any other law for the time being in force, the detention of any abducted person in a camp in accordance with the provisions of this Act shall be lawful and shall not be called in question in any Court.

9. *Protection of action taken under Act*

No suit, prosecution or other legal proceeding whatsoever shall lie against the Central Government, the Provincial Government or any officer or authority for, or in respect of, any act which is in good faith done or intended to be done in pursuance of this Act.

As is evident the Bill, although it may indeed have been short, was not as simple, straightforward or innocent as the Minister would have the house believe. More than 70 amendments were moved by 20 members in an extended debate on the Bill that took a full three days to pass. Every clause, sub-clause and section was discussed threadbare, and serious objections were raised on everything from the preamble to the operative clauses. The main objections related to the definition of abduction, and the time-frame to which the Bill referred (1 March, 1947 and 1 January, 1949); the virtually unlimited powers given to the police with complete immunity from enquiry or action and no accountability at all; the denial of any rights or legal recourse to the recovered women; the question of children; the constitution of the tribunal; camp conditions and confinement; forcible return of unwilling women; unlimited duration for the Bill to remain in force; and the unequal and disadvantageous terms of the agreement for India vis-a-vis Pakistan.

The amendments moved by members sought to mitigate man of the gross irregularities they pointed out, and to qualify or modify certain other procedural aspects that were set out. But despite their strenuous efforts the Hon'ble Minister declined to incorporate a single amendment or modification proposed (bar one, limiting the duration of the Bill to December 1951) and it was passed, unchanged, on 19 December, and notified in the Official Gazette on 28 December, 1949.

But more on this later; we will turn now to the women them-selves.

## II

Even were it desirable, it would be difficult to present an accurate profile of the abducted woman during that turbulent time. From the official figures quoted earlier, it is clear that of those recov-ered, the majority were below the age of 35, and primarily from the rural areas. From what we have been able to gather through interviews and some documents, however, the circumstances of their 'abduction' varied widely. Some were left behind as hostages for the safe passage of their families; others were separated from their group or families while escaping, or strayed and were picked up; still others were initially given protection and then incorpo-rated into the host family; yet again as in the case of Bahawalpur State, all the women of Chak 88 were kept back, and in Muzaffarabad district of Azad Kashmir, it is said that not a single Sikh male was left alive, and most of their women and young girls were taken away to the provinces. Some changed hands several times or were sold to the highest or lowest bidder as the case might be; some became second or third wives; and very, very many were converted and married and lived with considerable dignity and respect. A Sikh schoolteacher we met had spent six months with a Muslim neighbour in Muzaffarabad after the October 1947 raid, before she crossed over safely to Srinagar; her younger sister who had been abducted could never be located, despite sustained efforts by the family and the International Red Cross. In the mid-Eighties she returned to Muzaffarabad where she stayed for six months, visiting every Hindu and Sikh woman who had remained behind, talking to them of their lives and circumstances. Of the 25-30 women she met, she informed us that only one could be said to be unhappy and in unfortunate circumstances. All the others, though nostalgic and distressed at not being able to meet their natal family freely, seemed to her to be settled and held in regard both by the community and their new families. And there were a few among them whose circumstances had in fact improved. "After all," she remarked "where is the guarantee of happiness in a woman's life anyway?"

It is by no means our intention to suggest that the predicament these women found themselves in was not traumatic or fraught with anxiety and uncertainty; merely that it would be false to presume that their lot was uniformly grim, their 'abductors' without exception 'bestial' or unreliable and craven, and to assert, as Mridula Sarabhai did, that recovery was "an effort to remove from the lives of thousands of innocent women the misery that is their lot today and to restore them to their legitimate environment where they can spend the rest of their lives with *izzat* [honour]". [15] Nor is it our case that the recovery effort should never have been made; going by the few accounts that exist and on the basis of the interviews we have conducted with women themselves and those to whose care they were entrusted, the majority of women recovered were rehabilitated in greater or smaller measure or restored to their families. Our purpose here is to look beyond these at the many discordant notes that were struck in the process of recovery; at the conflicting claims that were made and voices that were raised; at the silence that was almost unfailingly imposed on the women after the event, and at what all these tell us about the particular vulnerability of women in times of communal violence when each one of their identities—gender, community and nationality—is set up against the other and contested.

Let us listen then to what the women themselves have to say of their experience. The first is an account by a social worker who was the Superintendent at Gandhi Vanita Ashram, Jalandhar, for several years, and worked with recovered women. The second is a reported case; and the third has been reconstructed from family accounts, letters and taped messages sent by the woman to her brother.

1. "Some time in 1950 I was required to escort 21 Muslim women who had been recovered, to Pakistan. They did not want to return, but the Tribunal had decided that they had to go. They were young, beautiful girls, and had been taken by sardars. They were determined to stay back because they were very happy. We had to use real force to compel them to go back. I was very unhappy with this duty—they had already suffered so much, and now we were forcing them to return when they just didn't want to go. I was told, *'Ey tan aiveyeen raula pa raiyan ne, enada ta phaisla ho chuka hai, enanu ta bhejna hi hai.'* (These girls are simply creating a commotion for nothing, their case has been decided and they have to be sent back.)

"The girls were desperate. The news got around and I received two anonymous letters saying, 'If you take our women away to Pakistan we will kidnap you too.' Those women cursed me all the way to Amritsar, loudly and continuously. When we reached Wagah, it was evening and we found that there were about 15 other jeeps that had also accompanied us—all belonging to their relatives! They were hoping that should any one of the girls manage to escape, they would pick her up and take her back. As far as I could see, they were all Sikhs. I told the Pakistan SP who was with me that to transfer them at this point into Pakistani jeeps was a risky business—the girls will raise a real hue and cry and we won't be able to restrain them. We had no lady police—in those days there were hardly any—and I won't allow the policemen to manhandle any woman, whether she's a Hindu or a Muslim. And if they resist, we will have no choice but to use force. Now our jeeps couldn't go across without permission. Finally, we managed to get cleared, and as soon as we reached Pakistan, these same women who had made such a commotion, became absolutely quiet. This the Pakistan SP had already told me, would happen.

"Naturally, as soon as we reached Pakistan, the women realised their complete helplessness—what else can you call it? It was complete helplessness, they had been transferred from one set of butchers (*kasais*) to another . . . what could they do ?

"When the jeeps came to a halt, the SP dismounted, went round to the back of the jeeps, opened the door and rained abuses on those poor women. He shouted at them and said, 'Now tell me, which one of you wants to go back to India? Tell me and I'll let you off right now to find your way back. Let's see how far you get.' They shouted back at me—after all, I was the one who had brought them—they kept saying, 'Why are you destroying our lives?' Earlier, when I had brought them from Jalandhar jail saying, this is a government agreement, our girls are also being returned, they had shouted at me: 'Who are you to meddle in our lives? We don't know you, what business is it of yours?'

"In Lahore, the camp for recovered Muslim women was in the Women's Penitentiary. When we reached there, the women got down and each one of them made a burqa of her chunni and emerged in parda. They knew that if they protested now, they would regret it."

**2.** S. is 58, a sturdy Punjabi woman from Mirpur (in Azad Kashmir). Abducted by Muslims when she was about 15 or 16 years old she lived in Pakistan till 1956 when she was recovered by the military at her brother's insistence, and brought to Jalandhar. She was happily married in Pakistan to a man in the police service, had three children—two girls and a boy—whom she brought with her.

S. was returned to India very much against her wishes. We were told that after she came back, she refused to see her brother, did not leave the ashram and socialised very little with the women there. She almost never spoke of her life in Pakistan, except to say that she had been well-treated and was content, and that her children were well looked after. In the ashram she educated herself, took a degree in Hindi Visharad, started to teach in a local school, and in May 1990 retired as its headmistress. She now lives in a house that she has built herself, with her widowed daughter and her son and daughter-in-law.

S. was eloquent about her present life, spoke with pride about having been able to stand on her own feet, and of being helped greatly by the ashram and the women there, but absolutely refused to speak of her past. "*Dafa karo*", she kept saying, "*hun ki yaad karna hai. Dafa karo. Main sab bhula ditta hai. Hun main izzat nal rah rahin aan, main kyon puranian gallan yaad karniyan ne. Mere baccheyan nu vi nahin pata. Hun sudhar nahin ho sakda, kuj nahin ho sakda.*" (Leave it. What use ·is it recalling the past? Forget about it. I've banished it all from my mind. I lead a respectable [honourable] life now, why look back to the past—even my children don't know anything about it. Nothing can be done now. It can't be resolved.) For years she believed in no religion and no god, till very recently, when she joined a Radha Soami sect.

3. K. was 16, and had gone to visit her grandparents in village Hattiyan Dupatta (Muzaffarbad Distt. of Azad Kashmir), when she was picked up by the Kabailis (tribals). She passed from one man to another, tried to commit suicide by throwing herself off the roof of her captor's house, but was caught and taken away by a *zaildar*. She was rescued by her parents' erstwhile neighbour, a *patwari* (village headman who keeps all land records), who kept her in his house for some time before he persuaded her, for her own safety, to marry his son who was in fact younger than her.

Her father went to Lahore, stayed there for three months and tried to trace her through the Red Cross, but failed. When they finally managed to make contact with her, he went again to Pakistan and tried hard to persuade her to return. She did indeed journey to Lahore to meet him, but refused to go back because she was carrying her husband's first child. Her father returned, heart-broken and minus his daughter, and died shortly thereafter.

K. had two sons and four daughters, commanded great respect in her family and community and according to the accounts of those who visited her, lived well and with great dignity. She had complete freedom, we were told, didn't believe in Islam, was not obliged to read the Koran or say her namaaz. The common description of her was that she was like a dervesh whose words had almost oracular importance. She never moved out without a pistol (is supposed to have shot dead three intruders who entered her house when she was alone), always kept a lathi by her side, was quite militant—and wrote reams of mystic poetry.

K's brother, whom we met, said she was filled with longing for her family after she met her father, and wrote and wrote and wrote, letters that spoke heartrendingly of the wall of separation that had come between them, of the misfortune that divided them forever.

*Who has aimed these arrows of separation?*
*Neither you, nor me.*
*He has released these arrows of separation*
*That forever divide you and me.*

When her brother wrote once that for them she was forever lost, she responded with, "How can you talk of purity and honour? How can you denounce me for what was no fault of mine?" When he visited her 40 years later, she sat guard by his bedside, all night, every night, for the two months that he stayed with her. But she did not visit them in India even once, nor did she ever return to their ancestral village in Muzzafarabad.

These three narratives (as well as the disputed cases heard by the Tribunal, and the several stories we were told of women who had managed to escape from the transit camps on both sides), offer clear clues regarding the particular circumstances of abducted women's lives and the individual adjustments they made in order to achieve a degree of equilibrium that would enable them to take up the threads of living again. At the same time they are an indication of the strong resistance by, and often refusal of, many women to conform to the demands of either their own families or their governments, to fall in line with their notions of what was legitimate and acceptable. Some women who resisted returning to their countries resorted to hunger strikes, others refused to change out of the clothes they had been wearing either when they were recovered or when they had been abducted. Their protest could be powerful and searing. One young recovered girl confronted Mridula Sarabhai thus: "You say abduction is immoral and so you are trying to save us. Well, now it is too late. One marries only once — willingly or by force. We are now married — what are you going to do with us? Ask us to get married again? Is that not immoral? What happened to our relatives when we were abducted? Where were they?. . . You may do your worst if you insist, but remember, you can kill us, but we will not go."[17]

The challenge posed by those 21 Muslim women to the social worker — "Who are you to meddle in our lives?" — was a challenge directed at the State itself, a State that had already lost any legitimate claims it might have made to intervene in their lives by its complete failure to prevent the brutality and displacement that accompanied Partition. "There was so much distrust and loathing for us in their hearts," we were told by a social worker who was Rameshwari Nehru's right hand person for eighteen years. "They would say—'if you were unable to save us then, what right have you to compel us now?' " To assurances that they were India's and Pandit Nehru's daughters and that the government was duty-bound to look after them, they retorted angrily, "Is this the freedom that Jawaharlal gained? Better that he had died as soon as he was born . . . our men have been killed, our homes destroyed."

For those who were recovered against their wishes, the choice was not only painful but bitter. Abducted as Hindus, converted and married as Muslims, recovered as Hindus but required to relinquish their children because they were born of Muslim fathers, and disowned as 'impure' and ineligible for membership within their erstwhile family and community, their identities were in a continual state of construction and reconstruction, making them, as one woman said to us, "permanent refugees". We were told that often, those women who had been abandoned by their families and subsequently recovered from Pakistan, simply refused to return to their homes, preferring the anonymity and relative autonomy of the ashram to a now alien family.

## III

In all, approximately 30,000 women, Muslim and non-Muslim, were recovered by both countries over an eight year period. Although most of the recoveries were carried out between 1947–52, women were being retuned to the two countries as late as 1956, and the Act was renewed in India every year till 1957, when it was allowed to lapse. Recoveries were more or less abandoned in the two or three years prior to this, largely because Mridula Sarabhai came in for some adverse criticism, and resigned. The total number of Muslim women recovered was significantly higher — 20,728 as against 9,032 non-Muslims.

On 16 January, 1948, Nehru made a public appeal through the newspapers, in which he said:

> I am told that there is an unwillingness on the part of their relatives to accept those girls and women (who have been abducted) back in their homes. This is a most objectionable and wrong attitude to take and any social custom that supports this attitude must be condemned. These girls

and women require our tender and loving care and their relatives should be proud to take them back and give them every help.[18]

Mahatma Gandhi who, after the Noakhali riots of October 1946, had resolved to go and "wipe away the tears of the outraged womanhood of Noakhali" expressed similar sentiments. He said,

> I hear women have this objection that the Hindus are not willing to accept back the recovered women because they say that they have become impure. I feel that this is a matter of great shame. These women are as pure as the girls who are sitting by my side. And if any one of those recovered women should come to me, then I will give them as much respect and honour as I accord to these young maidens.[19]

Quite early in the recovery process, social workers came up not only against resistance on the part of families or of the women to be claimed, but also against those whose status could not easily be determined. These were the disputed cases, and generally consisted of those who said they were in either country out of choice, had voluntarily stayed back, or had been married to either a Hindu or a Muslim as the case may be, before 15 August, 1947. There is no doubt that many were compelled or coerced into saying so for a variety of reasons, but it is also clear from the cases that came up before the joint tribunals that there were enough who protested against forcible recovery in the only way open to them—refusal to comply.

In a letter dated 3 March 1948 to K. C. Neogy, Jawaharlal Nehru wrote:

> I have just had a telephone message from Sushila Nayyar from Patiala. She told me that a great majority of the (Muslim) women recovered refused to leave their new homes, and were so frightened of being taken away forcibly that they threatened to commit suicide. Indeed, last night 46 of them ran away from the camp through some back door. This is a difficult problem. I told Sushila that she can assure these women that no one is going to send them forcibly to Pakistan, but we thought it desirable for them to come to Delhi so that the Pakistan High Commission and others could then find out what their desires were. This would finally settle the question. In any event I assured her that we would not compel any girl to be sent to Pakistan against her wishes.[20]

The question could not so easily be laid to rest, however, for the issue became a matter of prestige for both countries: how many Hindu and Muslim women were returned and in what condition, and how the authenticity of conflicting claims was to be established gradually took precedence over the humanitarian aspects of recovery. The issue, in addition to being focused on the identity of the women as, of course, being either Muslim or Hindu, also extended to their being citizens of their "respective countries", needing to be reclaimed. Kamlabehn Patel, who worked in the Lahore camp for four years in close association with Mridula Sarabhai, said to us: "The identification was done according to the countries they belonged to, this one is Indian, this one a Pakistani. Partition was internally connected with Islam, the individual, and the demand for a separate homeland. And since this label was attached, how could the women be free from it?" Speaking of the disputed cases, she continued, "The government of India said any person abducted after the 31st of August, either women or children, must go to their respective countries, whether they desire to or not."[21]

The major part of the recovery operation extended upto 1952, although as mentioned earlier, women were being claimed and returned as late as 1956 through official channels. The public appeals made by Gandhi and Nehru indicate that the number of families unwilling to accept women who had been 'defiled' by the Muslims was by no means insignificant. According to one social worker, the problem became so pressing that the Ministry of Relief and Rehabilitation was constrained to print and distribute a pamphlet that sought to educate the public on the subject: it said that just as a flowing stream purifies itself and is washed clean of all pollutants, so a menstruating woman is purified after her periods. Similarly, the All India Women's Conference Report of its 21st session in Gwalior mentions that the Delhi Branch organised public meetings in different localities during Recovery Week in February 1948. It says, "Some of the office-bearers and a few members did propaganda work in connection with abducted women by going about in a van through streets of New Delhi and speaking to the public on loudspeakers." No details of this propaganda are given but one can guess its contents without being too far off the mark.

The anticipation of just such a rejection by the very family and community that was to provide them succour was one reason why many women resisted being recovered. Kamlabehn says, "The women who came to our camp put us this question: 'Where will we go if our relations don't keep us?' And we used to reassure them that, you are India's daughter, Pandit Nehru's daughter, and as such the government is duty-bound to look after you. We shall keep you in a camp."[22]

Pregnant women were obviously more vulnerable than others. Kamlabehn told us that lists of all the pregnant women would be made and sent to Jalandhar; there, the women would be kept for three months or so, be given a complete 'medical check-up' (a euphemism, we soon learnt, for abortions, illegal at the time) and only then be presented to their relatives, "Because," she said, "if they came to know that the woman is pregnant, they would say, let her stay in the camp and have her child."

Meanwhile the government passed an ordinance to say that those women whose babies were born in Pakistan after Partition would have to leave them behind, but those whose children were born in India, could keep them. According to Kamlabehn: "For the government this was a complex problem. In Indian society, a child born to a Hindu mother by a Muslim father was hardly acceptable, and if the relatives of the women did not accept such children, the problem of rehabilitation of a large number of women and children would arise." A special conference was held in Lahore to discuss the implications of this, where the majority of social workers felt that it would be wise to leave all such children with their fathers instead of allowing their mothers to bring them over to India where, eventually, they were likely to end up in orphanages. A senior civil servant, a joint secretary in the Ministry of Relief and Rehabilitation, said the only practical solution was to treat such children as "war babies" and not be guided by emotional considerations while arriving at a decision in this regard. It was only a sharp difference of opinion between Rameshwari Nehru and Mridula Sarabhai on the issue, and the insistence of those social workers who opposed such a callous solution to the problem, that saved the day for the women. A compromise was arrived at whereby the women would take their children with them to Jalandhar and, after 15 days, decide whether they wanted to keep them or not. "It was our experience," says Kammobehn, "that most of the unmarried young mothers were not keen to part with their infants. . . and older women were not keen to take their children, for they had other children earlier."

When the question of separating women from their children arose and was sought to be decided "practically" and "unemotionally," Kammobehn told us,

I said to Mridulabehn that I would not attend this meeting because my opinions are the opposite of yours. I will say frankly what I feel about this matter at the meeting, otherwise I will not come. . . Mridulabehn was worried about the future of these girls: how to settle them, who will marry them? Rameshwari Nehru was of the opinion that if they were Muslims themselves, why should they leave their children in India? So I said in the meeting: the soldiers responsible for their birth go back to their respective countries and the infants have to be brought up by their mothers. Nobody separates them from their mothers. The stalwarts and the seasoned social workers like Rameshwari Nehru should therefore visit Lahore and impart necessary training for separating the child—on our part we have neither the strength nor the capability for that work. If all of you do not approve of my suggestion, I would like to dissociate myself from this work.

Before long, strong differences between Rameshwari Nehru (who opposed forcible recovery) and Mridula Sarabhai (who wished to press on) began to surface; Mridula Sarabhai believed that no woman could be happy with her abductor, Rameshwari Nehru, not so. Within a few months of recovery work having been undertaken systematically, she advised the government to stop it altogether because she was convinced that "we have not achieved our purpose. . . Figures alone are not the only criterion against which such work should be judged." Viewed from the "human and the women's angle", as she proposed to do, removing them (the women) from the home in which they were now settled would "result in untold misery and suffering". From what she could gather, the number of such women was "appreciably great"; moreover, there was no way of ascertaining what happened to them once they were recovered and returned. "By sending them away we have brought about grief and the dislocation of their accepted family life without in the least promoting human happiness," she said. And finally, the woman's will was not taken into consideration at all; she was "once again, reduced to the goods and chattel status without having the right to decide her own future or mould her own life". Her pleas found few supporters and little sympathy within officialdom, however, and in July 1949 she resigned as Honorary Advisor to the Ministry of Relief and Rehabilitation.[23]

It would be incorrect to claim that the social workers all spoke in one voice, or that they did not also subscribe to prevailing notions of 'difference' between Muslims and non-Muslims in the matter of 'honour' and acceptability, and of social—and government—responsibility in the task of restoring these women to a life of 'dignity'. Indications are that they carried out the search and 'rescue' missions with some perseverence, especially in the first flush of recovery; in time, however (and this factor assumes significance in the light of what is discussed later) and with first-hand experience of the implications of their actions, they began to express their disagreement with decisions that they believed worked against the women and rendered their situation even more precarious. Indeed, when it seemed to them that the women's plight was particularly poignant, more than one social worker admitted to having 'helped' them 'escape' the police and bureaucratic net. In December 1949, Mridula Sarabhai was constrained to point out that "the approach of the people *and even the social workers* is not correct. Public opinion must assert that the honour and dignity of women will be respected and that in our country abduction will not be tolerated", as it was "in itself, immoral, apart from its being criminal. . . ."[24]

These differences direct us to examine the role played by social workers in the recovery operation, and the triangular relationship that developed between the government, the women to be recovered and the intermediaries. That this relationship was ambivalent and became increasingly troubled is, we would suggest, precisely because the government's construction of the abducted woman's identity was being called into question. It was a construction that defined her, first and foremost, as the member of a community and then invested her with the full responsibility of upholding community honour. Second, it denied her any autonomy whatever by further defining her as the victim of an act of transgression which violated that most critical site of patriarchal control—her sexuality. For an elaboration of this, however, we need to return to the Bill, the circumstances under which it was formulated and the debates around it.

The Recovery Operation of the Government of India, albeit humanitarian and welfarist in its objectives, was nevertheless articulated and implemented within the parameters of two overriding factors: first, the relationship of the Indian State with Pakistan and second, its assumption of the role of *parens patriae* vis-a-vis the women who had been abducted. As the former, it was obliged, as a "responsible and civilised" government of a "civilised" country to rightfully claim its subject-citizens; as the latter it was morally bound to relocate and restore these same subjects to their family, community and country. This dual role and responsibility simultaneously cast Pakistan itself as the abductor-country and India as the parent-protector, safeguarding not only her women but, by extension, the inviolate family, the sanctity of the community, and ultimately, the integrity of the whole nation. Additionally, and recurrently, the moral, political and ideological importance of India's secularism was upheld as an ideal that had to be vigorously championed and defended; it was this, more than anything else, that enabled the Indian State to *define itself in opposition to the Pakistani one.*

"For me," said Mridula Sarabhai, "recovery work is not only a humanitarian problem, it is a part of my political ideology. The policy of abduction as a part of the retaliatory programme has given a setback to the basic ideals of a secular state and Janata Raj." Her statement is pertinent not only because it reflected, in general terms, the government's—and the Indian State's—own image of itself, but because she was, practically speaking, the driving force behind the moving of the 1949 Bill. Just as earlier, the Inter-Dominion Agreement of November 1948 had been based largely on a 14 page document drawn up by her and handed over personally to Liaquat Ali Khan.[25] Her proximity to Gandhi and Nehru invested her with an authority, minus political accountability, that she brought into full play on the issue of recovery, which operation bore her stamp as much as it did that of the government's.

For the government, as for many leaders, Pakistan's intentions as far as the restoration of women was concerned, never quite squared up with its performance. They disallowed the MEO from conducting recoveries after July 1948; were tardy in promulgating an ordinance based upon the November 1948 agreement; appeared not to be co-operating on the speedy recovery of those whose details had been furnished by the Indian government; desisted from taking action against those government servants who were supposed to have possession of 2000 women; and failed to ensure that their police and social workers honoured the spirit and letter of the Agreement. Members of the house continually urged the Minister to impress upon the government the need to put greater pressure on Pakistan for this purpose. One, Smt. Durgabai from Madras, even went so far as to say, "Thanks to the leadership in our country, we have been able to get social workers who are not only public-spirited but non-communal in their outlook, and therefore, they are inspired by the noble example set up by the Father of the Nation and also other leaders whose support and help are available· in plenty for recovery activity. . . " And another, Pandit Thakur Das Bhargava, declared ". . .so far as we are concerned, we know how to honour our moral obligations. . ."[26] implying of course, that the Pakistanis did not. Although some concessions were made regarding moral lapses on the part of the Indian people—"We are not the monopolists of virtue and the people in the other dominion are not the monopolists of vice—we are as guilty as they have been"[27]—no one seriously questioned their own claims of being secular, non-communal or motivated by anything other than humanitarian and noble considerations. The terms within which the debate was conducted, however, reveal individual as well as commonly-held biases that make it clear that the communal dimension of the issue was never lost sight of and that it crystallised around questions of forcible conversion, marriage, children and the legitimate family, forcible return and recovery and, marginally, fundamental rights. It should also be mentioned that although the Bill under consideration referred to Muslim women abducted by Hindus and Sikhs, it seemed to be Hindu and Sikh women in Pakistan who were the real subjects of the discussion.

It was generally assumed that all abducted women were victims, being held captive, wanting nothing more than to be restored to their original families as soon as possible. "Women or abducted persons are rescued from surroundings which, prima facie, do not give them the liberty to make a free choice as regards their own lives," said Gopalaswami Ayyangar in Parliament. "The object of this legislation is to put them in an environment which will make them feel free to make this choice."

Smt. Durgabai, supporting the move, went a little further:

> Questions are asked: Since these women are married and settled here and have adjusted themselves to the new environment and their new relatives, is it desirable that we should free them to go back? May I ask, are they really happy? Is the reconciliation true? Can there be a permanent reconciliation? . . . Is it not out of helplessness, there being no alternative, that the woman *consents or is forced to enter into that sort of alliance with a person who is no more than the murderer of her very husband, her very father or her brother? Can she be happy with that man?* . . . Is she not the victim of everyday quarrels in that house? The social workers can testify. . . that such a woman only welcomes an opportunity to get back to her own house . . . Sir, it may be that she has refused to go back, But on what

grounds is this refusal-based? On a fear complex, on the fear of social customs and . . . that her relatives may not take her back.

Other members disagreed and demurred at the arbitrary powers being given to the Tribunal to decide who was or was not abducted and should be sent back. Smt. Purnima Banerji cautioned the government against being over-zealous:

> Time has passed and in between (these girls) have lived in association with one another and have developed mutual attachment as . . . couples. . . Such girls should not be made to go back to countries to which they originally belonged merely because they happen to be Muslims or Hindus and merely because the circumstances and conditions under which they had been moved from their original homes could be described as abduction.

Shri Mahavir Tyagi in fact, declared that such a recovery was the real abduction, legally speaking; ". . .my feeling is that already violence has been committed on them once. . . would it not be another act of violence if they are again uprooted and taken away to the proposed camps against their wishes?" To this the Minister replied, ". . .there has been hardly any case where after these women were put in touch with their original fathers, mothers, brothers or husbands, any one of them has said she wanted to go back to her abductor—a very natural state of feeling in the mind of a person who was, by exercise of coercion, abducted in the first place and put into a wrong environment." Despite the urging of some members that some mechanism be devised to ensure that no unwilling woman was forced to return to her country, the Minister declined to do so, simply giving his verbal assurance that no compulsion or coercion would be used, and adding, "I have not come across a single case of an adult abducted woman who had been recovered and who was pushed into Pakistan against her will." The clause in question was put to the vote, and passed by the house.

The two governments had agreed that neither forced conversions nor forced marriages would be recognised by either government. It followed that all children born of such unions would then be illegitimate, and for the purpose of the Bill were defined as "abducted persons" if they happened to be born to any woman within the time-frame set out in it. Now, those very members who had protested that no forcible recovery or return could be countenanced, and those who believed that every abductor had been guilty of a "shameful crime", was a murderer and could not be relied upon to provide either security or dignity to the woman he had forcibly converted and married, found that there were no grounds for their children to be treated as abducted persons. Why should they all be forced to go to Pakistan? they asked.

> You must realise," Thakur Das Bhargava declared, that all those children born in India are the citizens of India. Supposing a Hindu man and a Muslim woman have married. Who should be the guardian of the offspring?. . . Now when a Muslim girl is restored, she will go to Pakistan; she may change the religion of that child. . . The child will be considered illegitimate and is liable to be maltreated and killed. Between father and mother, who is entitled to guardianship?. . . If the father insists that he would look to the interests of the child and will see that it is properly brought up, I do not understand why, by executive action, that child should be given to Pakistan merely because we have written these words here in the ordinance.

Other members differed. "Our society is different from Muslim society," said Brajeshwar Prasad from Bihar. "My friends (Pt. Bhargava and Jaspat Roy Kapoor) made the suggestion that the children of such abducted women should not be allowed to go back to Pakistan. May I know whether these children are regarded as legitimate? They are illegitimate in the eyes of the law . . . our Hindu society has no place for illegitimate children." He went on to say, "I do not know how a child born of a man and a woman can ever be illegitimate . . . but we have to take facts as they are. . . such children if they are to live in India, will remain as dogs . . .

Yet others cautioned that if the government did indeed regard such marriages as illegal and, consequently, the children as illegitimate then, according to the law, only the mother could be their legal guardian. Those who professed to speak on behalf of the abducted women admitted that the abductor had been guilty of

> highly reprehensible conduct; but let us look at the question from the point of view of the abducted woman. The children to her are a sign of her humiliation, are unwanted, and if she returns to Pakistan. . . I think we may feel almost certain that they will not be treated as members of their mother's family . . . Why should they not then be retained in this country where their father, *whatever his original conduct might have been*, is prepared to claim them as his own?

Moreover it was the opinion of yet others that if the Pakistan Ordinance had no provision for the return of children, why then should the Indian one? Once again the Hon. Minister assured the members that ". . . the mere inclusion of children in the definition of abducted persons does not mean that those children are necessarily sent away to the other dominion", for he too believed that, ". . . children born after 1 March, 1947 would not be welcome in the original homes of these abducted persons when they go back . . . in 90 cases out of 100". Indeed, as we saw from the statements made by social workers earlier, government policy in its implementation actively discouraged women from taking their children with them, and forced those who were pregnant to have abortions done before they returned to their families. Of the children born to mothers in Pakistan and recovered by India, only 102 had come to India as of July 21, 1952. The total number of women recovered from there at this time was 8,206.

The recovered women themselves, although promised a "free" environment and "liberty" were, by the very terms of the Bill, divested of every single right to legal recourse that they were entitled to. The writ of habaeus corpus was denied (could this be because it was precisely such a writ that had resulted in a Punjab High Court ruling in Lahore in 1948, upsetting a decision reached at the Inter-Dominion Conference in April 1948, that abducted persons were to be returned to their families "whatever their own wishes may be"?); their marriages were considered illegal and their children illegitimate; they could be pulled out of their homes on the strength of a policeman's "opinion" that they were abducted; they could be transported out of the country without their consent; confined in camps against their wishes; have virtually no possibility of any kind of appeal (bar the compassion of the social worker or the generally unsympathetic authority of the Tribunal); and, as adult women and citizens, be once again exchanged, this time between countries and by officials.

At least three members referred to the gravity of the measures proposed and pointed out that they violated the fundamental rights granted by the Constitution that was going to come into effect the very next month (January 1950). They warned that the Supreme Court could not countenance the denial of the writ of habaeus corpus, and that it was the right of every Indian citizen — which these women were — to choose to remain in India; by law and by right they could not be deported without their consent. Mahavir Tyagi pointed out:

> These women are citizens of India . . . they were born in India itself . . .
> they have not yet gone to Pakistan. . . . In taking them to Pakistan
> without their consent, even if the agency be the police or the sanction be

the proposed Tribunal, shall we not contravene the fundamental rights sanctioned by the Constitution? . . . The fact that their husbands have gone to Pakistan does not deprive the adult wife of her rights of citizenship. They have their own choice to make.

To this the Minister replied that he had in fact, himself proposed an amendment that would extend the powers of the Tribunal and allow it to determine not only whether the women were abducted or not, but whether she should be sent to Pakistan or allowed to stay back. On the issue of habaeus corpus, he replied, "If the interpretations should be that what we have provided in this particular Bill is not quite in accordance with Article 21 or any other provision of the Constitution, then of course the remedy for a writ of habaeus corpus will remain."

As mentioned earlier, the Bill was passed in toto, with no modification of its clauses. When the debate on it was over and some officials had adjourned to the Ministers' Room in Parliament House, "an excited Mridula Sarabhai said to the Minister, 'Thank God, Sir, it's all over, and the women in both the countries are going to be grateful to you.' "[28]

## IV

Why, it may be asked, did the Indian government bend over backwards in its efforts to reclaim women, sometimes several years after their abduction had taken place, and through such extraordinary measures as were proposed in the Bill? Why should the matter of *national* honour have been so closely bound up with the bodies of women and with the children born of 'wrong' unions? The experience of Pakistan suggests that recovery there was neither so charged with significance nor as zealous in its effort to restore moral order. Indeed, informal discussions with those involved in this work there indicate that pressure from India, rather than their own social or political compulsions, were responsible for the majority of recoveries made. There is also the possibility that the community stepped in and took over much of the daily work of rehabilitation, evidenced by findings that the level of destitution of women was appreciably lower in Pakistan. We were told that both the Muslim League and the All Pakistan Women's Association were active in arranging the marriages of all unattached women, so that "no woman left the camp single". Preliminary interviews conducted there also hint at relatively less preoccupation with the question of moral sanction and 'acceptability', although this must remain only a speculation at this stage.[29]

Nevertheless, some tentative hypotheses may be put forward. For India, a country that was still reeling from Partition and painfully reconciling itself to its divided self, reclaiming what was by right its 'own' became imperative in order to establish its credentials as a responsible and civilised state, one that fulfilled its duties towards its citizens both in the matter of securing what was their due, and in confirming itself as their protector.[30] To some extent, this was mirrored in the refugees' own dependency in turning to the *sarkar* as their *mai-baap* (parent) at this time of acute crisis.

But the notion of 'recovery' itself as it came to be articulated cannot really be seen as having sprung full-blown in the post-Partition period, as a consequence of the violence that accompanied the exchange of populations.

If we pause to look at what had been happening in Punjab from the mid-nineteenth century onwards with the inception and consolidation of the Arya Samaj and the formation of a Punjabi Hindu consciousness, we might begin to discover some elements of its anxiety regarding Muslim and Christian inroads into Hindu-ness and the erosion of Hindu dharma values and life-styles through a steady conversion of Hindus to these two faiths. With the creation of Pakistan, this anxiety found a new focus, for not only had it been unable to stem conversions to Islam, it had actually lost one part of itself to the creation of a Muslim homeland. Recovery then became a symbolically significant activity (its eerie resonance in the current frenzy to recover sacred Hindu sites from the 'usurping' Muslims, is chilling), just as earlier the *shuddhi* programme of the Arya Samaj, even if it resulted in bringing only one convert back into the Hindu fold, served to remind the Hindu community that losing its members to Islam or Christianity was not irreversible. Recovering women who had been abducted and forcibly converted, restoring them both to their own and the larger Hindu family, and ensuring that a generation of newly born Hindu children was not lost to Islam through their repatriation to Pakistan with their mothers, can be seen as part of this concern. Because, in fact, such a recovery or return might not be voluntary, necessary legal measures had to be taken to accomplish the mission. In one sense, it would seem that the only answer to forcible conversion was—forcible recovery.

This unhappiness and, indeed, outrage at forcible conversion is palpable through all the debates on abducted women, and the extension of the definition of the term to *any male child below the age of 16*, further indicates the depth of the disquiet. Although the State, especially one that called itself secular, could not be seen to be subscribing to this anxiety, it could certainly act in the national interest and in the interest of its male citizens and their communities, by upholding their honour; in this case, through restoring their 'sisters' and its own subjects to where they belonged—with their respective Hindu or Muslim families and in their own Hindu or Muslim countries.

By becoming the father-patriarch, the State found itself reinforcing official kinship relations by discrediting, and in fact declaring illegal, those practical arrangements that had in the meantime come into being, and were *functional and accepted*.[31] It was not only because abduction was a criminal offence that it was sought to be redressed—its offence was also that, through conversion and marriage, it transgressed prescribed norms in every respect. (After all, as one Member of Parliament pointed out, the government was nowhere near as anxious to take action against the abduction of Muslim women by Muslims or Hindu women by Hindus, because here no offence against community or religion had been committed, no one's honour compromised.) This was why such alliances could neither be socially acknowledged nor granted legal sanction, and why the children born of them would forever be 'illegitimate'.

This reinforcement of the legitimate family required the dismembering of the illegal one by physically removing the woman/wife/mother from its offending embrace and relocating her where she could be adequately protected. It also entailed representing the woman as ill-treated and humiliated, without volition or choice and—most importantly—without any rights that might allow her to intervene in this reconstruction of her identity and her life. Only thus could social and moral order be restored and community and national honour, vindicated.

It is rather unlikely that we will ever know what exactly abduction meant to all those women who experienced it because it is rather unlikely that they will ever talk of it themselves, directly; society still enjoins upon them the silence of the dead around an event that, to it, was shameful and humiliating in its consequences. Yet society and State, father, husband and brother, virtually to a man, placed upon women the special burden of their own attempt to renegotiate their post-Partition identity, 'honourably'.

## Notes

This essay is part of an on-going study of women's experience of Partition, with a focus on Punjab. Over the years, we have had the opportunity of discussing aspects of the study with a variety of people from an equal variety of disciplines. While our own perspective is clearly one that draws on feminist theory and research methodology, we have benefitted from the views of sociologists, historians, political scientists and anthropologists. Among those who have helped greatly in clarifying our own understanding are Amrita Chhachhi, Paola Bacchetta, Deepak Mehra, Veena T. Oldenburg, Bina Agarwal, Shahnaz Rouse, Dr K.L. Nadir and Vasantha Kannabiran. Veena Das has been a source of encouragemen and support throughout. A parallel study is being carried out in Pakistan by Nighat Said Khan.

[1] The various reports on communal violence, over the last ten years or so, by the PUDR, Independent Initiative on Kashmir, the PUCL and citizens and human rights groups; Uma Chakravarti and Nandita Haksar, *The Delhi Riots: Three Days in the Life of a Nation* (Delhi: Lancer International, 1987); Amrit Srinivasan, "The Survivor in the Study of Violence" in Veena Das (ed.) *Mirrors of Violence: Communities, Riots and Survivors* (Delhi: Oxford University Press, 1990); Veena Das, "Our Work to Cry, Your Work to Listen" in Das (ed.), *Mirrors of Violence,* op.cit.; Gyanendra Pandey, "In Defence of the Fragment: Writing About Hindu-Muslim Riots in India Today", *Economic and Political Weekly,* Vol.XXVI,1991, among others.

[2] Gyanendra Pandey, "In Defence of the Fragment", op.cit.

[3] A detailed account of the nature and circumstances of this violence is to be found in our "Surviving Violence: Some Reflections on Women's Experience of Partition", a paper presented at the IVth National Conference of the Indian Association of Women's Studies, Jadavpur (Calcutta), February 1990.

[4] Our discussion has also benefitted from the findings of the Pakistan study, carried out in West Punjab and Sind. Although detailed information has still to be analysed, a preliminary examination of it suggests some critical differences and also, unexpected resonances.

[5] M.S. Randhawa, *Out of the Ashes: An Account of the Rehabilitation of Refugees from West Pakistan in Rural Areas of East Punjab* (Bombay, 1954).

[6] Satya Rai, *Partition of the Punjab* (Bombay: Asia Publishing House, 1965).

[7] Constituent Assembly of India (Legislative) Debates, December 1949.

[8] Confidential papers of Evan Jenkins, IOL/R13/1/176

[9] Ibid., March 1947.

[10] Constituent Assembly Debates, op.cit.

[11] Ibid.

[12] Satya Rai, *Partition of the Punjab* (Bombay: Asia Publishing Housing, 1965).

13 Aparna Basu, *Rebel With a Cause: Mridula Sarabhai, A Biography* (Delhi: Oxford University Press, 1995).

14 Constituent Assembly Debates, op.cit.

15 Aparna Basu, op.cit.

16 The Gandhi Vanita Ashram in Jalandhar was set up for the rehabilitation of destitute women, after Partition. Subsequent to the signing of the Inter-Dominion Agreement on the recovery of abducted persons, it was designated the receiving institution for women recovered from Pakistan; its counterpart in Lahore was Sir Ganga Ram Hospital.

17 Aparna Basu, op.cit.

18 Appeal published in *The Hindustan Times*, 17 January, 1948. *Selected Works of Jawaharlal Nehru*, second series, Vol. 5 (Delhi: Jawaharlal Nehru Fund, 1987) p. 113.

19 Quoted in G.D. Khosla, *Stern Recokning: A Survey of the Events Leading Upto and Following the Partition of India*. (Delhi: Oxford University Press, 1949, rpt. 1989).

20 *Selected Works of Jawaharlal Nehru*, op.cit., p. 114.

21 Kamlabehn Patel in a personal interview.

22 Kamlabehn Patel, personal interview and her book, *Mool Suta Ukhadelar*, (Bombay-Ahmedabad: R.R. Sheth & Co., 1985).

23 Private papers of Rameshwari Nehru, Nehru Memorial Museum and Library, Delhi.

24 Report of the Relief and Rehabilitation Section, presented at the Indian Conference of Social Work (Delhi Branch), December 1949.

25 Aparna Basu, op.cit.

26 Constituent Assembly Debates, op.cit. Unless otherwise stated, all quotations in this section are taken from the Debates.

27 Gopalaswamy Ayyangar in the Constituent Assembly.

28 Aparna Basu, op.cit.

29 We owe this information to Nighat Said Khan, researching the Pakistan experience.

30 Organisations like the RSS and Akhil Bharatiya Hindu Mahasabha, for instance, were clamouring for the return of Hindu women, and the Hindu Mahasabha even included the issue of the recovery of women in its election manifesto of 1951.

31 We are grateful to Veena Das for having drawn our attention to this; for an elaboration of this point, see Das, "Of National Honour and Practical Kinship", in her book, *Critical Events:* (Delhi: Oxford University Press, 1995).

# Rape and the Construction of Communal Identity

KALPANA KANNABIRAN

## Introduction: gender and identity formation

When I was doing field work in southern Tamil Nadu, I came across a banyan tree that was a pilgrimage centre for people from all over the Karisal Kadu or black cotton soil belt. This entire area, which stretches from Virudunagar to Tirunelveli, is inhabited by Telugu immigrants. Some of them came as part of the Vijayanagar retinues, while a large number migrated during Muslim conquests in Andhra. Memories of "Muslim aggression" are clearly etched in their minds. This banyan tree, I was told, was worshipped for a particular reason. The story is recounted of a woman who was raped by Muslim marauders who then pursued her on horseback. She ran as far as the banyan tree, embraced it and was absorbed by it. She is now a symbol of virtue and a constant reminder of "the violation of the Telugu people". My grandmother tells the story of how women in south India started wearing blouses, because "the Muslims" would grab their breasts.

These stories can scarcely be dismissed as tales of a past that have no bearing on the way communities experience each other today. They are built into the present and structure perceptions of and experiences with communities perceived as opposing dominant interests. This paper will look at the manner in which the identity of a community is constructed on the bodies of women. It will also look at the ways in which proprietorial rights over women are defined by placing them within the family and community or challenged by removing them from the realm of family and community. Aggression on women can then be legitimised by "proving" their lack of community or family status. Both these processes are integral to identity formation which is defined by and through the aggression on women. This aggression is mediated by caste and community especially in situations where there is a precipitation of caste and community interests. In an atmosphere charged with polarised interests, women of particular communities are targetted for attack.

Most commonly there are two ways in which identity formation takes place. The first is through the rape of women of minority groups — religious as well as caste — which signifies the rape of the community to which the woman belongs and is justified by demonstrating its inherent immorality. It is also an assertion of difference and separateness and a reinforcement of the aggressor's position in the right. The second is through allegations, by the dominant group, of rape and aggression against their women by men of minority communities, an allegation which serves to justify dominant caste/community hegemony, by demonstrating the "lack of character" of minority men who show scant respect for women. This then creates a condition for the total refusal of safeguards — constitutional or otherwise — for women of these minority groups.

Public/political discourse on women first classifies them by caste and community, creating hierarchies so that different classifications co-exist and separate the 'normal' from the 'abnormal' within and between levels. Those who are perceived as being outside the normal cannot assert a legitimate claim to protection from the State, not just the women, but the communities they belong to as well.

To extend this argument, while the predicament of minority and dalit women is much the same, they are situated at different levels. Women of minority communities are located outside the Indian State, as it were. Constructing their 'otherness' then is the beginning and the end of constructing the 'otherness' of their community vis-a-vis the "Indian community". Dalit women however, exist within the Hinduised Indian State and their otherness is constructed in a manner that reinforces the upper caste Hindu norm — it is categorised essentially as an undesirable 'aberration' within Hindu society, one that destroys the 'Hindu fabric' from within. The upper caste Hindu therefore sees himself as being threatened and under attack on two fronts from the outside, by 'immoral minorities' and from inside by 'unclean castes'; and women form the core target in both the perception of this threat as well as the use of violence to suppress it. The threat to the community is defined as a threat to the chastity of women of the community/caste; this threat is then challenged through aggression against women of these groups.

Since the struggle for hegemony/power is carried out on women's bodies, establishing control over women through rape becomes a legitimate means of carrying out this struggle.[1] In this paper I will examine one specific instance of such rape and the ensuing dominant discourse on the issue.

### Rameeza Bee's rape

Rameeza Bee was eighteen years old when she was gang-raped by four policemen, one Hindu and three Muslim, and her husband beaten to death, in 1978.[2] There was public protest over her rape and the death of her husband, Ahmed Hussain. The police treated the angry crowd as an unlawful assembly and opened fire indiscriminately, resulting in further loss of life. After the firing, a commission of enquiry was set up with a sitting judge of the Andhra Pradesh High Court, a Muslim from a fairly affluent feudal background being appointed to constitute the one-man commission. This was the time when the Bhargava Commission was enquiring into so-called 'encounter' deaths during the Emergency. (In 1975, Prime Minister Indira Gandhi declared a National Emergency in India to counter "terrorist" activity and "lawlessness". A repressive eighteen months followed, during which all access to judicial redress was blocked, and there was total suspension of civil and democratic rights.) The terms of reference of the Commission were confined to the assault on Ahmed Hussain, the causes of his death and the rape of Rameeza Bee.

By itself, a commission of enquiry is inquisitorial in nature and cannot pronounce an enforceable judgement. The state government did not take any steps to assist the Commission in the conduct of the enquiry apart from providing the infrastructure. There were no instructions from the home secretary to the police department to assist the Commission in procuring witnesses, etc.; on the contrary, the government went out of its way to shield the delinquent policemen. As a result, the police department tried to exploit the bias against Rameeza Bee on account of her alleged 'prostitution', and against Ahmed Hussain who they alleged was a pimp. No effort was made to prove that she was not raped. The forensic experts had been bought over and the Special Branch had intervened in the preparation of the postmortem report on Ahmed Hussain which said that he died of cardiac arrest. Justice Muktadar found the policemen guilty of the offences of rape, assault and murder with a common intention to commit all three. He recommended that they be prosecuted. An investigation was conducted and chargesheets filed against them. The accused then moved the Supreme Court of India on the plea that since a sitting judge of the AP High Court was the one-man commission of enquiry, his subordinate judiciary was likely to be biased in his favour. The matter was transferred to the district judge of Raichur, Karnataka state, who acquitted the policemen. This was made possible because the evidence recorded in a commission of enquiry cannot be used in a prosecution. At this point a women's group, Vimochana of Bangalore, filed a review petition and compelled the state government to prefer an appeal, which was dismissed.

### Official discourse on Rameeza's rape

What was Rameeza's background? To quote her:

> When I was a young girl I was married to a person. I do not remember how old I was at the time of my first marriage. I do not remember how long ago I was married to my first husband, but I left him about a year and a half ago. I reached puberty about a month and a half ago from today. . . My first husband did not like me and I did not like him. I left my first husband and got married to Ahmed Hussain. I was in love with Ahmed Hussain before I reached puberty . . . Both Ahmed Hussain and I used to go for agricultural labour.

Rameeza Bee was picked up by two policemen while her husband was answering a call of nature. In her cross-examination, set up by the commission of enquiry to investigate the case, this act of her husband's which had no bearing on the case, whatsoever, became a crucial factor, as is evident from Rameeza's replies:

> I did not tell Mr. Bari that my husband went into a graveyard for purposes of answering the call of nature. Where my rickshaw was standing I saw a graveyard. . . I do not know whether Muslims respect Muslim graveyards or not. I do not know also whether the Muslims put flowers on the graves and whether they perform *fateha* and I do not know that Muslims consider it a bad thing in desecrating the graveyards by answering calls of nature or urinating there.

Rameeza was not the only one to be subjected to questions regarding her knowledge of Islam. Malan Bi, mother of the deceased Ahmed Hussain, also had to defend herself against accusations of procuring girls for brothels. An important part of Malan Bi's cross-examination, however, had to do with the validity of Rameeza's marriage to Ahmed Hussain from the standpoint of Islamic law:

> I know that according to the principles of Islam a marriage cannot take place unless the nikah is performed. At my marriage, nikah was performed. No nikah was performed at the marriage of Rameeza Bee to Ahmed Hussain, but before four respectable persons, garlands were exchanged and betel nuts distributed. I know that in Islam the relationship between a man and a woman without the performance of a nikah is illegal. I do not know whether my brother Imam Saheb is keeping Sambakka without performing any nikah with her.

Demonstrating the illegality of Rameeza's marriage on the one hand, and furnishing proof of her complicity in and links with prostitution on the other, served to prepare the ground for the argument that her rape did not constitute a violation of any kind — either of her person or of the law — and that being a prostitute rationalises rape, which then ceases to be an offence.

The crucial testimonies for the defence in Rameeza's case were those of Qutubuddin and a couple of women who asserted that Rameeza was, like them, a prostitute by profession. The testimonies of both women point very clearly to the fact that they were set up by the police. Qutubuddin, the uncle of Ahmed Hussain's first wife, Shahzadi Bi, says in his testimony,

> I work as a mason wherever I get a job. . . I have given up my mason's job and am now selling fish and mangoes. The Transport Minister telephoned Ali Saheb, Panchayat Board member, and he contacted me to get all this information.

And what is the 'information' he procures?

> Rameeza Bee had married another person about two years ago. . . I learnt that she was married a second time at Mandlam. . . Why should I now say as to how many men Rameeza Bee got married to and with whom she had been living? I got to know that she got married to a man named Noor Ahmed. I personally do not know anything about the second marriage of Rameeza Bee with Noor Ahmed. It is all hearsay. I do not know whether Rameeza Bee got married to Ahmed Hussain. . . The character of Rameeza Bee is wayward. I have only heard and did not see about the behaviour or bad character of Rameeza Bee. I heard that she was friendly with the son of one Sattar. And also she was friendly with Rahmatulla. I have not seen Rameeza Bee with these people at all.

According to Ahmed Hussain's first wife, Shahzadi Bi, however:

My husband was a mason. While working as a mason, he started the business of selling stones. My husband was never acting as a pimp or indulging in immoral traffic. My mother-in-law was working as a midwife in Nandikotkur. I came to know of my husband's death through Qutubuddin. Qutubuddin also told me that the government is giving a compensation of Rs.2000. A policemen had also come to my house. Qutubuddin brought me to Hyderabad for filing the petition. . . I do not know what language the petition is in. I also did not say anything about Rameeza Bee. If she says she does not lay claim to the compensation given by the government, but I am entitled to the compensation, I am quite happy. . . They brought me here representing that they will get me Rs. 2000.

Although Shahzadi Bi's testimony exonerates Rameeza and Ahmed Hussain and Malan Bi, and is clearly based on facts, it was marginalised in the trial. The entire evidence for the case was built around the fact that Rameeza Bee was a prostitute, or that she had, in any case, married so many times that the fact of rape itself was inconsequential.

Further, from the point of view of the State,[3] non-conformity on the part of Muslims to the tenets of Islam justifies the aggression perpetrated on them by the State in collusion with the dominant community. Conformity to Muslim religious law in this case is defined and assessed by the State and its agencies, not by the minority community. The agencies of the State were therefore communalising an issue that had nothing to do with religion. Before going into the complicity of the State in legitimising majority domination, there is a further dimension to this entire case that needs elaboration. Among the political parties that supported Rameeza, were the Left groups and the Majlis Ittehadul Mussalmeen, which is a Muslim fundamentalist organisation. It would be useful to look briefly at the history of this organisation.

Unlike the rest of Andhra Pradesh, Hyderabad before Independence was a princely state governed by the Nizam, part of the British Paramountcy. The Nizam's state of Hyderabad spanned most of the Deccan plateau, with a total area of approximately 82,000 square miles. It had a predominantly Hindu population, while Urdu-speaking Muslims accounted for 12 per cent of the entire population of the state. Feudal ownership of land by the zamindars and their proprietorial rights over peasants made the Telengana an area with the greatest feudal exploitation in the Nizam's government. In 1947, when the Indian Union declared Independence, the Nizam refused to join the Union and instead attempted to establish Hyderabad as an independent state. At this point, the Ittehadul Mussalmeen, which started in 1927, became active through its para-military wing, the Razakars. The Ittehadul Mussalmeen was set up to protect the political and cultural rights of the Muslims and to ensure their continued dominance. Between 1940 and 1946, the organisation had built up a corps of armed volunteers who had been given regular military training. These armed volunteers were the Razakars who let loose a reign of terror in the city and rural areas immediately after Independence, to continue what they perceived as Muslim hegemony. In September 1948, the Indian government sent in the Union Army, forced the Nizam to surrender and disbanded the Razakars.[4] A revived Majlis Ittehadul Mussalmeen was now supporting Rameeza.

One argument, and a quite valid one given the history and politics of the Majlis, is that the Majlis was trying to communalise the issue. Far more significant, however, is the fact that the interest of the Majlis in the case put the State on the defensive, and Rameeza, quite literally became the ground on which the battle for hegemony was fought all over again. And we know by now that this battle had had a long and tortuous history in Hyderabad. I would contend that the arguments of the defence and the rhetoric of the Ittehadul Mussalmeen addressed and reinforced each other, and the fact of Rameeza's rape or Ahmed Hussain's death was lost in the process. The entire experience — the defence, the marginalisation of protest and the marginalisation of the recommendations of the commission — is a lesson in minority experience.

### Understanding Rameeza's experience

Although it is impossible to generalise from one instance, the Rameeza Bee trial brings into focus important issues pertaining to the functioning of state apparatuses in India and the norms that govern them. These norms are set by the majority community, that is upper caste Hindu, and no Muslim woman (or dalit woman as we see in instances of upper caste violence) can register any grievance especially against the agencies of the State.[5]

While theoretically, the power to set up norms for governance undoubtedly rests with the State, we are speaking here of a situation that is far more complex than appears to be at first sight. To begin with, although secularism is the basis of the Indian State, a consideration of national communal politics and nationalism both in the colonial and post-colonial periods unearths serious contradictions between professed ideology and practice in India.[6]

After Partition, policy-makers in India defined secularism not merely as a separation of religion and politics, but as a separation of religion from public affairs, merely and insisted that religion remain a private matter for the individual. Alongside this effort there was also a keenness, especially on Nehru's part, to win the confidence of the Muslims who were still feeling besieged by the events surrounding Partition. The common civil law was therefore set aside; religion was separated from politics, but not from law — which in fact was more crucial to the secular identity of the State.[7] The Muslims also perceived secular law as a threat to their interests, a continuation of their already grave dispossession. The loss of privileges and dim material prospects were reinforced by the communal atmosphere that prevailed in the country and its effect on Muslims. For one thing, their loyalty to the country was suspect. With Hindu communalism and militancy finding a raison d'etre in the massive influx of refugees from west Punjab and east Bengal, there was a greater and more vigorous insistence on Muslims to prove that their sympathies did not lie with the secessionists in Kashmir or the Razakars in Hyderabad.[8]

For the minorities, as for the Indian State, compensation for material dispossession could be sought through the exercise of control over women. This was made relatively easy by enshrining freedom of religion as one of the fundamental rights in the Indian Constitution. The corollary of the right to freedom of religion was that each community in India would continue to be governed by its own personal laws. These laws govern all matters relating to the family — marriage, divorce, custody and guardianship, succession and inheritance, and adoption. So while we have the elegantly enunciated ideal of secularism on the one hand, political practice in India, the politics of the Indian National Congress as well as that of other major national parties, has been structured along communal and caste lines, to the extent that hierarchies within, say the Congress, have more often than not, replicated hierarchies outside. In this context, the Indian State, which with minor exceptions has been constituted by the Congress throughout the post-colonial period, has absorbed the dominant upper cast Hindu norms of the Congress, along with the ideal of secularism. This is demonstrated in instances where, although the agencies of the State itself are not directly responsible for acts of violence, their complicity with the aggressors is established by refusing to press charges against those of the dominant group responsible for the violence. This, as I have asserted elsewhere, is also true for dalit women.[9]

What implications does this have for women? Let us take Rameeza's instance. She was a victim of gang-rape. First she had to prove that she was not a prostitute; second that she was not a woman of loose character who had married several men before cohabiting with Ahmed Hussain; third, that she was in fact legally married to Ahmed Hussain; fourth, that she was a good Muslim and knew and respected the tenets of Islam, as presented by the Hindu State, and so on. The fact of rape in her case is lost in a maze of considerations that in no way disprove the rape; on the contrary, they effectively justify it.

Given the fact that women are trapped in battles of identity and that their access to secular criminal and civil justice is limited in serious ways by the aggressive identity politics that is legitimised by the State we, as feminists, need to comprehend the complexity of the situation. A serious consequence of the official definition of secularism is that it places women firmly within the family and community. In doing this it denies them equal citizenship and access to democratic, civil and criminal justice systems; and by legitimising male control within the family and community, it pushes all those women who cannot be placed within the family outside the purview of law, thus sanctioning all manner of aggression against them without providing any access to democratic justice. This denial of access has serious consequences for all women, especially family women: all that needs to be done in instances of aggression or rape in their case is to prove that they are not the property of any man — that they are prostitutes. And a prostitute, or worse still, an independent single woman, by definition, has no constitutional or democratic rights in this society.

### Notes

This paper emerged from discussions I have had with Vasanth Kannabiran on questions of violence and women, and was originally intended to be jointly written. It has also been infinitely enriched by discussion with K.G. Kannabiran who appeared in the Muktadar Commission of Enquiry on behalf of all political parties and civil liberties organisations. The discussions on and reactions to my paper by Rhoda Reddock and my friends at the South Asian Feminist Workshop at Colombo forced me to clarify and sharpen my argument.

1   The category of rape includes every act of sexual aggression on women.

2   Details of the Rameeza Bee case have been obtained from the proceedings of the Muktadar Commission of Enquiry.

3   The case presented by the defence is, in my view, also the case presented by the State. The State's complicity with the defence is established by the fact that although it was instrumental in setting up the Muktadar Commission of Enquiry, its agencies in fact transgressed every limit in order to render its proceedings and outcome, ineffectual.

4   Stree Shakti Sanghatana, *We Were Making History: Life Stories of the in the Telengana People's Struggle* (Delhi: Kali for Women,1989), pp. 1–15.

5   In this process, although three of the four policemen who raped her were Muslims, they get absorbed in this identity of the State by virtue of being the law-enforcing arm of the State. The judge, also a Muslim, who is by his own admission increasingly disturbed by the plight of poorer women of his community, is condemned to silence and ineffectuality. He can only bring to the surface the reality of minority experience, but has no real power to act on the basis of the facts presented before him.

6   See Sarvepalli Gopal (ed.), *Anatomy of a Confrontation: The Babri Masjid–Ramjanmabhumi Issue* (Delhi: Penguin Books, 1991); and K.N.Panikkar (ed.), *Communalism in India: History, Politics and Culture* (Delhi: Manohar, 1991).

7   Sarvepalli Gopal, "Introduction" in Sarvepalli Gopal (ed.), op. cit.

8   Amiya Kumar Bagchi, "Predatory Commercialization and Communalism in India" in Sarvepalli Gopal (ed.) op. cit. p. 199.

9   Vasanth Kannabiran and Kalpana Kannabiran, "Caste and Gender: Understanding Dynamics of Power and Violence", *The Economic and Political Weekly*, XXVI,37, September 14, 1991, pp. 2130–33.

# Gender, Nationalism(s) and Cultural Identity
## Discursive strategies and exclusivities

SHAHNAZ ROUSE

This paper addresses the question of the construction of the nation-state and Pakistani nationalism; more specifically, it focuses on those aspects which I feel are central to ongoing debates around gender and women's location in today's Pakistan. What I propose to examine are certain critical aspects of the emergence of Muslim nationalism in colonial India, and the ways in which they have mediated gender disputes and debates in contemporary Pakistan. It is my position that the construction of a Muslim identity in colonial India and the demand for Pakistan necessarily evoked a contradiction, one which transgressed and confounded any clear-cut demarcation between supposedly 'secular forces' and religious ones. It is also my position that this contradiction became most pronounced in the aftermath of independence. I would further like to argue that while this process has parallels among other religious and ethnic communities in united India, it is accentuated and immediately problematic in the Pakistani context. Lastly, I wish to suggest that the inability to confront the very basis of Pakistani nationalism as problematic has generated certain untenable positions whereby debates on gender within Pakistan are circumscribed and confined.

## I

A particularly vexing issue in discussions of gender and nationalism(s) in Pakistan centres around the very basis for the country's creation. While different interlocutors might rationalise this on diverse grounds (e.g. fears of a minority community, aspirations of a rising Muslim middle class, etc.) an indisputable factor in the demand for a Muslim homeland in post-colonial India was the prior creation of a constituency for this entity. This creation was grounded in the collective consciousness of a group perceiving itself as Muslim, with a heritage, culture, and tradition(s) different from those groups from which they wished to separate. In order to articulate their political demands, Muslims had to be *defined*. This is not unusual; it was just such a process that led to a European identity, and its Other: the Orient and Orientalism. A corporate self could only exist by virtue of separation and self-conscious redefinition.

Despite their political disagreements — they supported the Congress, opposed the British, considered themselves constitutionalists and secularists, sought social reforms and/or opposed certain reforms — Muslims nevertheless represented a coherent, recognisable body, separate and distinct from Hindus, Christians and others. Religious redefinition served crucially as a *marker* of that difference and subsequent cultural identification. It is this point that I really wish to underscore: Indian Muslims, prior to the colonial period, were not particularly concerned about defining themselves discursively in religious terms. Religious practice was customary: a vast range of borrowed practices and ideas interpenetrated the community and were acknowledged as 'Islamic' and/or Muslim by their practitioners. Under colonialism, on the other hand, Muslim 'reformists', e.g. the Deobandis, sought to reconstitute religious ideas and Muslim identity by stressing the *sacred texts* of Islam, utilising them to replace customary practices.

Partha Chatterjee in an article on "The Nationalist Resolution of the Women's Question"[1] details this process in the context of debates over social reform in early and mid-nineteenth century Bengal. Teasing out the contradictory pulls on nationalist ideology in its struggle against colonial domination, he suggests that this resolution "was built around a separation of culture into two spheres — the material and the spiritual".[2] In the former, European techniques, structures, etc., were to be adopted; the latter was to constitute the holding line against colonialism. By virtue of this separation, accommodation to/with colonialism could be rationalised and resistance to it mounted, simultaneously. The spiritual was to constitute the 'superior' arena of resistance, and also construct the specific location that women were to occupy. Chatterjee also makes an analogy between the material/spiritual and outer/inner realms: the outer is the public world where supposed contamination occurs, the home is that which is *authentic*, pure, and sacred.

This set of dichotomies is critical to understanding the nationalist project and its implications for women. For unlike the commonly held separation between 'tradition' and 'modernism', this suggests the necessary maintenance of a balance — constantly shifting and reformulated — between the two, where 'modernisation' occurs in the material/outer/public world while 'tradition' is maintained in the spiritual/inner/private/home. This manner of understanding nationalist constructions is enormously useful not only for the context in which Chatterjee evokes it — that of Bengali social reformism — but, as significantly in the context of Muslim nationalism, leading eventually to the creation of Pakistan.

In the Muslim context, this construction is clearly evident not only in the writings of significant Deobandis (see Barbara Metcalf's recent translation of Maulana Ashraf Ali Thanawi's *Beheshti Zewar*),[3] but also in Syed Ahmad Khan's insistence that while Muslims enter 'modern' education, they maintain the privileged space of the Shariat (Islamic Law) against British encroachments. In other words, debates among Muslim reformers are better understood within the framework Chatterjee sets out than in terms of the artificially constructed dichotomy, modernist[4]/traditionalist. The Deobandis, for example, emphasised the significance of women's education and knowledge of the Koran, Hadith and Shariat as necessary, both for the advancement of the Muslim community and the maintenance of its cultural heritage. Women were to be brought into the 'modern' world through education, that would enable them to preserve and protect their cultural heritage and pass it onto their children in their role as mothers and caretakers. In adopting this position the Deobandis, far from denying women agency, acknowledged and sought their individual commitment to the reconstituted Muslim community. They also sought to stress the class nature of their concern, arguing that by educating themselves in this manner, women would ensure their families joined the ranks of the *ashraf* (the rising middle class).

The Deobandi position, therefore, far from being in opposition to the constitutionalist–nationalist one, can be seen to complement it through an insistence on women's active agency in the social process, resistance to cultural encroachment, contribution to a middle class agenda and struggle for hegemony in a rapidly changing class equation. While invoking women's autonomy and empowerment, both scripturalists and so-called 'secular nationalists' sought to position women in a broader project. Indeed, their invocation and involvement was central to this project.

From its very inception the nationalist framework contained within itself a contradiction: a separation of the material from the non-material; a privileging of the latter as the site to be preserved and protected; women's central position in the maintenance of the cultural domain; and yet, their incorporation into that domain through using the means of the material realm. Those in the forefront of the construction of a Muslim Nation sought not to reject modernism but to selectively utilise it in ways that would both fulfil the middle class desire for hegemony, while preserving control over women, albeit utilising different mechanisms for such control. While feminists have argued that nationalism under colonialism was a male project centred around male desire, it could not have been adequately accomplished without the active participation of women.[5] That such participation was forthcoming is evident from historical and other documents.

The construction of a national identity is critically related to the nature of classes in the colonial and peripheral State. In an illuminating article entitled, "Class, Nation and State: Intermediate Classes in Peripheral Societies,"[6] Aijaz Ahmad argues that we must comprehend the critical location of the middle strata in peripheral societies as itself an outcome of the distorted process of capitalist development. Unlike the metropoles where the bourgeois class developed organically, in the peripheries one finds a comparative "weakness of the polar classes, namely the owners of large scale private property on one hand, the peasantry and the working classes on the other".[7] Nationalist struggles, therefore, represent the "drive for hegemony on the part of the intermediate classes and stem, principally, from the overwhelming role of the State in all aspects of the peripheral societies, including the economic, and from their powerful presence in apparatuses of the State."[8]

In this drive for hegemony, one can discern a "whole range of disparate and mutually contradictory ideologies",[9] which may on the surface seem oppositional, but which are nonetheless "united in viewing the State as the principal agency of social transformation".[10] It might also be added that a close reading of the respective positions of distinct fractions of the intermediate classes reveals the artificiality of the commonly held distinctions between `traditional', 'modern' etc., An analysis of peripheral, intermediate classes is crucial to any examination of the formation of the nation-state, nationalism(s) and the construction/location of gender. Such an analysis, Ahmad points out, must delve into the following aspects: (*i*) the historical genesis and the contemporary form of the peripheral State; (*ii*) the manner in which this State rose, historically, prior to the emergence of a full-fledged bourgeois class and still continues to guide and even dominate that class; (*iii*) the 'overdevelopment' of the State in relation to the largely disenfranchised civil society; and (*iv*) the presence of personnel from the intermediate classes in the actual exercise of power of that State. Ahmad states:

> The crux of the matter is that the social formations [of the periphery] are, by and large, transitional in character, where capitalism is dominant but not universal and where a variety of non-capitalist forms exist not only alongside capitalism, occupying their own effective space, but also intertwined with the capitalist mode itself, with profound effects on the social relations of capitalist production, per se. The balance of class powers, and hence the modalities of class struggle in such peripheral formations, have characteristics that correspond to this transitional character of the systems of production. Likewise, the genealogy of the capitalist state in the periphery ought also to be studied not so much on the theoretico-abstract level of the capitalist mode of production as such, but in relation, fundamentally, to the specific modalities of the transition as it has unfolded in the actual histories of these formations.[11]

The politics of nation-building in peripheral societies, then, is not an aberration from some idealised 'norm' seen through the prism of the European nation, but a direct consequence of their specific insertion into the capitalist system. Furthermore, given this particularity, the struggles and contestations over the State can only be understood historically in the light of concrete possibilities and limitations within the intermediate strata.[12]

When and if we combine this perspective with our prior insight gained from Chatterjee, it leads to a realisation that the *process* we are witnessing — i.e., an attempt by the intermediate strata to establish its hegemony over the State and civil society — is identical regardless of the discourses of its various fractions on nationalism. That there are different ideologies constructed from within these fractions speaks their attempts, at different historical periods, not only to carve out a space for themselves, but also to serve the broader interests of reproducing the capitalist mode ·itself while simultaneously repressing alternative fractions, striving for position and authority both at the level of the State and civil society.

Applying these two frameworks to the Pakistani context necessitates an understanding of how the very logic on which Pakistan is based, rests on validating a *religious identity*, whereby that nation is constructed. In the absence of such a recognition, we will continue to talk of Pakistani fundamentalism as an 'irrational' departure from the visions of Pakistan's creators. My argument is that far from being a departure, it represents a culmination, the coming to fruition of the contradictions contained within Pakistan from its very inception. Failure to acknowledge this leads feminists into the cul-de-sac of speaking to a 'true' Islam which grants women equality. In so doing, they reproduce the modern/traditional dichotomies that constitute part of colonial categorisations, and at the same time remain within the discursive framework produced during the colonial period and strengthened since independence, whereby 'Islam' has been reified, transformed into an ahistorical expression of a sacred text, rather than being seen as itself the product of contestations among various hegemonic/anti-hegemonic forces in society. Rather than displacing fundamentalist rhetoric, such an approach grants it a salience and privilege it does not deserve.

This view of fundamentalism as a contemporary departure from what was the idealised vision of the supposed secular creators of Pakistan is itself linked to an inadequate historical exposition of the very significant contradictions within the Pakistan movement. I would like to briefly examine this construction. Part of the problem, as I stated above, stems from an inscription of a particular ideology through the production of a history of the 'Pakistan movement'. Given the basis of Pakistan's existence in religion, its official history had to be written so as to separate not only Muslims from Hindus, during the colonial period but also Pakistan from India, post-independence. It also had to justify the hegemonic position of that fraction of the intermediate classes that took over after independence. This meant two things: first, an insistence on Pakistan's 'Muslimness', initially in separation from Hindus, and later stressing its relation to the *Muslim maghreb* — Iran moving west (and most recently centering on the Saudi connection thanks to petro dollars). This project could not be new — it had already been constituted in embryonic form in pre-Partition India, and was exemplified not merely in the writings of those forces termed 'religious' but also in those of a figure like Jinnah who stated that Indian Muslims had a different history, culture and language from Indian Hindus.

Secondly, the construction of a narrative of the Pakistan movement sought to establish the hegemony of one class fraction by suggesting a sharp divide between modernists and religious forces rather than point to the contradictory elements and ideas incorporated within the movement, while understanding its unity in terms of class interests and representation. Syed Ahmad Khan and Jinnah are portrayed as our great leaders who sought simultaneously to protect Muslim cultural identity from colonial and Hindu encroachments, while propelling the Muslims into the 'modern' world. Without asking what this cultural identity consisted of, how it was formed and how it came to be positioned socially and ideologically, this separation is seen as evidence of the commitment of this strata to progress, enlightenment, rationality and by implication, particularly in Jinnah's case, of women's equality.

This historical fiction denies the insistence on the centrality of Shariat in family law, to which both individuals subscribed. It is further facilitated by the fact that Maulana Maudoodi (and the Jamaat-i-Islami), later positioned discursively as the nemesis of the secularists, opposed the creation of Pakistan and Jinnah in no uncertain terms. Such historical (re)construction has totally distracted attention from debates within the Muslim League and its position on women.

A number of elements can now be highlighted:

1. To speak of Muslim fundamentalism as an aberration of a 'secular norm' is a fallacy: Muslim nationalism was grounded in a selective adoption of 'modern' ideas tied to a key reformulation of the sacred/spiritual/inner realm. It was precisely the existence of this latter aspect as a key marker of Muslim identity that laid the ground for the eventual demand for Pakistan.

2. In the course of the evolution of this separation between the

two realms, scripturalist views came to dominate. It was by reference to the sacred texts of Islam, rather than customary practice, that Muslim identity was to be constituted and separated from that of other religious communities in India. It would also serve as the means for the maintenance of specific institutional structures that could be held despite British encroachment in other material realms.

3. This separation would also legitimise demands for 'Muslim' representation in education, administration and other public institutions. In this way middle class, non-religious Muslim interests[13] were well served by religious separation.

4. Nationalism both assumes and posits a homogeneity of interest among the community in question. This is as true of 'larger' nationalisms, e.g. Indian anti-colonial nationalism, as it is of nationalisms within independent ex-colonies (Sindhi, Muslim, etc.). While this is certainly understandable (given the continued persistence of imperialist intervention and the necessity for forging a common alliance against it), it serves as a powerful mechanism of control for the community in question by serving to silence oppressed groups within it, at best subsuming their interests within the broader national grouping. As such, it is a mechanism as potent and readily used by liberals as the religiously orthodox.

In discussions regarding Muslims in colonial India, diverse positions have been read in several different, often contradictory ways: first, as being anti-colonial or collaborationist with the Raj. For instance, the Deobandis have been seen as progressive (in so far as they are held to have remained staunchly anti-colonial, itself a problematic assumption), whereas Syed Ahmad Khan, who remained a civil servant throughout his life, has been viewed as reprehensible. An alternative approach has been to categorise the nationalist divide along modernist and religious lines. In this light, Syed Ahmad signifies progress and modernity, whereas the mullahs (Deobandis among them) are seen to constitute the forces of regression and darkness.

If we re-enter gender into the frame, using it as our central divide, new questions emerge: what was the position of each of the two groups vis-a-vis women? How were women incorporated and addressed by the religious versus the modernist elements? Is there indeed a radical disjunction between the two groups or were they perhaps closer than previous scholarship suggests? What were the nuances and distinctions within the religious forces and within the modernists? What were their underlying assumptions? Which communities/classes did they hail from? Whom did they speak to, and whom did they speak for? How did their position differ from that of the colonialists? Seen in this way, Muslim nationalism necessitates a reinterpretation.

Both modernists and religionists focused their activity on the Muslim community, using religious identity as a primary basis for organising resistance-cum-accommodation to colonial rule. Culture — Muslim culture — was the raison d'etre of their efforts. In the public realm, membership in colonial institutions was accepted and even encouraged by both elements. Islamic identity was, however, to be maintained in the private realm, i.e., in the family. Both groups favoured education for women but segregated education, emphasising religious content and domestic training. Muslim identity and respectability were seen to reside in the 'protection' (read segregation and seclusion) of women. Cultural and national assertion was to be achieved at the expense of women.[14]

The prime beneficiaries of these moves were clearly Muslim men. When a vote was taken at Aligarh on women's education during this early period, it was soundly defeated. Syed Ahmad specifically indicated there was no question of women's progress *alongside* men: ". . .there could be no satisfactory education. . . for Muhammadan females until a large number of Muhammadan males [had] received a sound education".[15] Interestingly, the Deobandis adopted an approach that spoke to women directly. Ashraf A. Thanawi's *Beheshti Zewar* sought to inform and convince women of Islam's egalitarian theological position on gender. The text repeatedly makes this point. It also marks a sharp break from Muslim traditionalism in which women were precluded from exercising independent judgement regarding the Koran and Hadith, being expected to merely *receive* the word, while living according to customary norms. *Beheshti Zewar's* emphasis on questioning rather than rote represents a radical break from customary expectations regarding women's religious learning. It is also unique (for the times) in its firm insistence on the positive benefits of women's education.

There is, of course, another aspect to this text. It sought to break customary hold(s) on Muslim women. While custom constrained women, it also provided them with a certain space and control in the private realm. Women upto this time were not regarded as the repository and 'guardians of virtue'.[16] By simultaneously departing from customary practice *and* justifying women's position according to and within Islamic, doctrinally established, social hierarchy, Thanawi sought to implicate women (of the ashraf or aspirants thereto) in the construction of an 'ideal Muslim' woman. Subordination was made palatable by emphasising women's own choice in the matter as well as by putting forth the argument that this location does not represent an inferior but rather a separate and different position for women, wherein the two genders complement each other as co-equals in their respective domains. This work, therefore, represents a significant 'cultural shift' among Indian Muslims whereby women's virtue resides in their practice of a doctrinally defined social role.[17]

Thanawi's emphasis is complemented by Syed Ahmad's adamant opposition to any intervention vis-a-vis the Shariat by the colonial state. Religious reformers alone cannot be held responsible for this shift in Muslim discourse — so-called modernists were equally implicated in the attempt to construct Muslim identity through this means. It is this struggle over the Shariat and its primacy that continues to plague women's struggles in Pakistan to this day.

Both Syed Ahmad and Thanawi spoke primarily to privileged Muslims. They sought to impress among women of Muslim upper classes their *duty* as Muslims. However, these women's lives were structured totally differently from women of other social strata. The latter often worked outside the home, and did not have the option of seclusion and segregation. Norms of honour, virtue, modesty were meant to percolate down to women of these other classes, to serve as standards by which they would live, judge and be judged. Segregation and seclusion thus also served as a mechanism whereby middle class women could exert control over those in lower social strata and position themselves as their 'betters', ideologically. Thus, while men remained at the pinnacle of the gender hierarchy, women of privileged strata also benefitted, relative to those with fewer resources.

This discussion should demonstrate the limitations of reducing an examination of different groups merely to their position in the anti-colonial struggle, or in terms of religion versus rationalism. A gender(ed) focus forces us to problematise these very terms and render them more complex.

## II

Part of the resistance to women's secular education in the nineteenth century was located in fears that women's virtue and, by extension, the identity of Muslims as a distinct group, would be lost. This viewpoint was articulated most clearly in the stiff opposition to 'permitting' women of one's family to study in missionary and government institutions — such study being seen as contaminating women, depriving them of their cultural beliefs.[18]

Early in the twentieth century, however, the Muslim salariat had grown as a consequence of structural transformations in the political economy. A shift in attitudes regarding women's education is noticeable among the second generation of Muslim leaders. Evident among the emerging Muslim salariat is a desire to marry educated women. The nationalist position among this same salariat — Jinnah included — saw women's incorporation into the struggle as essential to its success. Since women constitute half 'the community', failure to involve them was seen to represent a loss of 'wealth', i.e., underdevelopment of community resources.

This turn represents a substantive break between 'modernists' and reformist co-religionists. While both support women's formal education, the former now bestow their approval on non-Muslim institutions, while the latter continue to stress Muslim ones. Despite these changes, Muslim women's entry into secular institutions was limited to a minute fraction. Education was a luxury most could not afford and customary taboos against it remained fairly strong.

The manner in which such taboos operated even among women receiving an education can be seen from Maskiell's study of Kinnaird women.[19] The first generation of Muslim women at Kinnaird College observed purdah; women attended sexually segregated schools; government schools and colleges were favoured over missionary institutions. Thus, while (more) women received formal education, they did so under a series of constraints whereby their 'difference' as women could be maintained.

Such biases were not only limited to Muslims. Maskiell argues that the Wood Despatch, instrumental in setting educational guidelines for all of India under the Raj, displays a similar attitude:

> The Despatch stipulated that the Universities of Calcutta, Bombay and Madras were to be at the apex of a hierarchical educational system for boys. . . it did not sanction a similar system for girls.
> [Further]. . . the provincial government treated women's education as a step-sister to men's education in the Punjab. Both the number of government institutions and public financial support lagged far behind that for males. [By] 1859, the provincial government established a vernacular education system for males; no parallel system was ever organized for females. The Lahore College for Women opened almost sixty years after. . . [the] Government College for men at Lahore.[20]

This demonstrates a correspondence of interest among the colonialists and local Muslim men (although each ascribed blame to the other for their steps).[21] A committee appointed by the Punjab University issued the following recommendation in 1927: "A special non-degree course should be designed for Indian girls. . . to train the general intelligence and character of any future wives and mothers, rather than to provide any professional qualifications."[22]

Further evidence of the British notion of women's education is provided in a letter written by the British Vice-Chancellor in 1936:

> Would it not be possible to make women's education of a far more practical kind. . . so that no woman can obtain any kind of degree or diploma without being really well trained for what is bound to be the main occupation of 99% of her sex?. . . education has got to fit people for the battle of life, but if education is going to unfit women for the places they will have to occupy in life, it will become harder and harder to obtain a strong public opinion in favour of female education.[23]

Here, too, we can see an amazing similarity between colonial official viewpoints, and those found among the Muslim reformers (both modernist and religious). The difference does not reside in their respective actions as much as in the rationalisations each group (of men) offered up for them: each is engaged here in a power struggle, vying for consolidation of its own position. Women are treated by each as appendages in this process.

We also see here another discordant notion, i.e., that educated women begin to challenge and abandon their 'given' roles as mothers and caretakers. Islamists often attack women's technical education on the same grounds, yet it is noteworthy that colonial administrators shared this concern. This further undermines the notion that the push for women's education was an attempt by modernists, nationalists, and/or colonial administrators, to single-mindedly transform the 'essential' Muslim woman. British colonial policy varied at different periods, as did the response of Muslims to it. We can neither congratulate the British for their 'enlightened' views on gender, nor see them as the only group who sought to exploit gender for their own purposes. The dichotomy, in other words, cannot be set up as British versus Muslim, nor even as British and modernists versus believers and indigenists. None of these polarisations are borne out once history — temporal and contextual — is drawn into the analysis.

The convergence I have pointed to did not occur by way of a clear-cut intentionality. Different groups worked at cross-purposes, yet all of them added up to a formidable opposition to particular types of learning for women. This last point deserves further elaboration, because it is in this respect that the Islamist position is predicated upon a reconstruction of the colonial process such as to collapse modernism, colonialism and feminism into one: it is imperative to their position that women's experiential circumstances never be permitted to enter the terms of the debate. Any criticism of their position is thereby invariably construed as the outcome of a denial of one's heritage and faith. Relatedly such opposition is seen as having its basis in external influences (whether from wrong thinking and practice within the community, or 'foreign' influences that seek to denigrate and transform the Islamic community'. Not only are colonialism, modernism and feminism elided, but yet again, Islam is denied historicity, diversity and context.[24]

Within the nationalist movement, it is instructive to look at the nature of women's involvement, but equally important to situate their activity in the context of public pronouncements and writings by significant Muslim figures involved.[25] The significant (best known) historical Muslim nationalist figures are men. For our purposes, most critical among them are Iqbal and Jinnah, both of whom continue to dominate the discursive scene in contemporary Pakistan.

Iqbal gave primacy to formulating a philosophical position that would guide Muslims in a colonial/capitalist context. For him, history represents "the implementation of ideas".[26] Iqbal argued that for Muslims, nationalism is "a sort of mental agreement in a certain view of the world".[27] While a feminist reading of Iqbal is possible, it is noteworthy that in commenting on European suffragettes, he stated:

> Superfluous women. . . are compelled to 'conceive' ideas instead of children. Recently they have conceived the inspiring idea of 'votes for women' . . . . The Suffragist movement in Europe is at bottom a cry for husbands rather than votes. To me it is nothing more than a riot of the unemployed.[28]

It is noteworthy that a man who conceived history as a playing out of ideas should be so appalled at women's attempts to achieve what he himself termed *khudi* (self-hood). His position is an indicator that the citizenship he espoused was to be available primarily to men. His quotation suggests that only men were supposed to 'conceive ideas': women's role in history was as loyal wives, sisters and mothers, faithfully following the Shariat, helping men implement their ideas.

Iqbal, like many prominent Muslims of the time, was attempting to justify Islam against the onslaught of "western civilization" and imperialism. Stopping there, one runs the risk of rationalising the systematic misogyny of his thought. Thus, suffragettes are "superfluous" women, their demand for representation reduced to an (unfulfilled) desire for husbands. In other words, it is childless women, unable to fulfil and occupy themselves (re)productively, who resort to such demands. "Unemployment", too, is equated with a lack of husbands and children. It is this logic that leads Iqbal to his solution: polygyny. That Islam permits polygyny demonstrates to Iqbal the "greater wisdom of the Shariat, and. . .the moral degradation of industrialised society".[29]

In the light of Iqbal's prominence as a thinker of repute in Pakistan, it is critical to underline how pervasive was Muslim (male) insistence on women's appropriate role as mothers, daughters, sisters, in short, their domestic role. Yet, during this same period, we see numbers of women participating alongside men in the anti-colonial struggle. This meant that women came out into the public realm, spoke to large crowds (on occasion), travelled (even if most often in the company of male relatives and family friends) to attend political gatherings, increasingly attended schools, colleges and universities, and when the demand for representation came up, pushed also for women's voting rights.

While it is certainly true, as some have argued, that such inclusion meant women agreed to the terms under which it was made possible, (thereby, in a sense, becoming complicit in their own subordination),[30] it is equally important to realise that this also meant concessions would have to be made to women, when and if representation and social policy were formulated, post-independence. We can neither reduce this experience to mere class privilege or women's manipulation by men, nor to naive and misguided behaviour on their part. For individual women this did mean a substantive change in their lives — certainly not total freedom, but a pushing back of some of the barriers of their oppression. Such changes occurred in conjunction with wider transformations in ideas and institutions of the time.

Jinnah's speech in 1944 is one indicator of such changes, at least among a certain segment of Muslim leadership:

> No nation can rise to the height of glory unless your women are side by side with you. We are victims of evil customs. It is a crime against humanity that our women are shut up within the four walls of the house as prisoners. There is no sanction anywhere for the deplorable condition in which our women live. You should take your women along with you as comrades in every sphere of life.[31]

While it can be argued that this position only pertains to privileged women (in that seclusion and segregation were most pervasive among the upper classes), there is another logic that explains this development.

Syed Ahmad Khan and the Deobandis represent the first phase of Muslim nationalist politics and also the views of the first generation of Muslim leadership. The second phase, in which Jinnah later dominates the scene is, in many ways, a direct consequence of that first period. Not only had the number of Muslims receiving modern (including western) education increased enormously, so had those entering bureaucratic service and the professions. The difference is generational.[32] Class background alone does not adequately account for the shift, nor was Jinnah singular in this transformation. Rather, one can see in it the logical outcome of colonial policy and related steps taken by different classes and communities in British India to cope with these changes.

Jinnah and the Muslim League thus represent a continuum with the immediate past, resplendent with their own contradictions which become evident in a perusal of League documents.[33] As early as 1908 (when the first Muslim League session was held at

Aligarh), issues of Muslim representation and identity, concern with overseas Muslims, and education, formed part of party discussions. The first mention of women comes indirectly in the League's fourth session (at Nagpur, 1910) in the context of restoration of 'Wakf alal aulad' held to be crucial to maintain Muslim property.[34] This concern was relevant only to propertied Muslims, but it did not necessarily lend itself to privileging women: such wakfs could be used to prevent women from realizing the inheritance they are entitled to under Islamic law.

It was not until the fifth session (Calcutta, March 1912) that we have the first direct mention of women's status and education:

> There has lately come into evidence a powerful development of opinion... in favour of emancipation of our women.... Female education is one of the crying needs of Muslim India. Purely through our own culpable neglect... Muslim women had sunk to a low degree of social degeneration. Some grew to look on them as commodities to be toyed with. They had no individuality of their own. They could not take part in the ordinary social and literary life of the nation — let alone the higher political and economic spheres... This regrettable backwardness... is a notorious cause of our social degeneration; and the betterment of their education...will be the most vital contribution to the cause of our national regeneration...[35]

This brief mention occurs after over two hundred pages of documentation of League sessions. Several factors are significant: first, the reference concerns one particular female member of the Bhopal royal family, and does not indicate a recognition of education for women, in general, as approximating that of men. Second, emphasis is placed on the Muslim 'community' and women's contribution to it.

In the League's tenth session (Calcutta, December 1917–January 1918), homage is paid to Hasrat Mohani (interned in a British jail) and to his wife, who had made an unsuccessful petition for his transfer to a jail closer to home. The speaker extols her:

> [She made the request so that] She would be in position to see him frequently and render him whatever services were permissible.... She never for a moment prayed that her husband might be released... it is a familiar sight in that part of the country to see Mrs. Hasrat in almost the tattered robes of a beggar covered by a burqa, leading her little daughter by the hand and wending her weary way from Aligarh to Faizabad to see her husband in jail....All honour to this brave and courageous lady who has set an example of wifely devotion, courage and fortitude of which the womankind of India may well be proud.[36]

As in Maulana Thanawi's *Beheshti Zewar,* the ideal Muslim woman for the speaker is one who stands by her husband: it is merely the context that has now been transformed. Nationalist politics requires a wife to move freely between home and prison: Mrs.Mohani does this, *appropriately clad in a burqa.*

This version of the ideal woman does contain within it the seeds of opposition to dominant Muslim ideology. By virtue of the *necessity* of women's involvement, limited access to the broader political realm is opened up for women. This departs radically from the Deobandi position, as expressed by Thanawi, wherein women were to be active agents, but remain confined to private quarters, though not necessarily to the domestic realm alone.

A shift on the question of gender can be discerned in the League's Extraordinary Session (Calcutta, 1920), when a number of women appeared on the speaker's platform. Later, the League adopted "Ladies and Gentlemen" as its preferred mode of address. In the early Thirties, the League passed a resolution favouring suffrage, representation and equality for women. It was compelled, over time, to adopt a progressive stand on women's issues as far as political representation and education went. While these changes initially (and primarily) benefitted only a select group of women, they later became the basis for women's involvement in the post-independence movement.

It is important to note, however, that the League's position on women was by no means monolithic or homogeneous. It claimed to speak on behalf of *all* Muslims, and contained diverse voices, not necessarily in agreement, on the shape of a future Pakistan and/or women's location within it. Jinnah's own position was not unwavering. As pointed out earlier, at times he spoke of cultural differences between Hindus and Muslims, giving credence, at least indirectly, to the Islamist position favouring the centrality of the Shariat in post-independence Pakistan. This latter idea was also favoured by Iqbal even though he saw it constructed and as functioning through a legislative body, not religious courts. The Pakistan Movement contained inherent contradictions which enmeshed even its secular leadership. I have dealt here primarily with their ideological manifestations but they have a material base as well. Those within the League leadership who foresaw a secular Pakistan, nonetheless envisioned it as a hierarchical, class-based society. It was this factor, combined with the ideological schisms within and outside the League, that was centre stage after independence and resulted in the rise of dictatorship and, ultimately, in Islamist policies instituted at the State level.

## III

The issue of gender in an independent Pakistan cannot be understood apart from struggles over control of the State. Immediately after independence, Pakistan had to deal with very serious material and human dilemmas.[37]

The question that arose immediately was how Pakistan's 'Muslimness' was to be expressed and concretised. Historical evidence indicates a lack of unanimity among political figures on this issue.[38] Feeding into this confusion was that fact that some *ulema* such as Maulana Maudoodi, who had staunchly opposed the very idea of Pakistan, had now migrated to Pakistan and were demanding that it be an Islamic State. Then, too, the Muslim League had given extraordinary powers to Jinnah well before independence. This tradition of centralisation continued after independence: Jinnah was elected by members of the Constituent Assembly rather than through direct elections. Despite such centralisation, however, the League did not have clear supremacy at the state level. These tensions help explain why Pakistan's Constitution was not formulated for many years, during which time various groups within and external to the State vied for power and control.[39]

It is this combination of factors, accompanied by those previously addressed that "compelled the ruling groups to maintain at least a semblance of unity".[40] During Jinnah's lifetime this took the form of officially including the term 'Muslim' in references to the State.[41] Immediately upon his death, Liaquat Ali (who did not enjoy as much popular regard) formulated the Objectives Resolution of 1949, which sought to appease the population by promising that Pakistan would simultaneously be a democratic state, in which minority rights would be guaranteed, and one in which "all Muslims would be able to build their life in accordance with the teachings and injunctions of Islam".[42] Going beyond this vague and ambiguous statement, *ulema* were employed as legislative advisors, and Islam was designated the State religion. Gradually the role of the Council of Islamic Ideology was strengthened. Rather than go directly to the people for support, those in power decided to use religious ideology to gain legitimacy. Religion was thus yoked directly to the State.[43]

Religious leadership, once again, was not unified: Individuals like Ghulam Ahmad Parwiz and Maulana Shabbir Ahmad supported and provided theological justification for Pakistan's creation. Others such as Maudoodi initially opposed it. All agreed, however, that Pakistan should have an "Islamic character", which meant giving primacy to particular (albeit divergent) interpretations of religious law by the State.[44] Such debates are significant both in terms of the politics of the time and of the struggle over State ideology and its institutional framework. Also noteworthy is the distinction between religious elements who worked within the State and those who continued to oppose it.[45]

While the diversity of ideological positions is itself noteworthy, what is striking is that what has generally (and erroneously) been construed as a straightforward struggle between secular (modernist) and religious (often labelled 'obscurantist') forces, is in fact better understood as a struggle between democratic and anti-democratic tendencies. Throughout Pakistan's turbulent history, this struggle has been evident in attempts by working Pakistanis to achieve the promise of social justice and equality. The downfall of Ayub Khan's regime was precipitated by these forces, Bhutto's ascension rested at least partially on their support, as did Benazir Bhutto's brief regime. However, it is precisely the desire of all Pakistani regimes, including those of Bhutto and his daughter, to deny and suppress such forces that partially explains the collusion between supposed secular bourgeois forces and Islamists.

The necessity to keep popular demands for democratic rights in abeyance has meant that the State has adopted a contradictory position vis-a-vis gender. By and large, early policy was one of 'benign neglect', whereby gender relations continued to be dictated by social custom and practice, and the economic and political policies of the State. At the same time, the pre-independence call to women to participate in nation-building continued after independence; in the forefront were women belonging to prominent political families, and those connected with religious groups.

While gender-related changes by successive regimes need to be understood in terms of the struggle for democracy, such an analysis has to encompass complexity. Early Pakistani regimes cooperated closely with the US and their policies resulted in the debacle of the late Sixties. Popular sentiment at the time was profoundly anti-imperialist. Oppositional forces, both Islamist and the left, used issues of national identity and anti-imperialism as rallying points. For women the consequences of such congruence elsewhere have been disastrous. In Pakistan, it meant that the left and religious right, both, denounced women who had achieved economic and social independence. The latter saw them as no better then prostitutes, traitors to their heritage; the former saw them as frivolous and victims of a consumerist, imperialist ideology. Thus two very divergent ideologies coincided in their construction of women struggling against a patriarchal social order as deviators from their respective 'truths'.

The consequences of such positioning at the popular level have been mixed. Thus, people demonstrated their desire for democracy rather than oppression by the State by supporting the women's movement during the Zia period, and by voting in Benazir Bhutto as the first woman prime minister of a Muslim nation. However, during this same time, the number of violent crimes against women (including rape) increased alarmingly.[46]

This suggests that there exists a commonly held distinction between opposition to State policies and personal action. In the former, where democracy is denied to all groups, women's rights are upheld. Simultaneously, at an individual level, where people act out their beliefs on a daily level, male privilege is upheld. Thus, while the State definitely helps set the limits of women's oppression, the latter is not simply reducible to being an outcome of State action.

State policies regarding women and changes introduced—starting with inheritance laws soon after independence, the Family Laws Ordinance under Ayub, the guaranteeing of equal rights to women, setting up a Commission on Women as well as a Women's Institute under Bhutto — while hailed as major gains by upper class women were, in fact, of minor import. Inheritance laws only benefitted propertied women; neither these nor the Family Law Ordinance (introduced by a military dictatorship) contained any sanctions against violence. Regulations introduced by successive regimes represented an attempt to cast the State in the role of patron of women's rights. It is this factor that explains the relative complacency of women activists through the Bhutto period. Thus, while Bhutto's regime signed the UN declaration on women's rights, set up a Women's Institute, and promised universal education for both genders, it did little to ensure that these measures had significance and/or permanence. Further, Bhutto's declaration of the Ahmedis as non-Muslim, his banning of alcohol in public places, and declaring Friday the weekly holiday, were a direct sop to Islamists, made necessary by his inability to effect changes in the socio-economic realm. The fact that State policies on women continued to remain within the aegis of Islamic law or were merely symbolic, was especially noticeable during Benazir Bhutto's term. Her predecessor, Zia ul Haq, had introduced far-reaching (negative) changes pertaining to women through his passage of the Ninth Amendment.[47] Ms. Bhutto did not once attempt to overturn these laws. Many PPP apologists argue that she had no choice, since she governed by means of a fragile coalition. This is too simplistic an explanation: her regime did not even take a symbolic public position against that amendment. Further, by entering into an arranged marriage, by beginning to cover her hair in public, she conceded the ideological battle to the Islamists in significant ways. These are not trivial issues in a Muslim country where Islamists seek to control every aspect of women's bodies and lives.

All this serves to remind us that the construction of gender in Pakistan cannot be understood as a struggle between secularist and Islamist forces, per se. Rather, it should be seen in the light of the struggle for democracy by sectors of the Pakistani population. This struggle is further complicated by a rift along gender lines, not always evident at the public level since men and women have often united to form a common front against successive regimes. It is more noticeable at the individual level where the discourses of nationalism, anti-imperialism and cultural authenticity coincide in situating gender transformation as a secondary issue, if not downright taboo. This coincidence occurs despite surface differences.[48]

## IV

By writing and speaking of women's position in Muslim society through a focus on 'the Veil' (i.e., the two-fold elements of segregation and seclusion), many academic observers[49] and Islamists have overlooked the diversity of women's experiences and their active participation not only in the national economy but also in the reproduction of individual households, thereby serving to obscure the fact that "patriarchy is almost infinitely adaptable".[50] It is critical to note that Pakistani women's lives and their experience of patriarchy is distinct depending on the class, geographical location and system of social organisation within which they are situated. It is this diversity that has, until recently, gone largely unrecognised.

One of the best kept secrets has been the contribution of Pakistani women to the economy. In this the State and Islamists have both been complicit. Official statistics have, in the past, consistently under-represented the economic contribution of women. This has occurred in a number of different ways: first, official census takers, invariably men, have interviewed male heads of households who find it socially and ideologically demeaning to acknowledge women's contribution to household resources. Second, women tend to be involved in the informal sector in large numbers — in home-based piece-work, as petty traders, and as unskilled workers in the service sector.[51] Much of this activity is mis-enumerated in official statistics. Third, the separation of 'productive' from 'unproductive' labour has meant that women's contribution in certain areas critical to household reproduction — e.g., fodder and livestock rearing, water and firewood gathering, food processing — is unrecorded. Last, women's work, even in the productive sector is often unpaid (wages, if any, often go to the male household member). As a consequence, women's contribution is again rendered invisible.[52]

This lack of acknowledgement has serious implications. It makes possible the reinforcement and reproduction of both Orientalist and Islamist stereotypes. In the former, women are represented as being totally segregated and marginalised by ('traditional') society; in the latter, Islamists are able to depict men as 'caretakers', when in fact women work longer hours and often contribute equally to the social reproduction of the household. Furthermore, this denial at the popular level permits economic decision-making to be controlled by men (although individual women may try to intervene in this process in a number of ways). At the level of the State, it constitutes a basis for denying women access to resources such as credit; it creates a divide between 'visible' and 'invisible' women workers, thereby hindering mobilisation; and finally, it

denies the vital contribution women make to the cheaper reproduction of capital, thereby repressing an understanding of the
interrelation between patriarchy and capitalism.[53]

Disinformation does not occur by way of statistical negation
alone. Women's socio-political contribution is also obscured in
scholarship, particularly in historical accounts. In tracing Pakistani history, the focus is on elite (largely male) history. This is
equally true if the frame of reference is 'Islamic' history, Muslim
dynasties in India, or the Pakistan Movement. The historical narrative is constructed from the point of view of those in charge,
seldom from the prism of those Christopher Hill referred to as
"the worm's eye-view".[54] Within this construction, then, primacy is
consistently given to dominant ideological groups. To the extent
that women have not been the dominant historical figures, their
contribution to history and their experience(s) are denied; only
upper class women have figured in such accounts. This problem is
not unique to Pakistan. As elsewhere, the valorisation of literacy
and the written word as primary sources in the writing of history,
has meant that women from other than the educated classes have
been conspicuously absent from official histories and, until recently, from most scholarly writing.

While some of this work is now being recuperated,[55] the absence
of certain voices from historical constructions has had serious
implications for contemporary women's struggles in Pakistan.
Some consequences that ensue from an ungendered discourse of
history are ennumerated below.

First, men are positioned as being the *first* feminists.[56] I would
argue that this is problematic when one re-views history in the
manner I have attempted here, and also if one specifies what is
meant by feminism. The claim that men were the first feminists has
been used over and over again to suggest a difference between
Third and First World women's struggles. Thus, it has been said
that for women in our part of the world, the struggle is not against
men but against imperialism which seeks to divide and rule. While
I would concur that 'divide and rule' has certainly been part of the
ruling class' strategy, the accompanying argument pertaining to
women's well-being needs to be rethought. Those male 'first
feminists' were propelled into that position precisely because of
their arrogation to themselves of the *right* to speak on behalf of
women. In the process they often quelled women's own voices.

In Pakistan, it has become commonplace in certain quarters to comment that women's struggles occurred within the framework of larger nationalist struggles and that this practice was hegemonic throughout the Third World. Rather than closely scrutinising the implications of this subsumption, such a view has *naturalised* the process. Further, it has been granted legitimacy by the oft-repeated statement (in the context of feminists in different parts of the Muslim world) that men and women share the same interests. Recent counter-narratives problematise these assumptions and suggest that they are unfounded. While this work is in an embryonic state, its implications are potentially devastating for constructions commonly in vogue and indicative of the violent manner in which women were subjugated to male direction and male desire in the nationalist struggle.

Marie-Aimee Helie-Lucas, an Algerian activist speaks on this theme in the context of the Algerian anti-colonial struggle and its aftermath:

> During wars of liberation women are not allowed to protest about women's rights, nor are they allowed to, before and after. It is never the right moment. Defending women's rights 'now' — this now being any historical moment — is always a betrayal of the people, the nation, the revolution, religion, national identity, cultural roots. . . Leftist Algerian men are the first to accuse us of betrayal, of adhering to 'imported ideologies', of westernism. They use the same terminology our government uses against the left at large. We are caught between two legitimacies: belonging to our people or identifying with other oppressed women. . .'.[57]

This then is the bind that Muslim women, Pakistanis among them, find themselves in all too often. I would argue that it is precisely the construction of 'national identity' and nationalist males who (in denying internal relations of domination and subordination) have been responsible for the current strength of fundamentalism, a development that has further problematised women's status and potential. By raising the issue of gender, women threaten both the nation and cultural 'authenticity'. This construction denies women's actual experiences as having any authenticity: she who speaks must necessarily be influenced by that very 'other'— the 'westerner'.

One can ask, as Helie-Lucas does: "Whom does silence benefit?" While understanding women's reluctance to speak (especially in public, and especially those who themselves are beneficiaries of modern secular education and thereby also have a certain stake in maintaining class privilege), it seems to me that we need to move beyond this question: *for women do speak*. They have in the past and they continue to do so today. They do not, however, in the vast majority of instances, speak from a theoretical or organisational position, or in a language readily perceived as feminist. By looking at 'public' women (those active in feminist politics, the professions, etc.), we are privileging a certain speech, we too are engaging in 'veiling' and silencing.

More work needs to be done on women's autobiographies, diaries, journals, fiction — all works that deal with the 'private', subjective realm. Margot Badran in her introduction to *Opening the Gates: A Century of Arab Feminist Writing*[58] presents evidence that women addressed issues of gender oppression at least concurrently with (and independently of) men discussing the same issues. What is illuminating in her discussion is the difference between men and women's formulations: men wrote from a perspective of mobilising national resources in order to combat foreign intervention; women wrote of their lived experiences; men's writing informed public debates; that of women has yet to be fully explicated and revealed. It is this restoration not only of women to history but of women's articulation of their own experience that must form the basis for rethinking previously held assumptions regarding 'feminism' in our part of the world. The delegitimisation of women's voices and experiences needs to be challenged squarely, because it is precisely their experience of their 'private' lives that demarcates the primary (though not the sole) realm of women's oppression and exploitation. Citizenship, too, must be rethought, not merely in relation to the vote and equal rights but in terms of human rights. An emphasis on (private) experience should serve to underscore the falseness of the claim that women's rights are either a marginal or an 'imported' issue.

## Notes

[1] Partha Chatterjee, "The Nationalist Resolution of the Women's Question", in Kumkum Sangari and S. Vaid (eds.), *Recasting Women: Essays in Colonial History* (Delhi: Kali for Women, 1989).

[2] Ibid., p.237.

[3] Barbara Metcalf, *Perfecting Women* (Berkeley: University of California Press, 1990).

[4] In Pakistan, we often erroneously label 'modernists', 'secular nationalists', conflating personal life-styles with political strategies.

5 See Cynthia Enloe, *Bananas, Beaches and Bases* (Berkeley: University of California Press, 1989).

6 Aijaz Ahmad, "Class, Nation and State: Intermediate Classes in Peripheral Societies," in Dale Johnson (ed.), *Middle Classes in Dependent Countries* (Beverly Hills: Sage, 1985).

7-11 Ibid., pp. 46–48.

12 It must be noted as well that the intermediate strata in peripheral societies assume a different shape, character and composition from classes in the advanced, industrialised centre precisely because of the distorted character of peripheral capitalism and its particular history in relation to the centre.

13 It is this factor that makes it imperative to understand the link between the dual meanings of the word 'representation': representation as signifying inclusion in any institutional or discursive realm must be preceded by representation of one's distinctiveness as a community. In India, the link between these two elements is seen clearly in the case made for, and support among minority communities, such as the Muslims, for quotas in representation (in the first sense).

14 I am not suggesting that women neither gained nor were not implicated in this process; rather that, on balance, women's agency was exercised within a larger framework which simultaneously benefitted the women participating in the process and served to resubordinate them.

15 Quoted in Ayesha Jalal, "The Convenience of Subservience," in Deniz Kandiyoti (ed.), *Women, Islam and the State* (Philadelphia: Temple University Press, 1990).

16 Barbara Metcalf, op. cit.

17 By way of illustration of the dual and contradictory address to women in this text, here are a few quotes taken from the very beginning of Metcalf's translation:

"In a short time, *God willing*, you will. . . become a *maulawi*. . .i.e. a scholar of Arabic. . . You will achieve the rank of a learned person, and you will be able to give religious opinions, as learned men do. You will begin to teach Arabic to girls, just as learned men do. . ." (Book Ten).

"[The Prophet Mohammad] was very gentle. . . At night he would do everything very softly, so that no one's sleep would ever be disturbed. . . When he was happy, he lowered his gaze. What young girl has ever been as modest as this?" (Book Eight).

18 Interestingly, it was the Anjuman-e-Humayat-e-Islam (Organisation for the Defence of Islam) and the Arya Samaj (Society of Aryas), communally based Muslim and Hindu organisations respectively, that established the first girls' primary schools in nineteenth century Punjab.

19 Michelle Maskiell, *Women Between Cultures: The Lives of Kinnaird Women*, Foreign and Comparative Studies/South Asian Series, no.9, Syracuse University Press, p.12.

20 Maskiell, ibid., pp. 16–17.

21 The British blamed Punjabi men, arguing that they envisioned a narrow domestic role for women and this was the reason why the provincial government was unwilling to lead the way in challenging existing social practices. But this is clearly misleading: British women frequently argued

against the government's position, both in the colonies and at home. However, the sexist bias of colonial educational policy is only a partial explanation for the limited availability of education (for both men and women). To quote from Maskiell: "Unless its own policy needs dictated innovation, as in the creation of a pool of English-literate candidates for government service, the late 19th century provincial government followed a very conservative social policy."

22  Maskiell, op cit., p. 46.

23  Quoted in Maskiell, *Women Between Cultures*, p. 48.

24  This position denies the transformative character of Islam and also its interpretive disputes as part of its historical trajectory.

25  Speeches and texts regarding women need to be understood and framed within the broader philosophical and political position taken by such men. See Mohammad Iqbal, *The Reconstruction of Religious Thought in Islam* (Lahore: Civil and Military Gazette, 1944); Mushirul Hasan (ed.), *Communal and Pan-Islamic Trends in Colonial India* (Delhi: Manohar, 1981); C.M. Naim (ed.), *Iqbal, Jinnah, and Pakistan: The Vision and the Reality* (N.Y.: Syracuse University Press, 1970).

26  Sheila McDonough, "Metaphors of Change in Early Iqbal" in Naim (ed.), *Iqbal, Jinnah, and Pakistan*, p. 119.

27  Ibid., p. 118.

28-9  Ibid. p. 116.

30  See Ayesha Jalal, "The Convenience of Subservience," op. cit.

31  Speech at Aligarh, 1944.

32  Generational differences here are seen as related to social transitions, not ageing.

33  See Syed Shariffuddin Pirzada (ed.), *Foundations of Pakistan — All India Muslim League Documents: 1906–1947*, Vols. 1 and 2 (Karachi and Dhaka: National Publishing House Ltd., 1970).

34  Ibid., Vol. 1, pp. 135–36; 180–83.

35  Ibid., pp. 222–23.

36  Ibid., pp. 404–05.

37  These included the establishment of a state machinery, a constitution, foreign exchange shortages, weak economic infrastructure, and resettlement of refugees. The first and the last, in particular, had serious implications for women.

38  See, e.g., Aziz Ahmad, *Islamic Modernism in India and Pakistan, 1857-1964* (London: Royal Institute of International Affairs, 1967).

39  For a creative account see Y. V. Gankovsky and V.N. Moskalenko, *The Three Constitutions of Pakistan* (Lahore: People's Publishing House, 1978).

40  Ibid.

41  In Pirzada, *Foundations of Pakistan*, Vol. 2, p. 571, we have an interesting account of a Muslim League Council meeting held at Karachi in December 1947. During this session, Maulana Jamal Mian introduced an amendment stating: "The word 'Muslim', wherever it appears in the resolution in the phrase 'Pakistan, a Muslim state' should be deleted." He said Pakistan could hardly take any pride in calling itself a 'Muslim state'. He found many un-Islamic things in it from top to bottom. [He added:] "The behaviour of the

Ministers is not like that of Muslims. . . The name of Islam has been disgraced enough."

42  See Government of Pakistan, *Objectives Resolution* (Lahore: Government Printing Office, 1949); see also I. A. Rehman, "Quaid vs. Theocrats" *Viewpoint*, Dec. 27, 1990. pp. 9–10.

43  The roots were thus laid for theocracy rather than democracy.

44  It was the Jami'yyat al-Ulama-i Islam which led the call for forming a Board of *Ta'limat-i-Islamiyya* (Islamic teaching), a demand granted by the Constituent Assembly's Basic Principles Committee. This board made the following recommendations:

> [that] the Head of State should be a Muslim, with ultimate power; that government should be run by an elite of pious Muslims chosen for their piety by the Muslim electorate; that the committee of *ulema* should decide what legislation was repugnant to the injunctions of the Quran and the *sunna* and was therefore invalid; that a Legislative Assembly, which they identified with the Islamic — in fact Arabian — *shura* should be empowered to demand the resignation of the Head of State in certain circumstances. (Aziz Ahmad, op.cit., p. 238).

45  Thus a schism arose within those adhering to a scripturalist position on Islam, with Maudoodi and the Jamaat-i-Islami taking the most extreme position.

46  Numerous journalistic reports in *Dawn* and *Viewpoint* give collaborative evidence. See also the *Human Rights Commission Newsletter* from Lahore.

47  The Ninth Amendment rendered all laws against women passed by his regime, legal, although many Pakistanis continue to regard this amendment itself as unconstitutional.

48  As part of the struggle for the State, however, different groups have carved out distinct socio-political positions. Until 1977, Pakistan's ruling classes positioned themselves as 'modernisers'. This meant pursuing an economic model patterned on advanced industrialised economies. The Islamists, for their part, argued (unlike the left) that the basic conflict was not between capitalism and socialism, but between 'Islam' and the 'West', as two distinct civilisational forms. Like Iqbal, they suggested that the exploitation of underdeveloped Muslim countries (Pakistan included) was not the result of material forces as such, but of the "westernisation" of Muslim leadership, which brought about civilisational decline. Maudoodi argued that "western progress" was to be lauded and indeed replicated, but its ideational corollary, "sexual license", was at the heart of the "moral decline" in the "west", and was to be avoided at all costs. The related development of universal adult franchise, too, was 'un-Islamic' and to be abandoned. In other words, one could comfortably adopt the capitalist model in the economic realm, but politically and socially, contain and control popular, democratic forces.

49  This includes Orientalists and western women scholars. In using the term Orientalist, I am referring to that segment which self-consciously positions rationality and civilisation over what it terms barbarism and irrationality. It also incorporates a universalising project, positing itself as offering a totalising approach towards social change and intellectual ideas. In Pakistan this is

loosely used to refer to those forces striving to take the capitalist path towards development and social change.

[50] Feminists, including Michelle Rosaldo, have made this comment.

[51] See Akmal Hussain, "Lifting the Veil" *Libas International* 4, No.2, 1991, pp. 59–60, 134.

[52] To the extent this bias is acknowledged, explanations vary. The primary reason given is one of inadequate statistical and economic methodology. Not only does this represent a male bias, but it masks social conservatism, wherein class and status reside in hiding women's economic contribution(s). In this, both men and women are equally complicitous. Altering statistical methods and economic categories alone will not result in error-free data; social attitudes need to be transformed as well so that women's work is not seen as attaching social stigma.

[53] The congruence between patriarchy and capitalism suggests that while neither is reducible to the other, one cannot address issues of economic exploitation without simultaneously understanding how the two intersect. Since capitalism is not merely a system of production but an economic system that must necessarily reproduce itself as cheaply as possible, patriarchy operates closely with it. A treatment of one without the other, therefore, means that one cannot address either adequately or completely.

[54] I have borrowed this phrase from Christopher Hill's well-known social history, *The World Turned Upside Down*.

[55] This work is still frightfully slow especially with regard to women from the lower classes. The recent publication of Rokeya Sakhawat Hossain's *Sultana's Dream* underlines the necessity of reintroducing gender into the writing of Indian Muslim nationalism. See my article, "Discourses on Gender in Pakistan," in Douglas Allen (ed.), *Religion and Political Conflict in South Asia*, for an extended discussion of the relevance of this text for the purposes of our current discussion.

[56] This is because, in most instances, nationalist men were the first public figures to speak of women's equality.

[57] Quoted in Enloe, op. cit., p. 44.

[58] Margot Badran, *Opening the Gates: A Century of Arab Feminist Writing* (Bloomington: Indiana University Press, 1990).

# Childhood and Role Models
# in the Andar Mahal
## Muslim women in the private sphere in colonial Bengal

SONIA NISHAT AMIN

## Introduction

The Muslim Awakening in late nineteenth century Bengal gave birth to a reform movement which eventually focused upon the condition of women. It was initiated and led by reformists belonging to both orthodox and liberal schools. The former in Bengal were considerably influenced by the ideas of the north Indian Deoband school; the latter, open to influences of the European Enlightenment, usually came from the western educated, new professional gentry, based in urban centres such as Aligarh, Calcutta and Dhaka. The Muslim polity, disempowered and decadent but reawakened with stirrings of new life, was compelled to turn its full gaze on the private sphere as one of the sites of renewal and empowerment. A similar process had occurred among Hindus and Brahmos several decades earlier.

The reality that met their gaze — the *andar mahal* (the private sphere) that had been the repository of weakness, ignorance and temptation—needed considerable reform. Striking changes occurred in the family during the late nineteenth and early twentieth centuries; some of these changes, both structural and ideological, ultimately and irrevocably reshaped the social contours of Bengali life and created a new personality in the Muslim community: the Muslim *mohila* (woman).

This essay is part of a larger work on the world of Muslim women in Bengal from 1876 to 1939 and the emergence of Muslim mohilas as a component of the new middle class. It draws heavily on narratives provided by women themselves, and on contemporary discourses in fictional and non-fictional literature — the latter comprises periodical literature and didactic texts.

### The andar and the bahir

In nineteenth century Bengal, the separation of the private and public spheres among respectable (*sharif*) Muslim families was spatially manifest in the division of the place of residence into an inner (andar) and an outer (bahir) world. This separation was physically better delinated in the houses of the well-born, upper class gentry, where the female members hardly ever ventured out of the andar mahal; in the houses of the less well-to-do the inner and outer would often be symbolically separated by a thin wall, fence, curtain, or sometimes even by a piece of furniture. The most important point was that the seclusion of women and privacy of family life be maintained in some manner or other. This 'separation', apart from its functional use, was the insignia of respectability and only those families lower down in the social scale, which had no choice but to discard even the last shred of respectability, did so.

The terminology ghar and bahir was in vogue right upto the early decades of the twentieth century; it was only in the 1940s that it began to drop out of popular parlance to be replaced by the unispatial *basha* (place of abode, usually a rented apartment) or *bari* (house). Women writers of the age—from Faizunnessa (1834–1903) to Sufia Kamal (b. 1911)—have all described the *antahpur* (Bengali equivalent of andar mahal) and lives spent inside these quarters

### The andar mahal of Shaista Ikramullah

A detailed picture of a typical andar mahal of the upper class is provided by Shaista Ikramullah (b.1915), a representative woman of the educated and urbanised Muslim aristocracy of the time, in the opening chapter of her autobiography, *From Purdah to Parliament*. She describes the residence of her maternal grandfather, Nawab Syed Mohammad (originally of the Dhaka Nawab family) in Calcutta, around 1915:

> I was born in Calcutta in my maternal grandfather's house. It was a very old-fashioned house, built in the style of Muslim houses of the nineteenth century. . . There was a small unpretentious gate which opened into a long gallery. At the end of the gallery at the left was a door. This opened into yet another uncovered gallery which turned into a courtyard. All around the courtyard were the various living rooms. . . with a deep verandah running through the entire length of them and each formed a separate unit. . . The smaller verandahs were arranged more or less in

the same manner. There was one used exclusively by young girls as their sitting room, for they were not supposed to make themselves too conspicuous. . . . There was an upper storey and another completely self-contained apartment. . . But as the windows of some of the rooms opened upon the lane, only young married couples were allowed to live in this part of the house.[1]

The verandahs, courtyards and kitchens, all referred to the layout of the traditional andar mahal. In a later chapter she describes two other residences in which she lived — in Liloah where her father worked as a government physician and later in Nagpur where her husband was a senior government officer in the British government. The 'modern' home at Liloah had no separate inner and outer quarters (and no self-respecting maid of the old school would agree to work there). The colonial bungalow at Nagpur was "modified and built on till it had taken on the look of the traditional Muslim house with the large enclosed courtyard and verandah".[2] Such passages point to the conflicts as well as adjustments taking place in traditional residences amid a changing life-style in colonial India.

*Faizunnessa's ghar and bahir*

The concept of ghar and bahir underwent a strange formulation (and violation) in the life of Nawab Faizunnessa Chaudhurani (1834–1903) of Pashchimgaon in Comilla. This unusual and gifted lady who was awarded the title of Nawab by the British for her philanthropy and her ability in administrating her ancestral zamindari, made brief references to her childhood in the andar mahal in the preface to her book *Rupjalal* (1876). Faizunnessa said that during her childhood her future husband Mahmud Ghazi once caught a glimpse of her. One must assume that Mahmud was allowed entry beyond the strict boundary of purdah into the andar mahal; but only because he was one of her relatives.

Later in life, separated from her husband, Faizunnessa returned to her ancestral home, and it is during this phase that she lived a life, very unusual for a Muslim woman of her time. "After breakfast she would go to the estate office, where she would first dispense with the *musafir-khana* (guest-house) accounts and then take up the estate records."[3] All this would of course be conducted behind a screen or purdah in keeping with the custom of female seclusion. "After disposing off with the various officials Faizunnessa would return to the andar. Here she would bathe in the private pond surrounded by walls. After lunch, a brief rest, and some more office work, she would retire to the privacy of her very own 'Faizun library'. The remainder of the day would be devoted to prayer."[4]

And so, at the very outset, one is presented with the picture of a woman who had the right to make the daily transition from andar to bahir, traversing the private and public domains. It is essential here to remember that Faizunnessa belonged to the elite — she was no ordinary woman — and that she had no family, so to speak, when she took over the management of her inherited estate (earlier, she had left her husband and returned to her paternal abode for good, because he went back to his former wife). The life of Nawab Faizunnessa was in many respects extraordinary. Here was a lady who apparently transcended the andar (observing purdah, nonetheless) and did not really have to operate within the conventional framework of the patriarchal family.

## The andar mahal of Rokeya, Nurunnessa and Monowara

The andar mahal, as experienced by Rokeya, Nurunnessa and Monowara, would perhaps be more more 'representative' of the age. Rokeya pointed to the andar mahal as being the woman's sole domain in her book *Aborodhbashini* (literally, women dwelling behind the wall), a collection of episodes of women's lives in seclusion, based on real life instances. In writing of her own childhood life in the andar in her father's stately mansion in Payraband of Rangpur district, Rokeya said, "From the age of five we girls had to observe purdah even from those of our own sex. Men were not allowed in the Antahpur so I did not have to suffer their oppression. . ."[5]

Nurunnessa Khatun (1882–1975), the most prominent fiction writer of the period discussed here, was born in an aristocratic family of Murshidabad. In her presidential speech delivered at the Bengal Muslim Women's Conference in 1926 (Bengali year 1333), Nurunnessa remarked that within the high-walled apartments of the andar of her childhood home the only glory of nature that her eyes could feast on were the stars at night. Syeda Monowara Khatun (1909–81) also referred to the andar mahal in her brief memoir *Smritir Pata*: "Purdah was very severe in the andar mahal in our household. Even a male servant of 13 or 14 would not be allowed in."[6]

*The impact of the ghar-bahir axis*

The concept of ghar and bahir continued well into the twentieth century — writers, male and female, testify to this. The highly popular social novels of the time, such as *Abdullah, Anwara, Zobeda, Goriber Meye* (not to mention the Urdu novels that were also popular in many homes at the time) were written against this background. In his autobiography *Batayon*, Ibrahim Khan painted a picture of the social and familial life of Muslim society in transition from the turn of the century to the 1950s. His accounts of early childhood set in a semi-rural environment in the district of Tangail clearly depict the rotation of life around an andar–bahir axis.

Abul Fazal (1905–83), a young writer of the Dhaka scene in the 1920s, lamented the fact that literary creativity would always be hampered in a society which provided no scope for its men to know the true feelings of its women. "When I set out to write I realized how little we know our own society, specially the domain of the family. . . So we would accost our mothers, aunts, sisters or cousins for glimpses of the unknown Muslim Antahpur."[7]

In her interview to the present author, Mrs Rokeya Khatun (born in 1908 in the village of Agarpur) recollected: "We observed purdah from the age of eight. Males with whom one could legitimately get married were not allowed into the andar." When asked about the spatial distinction between the andar and bahir among the less well-to-do, she said that the economically disadvantaged also tried to maintain the distinction, however faint. Some other terms like *bhitorbari* and *bahirbari* were also used to mark the different spheres.[8]

As the traditional family began to break up with the beginning of urbanisation, professionalisation and upheavals in the socio-economic and ideological world of the Muslims, the significance of andar-bahir began to diminish. In the nuclear family of a civil servant, lawyer, doctor or teacher where the wife would accompany the husband to his new posting, taking up residence in English-style houses in burgeoning towns or remote spots, other priorities took the place of andar–bahir and by the 1950s the word had slipped out of use, used only occasionally in the urban context.

## The structures of traditional family life

### The religious basis

The institution of the Muslim family, with its emphasis on segregation and subordination, played a crucial role in maintaining the Islamic patriarchal order, and the andar was a key element within it. Theoretically, Islam affirmed the potential equality of the sexes, so the roots of gender inequality in Muslim society had to be sought elsewhere.[9] "The existing inequality does not rest on an ideological or biological theory of women's inferiority, but is the outcome of specific social institutions designed to restrain her power: namely segregation and legal subordination in the family."[10]

The new social order and polity created by Prophet Muhammed in the seventh century — a patriarchal, monotheistic state out of warring and polytheistic tribes with certain matrilineal traits — could exist only if the tribe gave way to the *umma* (or social order). The Prophet realised that the tightly controlled patriarchal family was necessary for the preservation of the umma. With patriliny came the importance of private property and the possession of family members: wives and children, and biological paternity of the child and, therefore, control of female sexuality. All of these would have to be exercised by the authoritative but benevolent patriarch. "One of the many devices the Prophet used to implement the umma . . . was the creation of the institution of the Muslim family, which was quite unlike any existing sexual unions. Its distinguishing feature was its strictly defined monolithic structure."[11]

The great strength of the Islamic code was that it was capable of preserving its essence long after the Islamic revolution of the seventh century, in the face of countless centuries and various cultural reincarnations. Far from its temporal and geographic origin in northern and eastern India where Islam had recreated the Muslim polity, the institution of the family fitted in quite well with existing patriarchal structures.[12]

### The patriarchal joint family

In dwelling on the lives of Hindu women in the early decades of this century, Margaret Urquhart in her book, *Women of Bengal*, depicted the lives of women in the Hindu antahpur. Many of her observations could well have been applied to Muslim society.

Urquhart observed that the English family did not closely resemble the Roman *familia* but the Indian household of the time was an almost exact replica of it.

The family, rather than the individual which served as the social unit in India, comprised not just one couple and their offspring but "a patriarchal group in its main stream and branches".[13] In such large patriarchal set-ups the control and regulation of an entire system required a hierarchical structure with authority vested in the person at the apex. As such these 'joint' or 'extended' families, traditionally found in both Hindu and Muslim communities, had a well-defined set of roles and relationships based on authority and obedience. Though the ultimate head was understandably the male patriarch, in matters of daily administration of the household, the mother or wife of the patriarch (most powerful breadwinner) would be in charge.[14]

Urquhart provided an economic explanation for the existence of the joint family and its gradual disappearance. In a society where land was the major source of wealth, it was deemed easier to maintain standard, status and prosperity if all the sons "lived by means of a common purse". Both Hindus and Muslims had laws of inheritance whereby all the sons got an equal share of the inheritance, and it was this, she suggests that cemented the structure of the *paribar* (family). But as the traditional sources of wealth and sustenance started to dry up with the changes attendant on colonial rule, the traditional family in both Hindu and Muslim communities underwent great structural changes.

### Daily life in the andar mahal

As in the Hindu household the mistress of the house would supervise servants and other female members who had not achieved supreme/sovereign status in the cooking of meals, cleaning, serving, handing out rations, washing, etc. In rich households there would be plenty of hours of relaxation which might be spent in storytelling, gossiping, sewing, reading religious texts or novels (the latter considered very mischievous by most guardians and moralist social critics), or watching an occasional performance by a magician or snake charmer.

Each stage of a woman's life was marked by a ritual to relieve the boredom of andar mahal life — ear-piercing, completion of the Koran, a doll's marriage, birthdays, weddings and religious festivals. Syeda Monowara recorded her memories of andar-mahal life at the turn of the century:

> Mother used to love listening to songs. Sometimes after the Zohr prayer she would summon all the maids to the verandahs and bid them to sing. . . . Mother would sometimes request particular songs. . . songs about weddings, the *lagan/holud* (turmeric) ceremony, the bridal toilet, the coming of the groom, songs of farewell. Sometimes Mother wanted to hear *marfati* (spiritual) songs, or ancient ballads, etc. Many of us would cry with emotion at the beauty of the legends — the pathos, the sorrow, the depth. Thus songs could be the vehicle for such superb storytelling, such as that of Princess Komolmoni.[15]

Shaista Ikramullah painted a vivid picture of daily life in the andar mahal of an upper-class family living in Calcutta in the early decades of the twentieth century:

> One sat and did one's sewing and reading, ate paan and received visitors on the verandah. . . There was one used exclusively by young girls as their sitting room, for they were not supposed to make themselves conspicuous even inside their own home. . . Nawab Syed Mohammad (her grandfather) perforce had to accept certain things for himself, but he was determined not to accept them for his womenfolk.[16]

As the social and economic structure changed and a greater number of Muslims started to enter government service, the familial and residential pattern also assumed new forms among the middle class. A simple correlation was discernible between the women who first came out of purdah and participated in some measure in public life and the transferable jobs taken on by the new liberal and educated Muslim men. A similar breakdown in the familial and residential pattern occurred in the case of the first Brahmo and Hindu women whose roles were changed by dint of access to public life.[17] Both in Hindu/Brahmo and Muslim households, vendors, barbers, masseuses, etc., from the outside formed the only link between the private and public spheres as well as between one family and another.[18]

Shaista pointed to the link between the private and public spheres: "There were the women vendors, the *choori-wali* (bangle-sellers), the *bisatin* (women who sold ribbons, buttons, etc.). . . But the selling of their wares was the least part of of these women's jobs. Their most important role was that of purveyor of news. They were, in reality, the news-carriers of the women's world."[19] Ideally, men had suzerainty over the public world and women over the private, but as happens in all patriarchal societies, man was the lord of his castle as well.

Regarding the division of power in the Muslim household, Shaista makes an interesting observation, worth quoting here:

> Actually women in Muslim households invariably had great influence and a much greater say in household affairs than their menfolk. The fact that they observed purdah did not mean they were non-entities, though I know this is the general impression in the West, and like many other impressions, it is an erroneous one.[20]

Other commentators would disagree with Shaista about power in the andar mahal. For instance, Urquhart states: "It is often said that behind the parda the power of woman is supreme. But this in so far as it is true, applies chiefly to women who happen to be heads of households."[21] She added that in a large family there would be a few who experienced power and several who might never experience any at all. The power of a wife would be restricted to control over her children and perhaps limited influence over her husband.

In this regard, the responses of women interviewees (born around 1918–20) varied somewhat, but most seemed to agree that their mothers and grandmothers led happy lives, though actual power resided with the men of the household. In fact the happiness stemmed partly from an acceptance of the ideology of male supremacy in all spheres. Mrs Islam said, "Mother had no decision-making power. Father was the all in all. But one thing my mother insisted on and that was my education."[22]

On many occasions women of the previous generation whose lives had been lived in the late nineteenth and early twentieth centuries, and whose daughters were to emerge as the future Muslim *bhadro mohilas* (genteel women), sensed the change in the air and passionately stood their ground regarding their daughters' education. In several cases it might have been a mother's dying wish extracted from male family members on her deathbed. Often guardians married off their young but talented daughters after being assured that the groom would see to the bride's education. This happened in the case of Shamsunahar Mahmud (1908–64) who went on to do a Master's degree and Fatema Sadeq (b.1918) who went on to do a PhD.

Rokeya Sakhawat Hussein (1880–1932) had her own formulation on power in the household. In her various essays where she propounds her theory of feminism, Rokeya forcefully demonstrated how women have been disempowered throughout history in the home and outside it, till they were reduced to the status of domestic slaves.·She substantiated her point with cases from the Bengal Muslim community in which she lived. In *Griha* (Home), Rokeya drew the startling conclusion that as women do not have any genuine power, or ownership of the house and its assets, they are in fact 'homeless'. It must be remembered, however, that while other writers were writing autobiographies or memoirs, Rokeya was formulating a rigorous theory of women's subordination.

## Childhood and growing up

The birth of a female child was not considered as auspicious as that of a male. Many families did not bother to announce her birth with the *azaan*, a compulsory religious custom with Muslims for a male child. In his memoir, *Batayan*, Ibrahim Khan drew a picture of his contemporary society extending over a period of about six decades. In it he recorded, among other things, many rituals, customs and attitudes of a society in transition. While describing his childhood locality (Tangail subdivision and its surrounding areas), he recollected an incident about the birth of a daughter:

> There was no harm in the birth of sons one after another, but the birth of consecutive daughters resulted in displeasure manifesting itself in negative names such as "Chhutiwala", "Pochi", etc. . . In a nearby village a woman, after giving birth to four daughters, was pregnant again. Her husband had threatened her that if she gave birth to a female child again he would divorce her and cut off her nose. When a daughter was born again, the mother prepared to leave rather than be divorced.[23]

A child would be born in a separate room, termed variously *shutika griho* or *atur ghar*.[24] This need not have been spatially separated for the purpose as it was for Hindu women.[25] Giving birth to daughters would not always be frowned upon (the Prophet's great love for his daughter Fatima would often be invoked, for instance). Women writing in the period have testified to happy childhoods, in spite of severe purdah and lack of education. The more fortunate of them who spent their early lives in sprawling houses set amid expansive grounds (before these families became urban dwellers in the truest sense of the word) have some happier memories. Rokeya recollects:

> Where may one find a comparison to our house and its grounds, shaded by forests on all sides? . . . We have no clock here but no task is left

undone. We rise to the cry of the morning birds; the call of the foxes signals that *maghreb* (evening) prayer is near. . . . Our childhood passed in bliss in the midst of shady forests in rural Bengal.[26]

Nawab Faizunnessa also referred to a happy childhood in the preface to *Rupjalal*. These women belonged to upper or middle class landed gentry (*shurafa*) whose power was on the decline, giving way to the new professional Muslim elite drawn along the lines of the Brahmo/Hindu *bhadrolok* (middle class). The traditional shurafa were gradually being replaced by a more modernised middle class forged by a convergence of a relatively lower but upwardly mobile class and a higher but downwardly mobile one. Realities for the new gentry were different; and though women from these households, precursors of the Muslim bhadro mohilas of the 30s and 40s, were fortunate not to experience hardships that the vast majority of children faced every day, many of them had to struggle hard later. The comfort and luxury of their earlier lives had become things of the past. Rokeya, Monowara, Mamlukul Fatema, and Sufia Kamal worked to make ends meet — often after their widowhood or separation — but as children, they seldom knew what hardship meant. Their early childhoods were spent inside the andar mahal, playing with dolls or romping round the garden, listening to stories and fairy tales told by grandmothers or other elderly inmates of the house, learning and reading religious texts and an occasional chidren's story book. As girls, they were also taught to help in household chores, in cooking, sewing, knitting and embroidery. From an early age, they were brought up with the 'ultimate' goal of a woman in mind, that is, the role of a wife and mother. Childhood in the late nineteenth and early twentieth centuries did not last long for a girl by present day standards. It would end virtually at the age of six or seven when she would be put in purdah and shortly afterwards, be considered ready for marriage.

Norms and concepts of what women's role should be, what womanhood comprises — woman in her wanton and chaste aspect, one juxtaposed on the other — and women's own internalisation of this ideology, all generated an engrossing and continual discourse on women. It was formulated in the mosques, at home, in the fictional and non-fictional literature of the time, in politics and in the world of culture — there was no aspect of life free from it.

*Religious heritage*

The mental world of the Muslims in Bengal was made immensely more complex by the extraterritorial culture of pan-Islam. At the apex of the ideological world stood the Holy Koran, considered eternal, immutable, and final by devout Muslims, governing every aspect of their spiritual and material lives. The all-embracing Islamic law or Shariat is difficult to define in a few words, but its foundational principles as expounded by eighth century jurists like Al-Shafi, were based on five sources: (*i*) the *Koran*; (*ii*) the *Hadith* (recorded sayings, views, explanations of the Prophet) and *Sunna* (model) behaviour based on the conduct of the Prophet; (*iii*) *Ijma* (consensus among the community of believers); (*iv*) *Qiyas* (analogical reasoning); and (*v*) *Ijtehad* (original thought or research based on or exercised through qiyas).

The Koran lays down a fairly clear and strict code of conduct for all believers, but, for centuries, critical passages were taken up by countless jurists, commentators and preachers to provide the inviolable model of female behaviour. Of late, many feminist scholars who happen to live under Muslim law, are making a through study of those Koranic passages; their researches claim to have found numerous distortions and manipulations of the provisions of original passages. These claims are based on the scope for an interpretation (*tafsir*) of Koranic provisions and the etymology of the Arabic language.

The Koran, revered as the word of God as revealed to Prophet Muhammed, remains the highest source of law and philosophy in Islam; but as happens so often, the substance of religious belief gets conveyed through more popular and comprehensible means. Thus, the various commentaries, tracts and manuals were significant tools used to explicate its message—in the context of Muslims in India, because of the fact that the masses did not speak or understand Arabic. Though not given the status of Shariat, a vast number of religious tracts and manuals subsequently developed in various regions of the Islamic world which explained, interpreted and, in many cases, added to the provisions of the Koran and Hadith. Unlike classics such as Bukhari's Hadith these forms of didactic literature appealed to the masses. Along with the spoken word of the mullahs (religious leaders), expressed in the form of the *khutba*, *fatwa*, and *waz*, they brought Islam to the homes of the populace, filtered through the prism of the mullahs' interpretive faculties.

## The puthi tradition

Through cultural forms such as the reading of *puthi* (*punthi* in Bengali refers to hand-written books, usually composed in simple verse), instructional manuals and advice of the elders, girls in most sharif families were raised to be model Muslim daughters, wives and mothers. Till the late nineteenth century *Nasihat-namas*, a special brand of puthi literature meant to be recited, were the most popular medium of didactic instruction. Many of these namas had Arabic titles but were actually written in Bengali.

The socio-economic conditions of colonial rule in Bengal from 1757–1857 (the period of Company rule), created an ethos of cultural decay and erosion. This, according to Anisuzzaman,[27] generated an ambience for the development of puthi style composition in *misra-bhasha riti* (mixture of Arabic, Bengali, Persian, Urdu and Sanskrit). These sagas point to a decline in the status of women judging by the deep distrust and conviction regarding their fickle and lowly nature displayed by the writers. 'Love' too is debased in these eighteenth and nineteenth century puthis and one may assume that these popular didactic texts must have created and reflected the existing discourses on women. *Tambiatunnessa*, written by the nineteenth century poet Maleh Mohammad, "a respository of advice to women", was one such work.

Garibullah, whose father hailed from Dhaka, composed several pieces centering around women. His *Imandar Nek Bibir Keccha* (Story of the Pious and Faithful Lady), written in the latter half of the nineteenth century, celebrated "the medieval devotion of a wife to her husband though her status and nature are otherwise debased".[28] The poet also eulogised the devotion, piety and chastity of women such as Bibi Fatema (the work was based on the Urdu *Tambiatunnessa*). In an appendage titled *Kolikaler Aurater Bayan*" (The Ways of a Woman of Kali Yuga), the puthi-writer derided the modern woman:

> Garibullah says what can I expound
> The vices of today's women in Kali Yuga bound.
> In neighbour's house they talk ill of spouse,
> Neglecting chores in the house.
> The women gather and heap abuse

On husband, home and whatever they choose.
Some say, 'He buys no jewels for me.
Accursed may his earnings be.'
They while the hours, work undone,
The women of Kali Yuga, shameless ones![29]

In *Harh Jwalani* (1864), a short playlet written in the form of a conversation, the writer Ghulam Husain bemoaned the advent of Kali Yuga in which the traditional family structure was breaking down, that is, the daughter in-law wanted to reign and the mother-in-law's power was on the wane. The alert, 'modern' bride did not want to accommodate her mother-in-law and the son acquiesced. The mother, turned out of the house, was forced to roam the streets, begging. The theme of the manipulative wife (often a second one), poisoning the ears of the besotted husband against the mother-in-law or step-daughter (the latter, pious and chaste) became a recurring one among male writers of the subsequent period. It also found a place in the characterisation of the step-mother of the heroine in Nojibar Rahman's social novel *Anowara* (1914). Such books were popular among the Muslim literati in town and village.

The Muslims of nineteenth century Bengal were a pre-domi-nantly 'rural' society, but as urban migration intensified, so too did cultural exchange between towns and villages. With the devel-opment of modern Bengali prose in the latter half of the nine-teenth century, the namas were replaced by a spate of instructional literature meant to be read rather than heard. Initially a lot of Urdu works were imported into Bengal from North India and some were even composed indigenously. In fact, till the '30s, Urdu was the medium of instruction in maktabs and madrasas (the dominant, indigenous educational institutions for Muslims in Ben-gal before the colonial system of education took over). From the early decades of the twentieth century, religious scholars started writing didactic manuals in Bengali, often taking into account the changing lifestyle of rising middle-class Muslims. One of the earli-est of these was written by a woman called Khairunnessa (1870–1912) who also contributed a few articles to the periodical, *Nobour*. She wrote *Shotir Poti Bhakti*, which was said to have been a slim volume "recording the duties of a good wife". [30]

By Faizunnessa's time there were a few prose works by Muslim writers, but poetry had by no means lost its popularity as a medium. While the upper classes were disposed to classical Urdu-Persian literature, the majority preferred the misro-bhasha works. Role models upheld in front of young girls were: Bibi Fatema (the Prophet's daughter), Bibi Rahima (wife of the Biblical prophet Ayub), Bibi Khadija and Bibi Ayesha (and other wives of the Prophet), Khaola, Umme Aban, Umme Amara (female warriors of the early Arab empire), Rabeya the mystic saint, Razia Sultan and Chand Sultana (heroic warriors closer to home), Gul Badan, Nurjehan and Jahanara (learned ladies of the Mughal Court), etc. They were all-time favourites and their popularity endures to this day. Each of these historical figures represented one important virtue that a young girl should emulate: Fatema's life was an example of filial love as was Jahanara's (who also exemplified scholarship); Bibi Rahima was the ultimate example of devotion to husband and God; Khadija and Ayesha also stood for wifely love and devotion, Khaola and other *biranganas* (brave women) were extolled for their valour in defending Islam and their own honour. Rabeya, the eighth-century Sufi, alone, was different in that she trod a homeless, hearthless, husbandless path — that of a saint in search of God's love. Interestingly, the few Hindu women extolled by Muslims were Sita, Savitri and Sati — all renowned for their wifely devotion.

Shamsunnahar Muhmud (1908–64), one of the early female educationists, wrote *Punyomoyee* (a collection of biographical accounts of eight pious Muslim women) when she was only ten or eleven years old. Kazi Nazrul Islam, the Renaissance poet of Bengal, wrote a glowing preface for this book which was published in 1925. Later, in 1932, Shamsunnahar wrote her most famous biography *Rokeya Jiboni*: a life of Rokeya Sakhawat Hussein who pioneered Muslim women's awakening. This became a school text in which Rokeya's life was held up as an example; the pantheon of ideal women now included a new type incorporated by Rokeya. The old pantheon and its deities remained — to it was added yet another element created by and creating the new woman.

At late as 1912 Maulvi Dewan Nasiruddin Ahmed's *Poti Bhokti* (Devotion to the Husband — in verse, and in 1926 also in prose) handed out *masahel* (rules) for girls and held up once more the examples of Hawa (Eve), Khadija, Ayesha, Sauda, Fatema, Asma binte Yezid, Umme Abban, Zobeda Khatun, Mumtaz Mahal, Romesa, etc.

### Didactic manuals

Alongside this, a new kind of manual started appearing on the shelves of Urdu-educated Muslim homes. One could, if one chose, start with the multi-volume treatise *Beheshti Zewar* (Ornament of Heaven) written in Urdu by Ashraf Ali Thanawi (of the Deoband school) in 1905. Its Bengali translation was published in Calcutta in 1925. Thanawi's work was part of the Muslim Reformist project, aimed at creating the new model woman whom he conceived of as the Heavenly Ornament. As North Indian texts by Muslim writers were imported, sooner or later, into Bengal, this book not only became popular, it spawned Bengali versions based on its style and content. *Beheshti Zewar* was on the syllabus at Rokeya's Sakhawat Memorial Girls School, and Monowara Khatun remembers her elders reading it when she was a child.

Soon Bengali manuals started to become more popular. Written in chaste prose they differed from their precursors in one important respect: they were meant to be read by girls themselves, comprehended intellectually, emotionally, and acted upon. Various elements went into the making of the new woman — to whom the manuals were addressed and whom they also aimed to construct — and she was by no means a monolithic entity. The important point was that the manuals were self-contained and self-sufficient, sole guides in the turbulent sea of colonial India, for the pious but practical Muslim girl.

Though older texts and models persisted, there was a shift towards comprehensive compendia which any *individual* girl whose faculties had been 'opened' (a condition the *Beheshti Zewar* insisted on) through education, could comprehend and interpret. All existing virtues were kept intact; but more practical instruction and advice on cooking, cleaning, child-rearing, home medicine, religious duties, marital duties and rights, travelling, shopping, posting letters, etc. were added. In short, the texts were meant to be the model and guide for the Muslim girl now re-formed, so that she could steer herself and preserve her tradition, religion and purity in changing times, contributing simultaneously to the growth of the Muslim polity by producing ideal citizens. With the availability of cheap printing facilities, such manuals and booklets were on the rise, but their content and quality varied considerably.[31]

Repressing what may be termed the conservative strand of

Reformism, the novelty of the didactic manuals lay in the agency given to the female reader, albeit an agency used in the end to preserve the pristine, timeless traditions of Islam. The emphasis in the manuals, such as *Moqsudul Momenin* (1932), had shifted from concrete examples (though they still held their ground) to abstract values of female domesticity and virtue which were specifically spelt out. New social conditions had called for new female personalities, and new role models. Thus it was that when M. Sanaullah in 1937 decided to write another manual for girls, he named it *Adarsha Balika* (the Ideal Girl). It was meant for young girls and the author takes them by the hand, guiding them along the way to 'ideal womanhood' chapter by chapter.[32]

## Concluding remarks

The andar mahal, the primary abode of women, was where young girls were trained for their future roles as wives and mothers. By the first few decades of the twentieth century the reality of andar mahal life, its ambience and ideologies, had undergone significant changes in response to challenges to the old way of life from both male reformers and women themselves. As the boundaries of andar and bahir shifted the andar itself was being reshaped; in the process, the modern Muslim middle-class Bengali woman, counterpart of the Brahmo bhadro mohila, was being re-formed and recast.

## Notes

1    S. Ikramullah, *From Purdah to Parliament* (London: 1963), pp.1–5.
2    S. Ikramullah, op.cit., p.66.
3    M.A. Quddus, "Preface to *Rupjalal* by Faizunnessa Chaudhurani", (Reprinted by Bangla Academy, Dhaka: 1984) p.x.
4    M.A. Quddus, op,cit., pp. xii-xiii.
5    Rokeya S. Hussein, *Aborodhbashini* in M.A. Quddus (ed.) *Rokeya Rochonabali* (Dhaka: Bangla Academy, 1973), pp.488–89.
6    Syeda Monowara Khatun, *Smritir Pata*, in *Ekkhon*, Sharadiya issue (BS 1396) no. 5–6 (Calcutta: 1989), p.12.
7    Abul Fazal, "Preface" to Fatema Khanum's *Shoptorshi* (Dhaka: 1964).
8    Interview with Mrs Rokeya Khatun (December 1990).
9    Fatima Mernissi, *Beyond the Veil: Male Female Dynamics in Muslim Society* (Bloomington: Indiana University Press, 1987).
10   Fatima Mernissi, op.cit., p.19.
11   Ibid, p.18.
12   One of Mernissi's arguments is that in pre-Islamic society there were several

matrilineal tribes with a variety of marriages and women's rights. In this light the thesis that women's position in *Jahilya* was uniformly deplorable needs to be re-examined.

13   Margaret Urquhart, *Women of Bengal* (Calcutta: 1925, reprinted New Delhi, 1983).

14   M. Urquhart, op.cit.

15   S. M. Khatun, op. cit.,p.28.

16   S. Ikramullah, op.cit.pp.3–8.

17   Meredith Borthwick, *The Changing Role of Women in Bengal: 1849-1905* (New Jersey: Princeton University Press, 1984).

18   S. Banerjee, "Marginalization of Women's Popular Culture in Nineteenth Century Bengal", in K.Sangari and S.Vaid *Recasting Women: Essays in Colonial History* (Delhi: Kali for Women, 1989).

19   S. Ikramullah, op.cit., p.23.

20   Ibid, p.66.

21   M. Urquhart, op.cit., p.42.

22   Interview with Meherunnessa Islam (November 1991).

23   Ibrahim Khan, *Batatyan* (Dhaka: 1967), p. 209–10.

24   N. Rahman, *Anowara* (Calcutta: 1914, Reprinted Dhaka: 1988), pp.215–18.

25   Some interviews stated that the conditions and rituals of confinement and child delivery etc., for Muslim women were not as severe as for Hindu women, while others insisted that things were not so different. The official records as depicted in Censuses and Statistical Accounts refer to similar practices in both communities.

26   Rokeya S. Hussein, op.cit.,pp.195–96.

27   Anisuzzaman, *Muslim Manosh o Bangla Shahitya* (Dhaka: 1964) p.138.

28   Anisuzzaman, op.cit.

29   Cited in Anisuzzaman, (translation by the present author).

30   Anisuzzaman, op.cit. (Khairunnessa's book, *Shotir Poti Bhakti* 1912, referred to by Anisuzzaman, could not be procured by the present author.

31   In addition to those mentioned in the text, are, *Taujihul Adas* (1925); *Moslem Poncho Shoti* (1926); *Moslem Nari* (1927); *Muslim Birangana* (1936); *Moqsudul Momenin O Stree Shikkha* (1932).

32   Maulvi M. Sanaullah, *Adarsha Balika* (Calcutta: 1937).

# Sexuality in the Field of Vision
## The discursive clothing of the Sigiriya frescoes

MALATHI DE ALWIS

> *As a woman I'll gladly*
> *sing for these women*
> *who are unable to speak.*
>
> *You bulls come to Sigiri*
> *and toss off little lovesongs*
> *making a big hullabaloo.*
>
> *Not one has given us*
> *a heart-warming sip*
> *of rum and molasses.*
>
> *Maybe none of you thought*
> *we women could have lives*
> *of our own to get through.*
>
> — Richard Murphy, *The Mirror Wall*[1]

## Positioning

I have deliberately appropriated the title of Jacqueline Rose's book *Sexuality in the Field of Vision*[2] because I find that it has important resonances with what I wish to present in this paper. Though I will not be discussing her use of psychoanalytic theories, I am very sympathetic to her attempts to pose the question of female sexuality as a starting point of her work — especially in her examination of its intransigent and fragile representations in cultural life.

In this paper, I hope to explore the articulation of certain notions of female sexuality with Sinhala Buddhist nationalism. My focus will be on a series of visual representations of women at a Sri Lankan archaeological site/sight[3] — Sigiriya. While Sigiriya is of crucial importance for the nationalist project in Sri Lanka today, its contemporary form and content, I would argue, can be best understood by reading it as a colonial production, subsequently appropriated and contested by nationalists. It is this contestation and simultaneous narrativisation of the nation by nationalist scholars which will be my central concern here. The process of nationalisation/narrativisation, though authoritative and forceful, was not without its contradictions and complexities. The Sigiri paintings exemplify one such site/sight of ambiguity and tension, a battleground upon which notions of sexuality, morality, purity and race, sparred and parried.

### Sigiriya: historical and archaeological site/sight

The Sigiri paintings are also a sight/site within a larger archaeological site which I will call the Sigiriya complex. I will first briefly contextualise these representations within this larger grouping.

The Sigiriya complex gets its name from an independent rock formation that rises up about 600 ft. from the coastal peneplain in the Central Province of Sri Lanka. The etymology of the word 'Sigiriya' locates it as a compound of the two words — 'Sinha' (lion) and 'giri' (rock).[4] Encroached on by the "demolishing hand of time" and the "slowly advancing jungle"[5] Sigiriya is suddenly 'revealed' within an authoritative and historical discourse to a Ceylonese[6] public in 1831. The revelation here is that Sigiriya is no longer merely an interesting geographical and geological formation with a few 'ruins' scattered upon its surface, but that it has a history — an extremely romantic and dramatic one at that. The honour of making this momentous 'revelation' goes to Major Jonathan Forbes of the 78th Highlanders.

This 'history' of Sigiriya is located in a fifth century Pali Chronicle called the *Mahavamsa*. George Turnour, a British Orientalist and civil servant in Ceylon, who first discovered this text and translated it into English in the early nineteenth century, claimed that it contained a chronological, continuous and 'authentic' history of Ceylon extending from 500 BC.[7] The 'discovery' of various 'ruins' upon the Ceylonese landscape from now on became identified with specific historical moments mentioned in this text while simultaneously serving as crucial markers of the 'authenticity' of this text and the 'history' it recounted.[8]

This 'reciprocal' authentication was especially exemplified in the 'discovery' of ancient capitals such as Anuradhapura, Polonnaruwa and Sigiriya which were described in the *Mahavamsa*. Major Forbes, who met George Turnour in 1827, was delighted to be informed that "notwithstanding the disparaging assertions of English writers on Ceylon, there were still extant continued native records of great antiquity", and even more to be told that "the sites of several of the ancient cities mentioned [in these records] were still unknown, or at least had *remained unnoticed by Europeans*"[9] (1841 Vol 1:4–5, emphasis mine). This information inspired him "to acquire some knowledge of the Cingalese language, and to search for those vestiges of antiquity which could further verify the native chronicles."

Forbes' 'discovery' of Sigiriya thus enabled him to reveal a link in the 'glorious' past of Ceylon. His memoirs, *Eleven Years in Ceylon* published in 1841, for the first time places the descriptions of his 'finds' on the Sigiri rock side by side with the newly found 'historical' narrative of Sigiriya. From now on the connection between the site on the ground and the citings in this 'ancient' text are consistently reiterated in all subsequent descriptions of visits to Sigiriya. For example, when British travellers, Mr and Mrs Gay, visit Sigiriya in 1912 they take along the *Mahavamsa* as their guide book: "After a long rest and a long good supper, we took our 'Mihavansa' [sic], and there under the brow of the great 'Lions Rock', read again the strange, fragmentary history of Kassapa and his crime."[10]

Let me now briefly outline a composite Sigiri history culled from various dominant readings of the *Mahavamsa*, a history also provided in most school textbooks and travel guides.[11]

King Dhatusena (459–77AD), rules in the capital of Anuradhapura. He has two sons—the hot-headed Kassapa by a wife of unequal birth, and his favourite Moggallana, by the anointed queen and thus his rightful heir. Dhatusena also has a beautiful daughter whom he adores. She has been given in marriage to his sister's son, i.e., his nephew, Migara, who is now the Commander of Dhatusena's army. One day, Dhatusena notices his daughter's "vestments trickling with blood"[12] and learns that Migara has brutally whipped her on her thighs "although she was blame-less".[13] Incensed, Dhatusena orders that Migara's mother, i.e., his sister, be stripped naked and burnt at the stake. Migara's entreaties prove fruitless and he vows to wreak vengeance on the king. Migara incites Kassapa, who has always resented the fact that he can never be king, to stage a coup d'etat. While they manage to take the king prisoner and Kassapa ascends the throne, they are unable to kill Moggallana who escapes to India.

Still bent on revenge, Migara convinces Kassapa that Dhatusena has hidden his treasures until Moggallana's return. Ordered to confess its whereabouts, Dhatusena walks into one of the irrigation tanks built by him and proclaims that this is his treasure. Furious, Kassapa orders his death. Migara gleefully complies by having Dhatusena stripped naked and plastered alive into a wall.

Kassapa, fearing the inevitable return of Moggallana, decides to seek refuge in the "inaccessible stronghold of Sihagiri".[14] At the summit of this rock, he builds a magnificent palace which resembles Alakamanda — the abode of the god Kuvera. Hoping to atone for his fearful crime of patricide, he also patronises Buddhism and founds a monastery at Anuradhapura. In the eighteenth year of Kassapa's rule, Moggallana returns to Lanka with an army of south Indians. Confident of victory, Kassapa descends to the plains to battle with Moggallana. However, during the battle a stretch of marshy ground causes Kassapa to turn his elephant to take another course. His troops misconstrue this move as a sign of retreat and break up in disorder. Kassapa realises to his dismay that his capture is imminent and slits his own throat on the battlefield.

After Moggallana attends to Kassapa's obsequies, he returns to Anuradhapura and sets up his kingdom there. He hands Sigiriya to the priesthood and, from then on references to it more or less disappear from the public record.

With the rediscovery of Sigiriya in 1831 and its reinscription within a 'glorious' historical narrative, the Sigiriya complex became a popular site of exploration and adventure — a challenge to European masculinity. Journals such as the ones published by the Royal Asiatic Society (Ceylon Branch) and the *Monthly Literary Register* contain innumerable articles that document the exploits of these various adventurers, travellers and colonial administrators alike, who 'discovered' ruined monuments and tanks upon the rock or actually accomplished the perilous ascent to the summit aided by the 'natives' who "went up [the rock] like cats".[15] The Sigiriya complex's transformation to that of an archaeological site occurred in 1895 when H.C.P. Bell, the first Commissioner of Archaeology in Ceylon, was commissioned by Sir Arthur Gordon, the Governor of Ceylon, "to carry to completion the survey of either Sigiriya or Yapahuwa".[16] Bell selected Sigiriya as it was of "higher antiquity and directly greater interest".[17] He began by systematically clearing the jungle, surveying and mapping the rock and its environs and later moved on to excavate and restore the 'ruins'. During this time, strong iron stays were bored into the rock and a sturdy wire ladder leading up to the fresco chamber was constructed in order to make the paintings more accessible to visitors. Almost a century later, Bell's biographers note that his work at Sigiriya was "the most dramatic of the episodes of [his] career, both in the actual danger and difficulty of the undertaking and in the peculiar interest of some of the discoveries made in the course of the excavations".[18] Bell's name also first became known to a wider public through his reporting of his work at Sigiriya to the RAS(CB) and it was also during this time (1898) that he was elected an Honorary Member of the Society; "in more ways than one Sigiriya was the peak of his career".[19]

### The Sigiri frescoes: (re)production & (re)presentation

Now, let me return to the Sigiriya paintings which are popularly identified as frescoes.[20] The best preserved are located in a horizontal pocket midway along the almost perpendicular western facade of the rock. They have been dated to the time of King Kassapa's reign in the fifth century. Though it is believed that there were around 500 depictions of women in this and other rock pockets, there are only 21 complete figures visible today.

The frescoes were first sighted in 1875 by T.H.Blakesley of the Public Works Department who viewed them through field glasses as he was unable to make the perilous climb upto the fresco pocket. However, in June 1889 Alick Murray, also of the Public Works Department, at the request of the former Governor of Ceylon, Sir William Gregory, enters this "hitherto inaccessible chamber" and takes tracings in chalk from 13 of the frescoes.[21] Murray's report of this whole enterprise reads like an adventure story. Despite the "absolute refusal of the resident chiefs and the local population to have anything to do with the disturbances of a rock chamber which they believed to be inhabited and protected by 'Yakkos' (demons) in spite of the strong appeal — nay, order — of the European Revenue officers of the district", Murray finally reaches the chamber with the help of three stone-cutters from south India. Unable to stand or sit on the chamber ledge, Murray gets a special platform fixed on with iron stanchions upon which he lies full length on his back to make the tracings. Inches away from a sheer drop of 160 feet, tossed about by fierce winds and pecked at by swallows, Murray works from sunrise to sunset for an entire week. The "terrified natives" keep watch below his perch expecting him to be done to death by the demons and are finally "constrained to admit at the end [of his task] that [he] had succeeded in frightening the demons away". Extremely conscious of his 'historic' contribution within the British archaeological 'project', Murray hermetically seals a bottle containing a current newspaper, a few coins, and a list of friends who had visited him in the chamber, and cements it into the wall "to be discovered by the archaeologists of some future era". The proceedings are then "concluded on a solemn note with a bhikku being permitted to chant a *gatha* for the preservation of the bottle, and Murray and his compatriots singing 'God Save the Queen'".[22]

However, though H.C.P.Bell "frequently praised [Murray's] 'pioneer work' he felt that the copies failed to give anything like a true presentation of the vividness and coarseness of the original colouring".[23] Bell's yearning for a reproduction of the frescoes "with a faithfulness almost perfect" was fulfilled in 1896–97 when D.A.L. Perera, the First Draughtsman of the Archaeological Survey produced twenty-two beautiful facsimiles in oils. In the face of Perera's "singular talent, unflagging patience and real courage", Murray's week-long adventure pales into insignificance. Yet, unlike Murray's case, the heroism of Perera is always mediated through the writings of Bell:

> Mr Perera spent nineteen weary weeks—practically five months—in the cheerless 'pocket' caves of Sigiri-gala working on day after day from morning to evening — exposed latterly to the driving force of the south-west wind, and sorely tried at times by inflammation of the eyes and attacks of fever—before the final touch could be put to the last of the twenty-two paintings.[24]

Perera's copies were then deposited and later displayed at the

National Museum for the comfortable viewing of a larger public:

> I did not, I admit, choose to scale a dreadful little bamboo ladder which
> mounted up from the long Gallery to the frescoé cave, swaying over
> vacancy as it went. Instead, I studied the ladies of Sigiri from the
> facsimile paintings at Colombo, which are admittedly marvellous in their
> accuracy.[25]

The making of the facsimiles was indeed a momentous achievement as these frescoes now became visually accessible[26] to an
extremely large number of people not only by being on 'view' at
the Museum but by being reproduced in various journals, magazines and newspapers.[27] Along with the increased visual access to
the frescoes there also arose a need to make meaning of these
paintings. Unlike the historical narrative that could be matched
with the Sigiri complex as a whole, there were no specific references to the paintings in the Pali Chronicles. Nevertheless, all interpretations of the frescoes attempt to inscribe them within the
larger historical narrative of the *Mahavamsa*. Travel writer Kishor
Parekh articulates this desire when she suggests that the paintings
of these "sensuous women of Sigiriya" were commissioned by
Kassapa "[the] princely parricide who feared danger but loved
pleasure".[28] Thus, implicit in the celebration of these paintings are
notions of beauty, royal patronage, secular pleasures and a refined
sense of aesthetics that is seen as a marker of Sinhala culture at its
zenith.

However, this incorporation of the Sigiriya frescoes within a
Sinhala tradition did not occur so easily. In 1897, when H.C.P.Bell
reported to the RAS(CB) that "artists trained in the same schools,
if not the very same hands, must have executed both Indian and
Ceylon frescoes" he caused quite a furore among the Sinhalese
literati of the time. C.M. Fernando commenced a heated debate
with Bell on this issue that spilled over into local journals and
newspapers.[29] Much chastened, Bell did not repeat these assertions in his 1905 report![30] There now seems to exist a consensus of
opinion among most Sri Lankan scholars as well as foreign art
historians, that though the Ajanta and Sigiri frescoes share some
similarities, they differ considerably in technique and colouring.
Some Sri Lankans scholars are even more ambitious in their
claims:

> The extremely perilous conditions under which the western face of the
> enormous rock was painted, the high quality of the technique adopted at

such an early period, the clear and beautiful line work, the mellowness of the shading, all contribute to placing the Sigiriya paintings amongst the *foremost wall paintings of any period in any part of the world* (emphasis mine).[31]

This notion of the 'superiority' of the Sigiri frescoes was also tacitly promoted by the State in an advertisement put out by the State Gem Corporation in the *Times of Ceylon Annual* 1973. The equation here was between the Sigiri paintings and gems. Interestingly, Kishor Parekh made a similar analogy a few years earlier by calling the paintings "jewels of Sinhalese culture" that had endured the "ravages of time".[32] In this advertisement, both commodities (touted for the consumption of tourists here) can "stand the test of beauty and quality". By calling upon men and women "of discerning taste", "connoisseurs", the advertisers not only attempted to justify the pricelessness of the paintings and the equally high cost of the gems, they also suggested that only a certain class of people can truly appreciate such products.

### The Sigiri frescoes: site/sight of sexuality

What makes the Sigiri frescoes most interesting is that they are not merely markers of a culture at its zenith, but also the only examples of an open celebration of the sensuality of the female body in Sri Lankan painting. I do not wish to speculate here whether the female figures are clothed or unclothed, merely to draw attention to the fact that in either case, the detailing of the female form — the voluptuous lips, the curving breasts, the swelling nipples — are clearly visible. As Margaret Miles has so aptly put it, "Some of the most puzzling historical images and the most difficult to interpret are those in which nude human bodies or nude parts of bodies play a central role in the visual communication." She gets to the crux of a feminist concern in such a context when she points out:

> [N]o pictorial subject is more determined by a complex web of cultural interests than visual narrations of the female body; such images are not susceptible to simple naturalistic interpretation. Moreover, with no other depicted object is it less safe to assume a continuity or even a similarity of meaning between its original viewers and the modern interpreter.[33]

Miles herself has done very interesting work on fourteenth century Tuscan religious paintings that depict the Virgin Mary with one exposed breast. Her major concern is to contextualise these paintings within their specific historical period. She notes that while the visual associations of a modern viewer to a bare-breasted Mary may consist largely of the soft pornography that covers the newsstands today, a medieval viewer would look at it quite differently. Through her sensitive exploration of the complexities of fourteenth century Tuscan culture, Miles shows us that these paintings had more to do with attempts to control women's power to nourish through breast-feeding, than with implying an overt eroticism.[34] Unfortunately, such sensitive work has not been done with regard to the Sigiriya frescoes. Undoubtedly, they are very old paintings and the only references to them occur in some of the 685 verses that were scratched upon a plastered wall facing the fresco pockets (which I will come back to later). I do not plan to posit a better way to read these paintings; my main interest here is to explore how these visual texts were 'narrativised' by a group of scholars in Sri Lanka.

The reason I have decided to concentrate on a somewhat narrow scholarly discourse is because I think that these scholars played a very important role in constructing a "collective identity" of the newly emergent nation-state in post-Independence Sri Lanka (late 1940s and through the middle 1950s). They were greatly interested in showing that the Ceylonese, too, were capable of being intellectuals and scientists and usually displayed their erudition by expounding on their 'indigenous traditions', trying to make meaning of their 'culture' and 'heritage'. In these scholars' world view, the majority of the archaeological and historical research on Ceylon, until the early part of the twentieth century, had been conducted by various British civil servants.[35] The results of their research were always published in English or other European languages for "the information and edification of their countrymen in their home countries".[36] The Royal Asiatic Society (Ceylon Branch), founded in 1845 and one of the major bodies that encouraged "antiquarian studies" was also seen as constituting itself as a very exclusive Society. Godakumbura notes that until the 1930s, the meetings of the Society were after-dinner gatherings which one was expected to attend in dinner-suits. He rather scathingly says that the "few natives" who were admitted were thoroughly Europeanised and lived apart from the majority of their countrymen "they had no roots in the soil; they had no contact with the common man". The State-run Archaeological Survey during this time also presented its findings in English and

thus had a limited audience. Since the Sinhala press hardly reported archaeological 'discoveries', and excavation sites were closed
off to the public with archaeological operations being conducted
within barbed wire fences, "the ordinary citizen had no idea of the
meaning and purpose of archaeology".

However, the consolidation of the nationalist movement and
the proliferation of Sinhala print capitalism in the 1940s, spearheaded the translation and publication of the *Mahavamsa* and its
commentaries, in Sinhalese. Many nationalist scholars were extremely fluent in Sinhalese and were thus able to communicate
their ideas about Ceylon's 'glorious' past in both Sinhala and
English. More and more people thus began to read about the
ancient monuments and to embark on pilgrimages to these sites. It
was during this time then that the Sigiriya frescoes were transformed into one of the many visual markers and sites of the newly-
emerging nation-state's cultural heritage. After Ceylon gained
independence in 1948 "the need to bring before the public with
greater emphasis the cultural heritage of the nation was served by
the appointment of an officer to handle matters connected with
publications".[37] Handbooks serving as guides to important archaeological sites were first reprinted and later freshly prepared in
both English and Sinhala. These books had brisk sales and were
soon out of print. Tourists were also catered to with the production of "first class picture postcards" of ancient monuments, sculp-
tures and paintings. However, I wish to propose here that the overt
sexuality and eroticism of the women in the frescoes did not make
the frescoes' transition to being part of a nation's cultural heritage, a very smooth one.

### Sexuality in the scholars' 'field of vision'

Roland Barthes wrote in *Image-Music-Text*, "all images are
polysemous; they imply, underlying their signifiers, a 'floating
chain' of signifiers, the reader able to choose some and ignore
others".[38] As Barthes went on to note, polysemy poses a question of
meaning, i.e., images become bound up with an uncertainty concerning the meaning of objects or attitudes. "Hence in every
society various techniques are developed, intended to *fix* the
floating chain of signifieds in such a way as to counter the terror of
uncertain signs".

I suggest that the most terrifying sign of all to Sri Lankan scholars was what they perceived as the sexual and the sensual. The exposed breasts of the Sigiri women ruptured the scholar's field of vision, bringing into recall identification, pleasure and distrust. When each scholar attempted to 'fix' both consciously and unconsciously, the meaning of this sign *he* (I use this pronoun deliberately as all the scholars involved in this discourse were male), was acting as a socially constructed being. Therefore, when he attempted to interpret these painting he drew on various concepts and ideologies with which he had been imbued in the continuous and dynamic construction of his socio-cultural being. In this context, it was unavoidable for him to ignore the 'larger' issues of his time such as race, religion, nationalism, etc. But this eagerness to discuss 'larger' and 'more pressing' issues, I suggest, was also an attempt to displace the scholar's anxiety about the overt sexuality of the Sigiri women.

By the late '40s and early '50s there were two major theories that had been propounded about the women in the frescoes. One was by an Englishman, an eminent archaeologist, H.C.P.Bell, and the other by the internationally known art historian, Ananda Coomaraswamy — half British, half Sri Lankan. Bell thought the frescoes depicted a procession of queens and princesses of King Kassapa's court, attended on by their maids, on their way to a Buddhist shrine north of Sigiriya.[39] He based his claim (and so did Blakesley and Murray[40] before him), on a division of labour, i.e., some women have been depicted as carrying flower trays while others are merely holding the flowers, and of colour, i.e., the women of "darker hue" carrying the trays were believed to be a different race.[41] Bell expands on this hypothesis in 1897 by noting that the serving maids "of unattractive mien" had been given a greenish complexion as a "badge of servitude" which clearly marked them off from the "high-born dames, their mistresses", who were "pale-yellow 'blondes' or orange-hued 'brunettes'".[42]

Bell was determined that these were portraits of real queens and princesses for each figure was "imbued with divergent traits in face, form, pose and dress, which seem to stamp it as an individual likeness". In his report to the RAS(CB) in December 1897, he waxed so eloquent on the various characteristics of these maidens that Governor Sir West Ridgeway in his vote of thanks for what he described as Bell's "maiden meditation" commented: "As your official chief I was rather shocked for a moment at your intimate acquaintance with the feelings of these ladies, and I began to fear a Breach of Promise case until I remembered how very much older they were than yourself".[43] Bell was convinced that the figures were not, as they appear to be, naked above the waist but "in reality fully clothed in a short-sleeved jacket of finest material. So thin, indeed, that the painter has occasionally contented himself by indicating it by a mere line of deeper colour".[44] He also suggested that the reason for the women being cut off at the waist by clouds was a purely practical measure that had been adopted by the artist in order to economise space due to the concavity of the rock surface.[45]

Coomaraswamy strongly disagreed with Bell on many points, noting that the frescoes contained no religious (read Buddhist) feeling,[46] rather they were "penetratingly sensual" and probably depicted Apsaras or divine women, the latter identification being based on the very fact that the women were cut off at the waist by clouds which he noted was a sign of divinity.[47] However, both scholars could not communicate in Sinhala and belonged to the colonial elite who wrote for and spoke to a more cosmopolitan audience in the metropolis as described by Godakumbura.

In 1947, Senarat Paranavitana, the first Sri Lankan Commissioner of Archaeology, defiantly challenged these two theories by writing a series of minutely detailed papers on the significance and meaning of the Sigiri frescoes. Paranavitana was a self-taught scholar and epigraphist, who gradually rose within the ranks of the Archaeological Department through sheer hard work producing a prodigious number of articles in both Sinhala and English on a variety of subjects. However, the Sigiriya complex was one of his favourite research sites. His intention was not just to decipher the meaning of the frescoes but to prove that King Kassapa was a God King modelled along the lines of the mythical god Kuvera who lived in Alakamanda.[48] His interpretation of the frescoes was crucial to his thesis. He completely naturalised the Sigiri women by asserting that they were really personifications of clouds. The 'golden-coloured' ones being "lightning princesses" and the 'lily-coloured' ones being "cloud damsels" who hovered around Alakamanda attending to every whim and fancy of Kuvera (as described in the Indian Sanskrit text *Meghaduta*).[49]

Though most Sri Lankan scholars were sceptical of this theory, the public was delighted and in 1974, a blockbuster film titled *The*

*God King* was made in Sri Lanka. Paranavitana never overcame his disappointment at being spurned by his scholarly audience however, and while in retirement during the 1960s he became rather crazed and professed to be able to read "inter-linear inscriptions", supposed to be inscribed in minute characters on many ancient stone epigraphs found scattered in various parts of the country.[50] His last book, *The Story of Sigiri* was based on translations of these inscriptions which *just happened* to prove every single point he had been trying to make about Sigiriya for much of his adult life. In his single-minded attempt to prove that King Kassapa was a God-King, and through his naturalisation and neutralisation of the women, Paranavitana avoided dealing with the overt sexuality of the Sigiri women. This was left to a few other scholars who were also trying to make meaning of the paintings around the same time.

The most vociferous denial of the sensual was from M.D. Raghavan, an ethnologist and assistant director of the National Museum in Sri Lanka at this time. He was horrified that Coomaraswamy found the frescoes "penetratingly sensual" and wrote rather despairingly in 1948:

> If Sigiriya art does nothing but express and communicate sensuous or sensual ideas, all our interest in the Sigiriya art would seem a waste, for Sigiriya art is truly great and could not possibly have been conceived or created to serve the sole purpose of exciting sensuous thought.[51]

He asserted that these paintings were "deeply symbolic" and suggested scenes of religious worship comparable to what can be seen at any Buddhist shrine today. According to Raghavan, these women were the wives and daughters of Kassapa, offering homage to the Buddha. The permanent representation of their worship on the rock was used by Kassapa to supplicate the Buddha in an effort to atone for the sin of patricide. Yet, Raghavan's efforts were interrupted by his own gaze: if the women seem rather sensual, he argued, "it is well to remind ourselves that a certain amount of sensuousness has formed part of the religious customs and observances of most countries, in the past". Seeming unconvinced by his own argument, he then attempted to re-define sensuality "as indeed any work of art which appeals to our sense of the beautiful", collapsing sensuality into beauty. Many of the women in the frescoes, he went on to point out, are mature "dowagers" and "matrons" who by wearing the tali and tilak like all well-married Tamil ladies, conclusively inform the viewer that they are respectable *wives.* Raghavan, like Bell, also stressed the fact that these women were not bare-breasted but actually wearing a cloth of "superfine texture" because of the incredible heat of the rock in the tropical sun!

Nandadeva Wijesekera, who claims to be the first Sri Lankan anthropologist, wove a complex theory of race in 1947, by proposing that the women depicted in the frescoes could be racially differentiated according to their varying hues of colour. By expanding on Bell's allusions to racial difference, Wijesekera labelled the women being served, the 'golden coloured' ones, as Aryan and the women serving, the 'dusky ones', as either Dravidian or of Negroid stock. The Aryan typology he culled from these paintings included the "more superior" features: long face, straight nose, delicate features and athletic body as opposed to the Dravidian typology: largeness of frame, thick lips, dark eyes and matronly features.[52]

In a slightly later paper, Wijesekera was more concerned about shedding "Fresh Light on the Sigiriya Frescoes", which consisted of yet another interpretation of the content of the paintings. I strongly suspect that this paper was written to counter the interpretation given by a popular novelist, Martin Wickremasinghe, in a more literary journal in 1938.[53] Wickremasinghe sought corroboration for the content of the paintings in classical Sinhala literature.[54] Rather haphazardly matching snippets of poetry with various segments of the paintings, he proposed that the frescoes depicted women participating in an erotic, aquatic festival. Wijesekera, who decided to debate Wickremasinghe (without actually naming him), based his argument on the premise that "festival occasions were never serious moments" and then did his utmost to prove that the women in the frescoes do not even betray a smile.

> Every one of those figures is portrayed in a studied pose of mental preoccupation. Do not some figures express poignant withdrawal from something strange and awe-inspiring, something awful and lamentable. The whole scheme is woven around such a central idea of deep loss or mourning, maybe for Kasyapa.[55]

P.E.P. Deraniyagala, director of the National Museum, writing in 1951, also reiterated Bell and Raghavan by pointing out that frescoes "strongly suggest that there was some feminine element incorporated in the religious ritual of those days and alluded to the fact that these women might be temple dancers.[56] In a later paper he also attempted to differentiate between the "sexually free" art of the 'west' and the more "spiritual" 'east', epitomised by the Sigiriya frescoes: "The female figure has always been treated with restraint and dignity [in Ceylon] there was less of a craving for the naked figure which has proved such a stimulus to western artists and especially their patrons."[57]

## Can the sexual be part of a nation's heritage?

These scholars' persistent de-sexualisation of the frescoes greatly facilitated the Sri Lankan government's response when vandals sprayed green paint on fourteen of the paintings and chiselled and hacked two of them—one on the head and the other, "above the waist", in October 1967.[58] The Minister of Cultural Affairs at the time, Mr Iriyagolla, is reported to have stated that this vandalism was tantamount to "stabbing one's own *mother* in the heart". If not for Raghavan's stress on the "maturity" and impeccable morality of the Sigiri women and many other scholars down the line who had also highlighted their religiosity and sobriety, Iriyagolla's statement would have sounded extremely ridiculous. The recourse to the symbolism of mother here further concretises the Sigiri frescoes' status as a national treasure which at this moment is made synonymous with the nation-state of Sri Lanka, invariably referred to as the Motherland.[59]

One of the main reasons for the puritancial and moralistic posturings of these scholars stemmed from a 'Protestant' Buddhist ethic that was being strongly promoted by Sinhala Buddhist revivalists in the new nation-state. These Buddhist revivalists were mainly petit bourgeoisie: small landowners, shopkeepers, minor bureaucrats, school teachers, etc., educated in Sinhala, and the 'organic intellectuals' of the rural areas; as well as those from the merchant and professional segments of the bourgeoisie educated in both English and Sinhala and concentrated in the larger cities. The latter group formed the intellectual core of the revivalists.[60] The now classic formulation of a Protestant Buddhist ethic was first coined by Gananath Obeyesekere in 1970. Obeyesekere's use of the meaning of this term was two-fold: (*i*) many of its norms and organisational forms were historical derivatives from Protestant Christianity and (*ii*) it was a protest against Christianity, and its associated western political dominance.[61] "Thus, for example, those very norms that were derived from Western Victorian Protestanism were thrown back at the 20th century West—Westerners [were] believed to be sexually lax, and there [was] a general condemnation of 'Western' values."

Unlike in the case of India, which Chatterjee has analysed so elegantly,[62] the discourse of Sinhala nationalists did not hinge upon the resolution of the 'Woman Question' which, in India, included such volatile issues as sati, child marriage, purdah and the ban on widow remarriage.[63] Nevertheless, the regulation of female morality was integral to the nationalist project. As the Anagarika Dharmapala, an influential leader of the Sinhala Buddhist revival put it, "the glory of woman is in her chastity".[64] Many of his injunctions concerning female chastity were mapped on the body. Dharmapala, in his *Daily Code for the Laity*, (1898) and in later newspaper articles which circulated widely advocated that Sinhala-Buddhist women wear the the Indian sari as a sign of their modesty, chastity and unique "Sinhalaness".[65] He specified a length for the sari, insisting that a woman's "black legs" should be completely covered. His injunctions on the osari blouse, in a society where many peasant women were often bare-breasted, were detailed and repeated. A blouse, Dharmapala wrote must be long, covering fully the woman's breasts, midriff, navel and back.[66] Dharmapala's own mother was the first to wear the sari in December 1884 on a pilgrimage to Bodh Gaya in India, and it soon became the standard "national" loe country dress for low country Sinhala women.[67]

## Counterpoint

The academic discourse on Sigiriya in no way held hegemonic sway over the entire population. One of the main reasons for this was the approximately 700 verses that were written in the so-called 'pure' form of Sinhala—Elu Sinhala, on the 'mirror wall' at Sigiri. It is believed that these verses have been written by visitors (mainly males) to Sigiriya between the eighth and twelfth centuries AD. Many of them are very sexist, but they also specifically take the sexual into consideration. Almost 60 per cent refer to the Sigiri women, often in extremely erotic and sensual language. Even today, they are constantly published in glossy magazines and newspapers along with photographs of the Sigiri women as in the following samples:

Ladies like you
Make men pour out their hearts
And you also
have thrilled the body
Making its hair
Stiffen with desire

The girl with golden skin
Enticed the mind and eyes,
Her lovely breasts
Cause me to recall
Swans drunk with nectar.

When you come to mind, the heart aches,
The blood boils and I cry aloud.
Your waist makes me bound to you in my heart.[68]

It is important to note, however, that many of the scholars discussed above were not aware of these verses until systematic rubbings were taken, translated and published by Paranavitana in 1957. Later scholars who were familiar with these verses, however, were careful to point out that "[t]here was no coarseness or vulgarity evinced in [the] comments" of these early visitors.[69]

Some of the more popular interpretations of these frescoes fluctuate between the prosaic and the fanciful. They run the gamut from proposing that Sinhalese monks, or Indian or Chinese 'mendicant' artists painted these women[70] to them being the work of "Kassapa's soldiers, relieving the tedium of their watch by painting 'pin-ups', 'topless' ones!"[71] Paulinus Tambimuttu who wrote in a popular journal soon after the restoration of the frescoes damaged by the vandals, concluded

Thanks to Mr Maranzi and Dr de Silva [the two restorers][72] visitors will continue to be delighted by the breasts of our Sigiriya ladies, which, according to Mr Arthur C. Clarke [a greatly cherished celebrity in Sri Lanka] are "as well developed as those of any of the current beauties of the Italian or Hollywood screens".[73]

Ironically, this celebration of sexuality in the frescoes is even today, tacitly promoted by an increasingly puritanical State in the face of an extremely lucrative industry: tourism. The State which constantly sends out communiques to its female employees—especially news readers on TV who enter the public's 'field of vision' daily, on how they should behave (modestly) and dress (be well 'covered')—blithely touts the bare-breasted Sigiriya women to the tourists.[74] This exploitation of sexuality to capture a specific consumer's 'field of vision' is especially marked when we consider the layout of the larger Sigiriya complex with reference to the fresco pocket. Visitors to the frescoes usually have to pass through a series of souvenir stalls that line the paths and stairways that ascend the rock. The most abundant items on display here are postcards of the Sigiri maidens and various souvenirs that are inscribed with their forms.[75] It has been argued that off-sight/site markers in the form of postcards, souvenirs or literature, when taken together, constitute a narrative sequence that leads the tourist to a sight/site with already well-formed preconceptions.[76] Therefore, 'sightseeing' actually involves a process of matching these preconceptions with the actual sight/site which leads to a site/sight's meaning always being mediated by its souvenirs. One begins the ascent of the rock with the sensual representations of the Sigiri women inscribed in one's mind. After about ten minutes of climbing, one finally arrives at the iron spiral staircase that leads up into the fresco pocket. Despite the seeming sturdiness of the staircase it is still a rather harrowing experience as the wind ferociously tears at one's clothing and if one looks down it is a sheer drop of 160 feet. The dimly-lit fresco chamber, adorned with these sensual women, at the top of the staircase thus offers a safe womb for the tired traveller as well as a pleasurable feast for the eyes.

## Conclusion

The dilemma the Sigiri frescoes present for the Sri Lankan State and its nationalist intellectuals today, is very similar to what was experienced by the scholars discussed above. The nation-state wants to posit a continuity with a glorious past and in this sense, Sigiriya is a perfect example — an elaborately constructed fortress with ingenious water gardens and mirror walls, displaying the finest paintings to be found in the whole of Sri Lanka. This historical continuity has been especially emphasised by the State with the increase in tourism from the 1970s onwards. But Sigiriya poses a specific dilemma in that the eroticism of the Sigiri women jars with the historical continuity that is being posited. As Partha Chatterjee has noted for India, in Sri Lanka too, one of the key ideological responses of nationalism to a colonialist critique of Ceylonese tradition was to latch on to the Orientalist dichotomy of the east as spiritual and the west as material.[77] The major terrain for this discourse was the colonised woman.[78] While the 'western' woman was portrayed as being sexually free, the Sri Lankan woman epitomised submission, chastity and restraint.[79]

The studied eroticism of the Sigiri women was not quite in keeping with this image of the modest and pure Sri Lankan woman. Nationalist scholars therefore attempted to discursively clothe and domesticate them. Their rhetoric revolved around whether the women were clothed or not, and on who 'owned' them. Since no male appears in the frescoes, attempts were made to deny that absence by insisting that the women had existed under some sort of patriarchy. They *had* to be the wives and daughters or handmaids of the king, who were involved in dignified activities such as religious ceremonies—paying homage to the Buddha on behalf of their king, or mourning his death. Any mention of the women's possible participation in an erotic festival was quickly silenced. On the contrary, they were swiftly drawn into the private/domestic realm to counteract the public gaze that was constantly on them.

With the proliferation of the tourism industry, the State's activities of exploiting the sexuality of these frescoes through advertisements, posters, postcards etc., fracture the nationalist scholar's moralistic rhetoric. Even though the women are discursively clothed and domesticated, they remain "exotic nudes" or "archaic erotica" for foreign tourists and the immoral "other" of the modest Sinhala woman.[80] I think this dilemma of embarassment, yet exploitation of the frescoes, echoes the seeming 'western' contradiction, now hegemonic to some degree worldwide, that constructs female sexuality as profane as well as powerful. Unfortunately, in this instance, the profanity as well as the power of the Sigiri frescoes has been manipulated by male scholars and a patriarchal State but . . . . the Sigiri smile lingers.

## Notes

I am greatly indebted to Lauren Berlant, Bernard Cohn, Jean Comaroff, Steve Hughes, Roz Morris, Tamara Neuman, Vijay Prashad, Jon Walters and especially Pradeep Jeganathan, for their incisive comments on earlier drafts of this paper. I also sincerely thank the participants at the conference on "Women: The State, Fundamentalism and Cultural Identity in South Asia" for their enthusiastic response and suggestions.

1 Richard Murphy's book of poems, *The Mirror Wall* (Newcastle-on-Tyne: Bloodaxe Books, 1989) was based on the 685 verses that were written by visitors to Sigiriya between the eighth and twelfth centuries, on a plastered, highly finished and glazed wall at Sigiriya (named the "mirror wall" by early archaelogists). These verses were systematically copied and translated by Senarat Paranavitana and are included in his two volume tome *Sigiri Graffiti* (London: Oxford University Press, 1956).
   The poem quoted is based on a verse that was believed to have been written by a female visitor to Sigiriya.

2 Jacqueline Rose, *Sexuality in the Field of Vision*, (London: Verso, 1986).

3 I use 'field' in the double sense of an archaeological locus or site as well as a focus of vision or sight.

4 P.E.P. Deraniyagala, "The Human and Animal Motif in Sinhala Art" in *Journal of the Royal Asiastic Society (Ceylon Branch)*, n.s., Vol 4(1), May 1955, p. 369.

5 R.H. de Silva, *Sigiriya* (Colombo: Department of Archaeology, 1971, p. 3.)

6 Though I use the more nationalist, 'Sri Lanka', I will resort to the colonial 'Ceylon' whenever I refer to the time periods in which it was used — the nineteenth and early twentieth centuries.

7 For a brilliant location and deconstruction of this text, see Jonathan Walters, "Positivist Paradise Lost: On the History of the Pali Chronicles of Sri Lanka", in Ronold Inden (ed.), *Post-Orientalist Approaches to the Study of South Asian Texts* (Delhi: Oxford University Press, forthcoming), and Pradeep Jeganathan, "Authorizing 'History', Ordering Land : British Colonialism, the *Mahawamsa*, and Anuradhapura", MA Thesis, University of Chicago.

8 Pradeep Jeganathan, "Authorizing History, Ordering Land: The Conquest of Anuradhapura" in *Unmaking the Nation: The Politics of Identity and History in Modern Sri Lanka* (eds.) P. Jeganathan and Q. Ismail (Colombo: Social Scientists' Association, 1995).

9 What constitutes "knowledge" here is European authentication, familiarity and appropriation. (Major Jonathan Forbes, *Eleven Years in Ceylon* (London: Richard Bentley, 1841, Vol 1: 4–5, emphasis mine). cf P. Jeganathan, op. cit. 1995.

10 Jennie Coker Gay, "Sigiriya : the Lion's Rock of Ceylon" in *Century Magazine*, Vol. 86, June 1913, p. 269.

11 Gananath Obeyesekere who did some research in the Sigiriya area has noted that there are several folk versions of this tale that provide different 'readings' of it—(G. Obeyesekere "The Myth of the Human Sacrifice: History, Story and Debate in a Buddhist Chronicle" in *Social Analysis*, No 25, Sept. 1989. However, we cannot ignore the fact that they too are being recalled and 'read' in the present.

12 Forbes, op. cit. Vol. II, 1841, p. 4.

13 R.H. de Silva, op. cit, 1971, p. 2.

14 Ibid.

15 Bethia N. and Heather M. Bell, *H.C.P. Bell : Archaeologist of Ceylon and the Maldives* (Wales: Archetype Publications, 1993), p. 85.

16 H.C.P. Bell, "Interim Report on the Operations of the Archaeological Survey at Sigiriya in 1895", *Journal of the Royal Asiatic Society (Ceylon Branch)*, Vol. 14

(46) p. 44.

17 Ibid.

18 Bell & Bell, op. cit., 1993, p. 83.

19 Ibid., p. 100.

20 Technically they do not fall into the category of frescoes as they have not been painted on a wet surface, but a dry one.

21 Alick Murray, "The Rock Paintings of Sigiri", in *Black and White*, No. 189, p. 183.

22 R.H. de Silva, op. cit., 1971, p 4. The sexual overtones of this project cannot be ignored as Murray cements a bottle into this womb-like chamber that is adorned with paintings of sensual women! The singing of 'God Save the Queen' is ironically double-edged in view of later interpretations that the frescoes depict King Kassapa's queens.

23 Bell & Bell, op. cit., 1993, p. 87.

24 H.C.P. Bell, "Interim Report on the Operations of the Archaeological Survey at Sigiriya in 1897" *Journal of the Royal Asiatic Society (Ceylon Branch)*, Vol 15 (48), p. 108.

25 Reginald Farrer, *In Old Ceylon* (London : Edward Arnold, 1908).

26 Though photography was utilised for purposes of archaeological recording in Ceylon since 1870, the inaccessibility of the fresco chamber provided 'limited' opportunities to photograph the paintings. An amazing photograph in Bell & Bell (1993) documents D.A. Perera photographing the frescoes while hanging in mid-air, 150 ft. above ground on a flimsy chair. Despite such heroism, Bell reports that the force of the wind impeded the shutter speed of the camera producing pictures that were "more or less blurred". Not to be defeated, the indomitable Perera nevertheless completed an "excellent little oil painting to scale" of the two fresco 'pockets' "after a week's 'rocking' in space"! H.C.P. Bell, Interim Report on the Operations of the Archaeological Survey at Sigiriya in 1896" *Journal of the Royal Asiatic Society (Ceylon Branch)* Vol. 15 (47), p. 257.

27 See Murray op. cit., p. 184, for an early example of this new development.

28 Kishor Parekh, "Sensuous Women of Sigiriya" in *Orientations*, Vol. 1(8), p. 32.

29 C.M. Fernando, "Sigiriya Frescoes" in *Journal of the Royal Asiatic Society (Ceylon Branch)* Vol. 15(48): 127-28.

30 Bell & Bell, op. cit., 1993, p. 97.

31 R.H. de Silva, op. cit., 1971, p. 19, emphasis mine.

32 Parekh, op. cit., p. 31.

33 Margaret R. Miles, "The Virgin's One Bare Breast: Female Nudity and Religious Meaning in Tuscan Early Renaissance Culture" in Susan R. Suleiman (ed.) *The Female Body in Western Culture* (Cambridge: Harvard University Press, 1985), p. 190.

34 See L.J. Jordanova, "Natural Facts: A Historical Perspective on Science and Sexuality" in C. McCormack & M. Strathern (eds.) *Nature, Culture and Gender* (Cambridge: Cambridge University Press, 1980), discusses the changing sites of eroticism in the female body in eighteenth and nineteenth century Europe. See especially pp. 49–50 on the eighteenth century emphases that sexual attraction was founded on the breast meshing with medical injunctions that women should breastfeed their children.

110   MALATHI DE ALWIS

35. R.H. de Silva, "Archaeology" in *Centenary of Education*, Vol. II, 1969 (Colombo: Government Press); and C.E. Godakumbura, "History of Archaeology in Ceylon" in *Journal of the Royal Asiatic Society (Ceylon Branch)* n.s., Vol. XIII 1969, pp. 1–38.

36. Godakumbura, op. cit., p. 20.

37. R.H. de Silva, op. cit., 1969, p. 1178.

38. Roland Barthes, *Image—Music—Text* (trs. Stephen Heath, New York: Noonday Press, 1977), pp. 38–39.

39. H.C.P. Bell, op. cit., 1896, pp. 242–260.

40. T.H. Blakesley, "On the Ruins of Sigiri in Ceylon" in *Journal of the Royal Asiatic Society (Ceylon Branch)* n.s., Vol. VIII 1876 pp. 53–61; and Murray, op. cit., 1891.

41. H.C.P. Bell, op. cit., 1896, p. 254.

42. H.C.P. Bell, op. cit., 1897, p. 117.

43. News of Bell's work at Sigiriya had got around by this meeting, and besides the RAS(CB) members, there were "75 ladies and 125 gentlemen present, certainly a record for a meeting of the RASCB upto that time" (Bell & Bell, 1993, p. 100).

44. H.C.P. Bell, *Archaeological Survey of Ceylon, Annual Report*, 1905, p. 17.

45. H.C.P. Bell, op. cit., 1896, p. 15.

46. Here, Coomaraswamy falls back on the puritan Buddhist notion that differentiated between the devotional/human and the divine/heavenly. Buddhism, which called for a moral and ethical way of living was divorced from the sensual pleasures of heavenly beings who were connected with folk religions and Hinduism.

47. Ananda Kentish Coomaraswamy, *Medieval Sinhalese Art* (New York: Pantheon Books, 1956 [1908]) p. 178 and also Coomaraswamy, *History of Indian and Indonesian Art* (New York: Dover Publications, 1965 [1927]), p. 67.
Bell also does allude to this possibility in a footnote, op. cit., 1896, p. 254.

48. Senarat Paranavitana, "The Subject of the Sigiri Paintings" in *Indian Antiqua: A Volume of Oriental Studies* (Leiden: E.J. Brill, 1947), pp 264–69. Paranavitana obviously wanted to at least elevate one Sri Lankan king to a higher status, thus elevating his cultural heritage as well. When he wrote for a more European audience in *The Illustrated London News*, he extended his comparison of Sigiriya to that of Xanadu. (April 3, 1954: 530-32).

49. See S. Paranavitana, "Sigiri : The Abode of a God-King" in *Journal of the Royal Asiatic Society (Ceylon Branch)* n.s. Vol 1, 1950, especially pp. 148-50 and 154-56.

50. S. Paranavitana, *The Story of Sigiri* (Colombo: Lake House, 1972), p. 5.

51. M.D. Raghavan, "The Sigiriya Frescoes" in *Spolia Zeylanica*, Vol. 25(2), December 1948, p. 66.

52. Nandadeva Wijesekera, "Sociological Background of Early Sinhalese Paintings" in *The Ceylon Historical Journal*, Vol. II (3 & 4,) Jan & April 1953, pp. 209–20. See also J. Comaroff & J.L. Comaroff, *From Revelation to Revolution* (Chicago: University of Chicago Press, 1991), Ch. 3, on 19th Century European racism and its bodily aesthetics.

53. Martin Wickremasinghe, "Identification of Sigiriya Paintings", in *Modern*

*Review*, July 1935. Other scholars were publishing in more scholarly journals like the *Journal of the Royal Asiatic Society (Ceylon Branch)*, *Spolia Zeylanica* (the journal of the National Museum), *Artibus Asiae* and *Orientalist*.

54  M. Wickremasinghe, op.cit, 1935, p. 29.

55  N. Wijesekera, "Fresh Light on Sigiriya Frescoes" in *Selected Writings*, Vol 12 (Dehiwela: tisara Press, 1983), p. 274.

56  P.E.P. Deraniyagala, "Some Side-lights on the Sinhala Monastery-Fortress of Sihagiri" in *Spolia Zeylanica*, Vol 26 (1), February 1951, p. 73.

57  P.E.P. Deraniyagala, op. cit., 1955, pp. 12.

58  Premadeva de Mel, "The Golden Ones of Sigiriya" in *Times of Ceylon Annual*, 1968.

59  For an extended discussion of the symbolism of 'motherhood' in Sri Lanka, see my "Seductive Scripts and Subversive Practices: Motherhood and Violence in Sri Lanka". Paper presented at a colloquium on "Violence, Suffering and Healing", Delhi University, 1993. Also Neloufer de Mel in this volume.

60  Gombrich & Obeyesekere, *Buddhism Transformed: Religions Change in Sri Lanka* (New Jersey: Princeton University Press, 1988), pp. 7-8.

61  Obeyesekere also suggests that it was a protest against peasant beliefs in demons, sorcery and magic, which were viewed as having corrupted the pure doctrinal Buddhism. The resurrection of this doctrinal Buddhism thus, also involved a demythologising of peasant beliefs and a rationalisation of their cults (see Obeyesekere, "Religious Symbolism and Political Change in Ceylon" in *Modern Ceylon Studies*, Vol. 1, 43-63).

62  Partha Chatterjee, "The Nationalist Resolution of the Women's Question" in *Recasting Women: Essays in Colonial History*, (eds.) K. Sangari and S. Vaid (Delhi: Kali for Women, 1989) pp. 233-53.

63  As Kamala Visweswaran has pointed out, the 'Woman Question' in India was the "usual shorthand to signify a range of issues concerning women which [were] also read as references to the nation. For example, British appeal to the degraded status of Indian women was one of the primary ways of legitimizing continued colonial presence"—"Family Subjects: An Ethnography of the Women's Question in Indian Nationalism", PhD thesis, Stanford University 1990), p. 65.

64  Ananda Guruge (ed.), *Dharmapala Lipi*, (Colombo: Government Press, 1963).

65  *Gihi Vinaya* (Sinhala) went into 19 editions by 1958 (Gombrich & Obeyesekere op. cit., 1988: 213-14).

66  For example in *Gihi Vinaya* (1898) & *Sinhala Bauddhaya*, 10/3/23 in Guruge (ed.) op. cit., 1963, pp. 37-38 and 85.

67  Gananath Obeyesekere, "The Vicissitudes of the Sinhala-Buddhist Identity Through Time and Change" in *Collective Identities, Nationalisms and Protest in Modern Sri Lanka*, (ed.) Michael Roberts (Colombo: Marga Institute, 1979), p. 305. Similarly, Dharmapala advocated the cloth and banian for men but this form of attire was not adapted as quickly or as widely as was the saree (Guruge(ed.) *Return to Righteousness: A Collection of Speeches, Essays and Letters of the Anagarika Dharmpala* (Colombo: Government Press, 1965) p. LXXVI)

68  Quoted in Premadeva de Mel, op. cit., 1968.

69  R.H. de Silva, op. cit., 1971, p.15.

70   Premadeva de Mel, op. cit., 1968.

71   D.B. Udalagama, "The Sigiriya Frescoes Restored", *Oriental Art*, n.s. Vol XV, (2), Summer 1969, p. 119.

72   Interestingly, the two restorers, Maranzi (sent over from Italy under the sponsorship of UNESCO), and Dr R. H. de Silva (Archaeological Commissioner at that time and an 'expert' on fresco paintings), continue Alick Murray's 'tradition' by burying two coins engraved with their names in that same fresco chamber (Paulinus Tambimuttu, "The Sigiriya Ladies" in *Times of Ceylon Annual*, 1970. This 'historic' second 'moment' of burial celebrates not a 'copying' but a "revivification" of the paintings to their "pristine beauty" so that generations can continue to "delight" in them (de Silva , "Restoration of the Sigiriya Paintings" in *Ceylon Today*, May-June 1968, p. 12.

73   Tambimuttu, op. cit.

74   Ironically, it is also the tourists, i.e., white women, who are now bestowed with the reputation of going about scantily clothed.  Bare- breasted white women on nudist beaches in Sri Lanka have now become the major attraction for the local population!

75   Recent excavations at the larger Sigiriya complex have unearthed miniature terracotta figurines (between 10 & 20 cm) that closely parallel the frescoes. Professor Senake Bandaranayake, Director of the Sigiriya Archaeological Project has interpreted these figurines as being 'art about art' or souvenirs that were meant to be taken away by visitors to Sigiriya around the seventh or tenth centuries AD (*Daily News* , Feb. 3, 1992).

76   Tamara Neuman, "Tourism and Authenticity: A Reappraisal of Dean MacCannell's *The Tourist*" (unpublished ms., 1989) p. 15.

77   Partha Chatterjee, 1989, op. cit.

78   Lata Mani, "Contentious Traditions: the Debate on Sati in Colonial India" in *Recasting Women: Essays in Colonial History* in K. Sangari and S. Vaid (eds.) , (Delhi: Kali for Women, 1989), pp. 88-126.

79   Kumari Jayawardena, "Feminism in Sri Lanka in the Decade 1975–85", in *Voice of Women*, Vol II, 1986.

80   This latter dichotomy was aptly illustrated on the cover page of the 1966 *Observer Pictorial.* A Sinhalese woman, her breasts decorously concealed by her jacket, was juxtaposed against the swollen-breasted Sigiri woman!

# Ethnicity and the Empowerment of Women

## The colonial legacy

JASODHARA BAGCHI

In India an authoritarian colonial state machinery, super-imposed on the so called 'pre-modern' societies of the erstwhile colonies, has now spawned fundamentalist onslaughts in which political groups have used religious idioms of the majority culture to spread violence against minority-culture communities.[1] The political protagonists of the majority culture, entirely on the analogy of the dominant cultures of the western rulers, tend to project themselves as the 'natural' inheritors of the Nation. Since, however, they are not convinced about their hegemonic status, they tend to ethnicise their own cultural identity.[2] Feminist inquiry into the socio-political history and mores of this phenomenon is extremely relevant. The negative impact of fundamentalism on the lives of women in society has been amply argued at different levels;[3] one of the prime targets of social injunctions is women since the regulation of women's lives and sexuality is one of the main props of any attempted fundamentalist reorganisation of society.

During the last one hundred years or so women have, in different contexts, protested against the way programmes of social cleansing that have invoked religious texts, have often been at the cost of women.[4] Women are specially vulnerable to this particular form of coercion because they symbolise the 'cultural' component of the nation-building process, and are the chief signifiers of community difference.

Given the widespread presence of fundamentalism in many post-colonial societies, it has become imperative for feminist scholars of different nationalities to examine the specificities of their own cultural identity as it was constructed under colonialism, and

how this has contributed to the later appearance of fundamentalism in their countries.

In *Chitrangada*, Tagore's poem/musical play about 'woman-
power' from the north-east, the princess of Manipur stipulates the
ways in which Arjuna the great macho hero must *not* approach
her:

> I am not the woman
> Who may be worshipped on a pedestal
> I am not the woman
> To be condescendingly allowed to follow:
> Only if you let me walk beside you
> And let me share your prosperity and adversity
> Will you get to know me.

This undoubtedly was the voice of the new woman in colonial
Bengal:

> I am Chitrangada
> Daughter of a sovereign prince
> Not a goddess nor a mere woman.

The alternative possibility of being considered a goddess became available to elite Hindu women who were supposed to have
entered the arena of 'modernity' under conditions that were
dictated by colonialism. The wide prevalence of Mother Goddess
worship was a phenomenon that has been noticed as part of social
life in the British city of Calcutta. It may have had many complex
sociological reasons, but one of the factors that was noticeably
present in militant nationalism was the equation between the
Mother Goddess, the Nation and colonised women.[5]

# I

A metonymic exercise will characterise this paper throughout, —
Bengali middle class women will be made to stand for Indian
women in general. One of the earliest regions to be thoroughly
colonised, Bengal represents that moment in our history when the
argument of modernist transformation had hit the psycho-social
life of upper and middle-class India. As a recent work by Vaid and
Sangari has shown,[6] the aspect of our social life that was most
seriously affected was the question of remoulding or recasting
women.

Womanhood became one of the most important signifiers of

colonial transformation; women were invested with the notion of authenticity that made them the chief conduit of nation building.[7] This process needs to be unravelled more than ever before, partly because there is a considerable overlap between the indigenous attempt at constructing a cultural identity, and the process of colonial state formation itself, which sought to keep communities apart with separate religious/scriptural laws. This is the terrain on which the status of women was debated, and the division of societies and nations along communal lines, made possible. A cultural identity, thus defined, meant that women's lives could make sense only in relation to their own community. Yet another metonymic exercise is used in this paper whereby the upper caste Hindu male elite will stand in for the Indian middle class. The common sense of the dominant ruling class culture in modern India today is that of the upper class/upper caste Hindu male elite. Bengal provides the first paradigm of colonial domination in India: Bengali Hindu elite, or the *bhadralok*, therefore, offer a suitable vantage point from which many of its singular characteristics may be examined.

The ambivalent position in which women are placed in regard to the fundamentalism latent within the world-view of this class arises from the disturbing fact that it is premised on a model of empowerment for women. Shakti, conceived as a female force, was one of the nodal points of a cultural identity that the upper caste Hindu male elite had defined for itself.[8] The emasculation and puniness that the coloniser's gaze had ascribed to these men[9] was sought to be overcome by the power of their mothers, both earthly and divine. The formation of a new class aspiring to hegemony was deeply linked with this gendering process, and on this question colonial history may be seen to enter into a dialogic relationship with the present.

The notional empowerment of women produces a complex problem. Women themselves often get drawn to fundamentalist configurations because of the so-called cultural authenticity that is supposed to reside in them, and because they are made to feel empowered. Feminist campaigns for social justice for women are in this reckoning seen to be an alien, westernised mode of intervention, out of place in the Indian context. Indian women were supposed to denote cultural purity and, as such, had nothing more to ask for. Much sentimentality also gets attached to the supposed empowerment; for instance, conch-shell bangles and sindoor are supposed to be authentic symbols of genuine womanhood. However, we are dealing here with something more complex than just an epiphenomenon of sentimentality: for the particular form of cultural identity that is constructed is also an instrument of class and caste hegemony.[10]

In the earlier, more simplistic, linear reading of the colonial response to women, an opposition was posed between progressive claims for women's emancipation by social reformers such as Raja Rammohun Roy and Iswarchandra Vidyasagar, and its reversal under cultural nationalism. In other words, the 'progressive' trend was supposed to have been reversed with the onset of the nationalist movement which turned its face away from a westernised reform package. In its place a refined image of pure Indian womanhood, culturally loaded against the stereotypical notion of a 'modern' westernised woman, was promoted. The purity of the caste Hindu woman was preserved in the 'inner sphere' and lent a special legitimacy to the elite class as a whole.[11] Even Tagore used the inner / outer dichotomy to locate his critique of militant nationalism.[12] A text such as Bhudeb Mukhopadhyay's *Parivarik Prabandha* illustrates the renewed emphasis on the family and the need to confine women.[13] The cultural authenticity of the domestic, married, nurturing and maternal woman was invested with a special glory and made to play a major role in the social reproduction of class.

The opposition between the 'liberating' influence of the modernising model of social reform on the one hand and the 'retrogression' of the politics of identity invoked by the nationalists on the other, is a recent ideological construct. It cannot be denied that in the discourse of social reform there is a strong presence of universalist rationalist argument about natural injustices against women. But it was not as unproblematically cast as later liberal assessments of social reform may imply.[14] For instance, Raja Rammohun Roy could use the arguments of pre-colonial Islamic rationalists in his *Tuhfat-ul-Muwahiddin*,[15] but when it came to widow immolation, his catechism was conducted entirely in high Shastric (scriptural) terms. In *Sahamaran Bishoye Prostab* (1817), the speaker and the respondent both argue entirely in the terminology of the shastras; the final advice to the speaker is that he should be able to interpret the scriptures impartially and desist from the wilful murder of women.[16] In other words, the juridical domain in which social reformers were constructing womanhood remained subject to personal laws that were based on religious scriptures.

In order to make demands of rationalist intention regarding the status of women and ground the social response on natural sympathy, Raja Rammohun Roy had to engage with Hindu orthodoxy, the main informants of the colonial State. Approaching the problem juridically would immediately mean engaging with it in terms of the scriptures which had been deliberately homogenised on the lines of text-based religions such as Christianity or Islam. This was the contribution of the cultural relativism of early administrators like Warren Hastings and Indologists like Sir William Jones. Since women's status could only be properly defined by religion-coded personal laws, social reform was heavily grounded in the shastras and Shariat.

The famous reformist impulse of Iswarchandra Vidyasagar regarding the status of women in Bengal thus was forced to continue with the process of high scripturisation. Vidyasagar's agitated denunciation of child marriage and widow remarriage had to be couched in scriptural terms. In his published tract on widow remarriage he first ascertained which of the *Dharmashastras* determined the appropriate dharma for kali yuga: having decided that it was the *Parashara Samhita,* he went on to locate the opposite sloka in defence of his argument.[17]

The passing of the Widow Remarriage Act in 1856 was a triumph for social reformers. While it would be mischievous to identify their struggle with mere intervention on the part of the colonial State, we have to face the fact that by locating the woman question in the juridical domain — and hence in personal laws based on homogenised scriptures — the reformers contributed to identifying the woman question with the purity of shastric injunctions. In the nationalist period, it was this domain that became culturally invested.

## II

In the post-Mutiny period, the growing conflict between rulers and the indigenous elite sharpened and ethnicised gender stereotypes. The division was not so much, as Partha Chatterjee would have it, between the 'inner' and the 'outer', as between the pure and impure. The public world of wealth and work that was some-how sullied with a sense of loss of power was the impure world; the private one was that of a purified Hinduism that was created even as reformers were trying to attain some social status for their women. A golden past of the Hindus was imagined, glorified and used to indicate the superiority of indigenous culture over the polluted culture of outsiders. In differentiating themselves from the rulers the elite defined itself as Hindu, while Muslims were categorised as the former rulers of Bengal.

The ethnicisation of indigenous culture that was part of the original scheme of the colonial administration led to a sharp demarcation in the self-perception of the two dominant religious groups, the Hindus and Muslims. It was 'difference' rather than identity that came into operation in this period and one of the chief markers of this difference was womanhood. Could we say that the good work done by the reformers in establishing women's rights was totally negated by the nationalists who tamed and domesticated womenfolk, hardly restoring the woman question?

The process was by no means so simple, nor were its politics simplistic. We cannot claim that social reform equals women's emancipation and cultural nationalism, women's enslavement. Occasionally left political idiom suffers from this dichotomy, and hence, the gender and class nexus also tends to get overlooked. The gender question for social reformers was applied to the upper caste and was therefore intimately related to the cleansed, purified Hinduism of the women who formed the backbone of the upper or at any rate, the socially upwardly mobile classes. The orthodoxy this generated around the gender question could easily be har-nessed to the cause of building up cultural identity along commu-nal lines.

Indigenous self-identity was increasingly beleaguered and threat-ened as the nineteenth century wore on. The earlier faith in State machinery to redress the wretched condition of women was problematised, and it became more imperative to project an empowered image of womanhood instead. This empowerment was, of course, diametrically opposed to that of socialist realism — it sought its validation and authentication in mythology, and in mythologising womanhood itself.

The resulting reformulation took place entirely on an ideolog-ical plane and succeeded in impeding the pace and changing the direction of reform. For instance, Rammohun Roy's arguments regarding the purity of widowhood created problems for Vidyasagar's campaign for widow remarriage. Şimilarly, widow remarriage itself militated against the cultural argument of Hindu nationalism.

The icon of empowered womanhood in the nationalist era may be reduced to the heroic woman /good woman that is goddess / mother syndrome, according to which the 'emancipated' bhadramahila seems to be in illicit collusion with western rulers. In standard fictional writings, the educated 'modern' woman is seen to stand for the dilution of values, and corruption.[18] Opposed to this is the ethnicised image of the pure Hindu woman, the Sati and the Savitri whose chastity became the proverbial means of protecting the health of the male community. A typical nationalist song would be:

> The wise Maitreyee, Khana, Lilabati,
> Sati, Savitri, Sita, Arundhati
> Many heroic women, the mothers of the best of heroes
> We are their progeny
> Tell o tell us when
> India will occupy the highest throne
> in the assembly of the world.

(Translation mine)

## III

Around the 1870s, about thirteen years after the proclamation of Queen Victoria as Empress of India, the ethnicisation of Hindus and Muslims began to rend the fabric of upper class Bengali society. By 1872, the first Census of the Lower Provinces of Bengal tabulated the strong presence of Muslims in the province.[19]

The Hindu intelligentsia that was imbibing western style education and social reform that accompanied it, tried its first institutional attempt at economic self-reliance, buttressed by cultural indigenism, by organising a national fair and calling it, the Hindu *mela*. The rhetoric of national regeneration followed the ethnicisation of the feminine that characterises the cultural nationalism of the Swadeshi movement. One of the songs composed on the occasion by Satyendranath Tagore (that won praise from Bankimchandra, the creator of *Vande Mataram*) had a whole stanza devoted to the chaste women of India, who remained exclusively devoted to their husbands:

Beautiful saintly and chaste women of India
Where will you find their likes?
Sharmistha, Savitri, Sita, Damayanti, dedicated
to their husbands,
Indian women nonpareil.

Then follows the usual refrain:

Let India be victorious
Victory to India
Sing the victory of India,
Why should you fear,
Sing the victory of India

(*Bagal, 1968: 113, translation mine*)

In the song, India is described as the heroic-wombed mother of heroes. The image of the 'heroic woman' stands for the incipient nation. At this point of time she is conceived entirely in Hindu terms, culled out of the history and mythology of Hindus. In her ethnicised empowered form she stands for the compensatory power that the Hindu male elite found themselves lacking. It is not surprising that the Hindu *mela* laid special emphasis on men's physical exercise. The organiser, Nabagopal Mitra, was himself a wrestling enthusiast. Predicatably, they invoked the physical courage of Kshatriya women specially in their attempt to preserve their chastity from raping Muslim invaders by committing *jauhar* (self-immolation):

Bravo, you Kshatriya women on this earth
How you suffered
Falling in the dustheap of yavanas
In despair and fear of losing chastity
Plunging with your life and care
Into flames of fire.

(*Bagal, p. 117, translation mine*)

A distinct gender edge thus emerged within Hindu nationalism that fed the later fundamentalisms and communal divisions.

In Bankimchandra's writings the ethnic edge of the power of women comes into play quite sharply. As I have argued elsewhere, the sense of humiliation and defeat at being ravaged by alien powers was fully ethnicised by Bankim into an anti-Muslim frenzy. In his last novel, *Sitaram*, Bankim's parable of an independent Hindu chieftancy is lit by the glow of the two women, Sree and Jayanti, who take on mythic proportions.[20] It is no accident of history that the militant nationalist movement took up the poem

*Vande Mataram* which was inserted as a song in the novel *Anandamath* as their political slogan; for not only is it the slogan of a political party, it was the slogan of Hindu fundamentalists during communal riots in Bengal.

It will be useful to recall the periodisation of Indian history that was read into the ten forms of Durga published in *Bangadarshan*, a journal edited by Bankim. Kali represented the stage when Indian society was wrested from non-Aryans by Aryans. Dhumavati, the desolate form of a powerless widow, represented the 'ignoble' phase of Muslim rule in India.[21] Whether or not for censorship purposes, Muslim rule stood for the kind of alienation that rightfully belongs to the British. The purity of Indian womanhood that was an obsessive theme with nationalists succeeded in doing a quick pirouette and acquiring an anti-Muslim stance. The high point in Bankim's novel, *Sitaram*, is when Sree and Jayanti lead the king, Sitaram, out of the palace:

> Just as the flood water gushes forth like a waterfall once the dam bursts, so the Muslim army rushed in once they found the door of the caste unlocked. But seeing Sree and Jayanti, the flood of soldiers stood still like a snake tamed by a mantra. The world-enchanting goddess forms, such extraordinary dress, the wondrous unheard of courage and the victory song, the tunes of which captivated the minds of all and sundry. The Muslim army made way for the women fearing them to be goddesses of the castle. They made their way through the Yavana army with the pointed edge of the trident (BR 1955).

The disbanding of the Muslim army by the strength and courage of feminine chastity was obviously a compensatory account of the vanquished race that never fought in the Mutiny. The weak Bengali male, considered feminine by the superior masculine power of the British, now takes up the cause of nationhood with the help of women in the form of chaste *sanyasinis* such as Shanti in *Anandamath* or Jayanti in *Sitaram*. The themes of renunciation and chastity, and the deification of womanhood into goddesses constantly flow into each other. As the nation is feminised in the form of a Devi, the domain of the traditional is harnessed to the service of social change, i.e., rapid polarisation and mobilisation of nationalist politics taking off as a mass movement, often quite militant.

The entire process of this surrogate empowerment of women through denial is quite complex, and not enough meaningful work has been done on it to explain the political momentum unleashed by the insidious control of the female. Veena Das has argued that in caste Hindu societies women hold the key to the ritual purity of the group and act as ·'gateways' to the caste system, hence female purity could act as a threat of power to the male.

> The dangers emanating from female sexuality were celebrated themes in song and fable in Hindu literature. At one level, the constant derogatory references to women may express the low regard in which they were held; but at another level, these references surely point to feelings of insecurity and fear with which men tended to regard the sexuality of woman.[22]

Controlling female sexuality could, therefore, be a theme in which wider participation of the community can be ensured. The point at which nationalism broke out of the shackles of a genteel westernised setting, it deployed images of Kali, a frightening symbol of vengeful femininity. One can hardly think of a more effective ploy to stare back at the horrified gaze of a typical orientalist. In an interesting section of her analysis of the nationalist iconography of woman, Tanika Sarkar has contrasted Bankim's reading of the image of Kali with that of Mukundadas, a popular poet who lent a powerful voice to the mass movement of Swadeshi:

> Bankim saw in her a measure of our shame, deprivation and exploitation; Kali is a have-not figure, a woman who has abandoned her femininity and even a basic sense of shame — 'She is trampling upon her own Shiva herself, alas, our Mother;' the woman on top signified the total collapse of the ordered world, a violence directed basically against the self. Other poets like Mukundadas, however, have, gloried in her power, in her capacity to destroy evil and transcend death.

The wrath of Kali also evoked a powerful image of the transformation of the rich country into a desolate, awesome cremation ground:

> Mother, come with your fierce aspect
> Come with your awful spirits
> Come and dance on this vast cremation ground
> Which is Bharat.

Through her thirst for revenge, through her insistence on the martydom of her sons, Kali would make a nation of heroes out of slumbering Indians. The two modes of representing Kali indicate, perhaps, an inner tension within nationalism — the principle of female strength versus the violence and destructiveness latent in it.[23]

The two aspects easily coalesce in Vivekananda's *Kali the Mother* in which he seems to exult in the more destructive image of Kali as an invocation for national regeneration:

> Dancing mad with joy
> Come, mother, come
> For terror is thy name
> Death is in thy breasts
> Thou 'Time' the All-Destroyer;
> Come, O mother, come;
> Who dares misery, love
> And bring the form of Death
> Dance, in destruction, dance
> To him the mother comes.[24]

## IV

The particular trend in developing the myth of female empowerment certainly has the potential of social mobilisation on a large scale. While the sacralisation of women's sexuality in the era of social reform remained confined to the great tradition of Aryanisation, accessible to the upper echelons of colonial society, the later emergence of the goddess as the vengeful deity, at war against the alien intruders on her pure domain, was capable of incorporating both the great and little traditions of Hinduism, thus reaching out to a large cross-section of people. This form of mythified empowerment caught the popular Hindu imagination and was fitted into the earthly equivalents of self-sacrificing mothers and wives. Within fifty years of the Act banning sati, the image of sati was back in circulation as a powerful nationalist symbol both in painting and in literature. Abanindranath Tagore's *Rajkahini* 'wrote' 'pictures' of Rajput princesses committing jauhar to protect themselves against Muslim attack. Padmini was a favourite subject for the Bengal School of painting. Our literature abounded in pure icons of mothers (Anurupa Devi's *Maa*) or wives (including co-wives as in Nirupama Devi's *Didi*). The interior of a Hindu household had to reflect this image of purity — the self-sacrificing wife who upheld the ideal of 'organic community' for the harmony of generational co-existence in a joint family.[25]

What does one do with this empowerment through deprivation? The status accruing to women through such empowerment is often flaunted as an indication of the truly high status of Hindu women. All mention of social inequity that women suffer in the dominant caste Hindu culture is, by this accounting, dismissed as a western import. The tea-drinking, mother-in-law baiting modern women of earlier days have been supplanted by images of cigarette-smoking, jet-setting feminists. The arsenal for this latest fundamentalist notion of women's empowerment is provided by the image of the pure vessel coming down from colonial times. Its presence cannot be simply wished away as a vestige of misguided feudal tendencies that the magic wand of modernisation will obliterate. For this convoluted empowerment is as much a part of the story of our 'modernisation' as it is of 'tradition', albeit an oft-invented one.

## Epilogue

The 'tradition' was invented yet again, under horrifying circumstances, on December 6, 1992 at Ayodhya. Uma Bharati and Ritambara, pure vessels of Hindu womanhood, sadhvis in short, danced, if not literally, certainly metaphorically, in ecstasy, as the five hundred year old Babri Masjid was systematically demolished. What better example of the grotesque grimace of history?[26] Empowered women were busy constructing Hindutva. In the end what did they construct: a nation or a graveyard?

## Notes

[1]   A.R. Desai, (ed.) *Expanding Governmental Lawlessness and Organised Struggles* (Bombay: Popular Prakashan, 1991).

[2]   Engineer, Asghar Ali, "Is India for Hindus only?." in *Expanding Lawlessness,* op. cit. (1991).

[3]   Bhasin Kamla, Ritu Menon and Abha Bhaiya, "Why Women Fear the Fundamentalists", (Sunday Review, *The Times of India,* January, 1991).

[4]   Jyotirmoyee Devi, *Epar Ganga Opar Ganga,* reprinted in *Rachana Sankalan,* edited by Subir Roy Choudhury and Abhijit Sen. School of Women's Studies, Jadavpur University (Calcutta: Dey's Publishing, 1991.)

[5]   Jasodhara Bagchi , "Representing Nationalism: Ideology of Motherhood in Colonial Bengal" *EPW* XXX 42/3, 1990, *Review of Women's Studies* 20-27 WS 65-72. Partha Chatterjee, "The Nationalist Resolution of the Woman Question" in Kunkum Sangari and Sudeshi Vaid (eds), *Recasting Women: Essays in Colonial History* (Delhi: Kali for Women, 1989).
Tanika Sarkar, "Nationalist Iconography: Images of Women in 19th Century Bengali Literature", *EPW* Nov. 21, 1987, pp. 2011-15.

[6]   Kunkum Sangari and Sudeshi Vaid (eds), *Recasting Women: Essays in Colonial History* (Delhi: Kali for Women, 1989).

[7]   Susie Tharu, and K. Lalitha (eds.), *Women Writing in India,* Vol. 1 (New York: Feminist Press, 1991).

[8]   Jasodhara Bagchi , "Representing Nationalism: Ideology of Motherhood in Colonial Bengal" op. Cit.

9  Sivaji Bandyopadhyay, *Gopal Rakhal Dwandwasamas* (Bengali) *Colonialism and Children's Literature in Bengal* (Calcutta: Papyrus, 1991).

10  Tanika Sarkar, "Gender Ideology in Bengal; Reflections on Birati Rape Cases", *EPW,* Feb. 1991, 215-8.

11  Jasodhara Bagchi , "A few words about Modern Bengali Prose Fiction from a Feminist Point of View" (Bengali) in *Bharat Itihase Nari,* (Calcutta: K.P. Bagchi, 1989, pp. 119-28).

11  Partha Chatterjee, "The Nationalist Resolution of the Woman Question', op. cit.

12  Jasodhara Bagchi, "Feminism and Nationalism: Tagore's *Ghare Baire*" in K. Radha *Feminism and Literature,* Institute of English, University of Kerala, Trivandrum, 1987.

13  Partha Chatterjee, "The Nationalist Resolution of the Woman Question", op. cit.

14  A. Salauddin Ahmed, *"Social Ideas and Social Change in Bengal, 1818-1835* (Calcutta, Riddhi: 1976, First pub. 1965).

15  Sumit Sarkar, "Rammohun Roy and Break with the Past" in *A Critique of Colonial India* (Calcutta: Papyrus, 1985).

16  Rammohun Roy, "Sahamaran Bissayak Prabartak Nibartak Samvad" in *Pratrodh* (ed. Debiprasad Chattopadhyay), Calcutta, rptd, 1991.

17  Benoy Ghosh, *Vidyasagar O Bangali Samaj* 3 vols., (Calcutta: Bengal Publishers, 1960).
Ishwarchandra Vidyasagar, *Marriage of Hindu Widows,* with an Introduction by Arabindra Poddar (Calcutta: K.P.Bagchi, 1976).

18  Partha Chatterjee, "The Nationalist Resolution" op. cit.

19  Rafiuddin Ahmed, *The Bengal Muslims 1871-1906* (Delhi: Oxford University Press, 1981).

20  Jasodhara Bagchi, "Positivism and Nationalism; Womanhood and Crisis in Nationalist Fiction: Bankimchandra's *Anandamath*", *EPW XX,* 43, 1985.

21  Jasodhara Bagchi, "Representing Nationalism" op. cit.

22  Veena Das, "Indian Women: Work, Power and Status" in B.R. Nanda (ed.), *Indian Women: From Purdah to Modernity* (Delhi: Vikas, 1976).

23  Tanika Sarkar, "Nationalist Iconography: Images of Women in 19th Century Bengali Literature", op. cit.

24  Jasodhara Bagchi, "Representing Nationalism" op. cit.

25  Jasodhara Bagchi, "A Few Words About Modern Bengali Prose Fiction", op. cit.

26  Amiya Kumar Bagchi, "Samrajyabad O Itihaser Bhyangchari (The Grotiesque Grimace of History, *Anushtup,* Autumn 1992).

# Hindu Nationalist Women as Ideologues
## The 'Sangh', the 'Samiti' and their differential concepts of the Hindu Nation[1]

Paola Bacchetta

In an earlier phase of scholarship on Hindu nationalism, women sometimes surfaced as symbols or as victim-bodies whom 'communalist'[2] males saw as part of their mission to protect or avenge. Today, since women have been more widely recognised as militants in 'communal' violence, it is often assumed that they act on the basis of their male counterparts' ideology. Here, I-hope to dispel that notion, for women have created, and their activism is supported by, a specifically feminine Hindu nationalist discourse. In what follows, I unravel one such discourse, that of the Rashtra Sevika Samiti (hereafter the 'Samiti'), and view it in comparison with that of its male counterpart, the Rashtriya Swayamsevak Sangh (hereafter, the 'Sangh'). The focus is on a thematic which for both is highly gendered, the 'Hindu Nation'.

This dismantling and comparative process has several functions: it should disclose the constitutive and thematic elements, of course; it should also reveal the differential modes in which men and women appeal to their own gender and are called upon to insert themselves into the same 'communal' conflict; finally, it should foreground internal mechanisms whereby Hindu nationalist discourse is fractionalised (here, along gender lines, but similar operations work to reach other sectors of society) while retaining unity enough to achieve ultimate common objectives.

The discursive unity is provided by a framework elaborated by the Sangh — the Samiti ideologues frame their own construction process within its context. They use some (but not all) of the same symbols and signifiers, and create some of their own. They are, indeed, profoundly related; yet, the two discourses simply cannot be reduced to one. Between them there are zones of convergence, of non-antagonistic divergence, and of complementary difference. And, there are points of antagonistic difference. The convergence is perhaps most evident. It can be explained by what Nicole Claude Matthieu refers to as the direct mediation of women's consciousness by men.[3] Here, Samiti ideologues reproduce elements of the Sangh's discourse in their own words, without modification. Areas of non-antagonistic divergence and complementary difference can be understood in terms of Gramscian modes of refraction.[4] Here, the Sangh's discourse, which occupies the dominant position in relation to that of the Samiti's (socially, politically and in its more extensive elaboration), is imperfectly assimilated by it, and imprecisely reproduced. Other divergences are the result of the Samiti's thematic expansion horizontally into areas unexplored by the Sangh, reflecting the separate concerns of women and men, and their differential locations within a gender asymmetrical society.

The antagonistic points are more difficult to understand. I attribute them to the Samiti's creative use of structural and subjective factors, and the Sangh's attitudes of acceptance, ignorance and sometimes devalorisation of the Samiti's discourse. By structural elements I mean the organisations' positions within their interrelations: each is somewhat autonomous, has developed somewhat separately, although the Samiti is technically subordinate to the Sangh. They also position themselves within the Hindu symbolic: it encompasses a range of representations of each gender that ideologues can draw upon and to which diverse interpretations can justifiably be assigned. Despite this potential, the Sangh's ideology leaves little space for women-actors to exist, and so the Samiti, in order to craft a Hindu nationalism which women can relate to, is obliged to exit the realm of the Sangh's discourse at some points. It is not suprising, then, that most of the antagonisms originate around questions of feminine and masculine identities, even if they extend into other domains.

Briefly, then, what I am arguing is that because of these differences, when women and men struggle for what they collectively call a 'Hindu Nation' they do not necessarily have exactly the same entity in mind. This will be the subject of the rest of the essay, but first, a few background notes are necessary in order to contextualise my discussion.

## The Sangh and the Samiti: some historiographical notes

Until recently, the Sangh was perhaps most known outside India for its implication in the assassination of Mahatma Gandhi. Today, it is notorious for its role in the wanton demolition of a sixteenth century mosque, the Babri Masjid in Ayodhya, in December 1992. The Sangh was founded in 1925 in Nagpur, Maharashtra, in a context of 'Hindu-Muslim' riots, the national movement for independence, and low-caste protest movements (which historically have been prominent in Maharashtra). The founder and first Sarsanghchalak (Supreme Leader), Dr. Keshav Baliram Hedgevar, played a key role in provoking 'communal' riots in the area.[5] He was also a peripheral member of the youth group of the Congress which functioned as an umbrella for a range of nationalisms. He left following disagreements on goals and tactics. The Congress advocated an all-inclusive, secular Indian nation, and Gandhian ahimsa (non-violence). In contrast, Dr. Hedgevar and his mentors envisioned a Hindu nation and favoured violence. Their main enemy was not the British, but rather Indian Muslims.

Dr. Hedgevar belonged to the most privileged four per cent of his society: he was an Andra (not Chitpavan) Brahman,[6] middle class and English-educated. Initially, he recruited young men almost exclusively from that milieu,[7] thus alienating low-caste activists. They read its Hindu nationalism as a Brahman plot to divide Muslims and low-caste Hindus in order to re-establish Brahmanical hegemony. On at least one occasion, Muslim and low-caste Hindu activists together physically attacked Dr.Hedgevar at a public meeting.[8]

The Sangh defines itself as a 'cultural', not a political, organisation. Despite its benevolent self-designation, one of its main activities from inception has been imparting para-military training and ideological indoctrination. Today it comprises over three million core members (swayamsevaks) who meet daily in shakhas (neighbourhood cells). It has over 37,000 local headquarters concentrated mainly in north and central India. Due to an aggressive recruitment campaign, it is spreading in the south (Kerala, Karnataka, Tamil Nadu), and has diasporic branches in 47 foreign countries; it is perhaps South Asia's largest international, micro-nationalist organisation ever.

The Sangh's structure is rigidly hierarchical with power flowing from the nation to region to state to city and thence to the neighbourhood level. Leaders are appointed, not elected. It has had four Sarsanghchalaks in all: Dr. Hedgevar (1925-40), Madhavrao Sadashiv Golwalkar (1940-73), Balasaheb Deoras (1973-94) and Rajendra Singh who was appointed in 1994 by Deoras due to his failing health. Until Deoras, each served a life term and appointed his successor on his deathbed. Each has oriented the Sangh in his own mode: Dr. Hedgevar gave it its structure, goals and technique; M.S. Golwalkar was its main ideologue; Deoras, who was trained personally by Dr. Hedgevar, shifted the Sangh away from its previous avant-garde style towards 'mass' recruitment. In nominating R. Singh, he translated his aspirations into practice. Singh is the first non-Brahman, non-Maharashtrian Sarsanghchalak, and is from the south where the Sangh is presently attempting to expand.

Around itself, the Sangh created its Sangh Parivar (network of affiliates or 'family organisations'). They include professional unions (for teachers, students, workers, industrialists, journalists, etc.) and issue-oriented organisations (cow protection, temple 'reconversion', and so on). It founded two political parties: the Jana Sangh (now defunct), and the present Bharatiya Janata Party (BJP). It has always had some presence in the Congress Party and engages in electoral politics in Kerala through its 'Hindu Front'.[9] These offshoots have allowed it to intervene in nearly every public domain, while retaining legitimacy in milieux where political ambition is associated with immorality, and spiritual goals with morality.

The Sangh defines its goals in spiritual terms: to 'unify' Hindus, and 'build' their 'character' in order to 'resurrect' the Hindu Nation. In this, it translates Brahmanical notions of spiritual self-realisation to the material plane and modifies them to fit its Hindu nationalist schema. In Brahmanism, realisation involves peeling back the layers of maya (illusion) which blind the individual to his unity with the One. However, for the Sangh, each Hindu is supposed to peel back the layers of maya that blind him to his 'essential' Hindu nationalist 'self' in order to 'resurrect' the Hindu Nation. The relationship between the self and the Nation are inscribed in the name: National (Rashtriya) Self (Swayam) Helper or Worker (Sevak) Organisation (Sangh). The term used for the self here is Swayam, the material-self-acting-in-the-world, as opposed to brahman or atman, the spiritual S/self in Brahmanism.[10]

The Sangh owns publishing companies, a distribution network and bookshops. It publishes in English, Hindi and many regional languages; the genres include political treatises, essays, biographies, journalistic pieces, short stories, etc. Recently, with its shift towards 'mass' orientation, it has developed more accessible forms such as posters, postcards, inland letter cards and comic books.

The Samiti was the Sangh's first family organisation. It was created in 1936 in Wardha, Maharashtra, in close geographical proximity to the Sangh. The founders were Dr. Hedgevar, and Lakshmibai Kelkar who became the first director (Pramukh Sanchalika). Its stated goals are to make women conscious of their 'divine identity'[11] , and to prepare them for the Hindu nationalist cause. The two organisations are 'parallel', but 'different' because women's 'field' is different from men's.[12] These notions are reflected in its name, its ideology and activities.

The name contains initials identical to the Sangh's (RSS), but in it the term swayam (self) is absent. The justification is that a man's self is individual, while a woman's "implies not only the individual self but also family, society, nation, religion and culture".[13] The "development of a man is the development of an individual", while the "development of a woman is the development of the whole society".[14] Here, women's self is relational, and merged in other (always bi-gendered) entities. In contrast, the male self is unitary, mono-gendered, not dependent on relations. There is a subtext to this, located in horizontal extensions of the theme. That is, the Samiti constructs elaborate models for the feminine self-acting-in-the world throughout its publications. In that sense, the nominative absence of 'swayam' represents a certain concession, but also disguises a non-concession, by the Samiti to the Sangh.

In its texts, the Samiti provides two divergent explanations of its founding; in both it assigns principle agency to Lakshmibai Kelkar. In an undated but post-1978 English language publication, it traces its origin to opposition to the Indian left and liberal women's movements of the 1930s. It explains that "due to western impact women were struggling for equal rights and economic freedom . . . There was every risk of women being non-committed to love, sacrifice, service. . . This unnatural change in the attitude of women might have led to disintegration of family [sic], the primary and most important unit of imparting good samskaras."[15] It goes on to state that L. Kelkar was introduced to the Sangh via her swayamsevak sons. She was interested in the Sangh's "way of working based on individual contact, mutual love and voluntary discipline".[16] Finally, she meets Dr. Hedgevar and proposes that she form the women's wing. Dr. Hedgevar, "gifted with divine vision, was convinced and he conceded to the proposal provided V. Mausiji accepted all the responsibility."[17] Here, it is the potential of Hindu femininity to go astray into feminism which renders the Samiti necessary.

In contrast, a 1989 Hindi language text cites L. Kelkar's increasing awareness of the sexual exploitation of Hindu women and the need to fight back, as the motivation.[18] It names two cases: in one, defenceless women orange-pickers lose their chastity to middlemen to whom they are in debt; in another, a woman is sexually harassed on the streets while her husband and passersby take no action. L. Kelkar links these instances to the abduction of Sita by Ravana in the Ramayana. She concludes that Hindu men cannot prevent outrages on Hindu women, so women must learn to defend themselves. Then she discovers that her sons know how to wield a lathi. She asks them to teach their sister and herself its use. They decline, saying they have vowed never to impart such knowledge to a non-Sangh member. So, she asks them to arrange for her to meet the Sarsanghchalak. Finally, after much insistence, she does meet Dr. Hedgevar. She tells him that women are exploited, defenceless, and asks if they can join the shakhas to learn self-defence. He refuses, but agrees that she can found a women's wing. This version adds that L. Kelkar had wanted the Sangh to include women. It attributes the need for the Samiti to Hindu women's oppression by ('unconscious') Hindu men, and the failure of Hindu men, including family members, to protect Hindu women.

The double explanation illustrates the performative nature of the discourse, in the sense of Bakhtin,[19] and its potential for fractionalisation. Each version reflects a different representation of gender relations in space and time, and the class and contexts of the Addressees. The English language text speaks to middle class women, whose class privilege provides a certain protection in the public space. Theirs includes the English language discursive space which the Samiti constructs as providing an exit for women from the 'Hindu Community'. When the text appeared, the present wave of the Indian feminist movement, which has a long history, was on the rise. In response, retrospectively, the Samiti represents the women's movement of the 1930s as 'western', and thus the wrong path for *Hindu* women. They are supposed to act in solidarity with Hindu men.

The Hindi version targets lower and lower-middle class women: it discusses male violence, women's vulnerability and Hindu male failure to protect. Its Addressees live those conditions; it proposes a solution which relies on their own agency. The link by analogy to Sita inscribes a positive symbolic meaning to the situation such that it exceeds individual and collective experiences. The text appears at the height of the current Indian feminist movement. Though it condemns feminism elsewhere in Hindi texts, the Samiti does not mention it in its account of the founding. In practice the Samiti has borrowed issues (dowry, health), adopted slogans (including in the Ramjanmabhoomi campaign) and modelled some of its projects on feminist ones (income-generating ventures, work in slums, etc.). Here, it appropriates elements selectively, but conveniently effaces all trace of its sources, perhaps because the feminist movement is its most threatening competitor.

The Samiti's major ideologue is L. Kelkar. She occupies a position similar to M.S. Golwalkar for the Sangh. She and Dr. Hedgevar agreed that the Samiti should not be an exact "imitation" of the Sangh.[20] He told her that he "knew nothing" about women[21], and L. Kelkar should determine "the basic principles and philosophy of women's life in Bharat".[22] It was to reflect "women's world view, her nature, her life ideals" which "in Bharat is quite different than that of men".[23] This accord on the notion of separate gendered concerns has contributed to the Samiti's relative ideological autonomy.

A biographical rendering of L. Kelkar is complicated by the Samiti's reconstruction of her in hagiographic terms, as a born saint in the sense of de Certeau,[24] and by the lack of other data. Yet, an analysis of the representations, as I have attempted elsewhere,[25] in and of itself tells us much about her and the Samiti. Briefly stated, the Samiti puts forth that she comes from a Nagpur-based politically-alert Chitpavan Brahman Date family with Tilakite leanings. She was 'conscious' of the national movement, and 'defended Hinduism' at the English-medium school she attended.[26]

At age fourteen, her family arranged her marriage to a wealthy Chitpavan Brahman lawyer, Purushottoma Rao Kelkar, and that brought her to Wardha. She was unhappy in his conservative, apolitical, joint family. Nearby was Mahatma Gandhi's Sevagram Ashram, a centre of activities for independence, but her in-laws confined her at home. The Samiti underscores her struggle to gain permission to be politically active.[27] It attributes her success to her perseverance and righteousness, and holds her as an example for sevikas to emulate, thereby diverging from notions of the young wife's ideal submission.

L. Kelkar's husband died in 1932, leaving her with eight children[28] including two daughters from his earlier marriage.[29] Through financial and emotional difficulties, she maintained her Gandhian activism until she founded the Samiti. There is no clear statement in the literature as to why she switched from one form of nationalism to another. But several texts mention that she met Dr. Moonje (Dr. Hedgevar's mentor, who told her of the orange-pickers' dilemma), much before 1934. If so, it is not unlikely that she was exposed to Sangh ideas earlier than Samiti founding narratives suggest.

Today, the Samiti has about one million members,[30] called sevikas, located in at least 16 states in India,[31] as well as in the diaspora, with concentrations in the same areas as the Sangh. The earliest were recruited among the women family members of the swayamsevaks, and such women still hold a disproportionate number of highly-placed posts. Yet, when the Sangh shifted towards 'mass' recruitment, it encouraged the Samiti similarly to expand its membership downwards, including outside the Sangh's confines.[32] This is a partial reversal of the previous mode of recruitment. For now, it makes inroads into villages by sending sevikas in to establish seemingly apolitical cultural programmes for women: puja and cookery classes, etc. They develop trust among village mothers, thus paving the way for their sons to be organised by the Sangh. Similarly, the Samiti recruits among women in bastis (urban slums) where it has created income-generating programmes.

Its internal structure is analogously rigidly hierarchical and based on geographical divisions. However, relationally, it is subordinate to the Sangh. The highest office, the Pramukh Sanchalika, also exists in the Sangh, and is also located below the

Sarsanghchalak. In all, there have been two Pramukh Sanchalikas. L. Kelkar was succeeded at her death in 1978 by Tai Apte, a Chitpavan Brahman, the widow of prominent Pune Sangh leader Vinayakrao Apte, and a niece of Lokamanya Tilak. Significantly, both women took up their posts in widowhood, and thus when physically (if not emotionally or spiritually) independent of an individual male counterpart. While widows do not necessarily play such roles in upper caste Hindu milieux,[33] in both instances the natal family backgrounds were supportive on such questions. Pune had been a centre of political activities, including women's reform movements, over the past two centuries, and many Chitpavan Brahmans were among its leaders. The Samiti valorises women whom it can construct as ascetics dedicated to the nation. This includes the post of pracharika (preacher, organiser, corresponding to the Sangh's pracharak) for women who wish to remain single and celibate, and dedicate themselves full time to the organisation.

The Samiti's basic unit is similarly the shakha, which meets daily, or in some areas, weekly. As in the Sangh, shakha members are divided into four categories: children, adolescents, adults and the elderly. They receive ideological indoctrination, paramilitary training (lathi-wielding, archery, karate, and sometimes rifle shooting), and play games devised to build "strength, courageousness, muscular development".[34] Many of these are identical to the Sangh's and involve physical fighting. National training camps are held annually to perfect their skills. Since 1945, there have been triennial all-India conferences.

The Samiti offers tutorial classes, discourses on selected Sanskrit texts, patronises the arts, and provides free medical care to poor women.[35] It has a history of intervention in the public space.[36] To cite just a few examples: it ran an underground network, organised above-ground demonstrations and hunger strikes, courted arrest, and put forth "fiery orators" in the Praja Parishad movement in Jammu of 1951–53.[37] It publicly protested the book *Red Flows the Ganges* (because of its unacceptable portrayal of the Rani of Jhansi) until it was banned in India in 1977.[38] It has continually organised boycotts of Muslim-owned businesses.[39]

Other activities are its local celebrations of the organisation's five "national festivals" to "remind people... of [our] glorious past [sic] with its relevance to the present".[40] They are designed to mark historical and essentialised time, to unify sevikas and attract recruits. They are drawn from other secular and sacred festivals, but are reinterpreted in the Hindu nationalist frame. They are: (*i*) Varsha Pratipada, to honour the "victory over the Shakas and Huns — the foreign invaders"; (*ii*) Guru Purnima, when puja is offered to the saffron flag and money is collected (*iii*) Rakshabandhan, when sevikas tie rakhi (sacred thread) to the flag and to each others' wrists to "encourage the feeling of brotherhood"[41]; (*iv*) Vijaya Dashmi Day (see below); (*v*) Makarasankraman, a "mark of love and friendship encouraging us to increase our capacity to work".[42]

Each corresponds to a Sangh festival in terms of its signifier, but the Samiti assigns many of them different signifieds. For example, for the Sangh, Varsha Pratipada falls on the birthday of Dr. Hedgevar, and "awakens in us the memory of our great epoch-makers".[43] The most striking, however, is Vijaya Dashmi Day, the founding day for both organisations. For the Sangh it marks the victory of the god Rama over evil (Ravana); for the Samiti, it is the victory of the goddess Durga over evil (rakshasas or devils). In the first case, the elimination of evil is due to masculine agency (Rama), while in the second, to feminine agency (Durga). In both cases evil is personified in the masculine. Here, reflecting more extensive tendencies in the Sangh's account, femininity is absent, while in the Samiti's, masculine and feminine elements co-exist.

Qualitatively, the festivals elucidate non-antagonistic divergence and complementary difference. But, quantitatively, they illustrate a process of erasure in the relation between the two organisations. For, the Sangh has an additional sixth festival, Hindu Samrajya Divotsav, to honour "the victory" of Hindu heroes "over the 800 year-old oppressive rule of the Muslims, under the virile leadership of Shivaji".[44] Shivaji has been an object of much dispute in Maharashtra, where several groups claim him as their own.[45]

The Samiti has one publishing company, Sevika Prakashan, in Nagpur, founded in 1953. It publishes in English, Hindi, Marathi and Gujarati. The genres include essays, periodicals, a 'biography' of L. Kelkar, her lectures on the Ramayana, some pamphlets (of Samiti songs, games), etc. It has no bookshops, no distribution network, and its materials are not sold in Sangh bookshops.

### The archive: sources, processes and logic

The materials for analysis are the Sangh and Samiti's Hindi and English language texts, from the earliest to the most recent. It encompasses all their genres. The logic is that publications represent the most fixed, least transient forms of their discourses, in the face of their respective dodging operations (see below). The Sangh elaborates its Hindu Nation primarily in political treatises and pamphlets. It is a major thematic. In contrast, the Samiti's notion is dispersed in an assortment of materials, and has been less central.

The Speaking Subjects of the Sangh's discourse are its highest level ideologues. The most thorough was M.S. Golwalkar, who wrote its first publication ever, entitled *We; Or Our Nationhood Defined*, in 1939. The Addressees have been swayamsevaks and potential members. The discourse is performed (again, in the sense of Bakhtin) with the aim of homogenising swayamsevaks and seducing new members. Its communicative capacity is maximal due to strategic operations which merit a few words of explication.

Sangh ideologues construct their discourse through a process of selectivity, recombination, rearrangement, reprioritisation, and reinterpretation of elements from other discourses in their context. They use western, Indian, and Hindu sources. Among the western elements is the thought of pre-fascist cultural nationalist, Joseph Mazzini.[46] Another is Hitler's Germany, wherein "race pride at its highest has been manifested".[47] The Sangh wrote that it was a good model to emulate.[48] But, after World War II, when it was criticised on this account, it took texts with such references out of circulation, denied that aspect of its past, and today condemns fascism. Despite a shift in signifiers, the basic tenets of its early concept of the Hindu Nation remain essentially the same.

From Indian history, the Sangh has drawn renowned figures (Shivaji, Tantia Tope, etc.), reinterpreted them as Hindu nationalist heroes, and essentialised them. On the model of nineteenth century revivalist movements with which it erroneously (and opportunistically) claims direct continuity, the Sangh places elements from sacred Hindu texts (Rig Veda, Bhagavad Gita, etc.) in its own. This operation is designed for legitimation: it renders the discourse familiar to Addressees, makes it appear as simply another religious discourse, while disguising its political nature.

Two incompatible conceptual grids traverse the Sangh's literature: binary and advaitic. In the binary mode, entities are divided into mutually exclusive halves, polarised, internally homogenised and hierarchicalised. An example of this is the Sangh's concept of the Hindu People, which it constructs in direct opposition to its negative Others (see below). The advaitic mode posits non-hierarchicalised diverse entities in a relationship of ultimate Oneness. The Sangh applies it sparingly, to pre-split entities, such as the ideal Hindu People.

The Samiti's discourse is designed to circulate among sevikas and potential members. Its communicative capacity is similarly maximal. It makes use of the same processes as the Sangh. However, it adds sources, selects different items from some of the same sources, and interprets some common elements differently. Where conflict exists with the Sangh, the Samiti does not name it; rather, it carries out its resistance subtly by omitting undesirable Sangh points and and investing the emptied spaces with its own. From the first texts, L. Kelkar was clear about what she was doing. She believed that "if someone is not satisfied with discussions and talk on a topic then he should read ancient books, classics, and search for the solutions in them".[49]

The Samiti's sources are from the Sangh, Indian nationalists and Sanskrit works. Contact with western sources has been minimal, via secondary materials (by the Sangh mainly). The Samiti draws from Tilak's notion of specifically Hindu national liberation.[50] From Swami Vivekananda, it takes the idea that women's condition is a nationalist issue, and that women are nationalist agents.[51] From Mahatma Gandhi, whose secular project it denounces, it extracts the view that women should determine their own future and the future of the nation.[52] His thought diverged from early nineteenth century nationalists for whom women were passive objects of enlightened male reform[53], and with turn-of-the-century nationalists for whom women's issues had largely "disappeared from the agenda".[54] Another source is V.D. Savarkar; his term, Hindutva, has been constant in the Samiti's literature, despite its disappearance from the Sangh's during its dispute period with the Hindu Mahasabha.[55]

The Sanskrit materials are the Ramayana, Bhagavad Gita and Devi Mahatmya. L. Kelkar wrote her own lectures of the Ramayana after being inspired by Gandhi's. She used the Bhagavad Gita and the Devi Mahatmya to formulate her ideal Hindu woman, including potentially violent qualities. Like the Sangh, the Samiti uses both a binary and an advaitic grid, and similarly assigns the binary to a wider zone. Finally, both discourses are dynamic, relatively polysemic, support internal contradictions and tend to escape fixity. I attempt to resolve the problems this creates for analysis by giving priority to major texts, and to points of repetition.

## The ideal Hindu Nation: its placement in time

### According to the Sangh

The Sangh makes a sharp distinction between "Hindu Rashtra" (Hindu Nation), which it valorises, and "Rajya" (the State, as a political apparatus), which it devalorises. Its Rashtra is "not a religious concept" nor a "political concept", but "a cultural and emotional one eternally asserting itself".[56] The "difference between them" is that "Rashtra is eternal and State is transitory" just as "according to Hindu conviction the Atma is eternal and only the bodies and their forms are changed".[57]

This de-emphasis on government, on the State as a political apparatus, echoes ideals put forth in ancient Hindu lawbooks, the Arthashastra and Dharmashastras.[58] But, in view of the fractionalisation of its domains via the affiliates mentioned above, ultimately its project also concerns a Hindu Raj. Moreover, it plays other political roles: it is a recruiting ground for future politicians, and a think-tank for their ideology. It prepares the social terrain for their success in electoral politics by forcing its issues into the public discursive space (for example, in the Babri Masjid-Ramjanmabhoomi conflict).

This use of the Arthshastra and Dharmasastras is limited to the surface; it diverges from them in its definition of the component parts of the nation. In the texts, the polity is composed of seven parts: the king, ministers, a territorially settled community, fortification, the treasury, an army and allies.[59] In contrast, the Sangh's Hindu Nation consists of three interdependent "indissoluble component parts"[60], which are Geography, Race and the combined units, Religion, Culture and Language.[61] These criteria correspond to theories of nation-state elaborated in western political thought, where they are commonly known as the Five

Unities. I shall discuss them in turn, but first a word on temporal categories.

The Sangh describes the Hindu Nation as *anadi* (without beginning). It is manifested in its ideal form in Satyuga, the glorified past and future.[62] At present, the Nation is in Kaliyuga, for the Hindu People have lost their self-knowledge. It will be 'resurrected' when all Hindus peel back the layers of maya which blind them to consciousness of their 'essential' selves and of the Oneness of the People and the Nation. The Sangh draws from the Hindu cycle of Yugas. It generally consists of four periods, but here it is reduced to two; it mirrors the nineteenth century Orientalist-designed opposition between a culturally-rich Vedic period which has been lost, and a degraded present.[63] The framework for this binary construction is not Hindu, but Christian thought, from which European fascism similarly drew. Here, the Sangh's project parallels the resurrection of its fictive ancient Nordic state and the Italian fascist recreation of its mythified ancient Rome.[64]

For the Sangh, the beginning of Kaliyuga corresponds to the exit from eternal time and entry into linear historical time. It attributes the shift to three factors: Hindu disunity, Muslim invasions, and British colonisation. Hindus became disunited after the Mahabharata War when a "sense of security spread its benumbing presence over the whole Nation".[65] Consequently, "the cohesive impulse resulting from the knowledge of impending danger ceased to function".[66] Then, "carelessness waxed and the one Nation fell into small principalities".[67] The principalities became vulnerable to "invasions of murdering hordes of Mussalman free-booters".[68] As in Nazi and Italian fascist thought the Sangh perceives peace as corrosive and a cause of decline.[69] Then, an "illustrious line of Hindu warriors" took up the challenge and "fought the enemy to the last drop of their blood" during an "800 Year War".[70] And, just as "the power of the invaders was entirely broken and the Hindu Nation was emerging victorious", a new enemy, the British, "with the help of the Mussalmans" began "taking possession of the land".[71]

This account is framed by categories established in nineteenth century colonialist historiography based on the work of James Mill. He divided the whole of India's history into three periods: a Hindu period characterised by staticity and "oriental despotism", a Muslim period where (homogenised) brutality reigned, and a British period of enlightenment and modernity. As Romila Thapar has pointed out,[72] such a division has no basis in fact or in logic. The criteria are inconsistent: the first two periods (non-'western') are defined in religious terms, and the latter ('western') in political ones. In colonialist historiography, within each category, a heterogeneity of practices and organisational forms were homogenised to place the British period in a positive light. The Sangh retains the categories, but rewrites their meanings. It assigns its Hindu period cultural and political excellence; it describes its Muslim period in terms of war between Hindu nationalists and Muslim rulers, followed by continued Hindu nationalist struggle against the British. *This reformulation of history is a key element in its strategy for hegemony.*

*According to the Samiti*

The Samiti adopts the Sangh's prioritisation of Hindu Rashtra over Hindu Rajya and, similarly, remains related to and distanced from the Hindu nationalist women who are in electoral politics. Many high profile BJP women were trained in the Samiti. They bring its ideology, discipline and stress on women's leadership into those domains, while the Samiti retains its image of aloofness from electoral politics.

The Samiti's temporal framework and categories are modelled after the Sangh's, but it adds selected elements to each period to render women visible and central. While women are nearly absent in the Sangh's Satyuga, for the Samiti, it was a glorious period for women. They were highly respected, had total equality with men, and excelled in every domain of life. Life revolved around the family, to which women were central.

The Samiti reproduces the Sangh's three reasons for the nation's downfall. Yet, here too, it adds elements horizontally and centralises them. The downfall was due to the marriage of Hindu men to "non-Aryan women" near the end of the Hindu Period, the subjugation of Hindu women to Muslim men in the Muslim Period, and the reification of Hindu women in the British Period.[73] Intermarriage destroyed the institution upon which the nation was based: the Hindu family. The changeover occurred

in the states of conservative or underdeveloped kings. . . In the Vedic period intermarriage between the three varnas was a common phenomenon. . . But Aryans never married the Dasas, the Sudras and non-Aryans, except for rare examples. . . Slowly this took root and the marriage of Bhima and Arjuna with Hidimba and Ulupi are examples of this. . . . Slowly when the ill effects of this unification came to light they began to condemn such intermingling as is revealed in the sacred texts which forbid marriage between Aryans and non-Aryans. . . The level of the Aryan women began to decline when the non-Aryans came into their homes. . . Since the non-Aryans were not well- versed in Sanskrit it was not possible to give them the right to study the Vedas or to perform other religious rites. . . Due to the prevalence of such evils as competition the right of women to study the Vedas was snatched away. . . Later the sacred thread ceremony too was lost. . . Women were married in their childhood.[74]

In the Muslim period, which as in British historiography the Samiti optionally calls "the middle ages", it reproduces the Sangh's discourse on "invasions" and "pillaging", but it stresses that "with wealth women were carried away too".[75]

In the British period, Hindu men contribute to the demise of Hindu women because they are mentally under British influence. One domain of male complicity is education: "the pattern of new education given by Macaulay was offending to all sacred things and to women too. . . She was denigrated to the status of a consumer article. . . Advertisements too offended her. . . ."[76] There, the 'unconscious' Hindu male is not explicitly named but is left to be inferred.

Finally, while for the Sangh each phase of decline is countered by examples of "national heroes" (who are overwhelmingly male), the Samiti has its own "nationalist heroines": Vadhrimati (of the Rig Veda), Rani Laxmibai of Jhansi (who fought the British in the War of 1857), and Bengali nationalists, Kalpana Datta, Vina Das and Pritilata.[77] Thus, the fate of women and of the nation are inseparable. And its resurrection depends upon women regaining what the Samiti posits as their original high status.[78]

In this historiography, the Samiti has recourse to sources alternative to the Sangh. As a result some of its affirmations actually conflict with the Sangh's notions. Its discourse on intermarriage is a case in point: it rests on a presupposed division between Aryans and Others. This notion has its origins in the "Aryan thesis" of nineteenth century orientalism, which the Sangh has always expressly refuted.[79] The thesis posits that Aryan invaders entered India from the north, settled, established a social system based on caste, assigned the highest roles to themselves, and subjugated the indigenous population. The Sangh calls it a British invention, devised to legitimise their Raj by arguing that Hindu rulers were similarly outsiders once.[80] It states that earlier Hindu nationalists, such as Tilak, who adopted it were simply operating on insufficient information.[81] A second point of contention is the role of the family in the Hindu Nation. For the Samiti it is central, for the Sangh it is peripheral. But more on this point below.

The Samiti's account corresponds more closely than the Sangh's to theories of social decline in the Arthashastra and Dharmashastras. There, it is the emergence of greed, the decline of morality, the appearance of ahamkar (a polysemic term meaning individualism, egoism, self-love, pride), and the neglect of dharma (duty, order) which lead to chaos.[82] The Sangh includes these as factors of "Hindu disunity", though it stresses Muslim and British domination. In the sacred texts, these personal vices lead to *varnasankara* (intermixing of castes, confusion of caste boundaries), *arajakata* (lawlessness) and *matsyanyaya* (the law of the sea according to which the big fish devour the small).[83] The Sangh does not consider these specifically, but the Samiti directly reproduces the notion of *varnasankara*.

This version also parallels strains of European fascist thought. Nazi theoreticians similarly maintain that Aryan women enjoyed a position of great respect in the ideal Aryan nation, although they define the position differently. They attribute German women's downfall to intermarriage with Jews which introduced impure blood and notions of women's inferiority into the Aryan 'community'.[84] They claimed that, "because Jewry was largely responsible for the degeneration of the German people, the woman problem could only be solved in the anti-semitic, National Socialist state."[85] Similarly, Samiti ideologues see their liberation as linked to the 'resurrection' of an anti-Other Hindu nation.

But, let us explore its component parts.

**The territory: symbolic space and material substance**

*According to the Sangh*

The territory has a symbolic and material dimension, and these are inseparable. As sacred space, it is symbolised by the goddess Bharatmata. Underlying this is the widely-held notion, among Hindus, of the land as Divine Mother. It was politicised in the nineteenth century when Bengal-based revolutionary and revivalist movements represented India as the goddess Kali. While she was a powerful unifying symbol, she was invested with a range of diverse signifieds. To some, she was a redeeming figure, and to others she symbolised the current desolate state of India under colonial rule.[86] Still others tended to interpret her cult negatively.[87] Within the spectrum of meanings, most pertinent for our focus is Ramakrishna Paramahansa's—M.S. Golwalkar had been a member of the Ramakrishna Order prior to fully committing himself to the Sangh and claimed to be deeply influenced by that experience.[88]

Ramakrishna's Kali was a very powerful figure. He interpreted her as "everything", containing "every attribute" and simultaneously asserted she was "nothing but pure love."[89] In her, he was able to synthesise elements of Vedantic and Upanishadic philosophy and bhakti devotionalism. He placed her centrally in his energy-matter monism, for he identified her both with the immaterial brahman and the material maya.[90] In contrast to more orthodox forms of Hinduism, he did not view maya as an obstacle to spiritual realisation. Instead, for him, Kali represented the path of working through and with maya, to achieve realisation.[91]

Since Ramakrishna's Kali is so central to his thought, and in view of M.S. Golwalkar's link to him, it is surprising that, while integrating the notion of the femininity of the territorial component, he rarely employs the signifier 'Kali' to refer to the Motherland. While studies on Ramakrishna's successor, Swami Vivekananda, reveal that the latter downplayed the role of Kali in his own thought, and while Kali's absence in the Sangh's discourse may reflect certain regional tensions,[92] it seems that her absence could also be due to less evident underlying factors. For, not only has the signifier 'Kali' been largely omitted, but so has the entire basis for it in the signified.

Briefly stated, the difference between Ramakrishna's Kali as the Motherland and the Sangh's Bharatmata is analogous to that of the Devi in her independent and domesticated forms.[93] The Sangh presents her as a chaste mother, victimised (by Muslims) and declares that she needs the protection of her "virile" sons[94], the "Men with the capital M".[95] Unlike Kali, Bharatmata is left with no warrior qualities of her own.

The image and the meaning the Sangh assigns to its motherland are not specific to Hinduism. As Andrew Parker et al. have amply demonstrated, in many nationalisms across the globe the territorial component is associated with, or symbolised as, a chaste female body, often a mother or a motherly figure.[96] The notion of her potential violation by foreign invaders is also widespread.[97] The idealised mother, because of her staticity, her asexuality, her perfection, and her potential victimisation, is a safe object of passion for her citizen/ sons. In Irigarayan terms, such a construction reflects a dominant form of gendered social relations in which the feminine is a space for males to realize their self-identity.[98] Perhaps what is unique in the Sangh's case, in relation to other nationalisms, is its process of continually narrowing the scope, and lessening the symbolic weight, of the feminine while expanding and reinforcing the masculine. For, as it splits off Kali's fierce characteristics from Bharatmata, it shifts them into the personality of the ideal Hindu male, where they are subject to nominative modification: Kali's feminine strength becomes male virility. This effacement of qualities which in many forms of Hinduism have been easily accommodated within symbolic femininity, are in their nominative transformation, their reassignment to the masculine pole (and at times their expulsion from the discourse altogether), an integral part of the processes at work in the Sangh discourse in general.

In yet another move to downplay symbolic femininity, the Sangh confines it to the nation's territory, and adopts the signifier, Bhagawa Dhwaj (the saffron flag) which it constructs in masculine terms to embody its ethical system. It must be remembered that various strains in the Bengali nationalist movement had used Kali to simultaneously represent the nation's territory, the unity of the people, and their ideals. In contrast, for the Sangh, the flag is "the highest, the noblest and the truest symbol of our nationhood", and the "guiding light" of the nation.[99] It is a "living symbol"[100], a "Guru"[101], under whose "sanctifying presence"[102] Sangh activities take place. The orange of the flag symbolises sacrificial fire (yagna).[103] The saffron tint represents the sunrise "dispelling darkness and heralding the coming of the light".[104] Indeed, the saffron flag is an ancient symbol, flown over sacred space, and temples, all over India. However, extracted from its sacred context, and seen through the perceptual grid of the Sangh's political value system where virility and manhood are the supreme components of masculinity, the Sangh flag on a pole, placed in the open spaces it uses for para-military training (fields, parks) stands erect as a phallus image. It represents culture in relation to the territory, nature.

In coherence with Bharatmata's symbolic dimension, the Sangh maintains that the material space is "mutilated" by the imposition of artificial, restrictive borders.[105] A recurring theme is Partition, or the events leading to and following the creation of Pakistan in 1947. The "memory" of "Partition" is re-evoked continually throughout time, throughout the Sangh's literature, to conjure up demonised images of Muslims ("Muslims on the warpath", "Muslim violence against Hindus", "Muslim rape of Hindu women", "Muslim pillaging of Hindu property" are repeated phrases). The purpose is to justify continual "retaliation" against Muslims. The events are presented in a schematic and one-sided manner. It does not ever indicate concern or even curiosity about how Muslims might have experienced the same events, or why Indian Muslims remained in India, for ultimately it has dehumanised them. They are constructed to represent a threat (or a promise, in so far as the Sangh's nationalism requires a threatening Other) of future violence.

The Sangh proposes a 'return' to the 'pristine state' of the territory[106], but delineates the 'pristine' borders inconsistently from text to text. At times its nation's space comprises the area of the present India, Pakistan and Bangladesh combined. Yet, on the postcards and posters it issued in connection with Dr. Hedgevar's Birth Centennial Celebration (1988), it portrays India's neighbouring countries from Nepal to Sri Lanka, from Pakistan to Bangladesh, as included in its domain. In one text it compares the Hindu Nation in its ideal state with the British Empire, and claims that "the sun never set over the Hindu empire in those days."[107] Simultaneously, it denies having territorial ambitions; however, nowhere in its various productions does it represent the Hindu nation as confined to the present borders of India.

For the Sangh, within the present 'restricted' boundaries, the Hindu territory is 'colonised' by sporadic Islamic enclaves: mosques. Each mosque is a "miniature Pakistan" violating the body of the Hindu motherland.[108] Elsewhere, I have shown that, in this conception, the mosque stands for a Muslim phallus and is read as a symbol of Muslim male sexual aggression.[109] For the Sangh, the presence of the phallus/ mosque denigrates the Motherland, and transforms her into a prostitute-like figure.[110] Such imagery reaches the Addressees in the emotional dimension, and underlies the passions evoked in events such as the destruction of the Babri Masjid.[111]

*According to the Samiti*

The Samiti reproduces Bharatmata but extends both her signifier and signified. It refers to her alternately as Bharatmata, Parvati and Durgadevi, and accordingly it assigns her a wider range of characteristics. The extensions are based on a reference the Sangh ignores: the Devi Mahatmya.[112] In it, Parvati, Durga, Kali, and other goddesses are diverse forms, embodying aspects of the same goddess. Similarly Bharatmata encompasses qualities which range from mild to fierce to potentially out of control. The Samiti does not represent her as victimised or in need of virile sons, even in her most benign forms. Instead, she is "the protector of society"[113], "the very source of all power"[114], and "the origin of all divinities".[115] This image is closer to many nineteenth century Bengali revivalist interpretations of Kali as the nation's territory, and certainly more affirmative of femininity than the Sangh's.

Bharatmata represents both the land and the characteristics Hindu women are to emulate. She is portrayed in her milder forms when linked to sacred geography and material motherhood, and in her fiercer forms in connection with the potential of women as citizens. As the land, she "offers us everything required for our growth and maintenance during our entire span of life".[116] Also, "the mountains are as if the breasts of our Motherland. . . as milk flows from the mother's breasts so do the rivers flow from the mountains".[117] Her motherliness is powerful, for it nurtures the entire society. She is the source which enables Hindu women "to generate innate power promoting divinity".[118] That power is "capable of destroying [sic] evil practices as well as tendencies".[119] But it is also potentially dangerous, and women "must have the discrimination to use it in a way benevolent to our nation".[120] This last statement contains much subtlety; it functions as a warning while appearing to promote feminine cooperation with Sangh ideals. Its hidden reference is to Kali, again in the Devi Mahatmya, who, after combatting the demons, celebrates her victory by dancing. In her enthusiasm, she loses control, until she looks down, realizes that she has almost trampled the god Shiva to death and suddenly stops. The notion that women's power, real or symbolic, is so great that it risks losing control and trampling masculinity, is antagonistic to the Sangh's depiction of things feminine and masculine.

The Samiti retains the Sangh's flag as a symbol, but reduces its status, extends its gender to include femininity and enlarges its meaning. The Sangh's flag is "the highest" symbol, but for the Samiti it is simply "a significant symbol".[121] For the Sangh, it replaces the ethical meaning of the territorial goddess, but for the Samiti, it exists parallel to the goddess as a reflection of the system she embodies. The Sangh associates it with divine masculinity (the "flag of God Himself"); but the Samiti leaves its gender ambiguous, unannounced, allowing it the possibility of including both genders. It does this at the level of the signifier in its English-language works, by translating Bhagawa Dhwaj as "the flag of the Divinity"[122] (instead of the masculine "God"). The bi-genderisation extends to the signified: regardless of language, the Samiti endows the flag with masculine and feminine characteristics.

The Samiti reproduces the Sangh's image of the flag and some of the meanings. Thus, its colour is as "orange rays of the rising sun, dispelling the darkness of the night"[123]; it is an "unbroken thread upholding our heritage and culture"[124]; it functions as a "mentor and guide in the task of national reconstruction".[125] Yet, it feminises each point. Thus, stressing form, it reads "two triangles" which resemble "our beloved motherland".[126] One triangle is larger, and stands for "material wealth and enjoyment", while the smaller one signifies "renunciation".[127] This must be read in view of the symbolic meaning of the triangle in Hinduism: as shakti, as a vagina, as a goddess. Within this configuration a number of inter-pretations which are affirmative of feminine power are possible.

The Samiti does not emphasise the material dimension of the Hindu Nation, yet it speaks of its boundaries and its violation by the presence of non-Hindus. Its "geographical dimensions are clear; starting from the northmost [sic] slope and not the southmost [sic] one as is thought generally — as accepted by the principle of 'Watershed Area' — of the Himalayas, to the southmost [sic] end of Hindu Mahasagar" (meaning Great Lake, Great Ocean or Indian Ocean).[128] Thus, it stretches from Nepal to Sri Lanka, from Pakistan to Bangladesh.

## The Hindu people and their Others[129]

*Hindus according to the Sangh*

The Hindu people are "by far the most important ingredient in the nation".[130] They are in Satyuga or Kaliyuga, according to whether they are 'conscious' or 'unconscious' of themselves as 'Hindus', in the Sangh's sense of the terms. It formulates them in binary opposition to its Others: that is, to those who do not conform to its identity models for ideal Hindu men and women. The models are based primarily upon cultural, not biological, arguments as, in the sense of Taguieff,[131] in modern forms of racism around the globe.

The ideal Hindu people in Satyuga is the most enlightened collectivity in the world; all Others remain in a state of barbarism until they come into contact with the superior Hindu civilization.[132] The Sangh speaks of the Hindu people almost invariably in directly masculine terms, and to a lesser extent, in neutered (and therefore masculine) terms.[133] They are the "sons of the soil", or the "men born in the land of Bharat".[134] Here, it simply erases femininity in the overall designation.

The Sangh represents the ideal individual Hindu male largely via characteristics associated by the British with Kshatriyas, when during their rule they attempted to construct the latter as a martial race.[135] He is virile, physically strong, fearless, a celibate, and most of all, an ardent Hindu nationalist. The most valorised male is the pracharak. Symbolic references for this model include Hanuman and Rama of the Ramayana, and Shivaji. In contrast, the 'unconscious' Hindu male is effeminate, materialistic, westernised, sexual, anti-national.[136] These qualities have been constant throughout the Sangh's literature. The two models are contrasted in the following Sangh story: Dr. Hedgevar (Doctorji to swayamsevaks) "had bought from an exhibition a couple of fans made of palm leaves and bamboo. . . One of them carried a picture of Chatrapati Shivaji, and on the other was a picture of the famous actor, Balgandharva in a female role. . . Doctorji explained, 'I intentionally bought these two just to show the contrast between the condition of Maharashtra some 300 years ago, and our present times.'"[137]

In its attempt to rewrite the 'proper' identities of Hindu men, the Sangh has circumvented forms of Hinduism which easily accommodated bi-gendered, bi-sexual and homosexual individuals or associated such qualities with saintliness. A growing body of social scientific and activist literature has brought the existence of such forms throughout the region and throughout time to the fore.[138] Consider, for example, in the context of the present study, Ramakrishna himself, who practised the *madhurya-bhava* (relating emotionally and spiritually to the deity as lover) of Radha towards Krishna[139] and described himself as having "a womanly nature".[140] Consider, also, Mahatma Gandhi who advised men to adopt feminine characteristics, and is respectfully called "Mother of our Nation" by many.

Until the shift towards 'mass' involvement, the Sangh rarely wrote of Hindu women. The change became visible when a chapter on them was added to the 1980 revised edition of M.S. Golwalkar's *Bunch of Thoughts*. It appears in a section entitled, "For Social Uplift"; others who need to be "uplifted" and are similarly allotted chapters here are "untouchables", "tribals" and "the poor". The chapter on women, "Call to the Motherland", centres on mothers of Hindu nationalist sons. It is addressed to the sons and speaks of women in the third person singular and plural. It lays forth a mother's ideal characteristics: she should teach her sons Hindu culture, bring out their virile qualities, spur them on to battle with the nation's enemies. She should serve "our needy sisters in society"[141] to make them "intimate with the true spirit of our national being";[142] and, she should be like Savitri "before whom even the Lord of Death accepted defeat".[143] Interestingly, in Hindu mythology with which Sangh ideologues are most familiar, Savitri is a wife, not a mother. She so demonstrates her loyalty to her husband, Satyavan, with her commitment to follow him to his death, that Yama, the god of death, grants him life again. Elsewhere in the literature, it rarely discusses women as wives, for the ideal swayamsevak has no wife; he is unmarried and his primary attach-ment is to his Hindu nationalist brothers and their common ideals.

Finally, a Hindu mother should not be 'modern', for that means negating "our cherished values of life".[144] Modern women are like prostitutes: they expose "their body more and more to the public gaze".[145] Here, it sets up a number of oppositions: 'traditional' versus 'modern', mother versus wife, asexual figure versus sexual figure, all of which it reifies in the process.

Sevikas appear only rarely in the Sangh's literature, and only recently so. Regardless of their age and marital status, it presents them as little sisters and as mothers. In its ideologues' family milieu, the mother is a more powerful figure than the sister. Thus, by adding the sisterly dimension to the motherly one, the Sangh tones down the power of women organised in a mode parallel to itself.

Besides the mass of sevikas, there are exceptional former sevikas such as Uma Bharati and Sadhvi Rithambara. Both women are orators of passionate speeches used to incite (militaristic) Hindu nationalist sentiments in the agitations which led to the demolition of the Babri Masjid. There are several ideological sub-tendencies in the Sangh, but there is a general agreement that such women should remain rarities. They are, however, welcome exceptions since their function in the public space is an active version of the passive Bharatmata's: they inspire machoised masculinity to 'protect' the 'purity' of Hindu Culture and of the Hindu Territory which they, as celibate chaste women, simultaneously embody.

The Sangh is ambiguous about women's roles in the public arena, besides the motherly and sisterly one. It has yet to officially pronounce itself on the question of national women political leaders. Until recently individual Sangh members voiced opinions largely against this possibility. Also, it was the subject of a debate in a major Sangh publication, the *Organiser*, from July to September of 1969, which was sparked off by an unsigned article on the editorial page, entitled "Women Rulers are Disastrous". It was meant to attack Indira Gandhi but extended its arguments to include all women.[146] Of a total of seven, only two articles stood in favour of women holding political leadership positions. They both evoked the Samiti's notion of women's "high position in the Vedic period" and figures like the Rani of Jhansi. The counter arguments were cultural, historical, psychological, and even biological. They asserted, for example, that "whenever women have been invested with absolute power they have caused absolute havoc", yet in India "though not very bright some of them have held posts of Ambassadors, Ministers of State and Cabinet Ministers, not to speak of the post of Prime Minister".[147] In western nations, "where feminine dominance over men is supposed to be overwhelming, women have been wisely excluded from that realm, and India should do the same".[148] The psychological arguments referred to "case studies. . . from Freudian point of view [sic]" on women over

50 years of age and on widows, which demonstrate that they are "frustrated. . . [with the] desire to take revenge or cling to power" and are "extremely receptive to the flatteries of young men"[149] The "physical changes in their bodies supply the motivation to their action and influence their process of thinking".[150] Although none of these opinions officially represent the Sangh, they reflect the mood and the subtext underlying the absence of an official discourse.

To conclude, ultimately the Sangh proposes a model for domesticated, motherly or sisterly femininity as the overwhelming ideal both at the symbolic and material levels.

## Non Hindu Others according to the Sangh

The Sangh has constructed a number of entities as its Others (Christians, Parsis, Jains, Jews, Sikhs, et al.) but, due to considerations of space, I shall limit the discussion to its primary enemy, Indian Muslims.[151] It formulates a 'Muslim Community' in binary terms, assigning to it terms which are antonyms of those of its 'Hindu Community'. Yet, it characterises the former, like itself, in overwhelmingly masculine terms; this is because, for the Sangh, males are the essential 'community' agents, regardless of the 'community' in question.

In the early literature there are two categories of Muslims: Muslims-as-Forcign-Invaders and Muslims-as-ex-Hindu-Converts. The former are the upper class and the leaders of fundamentalist groups. It holds them responsible for the downfall of the Hindu Nation, the "vivisection" of the Hindu nation's territory and the creation of Pakistan. It depicts Muslims-as-ex-Hindu-Converts as their lower class allies converted by bribery, by the sword or because of greed. In both categories, it portrays Muslims as anti-national, sexually overactive, lusting after and raping Hindu women and symbolic femininity (Bharatmata).

Since opening itself to the 'masses', the Muslims-as-ex-Hindu-Converts have become targets for its "reconversion" programmes, and a new model, termed "Hindu Muslims" has surfaced to accommodate them. The Muslims here are 'modern', 'progressive' and the Sangh claims that some get their daughters married to swayamsevaks so that they can escape the "evils of Islam".

The image of Muslim women depends upon their proximity to or distance from men. It depicts those who are close to Muslim men as prostitutes, baby factories for the (again, male) 'Muslim Community' or as the victims of "Islamic evils"—which it names as polygamy, talaq (unilateral divorce) and Muslim male corruption. In yet another set of Sangh images, Muslim women are desirous of ideal Hindu men who are either too chaste and too dedicated to the Hindu Nation to desire them, or who heroically agree to marry them. In sum, it represents them as the potential or real communal and sexual property of Hindu men.[152]

What is striking here is that, while the Sangh excludes sexuality from its ideal Hindu models, it projects it onto Muslims.

*Hindus according to the Samiti*

For the Samiti, too, the Hindu people are in Kaliyuga, in an 'unconscious' state, and must be brought back into Satyuga, into 'consciousness' of themselves. Unlike the Sangh, its Hindu people is a bi-gendered entity. They are the sons and daughters of the motherland.

It has chosen the elephant-headed god Ganesh[153], whose name means literally "god of the collectivity", as a symbol of the people. Ganesh is a recurring figure in Hindu mythologies, and is subject to numerous interpretations. In some he is the son of Shiva and Parvati, or the androgynous parthenogenic son of Parvati alone. In still other, rarer cases, he is represented as feminine, with or without parents, with or without a consort, as Vinayaki, and/or as one of the 64 yoginis of the shakta and tantrika sects.

In the Samiti's version, Ganesh is the androgynous son of Parvati. She created him alone from her bodily dirt to serve as her protector. Such a representation is not homogeneously masculine. For here, because Ganesh was created without male intervention, he lacks what in this form of Hinduism the male is said to provide: bones. In that sense, he is male but not fully so.

Ganesh also exists in a relationship of conflict to Parvati's male consort, Shiva. In the pertinent mythology, she requests him to refuse entry to all while she is bathing. In compliance, he bars the doorway for Shiva who, consequently, beheads him. When Parvati learns of this, she obliges Shiva to bring him back to life. However, since Ganesh's human head cannot be found, Shiva replaces it with an elephant's head. Interestingly, the figures of the intruding male, the potentially victimised mother and her sacrificing protective son recur in the Sangh's construction of the series constituted by Muslim aggressors/Bharatmata/sons of the soil. For the Samiti, Ganesh is "auspicious. . . showers happiness, banishes agonies, sorrows and calamities", and thus is worshipped by the women's organisation "at the beginning of every rite".[154]

Men are not a major thematic in the Samiti's literature, but when it does discuss them, it represents them differently from the Sangh. They are not unconnected to women as *sannyasins* in the material world; instead, they are located in the *grihasthashrama* as good husbands (of Hindu wives), good sons (of Hindu mothers), and good nationalist leaders or citizens. The Samiti does not idealise virility or machismo, nor does it represent 'unconscious' Hindu males as effeminate; instead, its negative Hindu males are those who harass women, who fail to respect Hindu femininity, or who intermarry with women outside their caste or religion.

The Samiti represents Hindu women widely: as mothers, wives, sisters, daughters, citizens, pracharikas, warriors and rulers. These are supported by Samiti interpretations of symbolic elements: Shivaji's mother, Sita, Savitri, Mira, Rani of Jhansi and others. Hindu women "pass through four phases of life: daughter, sister, wife and mother".[155] These correspond to the ashramas (stages of life) theorised in upper-caste Hinduism and generally associated today with men: *brahmacharin* or celibate student, *grihastha* or householder, *vanaprastha* or forest-dwelling hermit, *sannyasin* or homeless wanderer. The Samiti's phases stress the woman's relation to her family (which is bi-gendered), to an individual man and to the nation, but it interprets the phases widely, including providing a space for some individual women to permanently exit the family to fulfil citizenly duty.

The symbolic reference which underlies the models is the goddess Ashtabhuja (literally the 'eight-armed one') which was configured by L. Kelkar. She is "an integral combination of Mahakali, Mahasaraswati and Mahalakshmi".[156] She represents, "Co-ordination of Strength, Intellect and Wealth"[157], carries weapons in her eight hands and, like the Samiti's Bharatmata, accommodates characteristics ranging from benevolent to fierce to potentially out of control. She brings to mind the transformative aspect of the goddess in the Devi Mahatmya. Her personality is a multi-faceted source from which individual sevikas can subjectively draw. She is a striking example of the Samiti's subtle use of the symbolic to legitimise and reinforce wider models for femininity.

For the Samiti, as for the Sangh, mothers are supposed to give birth to sons, educate them, send them to battle, but, for the Samiti, mothers also have a primary role in the sons' self-realisation, and are direct agents in the resurrection of the Nation.

There are several models for the ideal wife, but the most elaborate is connected to the figure of Sita. She evokes a sense of duty in her husband, is loyal to him, brave, chaste, puts national interests above her personal interests and expects her husband to do the same.[158] The Samiti also inserts characteristics and a value system connected to the ideal wife which indirectly empower her within the context of the heterosexual couple. It reinterprets the concept of pativrata (in which the wife looks unconditionally upon the husband as god and is exclusively dedicated to him), such that not only her husband but, the Nation too, is her god.[159] Thus, it divides the wife's loyalties and responsibilities. It creates a space for her to resist unconditional devotion to her husband by asserting that his status as divine depends upon his good (husbandly *and* Hindu nationalist) behaviour. Thus, it gives wives the right to evaluate their husbands, and it institutionalises this reinterpretation by rewriting the rituals associated with normative pativrata. In it, the wife is expected to fast in order to ensure the well-being of her husband; the Samiti however recommends "fasting on the eleventh day for society" because "God is in society".[160] In so far as society is bi-gendered, and the wife is a member of it, she and all Hindu women are included in the beneficiaries of her fast. The Samiti stresses that there should be no conflict between these two loyalties, and where there is, reconciliation should be the goal. Yet, when that is impossible, it gives her the right to transfer that loyalty to the Nation. Obviously, such a situation would rarely, if ever, arise in cases where the husband is a swayamsevak. However, if it did, women would be free of the *individual* Hindu male but remain bound by the Rule of the *collectivity* of Hindu nationalist males.

Ideal sisters are sevikas. They are the younger sisters of the swayamsevaks as mentioned above, and they are the elder sisters (or mothers) to non-Hindu nationalist Hindus (women and men) who are not yet 'conscious' of themselves. They occupy various positions in relation to each other, based on age but also on avowed caste and class factors. Often their positions in the Samiti's internal hierarchy are not uninfluenced by their status outside the Samiti in the world, or by the position of male family members in the Sangh.

Ideal daughters are the children of Bharatmata and/or Ashtabhuja. They are supposed to emulate the qualities of their symbolic mothers, which potentially provides them a space for resistance to the values of their biological and social mothers, if the latter's values cannot be accommodated within the context of Bharatmata or Ashtabhuja's symbolic meanings.

I have discussed above the Samiti's encouragement of feminine warrior and leadership qualities, via para-military training and *bauddhik* (intellectual discussion) sessions, and pointed to the presence of former sevikas within the leadership positions of the Sangh Parivar. The Samiti has several symbolic references for such women: as warriors it mentions Vishpala, Vadhrimati, Durgavati;[161] as rulers it cites Rani of Jhansi [162], Devi Ahilyabai Holkar (of Indore) and Queen Chennana[163], for example.

The pracharikas are exceptional women, for the majority are to realise themselves in the *grihasthashrama*. The position provides a highly respected space to single women who see themselves as, in the words of one of my informants, "married to the Nation, not to any man".[164]

The Samiti's relational modes include those modelled upon familial ones (sisters, mothers, daughters, etc.), as well as positional linkages (leader/follower, teacher/student, etc.) The images of 'unconscious' Hindu women range from unknowing victims, to 'modern' women, to feminists, prostitutes, traitors.

## Non-Hindu Others according to the Samiti

The Samiti's major Other is similarly the Muslim community; it threatens the Hindu Nation and Hindu women. Yet, the term is assigned a bi-gendered meaning; the community is comprised of men and women. There is only one model for Muslim men, and it is thoroughly negatively connoted. They are overwhelmingly depicted in terms of violence: as rapists, rioters, murderers. It views not only Muslim men but also Islam as fundamentally, essentially degrading to women. In contrast, Muslim women are assigned a spectrum of images; but, these too are overwhelmingly negatively connoted. They are represented as weak, victimised, socially and ethically inferior to Hindu women and as a threat to the unity of the Hindu family.

The Samiti borders on constructing them as biologically inferior when it depicts them as non-Aryan, as noted above. In most of these images, it assigns impurity and sexuality to them. The Samiti's representations of Muslims, both men and women, are more rigid in their anti-Otherness than the Sangh's.·

## Religion, Culture, Language

### According to the Sangh

For the Sangh Hindu religion, culture and language exist in their ideal state in Satyuga; they are eternal, inseparable, 'undefinable' emanations of the 'Ultimate Reality'.[165] Each component exists in binary opposition to its negative Others. The Hindu religion, which is "the very life-breath of the people"[166], is "the only religion of the world worthy of being so denominated".[167] In contrast, Islam and Christianity are religions of "debased civilizations".[168]

Here, the Sangh reproduces notions from the well-known book by Arya Samajist Har Bilas Sarda, *Hindu Superiority: An Attempt to Determine the Position of the Hindu Race in the Scale of Nations.*[169] It was written to resist colonial racism at a time when race was naturalised by western science in the service of colonialism. Sarda remains within the original race paradigm and simply inverts its principal terms. His thesis is that the Hindu Race is superior to all others; it preceded the great ones and colonised the weaker ones. He draws from nineteenth century Orientalism, and from non-academic sources such as the Theosophists, quoting them in and out of context.

The Sangh characterises Hinduism as "naturally secular", and "naturally universal". It believes that Hinduism is the "mother" of all religions, and that every religion, every god or goddess of other religions can be accommodated in the Hindu pantheon. These aassumptions are grounded in notions of Hindu superiority as cited above. The practical implications are that the Sangh expects its 'Hindu-Muslims' to 'realise' that Allah is one god in the Hindu pantheon, for the sake of 'national integration'. This allows the Sangh to posit its version of Hinduism as a tolerant, all-inclusive religion, capable of accommodating Islam. Paradoxically, here, it negates the basic beliefs of Muslims while claiming moral superiority over them. It does not accept that for Muslims Allah is the only god, and not one of many gods. Such a proposition either denies or denigrates difference, and excludes the possibility of diverse belief systems co-existing peacefully.

For the Sangh, Hindu Culture is "but a by-product of our all-comprehensive religion", and the creator of "the peculiar Race spirit"[170] of the Hindus which it refers to as *chiti* (spiritual consciousness, in many forms of Hinduism). The Sangh's definition of *chiti*, however, is political. It is as a type of higher law within which Hindu nationalist dharma (duty, order) is worked out. It is made to correspond to the concept of the people's spirit which exists in both Mussolini's[171] and Hitler's[172] brands of fascism. It presupposes an ideal unitary, uniform cultural heritage in India which represents the essence of the Hindu Nation and which defies time. Here, non-Hindu religions are posited as the corrupters/destroyers of the Hindu Nation.[173] In that sense, they occupy a position similar to the one assigned by Nazi ideologues to their entity, 'the Jews', in relation to *volkgeist*. Again, it is through effacement and replacement at the level of the signifier that the Sangh manages to disguise a specifically fascist concept, to designate it as a timeless 'Hindu' one and thereby render it acceptable to its Addressees.

For the Sangh one immutable element of Hindu culture is *varna-vyavastha*, the division of society into a system of orders or castes. This "four-fold arrangement" reflects the unity of the "Hindu People" as "the Virat Purusha, the Almighty manifesting Himself".[174] In the early Sangh literature, caste is interpreted as in the Manusmriti: designated by birth for one's lifetime. Later, in a concession to the 'masses', it continues to speak of a four-fold division (and to name the dividing categories as Brahman, Kshatriya, Vaishya, Shudra), but proposes that one's positionality in it should depend upon merit. It retains the notion that "not equality but harmony" leads to the highest state of society.[175] It holds that it is against caste 'discrimination', both positive and negative, on the grounds that it might 'divide' the 'Hindu Community'. It has consistently opposed reservation" (a form of affirmative action designed to 'reserve' posts in the public employment sector and in educational institutions for members of collectivities which have not had access to them). This must be read contextually, keeping in mind the Sangh's history, and the upper caste background of its leadership and a good deal of its membership. Finally, it amounts to a disguised form of support for a hierarchical ritual and social status quo.

For the Sangh, the language of the Hindus is Sanskrit, "the

language of the Gods".[176] It is "an expression of the Race spirit"[177], and is "common to all from the Himalayas to the ocean in the south".[178] In its later literature, it foresees a Sanskritized form of Hindi as a possible intermediary until the use of Sanskrit becomes generalised.[179] In this project (which would also exclude other Indian languages presently recognised by the secular Indian state) caste, class and regional biases are quite evident. Sanskrit has largely been monopolised by Brahman males, and Hindi is a language of north and central India. The Sangh represents Urdu (identified with Muslims) as the diametric opposite of Sanskrit, and argues that it is an anti-national language.

Finally, the Sangh seeks hegemonic control in defining *the* Hindu religion, culture and language. Its ideal Hindu people are essentially a "homogeneous people".[180] The nation's resurrection requires the elimination of "all such habits, superstitions and tendencies which" in its opinion "had devitalised our nation during the last several centuries", such that the "sublime, life-sustaining values of our national culture", as the Sangh defines them, can be "cultivated".[181] In its future nation, its particular Hindu religion/culture/language "commands. . . every action in life, individual, social or political".[182] Ultimately, what it has in mind is an entity which it will define and redefine at will.

### According to the Samiti

The Samiti puts forth only a vague definition of Hindu religion and culture. Similarly, Sanskrit is the language of the Hindus, and "the vehicle of cultural unity".[183] Hindu culture is "divine",[184] "the entire structure of Hindu life is built on eternal truths; on the findings and experiences of the great Rishis. . . it is stern regarding the fundamentals, but very elastic regarding the externals and non-essentials".[185]

At the social level, some of those fundamentals are the *purusharthas* (goals of life), *varnashrama dharma* (the fulfilment of the duties particular to each order or caste by its members), and the principle of unity in diversity. The *purusharthas,* which in Hinduism consist of *dharma, artha* (economics and politics), *kama* (pleasure) and *moksha* (spiritual liberation or realisation), are the "basis upon which the individual and society attain coordination".[186] They are a "set of values and guidelines which enable a Hindu to lead a meaningful, purposeful and harmonious life" in the material world.[187] The Samiti's emphasis on the material world and self-realisation in it, parallel the Sangh's at the level of the signifier, but serve a different function. The women use these notions directly to affirm the positive qualities of femininity; they also use them indirectly to encourage male circumvention of forms of ascetic Brahmanism which devalorise the material and demonise women as temptations which threaten to divert a man from his spiritual path.

For the Samiti, *varnashrama dharma* is necessary to "maintain the quality and texture of an integrated life".[188] It has "imparted to the whole of Bharat a strong and stable cultural unity that has through ages stood the shocks of political revolutions and foreign invasions".[189] Today, the Samiti, like the Sangh, rarely writes of caste, and when it does, its statements are ambiguous. On the one hand it feels untouchability should be eradicated in order to prevent conversion to other faiths;[190] elsewhere, it links caste to the concept of "unity in diversity", this concept to social hierarchy, and social hierarchy to birth. Thus, "Bharat presents human evolution in all its states and stages from the lowest to the highest" while "the vast variety contains and exhibits a common thread of life".[191] One's position in it seems to be determined at birth: "persons not blessed by god are not inclined to do any good work, as they have not done any in their past lives";[192] in that sense the Samiti has a more rigid conception of caste than does the Sangh.

## Interrelations of the Component Parts

*According to the Sangh*

For the Sangh, there are two primary types of interrelations among the components: mother/son and brother/brother.

The mother/son relation involves the territory (Bharatmata), and the Hindu People (a masculine entity); the latter are to become one with the former. In this sense, the return to the idealised past/future of Satyuga is linked to the Swayamsevika's regressive return to a symbiotic relation with the Mother(land). The combined components, Hindu religion/culture/language, operate as a Third to mediate relations between the mother and the son, ensuring that their bonding remains filial and non-heterosexual.

The swayamsevaks' interrelations are brother/brother relations.

Bharatmata functions as a Third to mediate their homosociality, in the sense of Irigaray,[193] and guarantees that their male bonding remains fraternal and non-homosexual. To reinforce this, the Sangh often uses homophobic images to describe its Hindu enemies; for example, it accuses Congress of "wooing the Muslims" and of "holding its enemies to its breast".

The Bhagawa Dhwaj, its symbolism and the place the Sangh designates for it, serves to amplify the homosociality which operates therein. It functions as an additional mediating Third between the swayamsevaks, thus allowing them to operate within a more fully masculine context which includes the symbolic level.

Finally, the Rule of the Sangh is a rule of sons and brothers, thus a Hindu nationalist form of filio-fraternarchy.

### According to the Samiti

For the Samiti, there are several types of interrelations at work: mother/children (of both genders), sister/sister, brother/sister, husband/wife, etc. They are consistently mediated by Thirds which are always either exclusively feminine (Ashtabhuja, Bharatmata) or simultaneously bi-gendered (Hindu culture/religion/language, Ganesh and the flag). Through the re-insertion of the feminine at every instance of the Hindu Nation from the symbolic to the social, the Samiti carves out a space for women. But this space also assures that they remain within the confines of the Sangh's network.

### Concluding remarks: or fractionalisation as unifying praxis

I have tried to show throughout this essay that the Sangh and Samiti have two different discourses on the Hindu Nation. I have also pointed out, from time to time, some of the internal debates and ambiguities within each of them, but these divergences and points of antagonism do not mean that Hindu nationalists are disunited.

There is some indication that, similarly, in Nazi Germany, women fascists engaged in debates in their journals and sometimes proposed women-affirmative notions contradictory to the official masculinist line.[194] They were allowed to exist but ultimately were not taken seriously when policy was in question. Evidence also suggests that in Mussolini's Italy, where some bourgeois feminists had converted to fascism, women interpreted the regime's position on gender differently from men.[195] There, too, women sought to create a space for women as agents and citizens. Their male leaders allowed this because their project, based on the family cell, required women's adherence. Neither in Germany nor in Italy, however, did women fascists elaborate a specifically feminine discourse to the degree that Hindu nationalist women have. This is certainly due to women's structural positions, a greater degree of pre-existing feminine solidarities and other contextual factors in India, but also to the existence of an infinitely wider range of representations of femininity in the Hindu symbolic which Samiti ideologues have been able to legitimately draw from. Finally, the regimes accept women's differential modes of perception (Italian fascism) or discourses (fascist Germany for a period, Hindu nationalism now) in so far as they are the means to assure women's complicity, albeit in different modes, with the overall project.

In that sense, the gendered fractionalisation of Hindu nationalist discourse is ultimately a function of its unifying praxis.

## Notes

[1] This essay is for Siddhartha. Those to whom I am grateful for feedback related to it are Siddhartha Gautam, Veena Das, Nicole Khoury, Deepak Mehta, Rajendra Pradhan, Ritu Menon, Amrita Chhachhi, Sheba Chhachhi, Kanchana Natarajan, Liliane Kandel, Shahnaz Rouse, and Maureen L.P. Patterson.

[2] This is in quotes to signify the problematic nature of such terms constructed within and for colonialist historiography.

[3] Nicole Claude Matthieu, "Quand ceder n'est pas consentir. Des determinants materiels et psychiques de la conscience dominee des femmes, et quelquesunes de leurs interpretations en ethnologie", in *Cahiers de l'Homme*, n.s. xxiv, Editions E.H.E.S.S., Paris, 1985, pp. 169–245.

[4] Antonio Gramsci, *Letteratura e Vita Nazionale* (Rome: Editori Riuniti, 1987), pp. 267–74.

[5] David Baker, "The Muslim Concern for Security: the Central Provinces and Berar, 1919-1947", in Mushirul Hasan (ed.), *Communal and Pan-Islamic Trends in Colonial India* (New Delhi: Manohar, 1985), pp. 237–39.

[6] The Sangh has often erroneously been seen as dominated by Chitpavan Brahmans. I am grateful to Maureen L.P. Patterson for information on family histories of the leaders.

[7] Founders referred to swayamsevaks as "Brahman youths". Dr. Moonje's Private Papers (New Delhi: Nehru Memorial Museum and Library), Diary entry, June 12, 1927.

[8] Ibid., January 28, 1926.

[9] Walter Andersen and Shridhar Damle, *The Brotherhood in Saffron* (New Delhi:

162 PAOLA BACCHETTA

Vistaar, 1987), 123–27; 157–247. K. Jayaprasad, *RSS and Hindu Nationalism* (New Delhi: Deep and Deep, 1991), pp.181–350.

[10] See Agehananda Bharati, "The Self in Hindu Thought and Action", in A.J. Marsella, George Devos, Francis L.K. Hsu (eds.), *Culture and Self* (New York: Tavistock, 1985), p.208.

[11] Samiti, *Preface to Rashtra Sevika Samiti* (Nagpur: Sevika Prakashan, undated but post-1978), p.1.

[12] Ibid., p.2.

[13] Ibid., p.6.

[14] Ibid., p.8; L. Kelkar, *Strivishayak Vicharon ka Sankalan* (Nagpur: Sevika Prakashan, undated but post-1986), lecture V.

[15] Samiti, *Preface*, p.13.

[16] Ibid., p.14.

[17] Ibid.

[18] Kelkar, *Strivishayak*, lecture IV.

[19] Mikhail Bakhtin, *Problems of Dostoevsky's Poetics*, ed. and transl. Caryl Emerson (Minneapolis: University of Minnesota Press, 1984).

[20] Samiti, *Srimati Lakshmibai Kelkar ki Jivani* (Nagpur: Sevika Prakashan, 1989), chap. IV.

[21] Ibid.

[22] Ibid.; see also Samiti, *Preface*, p. 15.

[23] Samiti, *Preface*, p.15.

[24] Michel de Certeau, *l'Ecriture de l'Histoire* (Paris: Gallimard, 1975), pp. 274–88.

[25] P. Bacchetta, "On the Construction of Identity in a Hindu Nationalist Discourse: Rashtriya Swayamsevak Sangh and Rashtra Sevika Samiti" (in French), doctoral thesis, Sorbonne, Paris.

[26] Samiti, *Jivani*, chap. I.

[27] Ibid., chap.II.

[28] Samiti, *Preface*, p.14.

[29] Samiti, *Jivani*, chap.II.

[30] The exact number is unknown even within the Samiti; no records are kept. This is an average estimate, drawn from several Sangh and Samiti texts and oral sources. It excludes diasporic branches.

[31] H.V. Sheshasdri (ed.) *RSS: A Vision in Action* (Bangalore: Jagarana Prakashana, 1988), p.151.

[32] This information derives from interviews with sevikas I carried out from 1986 to 1990 in Ahmedabad, Pune, Nagpur.

[33] Lynn Gatwood, *Devi and the Spouse Goddess: Women, Sexuality and Marriage in India*, (New Delhi: Manohar, 1985), 86; Lata Mani, "Contentious Traditions: the Debate on Sati in Colonial India", in Kumkum Sangari and Sudesh Vaid, *Recasting Women* (New Delhi: Kali for Women, 1989), pp. 88–126.

[34] Samiti, *Aao Khel Khelen* (Nagpur: Sevika Prakashan, undated), unpaged.

[35] Samiti, *Preface*, pp. 8–9.

[36] This is also the case with women from other Hindu nationalist groups. P. Bacchetta, "From the Mother Goddess to the Warrior: the Shifting Place of Women in Communal Riots and Communal Discourse in Contemporary Ahmedabad, Gujarat", (in French), D.E.A. thesis in Sociology, Sorbonne, Paris, 1986.

37  Sheshadri, *Vision*, p.153.

38  Ibid.

39  This information is from interviews with sevikas cited above.

40  Samiti, *Preface*, p.7.

41  This is an example of the Samiti adopting a masculine signifier but assigning it a signified which includes the feminine.

42  Samiti, *Preface* pp. 7–8.

43  M.S. Golwalkar, *Bunch of Thoughts* (Bangalore: Jagarana Prakashana, 1980 ed.), p.517. Dr. Hedgevar, in the title of one of his biographies, is referred to as the 'Epochmaker'.

44  Golwalkar, *Thoughts*, (1980 ed.), p.517.

45  Rosalind O'Hanlon, *Caste, Conflict and Ideology: Mahatma Jotirao Phule and Low Caste Protest in Nineteenth-Century Western India* (Cambridge: Cambridge University Press, 1985), pp. 176–86; 295–6. Most pertinent here are the Tilakite and non-Brahmanist positions. Tilak, a Chitpavan Brahman, has been widely accredited with reviving the memory of Shivaji. In his interpretation, Shivaji fought against Muslim domination and for India'a unification. But earlier, the Maharashtrian non-Brahman leader Jyotirao Phule had stressed that Shivaji, as a Maratha, was a non-Brahman. His fight was against usurpers, his success was due to his low caste army, and he signified that Maharashtra belongs to non-Brahmans. The Sangh's version reproduces Tilak's anti-Muslim component, and rejects Phule's emphasis on caste power relations.

46  M.S. Golwalkar, *We; Or Our Nationhood Defined* (Nagpur: Bharat Publications, 1939), ii-iii.

47  Ibid., p.35.

48  Ibid.

49  Kelkar, *Strivishayak*, lecture I.

50  Samiti, *Jivani*, chap.I.

51  Kelkar, *Strivishayak*, lecture VI.

52  L. Kelkar, *Pathadarshini Sriramakatha* (Nagpur: Sevika Prakashan, 1988), chap.I.

53  Madhu Kishwar, "Gandhi on Women", in *Economic and Political Weekly*, vol. XX, no. 40, Bombay, 1985, pp.1691–1702.

54  Partha Chatterjee, "The Nationalist Resolution of the Women's Question" in Sangari and Vaid, *Recasting Women*, op.cit,. pp.233–53.

55  This is an example of a Gramscian temporal delay on the part of the Samiti in the assimilation of the Sangh's discourse.

56  K. Suryanarayana Rao, *Hindu Rashtra, Not a Mere Slogan but a Vibrant Reality* (Madras: Vigil, 1990), pp. 3–5.

57  Ibid., p.6.

58  David Miller (ed.), *The Blackwell Encyclopaedia of Political Thought* (Oxford: Basil Blackwell, 1987), p.206.

59  Ibid., p.207.

60  Golwalkar, *Nationhood Defined*, p.33.

61  Ibid., p.18.

62  Ibid., p.67.

63  The notion of the Vedic period as a Golden Age is attributed to William Jones

and H.T. Colebrook of the Asiatic Society of Bengal.

64 Umberto Silva, *Ideologia e Arte del Fascismo* (Milan: Gabriele Mazzotta Editore, 1973), pp. 64–6.

65 Golwalkar, *Nationhood Defined*, p.9.

66-68 Ibid., p.58, 9, 10.

69 Joseph Dunner (ed.), *Dictionary of Political Science* (London: Vision Press, 1964), p.180.

70 Golwalkar, *Nationhood Defined*, p.10.

71 Ibid., p.11.

72 Romila Thapar, *Ancient Indian Social History: Some Interpretations* (New Delhi: Orient Longman, 1978), pp.4–23.

73 Kelkar, *Strivishayak*, lecture I.

74 Ibid.

75 Samiti, *Deep Stambh; Rashtra Sevika Samiti Akhil Bharatiya Trayopdesh Traivarshik Sammelan 1986*, Pune, 1986, p.47.

76 Ibid.

77 Samiti, *Pratah: Smaraniya Mahilaaen* (Nagpur: Sevika Prakashan, 1990), pp. 30, 52–4, 63.

78 Samiti, *Preface*, p.4.

79 See Golwalkar, *Nationhood Defined*, pp.6–9; See also an unsigned article entitled "British Motive in Planting the Aryan Invasion Theory", in *Organiser*, August 19, 1990, pp. 53–4.

80 Golwalkar, *Nationhood Defined*, pp. 6–8.

81 Ibid.

82 Miller (ed.), *Blackwell Encyclopaedia*, pp. 205–8.

83 Ibid., p.206.

84 Leila J. Rupp, "Mother of the Volk: Images of Women in Nazi Ideology", in *Signs: A Journal of Women, Culture and Society*, vol.3, no.2, 1977), pp.362–79.

85 Ibid., p. 365.

86 David Kinsley, *Hindu Goddesses, Visions of the Divine Feminine in the Hindu Tradition* (Delhi: Motilal Banarsidas, 1987), p.181.

87 David Kingsley, *The Sword and the Flute: Kali and Krishna* (Berkeley: University of California Press, 1975), p.81.

88 In 1936 he became a student of Swami Akhandananda, a disciple of Ramakrishna. The Swami died in 1937. The Swami had requested that he never cut his hair, and Golwalkar faithfully complied. This is popularised in a Sangh comic book; see Swanand, *Shri Guruji*, (Jaipur: Gyan-Ganga Prakashan, undated), p.21.

89 Lynn Gatwood, *Devi and the Spouse Goddess* (New Delhi: Manohar, 1985), p.173.

90 Ibid., p.174.

91 Ibid.

92 Andersen and Damle, *Brotherhood*, p.30.

93 D.D. Kosambi, *Myth and Reality* (Bombay: Popular Prakashan, 1962), p.86; Wendy Doniger O'Flaherty, *Sexual Metaphors and Animal Symbols in Hindu Mythology* (Delhi: Motilal Banarsidas, 1981), pp. 77–129; Gatwood, *Devi*, p.206; Kinsley, *Goddesses*, p.5.

94 Golwalkar, *Thoughts*, (1980 ed.), p.588.

95  Ibid. "Men with the Capital 'M' " is the title of a chapter in the book (pp.570–88).

96  Andrew Parker, et al. (eds.), *Nationalisms and Sexualities* (New York: Routledge, 1992), pp.1–18.

97  Ibid., p.6.

98  Luce Irigaray, *Ethique de la Difference Sexuelle* (Paris: Minuit, 1984), pp.17–18.

99-106  Golwalkar, *Thoughts*, (1980 ed.), p.123-27; p.515-54.

107  Sangh, *Sri Balasaheb Deoras Answers Questions* (Bangalore: Sahitya Sindhu, 1984), p.8.

108  Golwalkar, *Thoughts* (1980 ed.), p.242.

109  P. Bacchetta, "Communal Property/Sexual Property: On the Construction of Muslim Women in a Hindu Nationalist Discourse", in Zoya Hasan (ed.), *Forging Identities: Gender, Communities and the State* (New Delhi: Kali for Women, 1994), pp.188–225.

110  Consider, for example, "Motherland has verily become an object of bargaining, only a land for enjoyment, Bhogabhoomi, just like a hotel". See, Golwalkar, *Thoughts* (1968 ed.), p.93; (1980 ed.), p.123.

111  See P. Bacchetta, "More of the Same: Nodal Narratives and the Use of the Lecherous in the Extension of the Hindu Nationalist Space", paper presented at Conference on Asian Studies, AAS, New Paltz, NY, October 16, 1993.

112  It is named in the literature. See, Samiti, *Preface*, p.55.

113  Kelkar, *Strivishayak*, lecture II.

114-16  Samiti, *Preface*, p. 48, p.47, p.54.

117  Samiti, *Prathah*, p.2.

118  Samiti, *Preface*, p.54,

119-28  Ibid., pp.31–52.

129  In early texts, the Sangh used the term "Hindu Race", and later "Hindu People". "Race" did not always indicate a biological entity; rather, it is an example of the unquestioned generalised reproduction of a current dominant signifier which was also used by contemporaries (including Mahatma Gandhi) who can hardly be called Hindu nationalists or racists.

130  Golwalkar, *Nationhood Defined*, p.21.

131  Pierre-Andre Taguieff, *La Force du Prejuge* (Paris: La Decouverte, 1987), p.645.

132  Golwalkar, *Thoughts*, (1980 ed.), p.73.

133  Luce Irigaray, *Sexes et Genres a travers les Langues* (Paris: Grasset, 1990), p.12; Dale Spender, *Man-Made Language* (London: Routledge, 1980), p.145.

134  Golwalkar, *Thoughts* (1980 ed.), p.107.

135  Ashis Nandy, *The Intimate Enemy: Loss and Recovery of Self Under Colonialism* (Delhi: Oxford University Press, 1983), pp.7–11; Ashis Nandy, *At the Edge of Psychology: Essays in Politics and Culture* (Delhi: Oxford University Press, 1980), p.78; Lloyd I. and Suzanne H. Rudolph, *The Modernity of Tradition* (Chicago: University of Chicago Press, 1967), pp.162–63.

136  Golwalkar, *Thoughts* (1980 ed.), p.316.

137  H.V. Sheshadri (ed.), *Dr. Hedgevar the Epochmaker: A Biography* (Bangalore: Sahitya Sindhu, 1981), pp.203–04.

138  On diverse aspects of these statements see Nandy, *Psychology*, p.38; AIDS Bhedbhav Virodhi Andolan (ABVA), *Less Than Gay: A Citizen's Report on the*

*Status of Homosexuality in India* (Delhi: 1991), pp. 48–57.

139    Swami Nirvedananda, *Shri Ramakrishna and Spiritual Renaissance* (Calcutta: Shri Ramakrishna Mission Institute of Culture, 1940 and 1978), pp.62–4.

140    Swami Ananyananda (ed.), *A Bridge to Eternity: Sri Ramakrishna and His Monastic Order* (Calcutta: Advaita Ashram, 1986), p.168.

141-145  Golwalkar, *Thoughts*, (1980 ed.), p.491-93, 488.

146    *Organiser,* July 26, 1969.

147-50  Ibid.

151    For a discussion of all the Sangh's (masculine and feminine) other Others, see my doctoral dissertation cited above.

152    See P. Bacchetta, "Communal Property/Sexual Property. . . " in Hasan (ed.), *Forging Identities*, pp.188–225.

153-57  Samiti, *Preface*, p.51-54, 4.

158    See L. Kelkar, *Sriramakatha.*

159    Kelkar, *Strivishayak,* lecture V.

160    Ibid., lecture IV.

161    Samiti, *Pratah,* chap. V.

162    Samiti, *Preface,* p.5.

163    Samiti, *Pratahsmaraniya,* chap.IX.

164    Interview detailed in P. Bacchetta, "All Our Goddesses. . . ", in Kamla Bhasin, N.S. Khan and Ritu Menon (eds.), *Against All Odds : Essays on Women, Religion and Development from India and Pakistan* (Delhi: Kali for Women, 1994).

165    Golwalkar, *Thoughts* (1980 ed.), p.72.

166    Golwalkar, *Nationhood Defined,* p.21.

167    Ibid., p.41.

168    Ibid.

169    New Delhi: Vedic Hindu Academy, 1906; reprint 1984.

170    Golwalkar, *Nationhood Defined,* p.12.

171    See Benito Mussolini, *The Doctrine of Fascism* (New York: Howard Fertig Inc., 1968), p.35.

172    See Adolf Hitler, *Mein Kampf,* transl. Ralph Mannheim (Boston: Houghton-Mifflin Company, 1943), pp.378–85. The concept was worked out by the Nazi theoretician, Alfred Rosenberg. See Robert Pois (ed.), *Alfred Rosenberg: Selected Writings* (London: Jonathan Cape 1970), pp.18–24; 34–7.

173    Golwalkar, *Thoughts,* 1980 ed.), p.137.

174    Ibid., p.48.

175    Ibid., p.31.

176    Golwalkar, *Nationhood Defined,* p.43.

177    Ibid., p.26.

178    Ibid., p.43.

179    Golwalkar, *Thoughts,* (1980 ed.), p.150.

180    Ibid., p.682.

181    Sheshadri (ed.), *Epochmaker,* pp.80–1.

182    Golwalkar, *Nationhood Defined,* p.22.

183    Samiti, *Preface,* p.26.

184-89  Ibid., pp.24–9.

190    This information is from interviews with sevikas cited above.

191    Samiti, *Preface,* p.22.

192 Ibid., p.53.

193 Luce Irigaray, *Ce Sexe qui n'en est pas Un* (Paris: Minuit, 1977), pp.167–68.

194 Claudia Koonz, *Mothers in the Fatherland: Women, the Family and Nazi Politics* (New York: St. Martin's Press, 1987), pp.115–17. While Koonz points to the existence of such a discourse, it has unfortunately not yet been the object of any in-depth study.

195 Victoria de Grazia, *How Fascism Ruled Women: Italy, 1922-1945*, (Berkeley: University of California Press, 1992), p.238.

# Static Signifiers?
## Metaphors of woman in contemporary Sri Lankan war poetry

NELOUFER DE MEL

Since 1983 the Sri Lankan civil war, which has raged in and ravaged many parts of North and East Sri Lanka has produced a national crisis of unprecedented proportions. All Sri Lankans have been affected, although factors of geographical location and class have sheltered some from the full and bloody impact of this war. Those living in the Central and Southern provinces have, by and large, escaped the atrocities and psychoses that attend the battlefields of the North and East, except when militants' bombs have exploded in the nerve-centre capital, Colombo. Recruitment to the armed forces, tapping mainly the unemployed semi-urban and rural youth, has permitted the Sri Lankan middle and upper classes to remain far removed from those losing their lives on the front line. But even for this middle class, the cost and consequences of the war in terms of political and economic instability, defence expenditure and therefore rising cost of living, erosion of democratic, civil and human rights, not to mention the grotesque loss of lives — the brunt of which has been borne by the poorer peripheral classes, has put this crisis at the top of the agenda in public and private debate.

Constructions of ethnic, class and gender identities take on significant personal and political roles at times like these. As the civil war continues, fought by the LTTE and the State with the support of sections of the Buddhist clergy, the media and the public have adopted ferocious communal positions and pitted a Sinhala Buddhist State against the Tamil civilian community and quasi-LTTE (Liberation Tigers of Tamil Eelam) State. Overdeterminate ethnic identities become central to both the Sri Lankan government and LTTE propaganda, and therefore, the overall war effort. Constructions of identities other than ethnic ones also become important in a scenario in which the government and certain sections of the Sinhalese population become polarised and oppose each other with violence, as at the height of the JVP (Janatha Vimukthi Perumana) insurrection in the South and the government's counter-campaign against it during the late 1980s. These identities, often overarching and stereotypical, of politicians, revolutionaries, foreign and neo-colonial capitalists, etc., are woven into the Sinhalese imagination through facets of popular culture such as theatre, cinema, popular song and literature.

These productions of identity which percolate down to us through such conduits are then re-articulated by us, often quite unselfconsciously. They are constructions which draw on productions of communal identity that have their historical roots in the early twentieth century emergence of nationalism and the class structures of the modern Sri Lankan State[1], and selected symbols, legends and religious practices of the past. The notion of the Aryan purity of the Sinhala race, and therefore Sinhala superiority over Tamil and Muslim 'invaders' and the '*thuppahi*' (debased) Burghers who constitute the ethnic minorities in Sri Lanka for instance, is based on the recuperation of a pre-colonial ancient past and selectively interpreted myths which tell of the Sinhalese as the authentic, indigenous 'sons of the soil'. There is, moreover, a need in this scheme to 'purify' this past further by the effacement of what is now embarrassing plurality, caste hierarchy, military aggression, personal ambition, violence, etc., that always existed in society. The move, then, is towards a pure, homogenous ethnic and/or racial group consciousness which argues for political and cultural dominance and supremacy, and particular geographical territories based on this selective past. These identities form a culture from which we exclude others, or which we use to consciously or subliminally differentiate ourselves from other communities and systems.

In such constructs of ethno-national identity and culture, the role of Woman has been, paradoxically, fundamental. Despite her continuing marginalisation in patriarchal society, her biological and historically social function of nurturing Mother for instance, has imbued woman with the notion of authenticity, permitting her to be used as a channel of culture and nation-building. It follows that at times of war and socio-political insecurity, the figure of the Mother becomes a central signifier of racial and cultural values, national pride and purity. Being intrinsically connected in this way to the concept of the nation's honour, it also follows that the rape of enemy women becomes, as Sunila Abeysekera has pointed out, "one of the most insidious weapons of war".[2] Thus, helpless mothers, younger sisters, wives and daughters in need of male protection that brave warrior sons, brothers, husbands and fathers are duty bound to give, feature regularly in popular songs and literature.

The focus of this paper will be on such metaphors of Woman as they function as signifiers in contemporary Sri Lankan war poetry, noting that they constitute complex, poignant and contradictory constructions of female identities through which overarching national and ethnic ones are formulated. My particular interest here is in how three Sri Lankan women poets negotiate these identities and view themselves as women, participating in, rejecting, and/or encoding in other ways, the traditional symbols of womanhood as they operate in our society. Jean Arasanayagam and Kamala Wijeratne write in English, but with radically different class and ethnic stances and can therefore be read in many ways against each other, and Sita Ranjani's Sinhala poetry complements her political activism.

A reading of their work, the internalisations and elisions of identity to be found, and the ambivalences they inhabit are, to my mind, useful for an appraisal of what goes on in the peripheral margins these poets inhabit as women.[3] The insights gained from such readings could in turn contribute to our understanding of problems like the internalisation of simplistic binary opposites, the effacement of diversity, the single issue, the need for a critical approach regarding these identities, and point to both the strengths and limitations of the 'political as personal'. It is crucial then to look at what is going on in the margins that women inhabit, problematise the margin, and see how the margin can shift the centre.

## Jean Arasanayagam

Crises of identity have taken on a new urgency in Jean Arasanayagam's current work. She has always been concerned with the Self, in terms of what it is to be a woman, adult, wife and mother. In a poem like 'Kindura',[4] she has given voice to a

feminist restlessness and sense of unfulfilled potential, identifying
with the figure of *kindura* whose 'folded wings/ Unruffled feath-
ers/ Suggests an immobility/ Of flight arrested'. (p.2) But while
the poems in the *Kindura* collection speak by and large of personal
love and betrayal, the passing of youth 'Time's Ambush' and
landscape 'The Valley', 'The Sanctuary — Kumana', there is none
of the overt anger and deep frustration that co-opt her feminist
awareness to an exploration of the broader personal/ socio-political
identities she inhabits today.

This frustration, which has its roots in Arasanayagam's growing
sense of alienation from the mainstream of society, is best mapped
through her responses to the changing status of the coloniser's
tongue in Sri Lanka, and through it her education and place in
society. Now, in an era in which, officially, English occupies secondary status and radical socio-political changes have made once
privileged families redundant, the evocative strengths of
Arasanayagam's poetry lie in her exploration of the many identities that constitute her as a woman who has increasingly become
part of an alienated political and cultural minority. Born and
brought up as a Burgher, a Christian, and married to a Tamil she
lives in a region of Sri Lanka where there is Sinhala Buddhist
hegemony. Much of her current work, then, is a statement of
resistance to this marginalisation in society. While she is acutely
aware that "each race perpetuates its own myth"[5] — in that history
is never innocent — she is able to cast a satiric eye on her own
westernised upbringing, even while acknowledging the marginali-
ty of the colonised in which

> page after page in the history book
> Had nothing to do with you and me,
> we were innocent, guilty neither of conspiracy nor sedition
> Led our ordinary lives, went to market, rocked babies
> In cradles, shot game, enjoyed our blood sports
> Put the animal out of its agony like gentlemen
>
> (*RW*, p.83)

Yet she remains angry at the situation in which, as she writes in
the poem, "it is only now that identity becomes important". (*RW*,
p.85). That this is precisely a reflection of her colonially privileged
past in which identity could be taken for granted, is something
Arasanayagam does not dwell on for long. In her poetry, this leads
to a somewhat uncritical yearning for the past as an era that was

secure, adventurous and enlightened, one that brought her ancestors, "ancient mariners/Through oceans to reach those lands as
yet unmapped/ And undiscovered." (*RW,* p.86).

Arasanayagam reinscribes here all the colonial metaphors of
dark, native territories tamed only by the bravery and scientific
know-how of the European coloniser. The reinforcing of this
particular mythology is very interestingly constructed in her work.
The active agency of her colonising ancestors in the epistemic
violence that finally made the island a colony, is effaced. In 'I Have
No Country', it is the sea winds that bring the ancestors to the
island (*RW,* p.86) and in 'A Journey Into Exile' a boat falls out of
the sun, drifts and is lost "In the high green wave/From which we
never returned." (*Kindura,* p.22) In 'Ancestors' she writes about
her Dutch ancestors' *tenantship* on the land (*RW,* p.25), which
implies a holding under a landlord rather than the colonial reality
of subjugating and governing native people. The poem itself is a
paean to the courage and determination to survive of those first
European merchants/colonisers in which even what she describes
as degenerate about her Dutch ancestors — "tables laden with
dish/ After dish of hot spiced Rijstafel" or "Seeing God in his
Calvinistic heaven/ Dressed in the velvet cloak of Elders" — finally
amounts to positive signs of Flemish culture.

This insistence on valuing one's European roots — "some-
where my ancestors whose name/Intrigues me slumbers in im-
mortality/Since I will not let him die completely" (*RW,* p.25) —
makes for an honest, non-essentialist acknowledgement of what
constitutes her, and is in keeping with explorations of their hybridity that many colonial writers subscribe to as being the essence
of the colonial condition.[6]

Arasanayagam's poetry, too, is an attempt to celebrate both her
European and Sri Lankan roots. Her poems recall her Dutch
legacy as well as the rural Sri Lankan countryside, the rich taste of
its spicy foods, village rituals and villagers like Reddi Nanda the
laundry woman — all important facets of her childhood in Maho.
She is too mature a poet to resort to a simplistic effacement of what
is now an embarrassing western ancestor, and a whole cultural
conditioning, just in order to survive in the Sri Lankan present.
Arasanayagam's work, her sense of alienation in contemporary Sri
Lankan society, is proof of this as she repeatedly valorises and
exoticises her Dutch ancestors, their voyages, dynamism, costumes,

foods, etc., while pointing to a hostile post-colonial present. But the burden of complex representation that falls on a creative writer also demands that, even as she rightly refuses to dismiss her colonial upbringing, Arasanayagam be more self-consciously aware of the privileges of the past that cannot be wished away, and the irony of her continued social (class) position, in that although largely eroded, colonial history even now locates her as privileged by virtue of her command of English. The glossing over of this in her work permits her a past that is comfortable and rich and therefore can be nostalgically viewed as colonialism which is politically over, and an anger at a loss of status which gets played out in her poetry, as she negotiates with contemporary transformed Sri Lankan society for the maintenance of that privilege.

One irony that Arasanayagam is acutely aware of is her victimisation for belonging to a Tamil family. She had to flee to a refugee camp following the attacks on Tamils by Sinhalese in the riots of 1983, and her book *Trial by Terror*[7] is an emotionally fraught treatment of the anguish, anxiety, moments of self-pity and affirmation of life she witnessed at the camp. The irony lies in her being branded a Tamil by a Sinhalese mob when in fact, as a Burgher and a Christian, she has never been given legitimacy in that Tamil family by her high-caste Hindu mother-in-law.

The majority of the metaphors of Woman that operate in Arasanayagam's current work then emanate from her responses grounded in this conflict — her desire to be accepted into particular personal, that is familial, and social identities on the one hand, and the rejection of her by her mother-in-law and society on the other. Her images of Woman are those of domineering Mother, and the Woman who possesses a body which is the site of sexual passion, but who suffers the bloody traumas of child birth in return — images that signify hardness, loss and pain.

Arasanayagam is unafraid to explore female sexuality in her work. She writes of the topography of the female body, positing it as a locus of sexuality and pain. Of her own labour she writes:

> The wounds half-healed still festering and bloody on my knife —
> Slit, hand-stitched body that had given birth . . .

(*RW*, p.31)

and this is refreshingly radical given the taboo status of sexuality in our cultural discourses.[8] But despite Arasanayagam's demystification of childbirth in her insistence on its pain, blood and afterbirth, despite the begetting of a monster child, as contemporary Sri Lanka is coded in her poetry, it is the fertile, reproducing, biological woman as Mother that she valorises in her work. "Woman, goddesses and their mythologies" (*RW*, pp.29–33), one of her finest poems, rich in evocative language, tone, and full of the enabling ambivalences that I find symptomatic of Arasanayagam's subject position, maps her response to a haughty and cold mother-in-law who visits at the birth of her granddaughter to "see only whether her son is happy". The only way Arasanayagam can combat this rejection, reassert her individuality and her *superiority*, is to invoke patriarchal notions of womanhood as they discriminate against the infertile woman and widow. Thus in stressing that in *her* body as child-bearing woman — "My womb, grown from her son's seed, leaving hers/ A barren cave, the frozen stalactites sculpted from time" (*RW*, p.32) who, once the wounds of childbirth are dressed, is "once more, green and fertile as the rainwashed/ Earth, stretching once more my arms to sun, to love" — resides the ultimate and only means of strength over her mother-in-law, Arasanayagam invokes the age-old notion of the inauspiciousness of barren, widowed woman.

One may well ask, what has a family feud got to do with war poetry? Its importance lies in the fact that the key to all Arasanayagam's socio-political positions lies in her personal psychobiography. This constitutes both the strengths and limitations of her work. On the one hand, of the ethnic riots and radical transformations in our society, she writes with a convincing personal anger and urgency. But on the other, her ability to view class and historical perspectives only in so far as they impinge on her personal life prevents her from seeing beyond the personal to the complexities of the contradictions she inhabits. For instance she categorically rejects caste hierarchy, perceiving herself the victim of its exclusionist structures. But there is obvious rapture to be found in her work with the drama of religious ritual (reinforced by her use of sensuous, exotic imagery and onomatopoeic language), which ignores the fact that it is through such rituals after all that these hierarchical structures of caste and patriarchy are disseminated and sustained in society. It is through her inability to participate in these rituals that Arasanayagam gauges her ostracism. She writes that her mother-in-law

Allowed me once, but barely once to enter the sacred
room, gaze upon her shrine with saints and gurus
And fold my hands in worship to those unknown gods
On whom she showered love, those goddesses of wealth
And learning, those powerful deities whose towering lingams
Curling trunks, lotus and veenas inhabited the world
Of her sacred legends and mythologies, where I, with
Human limbs and eyes, whose sacrifice of blood fell
On those empty stone altars where not one single god
Would turn its eyes, belonged not to a single of her rituals . . .

(*RW*, p.29)

Similarly, she indexes Jaffna only in terms of festivals and rituals as
practised there, as in 'Letters from the North', or deserted/
destroyed ritual places like 'Ruined Gopurum'. (*Kindura*, p.25)

Arasanayagam's personal insecurity and sense of helplessness
in a hostile society informs the predominant images of grieving
mother and bruised woman that figure in her poetry written on
the civil war and the JVP insurrection. In the poem 'Goyaesque
Etchings from the Disasters of War', one scene depicted is of "A
woman drag(ging) her injured son/ In a gunny bag through the
forest' crying 'Puthe, why did they do this to us?'", while another is
of a woman who "sleeps like a foetus/ Curved over her four day
old infant . . . (while)/ The milk seeps out faintly trickles/ As from
a snapped stalk in the forest/ Nipples like stalk/Wounded stalks."
Thus the country, Sri Lanka, is personified in the poem 'Ward 31'
as a woman whose sexual encounters are deadly as

thighs raised spread open to Death's
Spectral coition as the poison seeps into them
Twisting in the last rites of orgasm

(*RW*, p.44)

after which, "Women hunch over creep back foetal into wombs/
Of pain gestate themselves pushing tears and gasping/ Breath into
their unclenching palms" while they give bloody birth to a monster child of terror and death.

For Arasanayagam, the body of the woman then is one which is
abused, oppressed, one that suffers pain. In 'Letters from the
North', written during the IPKF occupation of Jaffna, it is the raped
blood of 'enemy' women, rape-impregnated embryos and the
'fondle or caress/ Leaving the needle patterns of tattoo marks/
Incised upon a thigh or breast' as women are frisked at innumera-

ble checkpoints that serve as metaphors of a brutal and tragic
Northern Sri Lanka. There is no valorisation here of the woman as
begetter of strong warrior sons who will defend the motherland
and uphold its values. In Arasanayagam's image of woman we see
a radical break from the popular use of the Mother image in
contemporary Sri Lankan propaganda of which there is an abun-
dance. *Rana Gi* or war songs which honour mothers of sons who
fight for the motherland and lovers who demand of their men that
they write of their bravery on the battlefield instead of "tales of
innocent love"[9], or government posters such as the one which
depicted a Sinhalese mother dreaming of her soldier husband
while breast-feeding her son with the caption, "Give of your breast
milk so that we may have soldiers for the future", served as useful
images with which to mobilise public support for the war effort.[10]
This propaganda continues in the publicity given in local newspapers to the stoic, proud, sometimes fatalistic reactions of mothers
whose sons are at the war-front. Nor are such productions confined to the Sinhala south. There is plenty of evidence that the
militant nationalist groups in the North also fabricate such female
identities, putting enormous pressure on Tamil women to produce brave sons; and when they are dead, to bear their loss with a
martyr's pride, or even, invoking the Goddess Kali, take to the
battlefields themselves.[11] All these have, as Serena Tennekoon
stated, the "pernicious objective of defining women as an intrinsic
part of military society."[12] For Jean Arasanayagam however, the
woman cannot be the glad participant, but rather the first victim of
a deadly, macho game. As she writes in 'Four Poems Without
Titles', "The lingam is a gun/ The yoni fills with blood."

### Kamala Wijeratne

If Arasanayagam signals a political consciousness which is governed entirely by the personal, it can be said of Kamala Wijeratne
that she constructs in her work, a socio-political consciousness
which subsumes the personal — the 'I' is never predominant in
her work — although of course, here too, the personal does
coincide with the political, as these larger constructs of identity
and ideology are always informed to some extent by personal
experience.

The concerns expressed in Wijeratne's poetry, too, are hopes
for peace in war-torn Sri Lanka. But there are significant paradox-

es to be seen in her work, as these hopes for ethnic reconciliation are undermined by the very images she uses in her poems,[13] which indicate that her predominant concerns are with the South of the country, the massacre of Sinhalese by the LTTE and the indifference of people and the state to the sacrifice of Sinhala life as seen in the poem entitled 'An Unmarked Grave'. (*Talent*, p.3) In her use of the *dagoba*, which stands "White and arresting/ A magnified water bubble/ Commanding a tank" as the *only* "Silent monument to a people's history" (*Talent*, p.17) — the image of the tank too is significant as it evokes memories of ancient and sophisticated Sinhala kingdoms — are justifications and therefore constructs of a Sinhala Buddhist tradition which, carrying hegemony, marginalises other minorities. Wijeratne's stance then is radically different from poet Sita Ranjani's which constantly argues in poems like 'Sun Blast Tomorrow' and 'Paraviyo Handathi' (ms) for an appraisal of both Sinhala and Tamil bloodshed and suffering.

Wijeratne's ambivalence towards the Tamil community is best seen in a poem like 'I Will Not Forget Dutugemunu'. (*Araliva*, pp.25–6)

Don't ask me to forget Dutugemunu
Dear brother of the North,
For I cannot and I will not;
You are asking me to forget my dreams
My glorious youth and twenty hundred years
Of gold-inscribed history.
The time we stalwart, brave
Faced the world unflinching,
For we owed it no money,
Sinewed arms accustomed to the plough
and the sword
We chiselled life out of stone.

The poem's tone is defiant in the face of what Wijeratne reads as Tamil aggression, taking issue — and while doing so blurring the distinction between terrorist and civilian in addressing the "Dear brother of the North" — with organised terrorism directed at the Sinhalese. The history of the Sinhalese is what is rich (glorious, ancient, gold-inscribed) in achievement. The evocations are of a self-sufficient economy, political strength, architectural and artistic heights. Tamil history in Sri Lanka on the other hand, is barbaric and primitive, being none of the above. Expansionist kings invade Sinhala territory:

> Sena and Guttika and a long line of invaders
> (I see Macbeth's gory glass in your hands)
> Elara was just but quite helpless
> To stop his marauding bands
> Dismantle monuments and raid
> Relic chambers . . . .

At best, Elara is decent (this allows for Dutugemunu's respect for the slain Tamil king, recalled later on in the poem), but ineffective, as Tamil thugs, vindictive and uncivilized, destroy art and desecrate the sacred shrines of the Sinhalese.

The superiority of the Sinhalese heritage, then, is a given, and worth defending in the most militant terms. This is where Wijeratne subscribes to the popular image of the pregnant or nursing mother who brings forth warrior sons to defend the (Sinhala) motherland.

> But you shall not hold the kris knife over me
> And say 'Love Me'
> I tell you my blood is pregnant
> With that which flowed in the infant
> Who bared his head to death
> And cried 'I will show you how to die'.

The poem's structure itself mirrors Wijeratne's ambivalence as it alternates between such militancy and offers of a peaceful co-existence. For Wijeratne then writes:

> But killing is not our creed, loving is:
> So here are my hands
> Held together in honourable 'Namasthe'
> If you like we will bury our quarrel
> And build another, bigger Dakshina Tupa.

That the reconciliation is imaged in terms of the Dakshina Stupa is significant. The explanatory note in *The Smell of Araliya* itself states that it is a "colossal mound built over the corpse of Elara by the victor Dutugemunu to honour his foe. He decreed that all passers-by should respect this shrine and that drums should be muffled and processions go silently." That the monument was built in the first place from a position of political strength which allows for such magnanimity is ignored by the poet. There is no space here for reconciliation with a minority that lives on and demands equality not as a gift, but as its inalienable right. Thus for Wijeratne, the problematic stance of placing the moral burden on the Other — "It is up to you whether we be friends" — while seeking this friendship entirely on Sinhala Buddhist terms, is not a matter of great concern.

When Kamala Wijeratne laments the loss of both Sinhala and Tamil blood, or the fracture of inter-racial relationships following the anti-Tamil riots of '83 then, significant elisions and overarching generalisations are to be seen in her work. In 'Farewell',[14] even as she voices her personal "misery and shame" at the "weight of history, its pages heavy with the grim saga of our war-torn races", she is ultimately able to negotiate that history only through an emphasis on the historical guilt of both ethnic groups and, more insidiously, through a trivialising of Tamil life. Confronted with a Tamil friend who does not lament the destruction of her home during the riots, Wijeratne writes:

> You did not sag
> for dispossession had made you free
> free of the water bill, the errant tenant
> and all the trammels that unleash the beast in man.

That the friend's existence is coded *only* in terms of such banalities and irritants of life, points to Wijeratne's inability and/ or refusal to rigorously confront the complexity of the ethnic strife the country is caught up in and moreover, to read the friend's refusal to lament as a possible protest against Sinhala hegemony. Again, in 'Come, give me your hand', (*Talent*, p.2), she writes of the "Sinhala dead/ Beside their Tamil counterparts". It is not just this relative status of counterpart given to the Tamil that is significant. Wijeratne's recourse to the humanistic notion of death as leveller — "The grass has covered each brown hillock/ And levelled one with the other" (*Talent*, p.2), allows her an escape from the harder reality of how a truly democratic, multi-cultural society can function in life.

In fact, let alone such avoidance, there is positive justification in Wijeratne's work, of even the most horrendous behaviour of the largely Sinhalese Sri Lankan military which completely denies the validity of the Tamil civilian's right to a dignified life: Take for instance the poem, 'For a Sinhala Soldier':

> They say you stole their jewels
> Snatched their TV sets
> Pocketed their radios
> Ransacked their houses for gold
> Raped their women
> Desecrated their gods.

You are sleeping a dreamless sleep, soldier
You have taken your booty and you are dead,
You have done all the marching you will ever do
You have done all the shooting you ever could
The land mine put paid to all your misdeeds, soldier.

Your mother still hammers the stone into road-metal, soldier
Her nailless hands bleed into the sand
The cadjan leaks in your house, soldier
The floor swells with the tide,
I don't hear a radio from within, soldier
I don't see an antenna on your roof.

They say you snatched their necklaces, soldier
Cleaned their houses of their goods
Your woman wears no gold necklace, soldier
And your son goes barefoot to school
You sleep the sleep of a dreamless soldier
You have taken your booty and you are dead.

(*Talent,* p. 6)

Rape and pillage then pale into insignificance compared to the sacrifice of life paid by the Sinhala soldier fighting for his motherland.

All this is reinforced through Wijeratne's recuperation of the usual images of women as Mothers who are duty-bound to beget courageous sons who will confront the enemy. The implication is that without them, women will be left helpless and unprotected. In 'I Will Not Forget Dutugemunu', or the poem quoted above, it is the helpless woman denied the protection of her sons and husband away at war, that is evoked. The bereaved mother, whose nailless hands bleed as she hammers road-metal while her cadjan roof leaks; her house in which radio and TV are not affordable commodities, gets flooded; the wife who has no jewellery — these are images that plug into (even as they comment on class stratifications in Sri Lankan society) the popular notion of man as protector and provider, on whom the woman is utterly dependent and who is emotionally non-existent once he is dead.

A poem in which Wijeratne does strike a convincing balance, and important for its presentation of the mother's voice is 'Mother of a Subversive' (*Talent,* pp.11–4). The poem, confronting current socio-political reality, is about a society full of informants where political idealism is thwarted, thousands of "flowering youth" subjected to "The interrogation (which) never ends", and many things, including the task of daily survival, are troped in terms of war —

the parents' duty being to prepare the son for the frontline of life, "recompensing (his) valour/ (For the) fight against the odds (he) was born to". The mother in this poem is also poor, but on the whole it is controlled and her poverty is not sentimentalised or over-stressed. The emotional complexity of the poem arises from the conflict between the justifiable position of the mother, who dreamt of a better future with her son as their "rudder in a tortuous sea", and the son, whose political activism shatters that dream. The mother's voice here is convincing as she is caught between understanding and regret, angry at those forces in society which corner her family, yet desiring peace at whatever cost.

The predominant signifier of Mother then is one in whom there is vested moral authority, and the grieving mother signifies in all these works, an affront and violation of what is sanctified in terms of accepted codes of behaviour, family, tradition, religion and, finally, the nation itself. Kamala Wijeratne's current hegemonic strand of nationalist discourse that makes such constructs, resonates across the board of popular cultural production where figures of virtuous but helpless women, and that of Mother in particular, are constantly co-opted as symbols of the nation.

A short analysis of the Mother figure in R.R. Samarakoon's play, *Duvili*, which enjoyed popularity throughout 1991–92, throws light on some of the significant aspects of the use of this figure in nationalist discourse. The mother in this play lives in the village. This is significant because it is symptomatic of the populist trend in Sinhala theatre today, that the village is always the innocent site of 'pure', authentic, indigenous values as opposed to the city identified with moral decay, vice and the evils of an 'alien' open market capital. The mother opposes the corruption and thuggery of her politician son and his urban family. Urban corruption is not only evident in the ruthless older generation comprising the politician and his virago wife, whose indifference to and rejection of the mother are severe markers of their degenerate values, but also in the younger generation, represented by sexually active grandchildren — their sexuality coded in the play as a particularly urban vice.[15]

In *Duvili* the mother figure gets co-opted as the voice of the Sinhala nation when news of the LTTE massacre of 150 civilians and the attack on the Sri Maha Bodi, one of the most sacred Buddhist shrines in the country, comes through. In a natural reaction, she is incredulous at this outrage to civilian life and Buddhism and warns aggressively from the centre of the apron stage, "Let those·who did this take one step further and see what happens!" The irony of seeing this mother as she opposes her son's thuggery on the one hand while herself militantly warning annihilation — not negotiation — on the other, is on the whole lost on local audiences who applaud these lines, participating in a collective notion of punishing the Tamil enemy. It is clear that the mother's moral authority, associated with steadfast, rural Buddhist values, is used in the play to legitimise military aggression against the Tamils. The danger here is that however abhorrent such attacks on religious shrines and civilian lives are, the blurring of the distinction between Tamil terrorist and civilian in the popular imagination makes the mother's militancy dangerous, for she comes close to inciting retaliatory violence.

Wijeratne's work inhabits an interesting ambivalence in that while symbols of motherhood are used to evoke responses of nationalist feeling among her readers, her work stops short of the kind of overt militancy we see in a play like *Duvili*. In fact her emphasis on the helplessness of women, shorn of their male protectors, ignores other affirmations in which women no longer only cry, but also participate and organise themselves in progressive protest against violence and war.[16]

Ignoring this agency of active protest against the war leads Wijeratne, as it does Arasanayagam, to seek refuge in a fatalistic resignation to contemporary events. Jean Arasanayagam begins 'Numerals' in a tone of bitter irony:

> Today a hundred and fifty shot
> Yesterday seventy blasted
> Even the poet becomes numerate

but finally asks, "What else is there to contemplate/ But death?" (*RW*, p.65), while in 'Checkpoint' Wijeratne declares:

> It's a burning by fire that we need
> When the purified spirit will rise
> From the black ashes
> And all offal will burn away

but ends with an abdication from personal involvement —

> It's not for me to do, perhaps the gods
> In their merciful wrath will do it . . .

(*Talent*, p.10)

This is a stance which indicates in effect, the complicity of such writers with the status quo in that, despite the hurt and threat of marginalisation, they remain privileged members of society who do not have to bear the brunt of violence in their daily lives, and so have a vested interest in not intervening actively for change. For, given the limited exposure of the general public to the work of these writers, their interventions remain essentially private.

## Sita Ranjani

Sita Ranjani's poems are deliberately activist in intent and tone, and given the language in which she writes, meant for a wider readership. For her the grieving mother is one who has been fooled by a corrupt and autocratic State. Such a State, propped up by the opportunistic agendas of sections of the bureaucracy and Buddhist clergy, makes for a society which subscribes to distorted values. In the poem she entitles 'Deformity', Sita Ranjani writes with biting satire of the proclamation made by the Ven. Elle Gunawansa that killing on the battlefield did not preclude attaining Nirvana as it was an act of defending the motherland — a declaration that was made into a song entitled 'Balasenagata Samaragi' (In Memory of Fallen Soldiers) and broadcast daily over the State-controlled radio station SLBC during 1989–90.

> There is no point crying dearest mother
> for ruined lives
> Didn't you know that one can attain merit by killing?
> While not in your wildest dreams did you imagine such a thing
> It was said.
> And traded for a hefty price
> By the inheritors of war
> Who filled their sacks.
>
> (ms)

Whether the perpetrators are revolutionaries or the State, however, the grieving mother as evocative symbol of national pride and matrix of personal/family relationships destroyed, remains in place. When writing of the despair of both the North and the South, it is the despair of the mother's voice that is evoked in 'The Dreams of the Mothers of the North' and 'Vikurthiya'. (ms) But we also note a significant desire to move away from the traditional role of womanhood as Ranjani and her generation of women take on activist roles for themselves. On the death of her mother, she writes

> When is it ever
> That a daughter is called upon
> To bear
> A mother's body for burial?
> Dearest Mother, it is because I cast off
> The umbilical cord that you never wanted to shed
> That I have returned
> To carry your body for burial today.

Patriarchy, which circumscribes women in this way, imposing rules of conduct, preventing them from participating in certain rituals (a daughter cannot be a pall-bearer at her mother's funeral) has to be torn down. But Ranjani is very aware of the tenacity of such patriarchy.

> It is because your funeral is their own
> That they beat their breasts so much.
> . . .
> These men who are restless to finish you off
> Would like to see my own demise
>
> Dearest Mother,
> I swear as I kneel beside your body for the final time,
> My death will be different from yours
> My final journey will not be as these men want it.
> This little bowered graveyard
> Will not be mine.

(ms)

The desire to cast off such patriarchal impositions on women, even though a concretised feminist struggle does not feature in her work, remains a powerful motivating and emotive factor in Ranjani's work. The stereotyping of women by patriarchy is categorically rejected. In the poem 'The Kiss', the sexual advances of a comrade are met with

> If this little kiss
> means the start of a love
> that is woman's heritage
> a love that is the destiny
> of a woman who is alone
> friend,
> I spit on your kiss.

There is obvious resentment here at being stereotyped in this way, an object of pity. But there is also a disturbing denial of the sexual in the poem. The love the poet declares for her comrades and seeks from them is of "the purest kind", one which is "treated with (great) respect" so that the kiss becomes an affront that has to be put in its place. And while one can argue the necessity of this as strategy — the exigencies of living and fighting together as a political group — the denial of love in its full complexity, the move to efface the sexual and invest love with purely the spiritual, the propounding of a platonic love for all, equally, sounds disingenuous. We can however locate her response in a larger Sinhala Buddhist morality which idealises the asexual woman as virtuous and suppresses the erotic in physical contact. Moreover, this is in keeping with what Jayadeva Uyangoda calls the moralistic discourse of the radical left, which de-sexualises the woman; she is ever, *sahodari* (sister).[17] What this re-inscribes, of course, is the patriarchal negation of female sexuality by holding up the asexual woman as steadfast, superior, ideal.

What insights can these poems offer to an understanding of the issues surrounding the constructions of female, personal and national identities that over-determine each other? For it is clear that in being co-opted as a trope in a wide and complex nationalist discourse, gender does not figure in these works as a single issue. The women poets I have looked at have, in the main, internalised patriarchal notions of women in their use of the Mother figure. For even if they, argue for the cultural and political independence of women as Sita Ranjani has, or contest the construct of the Mother as stoic and glad participant in war, as Arasanayagam, does they continue the practice of investing in the persona of the Mother, the *totality* of a woman's identity. In so doing, they have made use of its powerful emotiveness as a symbol in their explorations of contemporary Sri Lankan nationhood. The structural form of many of Sita Ranjani's poems indicate such co-option of the mother figure as a central signifier — they take the shape of letters written by mothers of the North to those of the South, a mother's lullaby, or the dreams of mothers of the North.

The political mobilisation of this mother figure is manifest in the Mother's Front which functions as a pressure group in Sri Lanka, a watchdog of human rights issues, disappearances, extra-judicial killings, etc. This points to a positive, unifying use of the mother image, as it also blurs the rigid distinction of the male/ public as opposed to the female/private or domestic space. Conversely, the manner in which the anger of mothers is used politically, draws heavily on the stereotype of the emotional, hysterical woman. This was exemplified at a recent Mother's Front rally (September 1992) when women, invoking the goddess Kali, heaped curses of revenge on the government and made a public, theatrical display of grief and tears. The political use of such an identity does not radically re-examine the place of women in Sri Lankan society, then, and this coincides with the equally uncritical re-inscribing of the signifier of Mother in the poems quoted, in which the figure is shown to exclude the possibility of economic and emotional independence, and, for those of Arasanayagam's and Wijeratne's class, political activism.

Such internalisations by those at the margins are frequent in history and point to the fraught nature of that space. In another context, Leopold Sedar Senghor, Aime Cesaire and Leon Damas, leaders of the Negritude movement which grew in the 1930s and '40s in Africa and the Caribbean as a decolonising response to British and French colonialism, re-inscribed constructs of the native subject's identity that had been imposed by the coloniser even as they sought to liberate themselves from colonialism. Leopold Senghor's formulation, we can say with hindsight, was fundamentally flawed, as he accepted the Orientalist notion, of the rational, intellectual European as opposed to the intuitive, rhythmic, spontaneous Negro. Thus he argued for the re-appraisal of the Negro not as someone who should have equal status but as one who could contribute to universal civilisation by bringing to mechanistic Europe the leaven of spontaneity and imagination.

What such internalisations prevent, of course, is a bringing to crisis point the colonising, male hegemonic centre, for Eurocentric and indigenous patriarchal blueprints of colonial/female identities remain firmly in place. Thus by perpetuating the very notions by which they are marginalised, women have complicity in their oppression. Of course, their re-inscribing processes incorporate continuous shifts in the emphases and parameters of these identities. Images come to mind of Arasanayagam's sexual woman, or a mother who is not a begetter of warrior sons, but one who, suffering pain, gives birth to terror, or Sita Ranjani's activist woman who spurns patronising sexual overtures. But however progressive these shifts are in themselves, we have to keep in mind that patriarchy too is never static; reacting always to the shifting margins, it re-sets its own goal-posts in order to continue its dominance over women.

The margins then, encompass many contradictions — take

Arasanayagam's demystification of childbirth on the one hand and her valorisation of the fertile woman on the other, or her dismissal of caste hierarchy even as she fetishises ritual through which hierarchy is disseminated and reinforced. The reading of such contradiction — not just plurality, but the contestation of diverse strands that make up identity — should be considered enabling, for it shows that we, as those doubly colonised, are constituted by the reality of such contradictions. The problem then lies in how we can consciously register this, without dismissing it as weakness, and articulate it in a way which forces the centre to examine its own contradictions, which its hegemonic position now permits it to fudge and ignore.

## Notes

[1] See Kumari Jayawardene, *Ethnic and Class Conflicts in Sri Lanka* (Colombo: Sanjiva, 1990).

[2] Sunila Abeysekera, "Identity Politics, the Women's Movement and the Recent Sri Lankan Experience." Paper presented at the South Asian Conference on 'Women: The State, Fundamentalism and Cultural Identity', Colombo 13–16 March 1992, p.8. (This story has not been authenticated.) A shrewd use of the emotiveness of the image of a raped woman was seen in response to the assassination of Rajiv Gandhi, which was explained as a revenge killing by a woman who had been raped by the Indian Peace Keeping Forces (IPKF) during their policing of Northern Sri Lanka from 1987–89. Seee Sitralega Maunaguru, "Gendering Tamil Nationalism: The Construction of 'Woman' in Projects of Protest and Control" in P. Jeganathan and Q. Ismail (eds) *Unmaking of the Nation: The Politics of Identity and History in Modern Sri Lanka* (Colombo: SSA, 1995).

[3] It must be noted that within the margin itself all women do not exist equally, as class, caste, regional hierarchies remain in place. But in so far as they are all confined and suppressed by a patriarchal society in a certain 'womanhood', it is essential that we look at women collectively as a group which is acted upon, rather than one which has the freedom of active agency, and is therefore relegated to the margins by the centre.

[4] Jean Arasanayagam, *Kindura* (Kandy: T.B.S. Godamunne & Sons, 1973). Pagination is from this edition.

[5] 'A Question of Identity', *Reddened Water Flows Clear* (London & Boston: Forest Books) 1991. Pagination hereafter is from this edition.

[6] One has to strike a cautionary note about uncritically accepting such celebrations of hybridity. For while hybridity is often posited as a site in which opposite and/or diverse inheritances come together in a syncretic acculturation, it remains a space in which the components that make up hybridity never mesh or mix *equally*. As I have shown elsewhere, a poet-playwright like Derek Walcott, who forwards hybridity as the only expression

of the 'authentic' identity of the Caribbean, does write in forms and images inspired by both European and African roots. But an analysis of his work shows that Walcott always privileges the European strands over the African in that abstract thought, "the inner life of poetry", is expressed in standard English; the commonplace or comic is represented in patois; and signs of African cultures in the Caribbean are symptomatically evoked through negative metaphors. This signifies, (even as the texts forward hybridity), a certain Eurocentricism in which hierarchical value is placed consciously or unconsciously (for this is grounded in one's education and upbringing and is invariably subliminal) on language registers and western traditions over those of the African 'native' continent. See Neloufer de Mel, "Responses to History: The Re-articulation of Post-Colonial Identity in the plays of Wole Soyinka and Derek Walcott", 1950–76, PhD thesis, University of Kent at Canterbury, UK, 1990.

7   Jean Arasanayagam, *Trial by Terror* (Hamilton: Rimu Books, 1987). Pagination is from this edition.

8   Arasanayagam admits, however, that the one constraint she feels when writing poetry in the Sri Lankan context is in the depiction of female sexuality, as its taboo status in ordinary social conversation makes her hesitant to express her feelings fully. (Interview with Neloufer de Mel. Kandy, 26 January 1992.)

9   For an analysis of a cassette called 'Rana Gi' produced by the Government of Sri Lanka, see Serena Tennekoon, "'Macho' Sons and 'Man-Made' Mothers", *Lanka Guardian*, 15 June 1986.

10   This poster appeared at the height of the war against the LTTE in 1986. See Malathi de Alwis, "Towards a Feminist Historiography: Reading Gender in the Text of the Nation." (Colombo, International Centre for Ethnic Studies) 1994.

11   Source for Tamil female identities. For similar uses of the Mother image in Tamil Nadu see C.S. Lakshmi, "Mother, Mother-Community and Mother-Politics in Tamil Nadu", *Economic and Political Weekly*, October 20–9 1990, pp.72–83.

12   *Lanka Guardian*, 15 June 1986.

13   The poems cited are from Kamala Wijeratne, *The Smell of Araliya* (Kandy: Wijeratne, 1983) and *That One Talent* (Kandy: Wijeratne, 1988). Pagination is from these editions.

14   Kamala Wijeratne, 'Farewell', *The New Lankan Review*, vol 2, 1984; p.55.

15   This is also reinforced through dress, particularly female clothing. A woman in a short skirt and T-shirt, embodying urban westernisation, signifies sexual availability. The same cultural code resonates in South India. M.S.S. Pandian shows how in M.G. Ramachandran's film "Vivasayee" (1967), dress functions as a similar signifier of sexuality and virtue. In the film the heroine's T-shirt 'incites' a peasant to molest her. Pardoning the peasant (for it was not his fault but that of the woman's dress) the hero covers her already covered bosom with a towel as if it were a saree pallu. When she falls in love with the hero, she comes to meet him in a saree which provokes him to break into song. Predictably, the song begins with the line, "This is how a woman should

be." See M.S.S. Pandian, *The Image Trap: M.G. Ramachandran in Film and Politics* (New Delhi: Sage,) pp. 86–7.

16  This is what Malathi de Alwis presents in an unpublished poem written in reply to Wijeratne's 'Bring Forth Women Children Only' which speaks of women who do nothing but "wail and grieve/Like Antigone . . . Over the rotting corpse/Of a dead brother". de Alwis writes that there are women who no longer only beat breasts but

> tired
> of picking up pieces of their lives
> are ready for Peace
> They have fasted
> They have marched
> They have yelled protest
> —No more violence!

17  Jayadeva Uyangoda, private response. I am grateful to Dr. Uyangoda for his comments on this paper.

# The Myth of 'Patriots' and 'Traitors'
## Pandita Ramabai, Brahmanical patriarchy, and militant Hindu nationalism*

Uma Chakravarti

### Prologue

Problems relating to the State, fundamentalism, cultural identity and women, have appeared with a poignant intensity in recent years in the Indian context, forcing the women's movement to confront issues of religion and culture within the experience of feminists in their own lives. These issues tended to take a back seat in the early stages of the women's movement when the focus had been mainly on the material and familial problems of women, isolating them from other institutions and practices in which women's lives were embedded. The movement then, dwelt on areas of commonality among *all* categories of women across class and religious differences, in an attempt to devise a 'secular' position in the understanding and practice of the women's movement.

In the Eighties increasing recourse to highlighting distinctive religious and cultural identities has forced the women's movement to recognise the power of religion in the everyday lives of women, as well as the fragmentation of women based on these distinctive identities. Exploring religious traditions, finding empowering strands and weeding out the 'good' from the 'bad' in religion and culture became an important part of the agenda of the women's movement. Simultaneously, the political use that could be made of the religious and cultural traditions of women (in which they were enmeshed, and which in many cases they cherished) were identified; attempts were also made to combat the divisiveness of these identities setting off one religious tradition from another which could split up the movement.[1]

*This essay is part of a larger work tentatively titled *Gender, Class, and Nation: The Life and Times of Pandita Ramabai.* I am grateful to the Nehru Memorial Museum and Library and Centre for Contemporary Studies for the grant of a fellowship that made this study possible.

Even these developments, however, were perceived as problems to be confronted in the case of 'those' women who were sometimes regarded as the 'objects' of the women's movement; the largely urban middle class women who were active in the women's movement were believed to be outside of religious biases. In recent years this view, too, has come in for criticism, partly a reminder of the painful times we live in and partly the unfortunate but deeply felt experience of being members of the 'minorities' (even though the agenda of the women's movement avowedly is to empower *all* categories of women) in the face of the rising tide of aggressive religious nationalism. The questioning of the inherent religious 'biases' of the women's movement in India,[2] where religion and culture are intertwined in ways which are difficult to disentangle, presses an urgency upon us to take a closer look at the relationship between religion, culture, nationalism and gender, the ways in which our recent history has constructed the 'nation', and the exclusions in this project. These exclusions are crucial in understanding what is regarded as 'acceptable' within nationalism and what position is occupied by gender in this structure of inclusions and exclusions.

It is within the framework of these questions that I will take a close look at a nineteenth century proto-feminist, Pandita Ramabai, whose life and work stand at the intersection of religion, nation and gender. Born in a Brahmana family and steeped in Brahmanical traditions, her own experience of life led her to make a break with the religion into which she was born, because she identified it as the locus of women's oppression, and adopt the religion of what was regarded by the 'spokesmen' of the nation as the religion of the colonial rulers.[3] Thereafter she was publicly proclaimed a betrayer and while she never gave up her work of alleviating women's oppression she was also a strong advocate of Christianity which she propagated with missionary zeal. In this capacity many of the women in today's women's movement might perceive her as a 'fundamentalist'.[4] For a variety of reasons the tension between gender issues and religious beliefs has led to a sense of discomfort among feminists with women like Ramabai. The question that needs to be posed is: Did the agenda of nineteenth century nationalism in India, predicated upon Hinduism, exclude both a gender critique of Hindu tradition and the incorporation of other religious systems and thus make of Ramabai a 'fundamentalist'? In what ways will the relationship between religion, nation and gender make for the empowerment of women or for their subjection to tyranny? These are some of the questions that feminist scholars need to explore.

## I

### The social context of gender in nineteenth century western India

#### 1. *Caste and gender in the pre-colonial State*

The construction of the image of Ramabai as 'betrayer' of her people and thus of the nation was primarily an achievement of B.G.Tilak. By the end of the nineteenth century Tilak had also successfully acquired the image of a fierce patriot. To understand the manner in which Tilak succeeded in making every major personality in Maharashtra, except himself, appear to be 'unpatriotic', thus neutralising them,[5] it is necessary to analyse the nature of social forces in the nineteenth century which were themselves a direct legacy of the Peshwai.

The most significant aspect of the Peshwai that needs to be stressed is that it marked the reassertion of the actual and hegemonic control of the Brahmanas. Even a cursory glance at the Poona Deccan region during the eighteenth century will reveal a close connection between the Brahmanas, especially Chitpavan Brahmanas (the sub-caste to which the Peshwa belonged), and economic, political, social and ritual power.[6]

The most notable feature of the political development in the eighteenth century was the successful entry of Brahmanas into military and financial roles, both traditionally regarded as alien to their *varna*.[7] Further even those who were not part of the military, financial or landed elite were privileged by virtue of their ritual status and shared the social power of the caste as a whole. The control of political and social power by the Chitpavans through their connection with the Peshwas was best expressed through the institution of dakshina which represented an informal alliance, between the Chitpavan Brahmanas and the State.[8] The dakshina, literally a gift, was the means through which the Peshwas extended support to the Brahmanas in their role as 'custodians' of Hinduism. It involved the distribution of enormous sums of money as charity to 'scholarly' Brahmanas. In return for such recognition the Brahmanas were unstinting in the support they extended to the State. The support was also attributable to the general policy of Brahmana *pratipalana* (protection of the Brahmanas) pursued by the Peshwas. Throughout the eighteenth century all categories of Brahmana men thus enjoyed land revenue remissions, exemption from transit dues, house taxes, forced labour, death penalty and enslavement.[9]

The Peshwa's usurpation of political power from the descendents of Shivaji in 1713 and the consequent Brahmanisation had consequences for other social categories too. The 'alliance' between the Marathas and Brahmanas, forged at the time of Shivaji, virtually collapsed. The marginalisation of the Marathas, especially of Shivaji's lineage at Satara, became a source of conflict which was postponed to the future since the balance of social forces lay at that time with the Brahmanas. Following the conscious process of Brahmanisation by the Peshwas, it appeared to nineteenth century observers that there were only two grand classes in Maharashtra— the Brahmanas and the rest.[10] This is of course a simplistic view but it does highlight the nature of the cleavage in the region and the dominance of the Brahmanas over the rest of society. Broadly the cleavage among the castes made for a correspondence between *varna* and *varga*, as there was a congruence of high caste with the upper class and of low caste with the lower orders.

The *varna-varga* congruence was likely to have been consolidated by the Peshwas who sought to create, at least ideologically, a Brahmanical kingdom where Brahmanic texts and rituals were reiterated and the Brahmanical social order was sought to be strictly upheld. In such a situation, according privileges to Brahmanas and suppressing other castes went together. In an important essay Fukazawa,[11] a historian of medieval Deccan, has argued convincingly that there was a close connection between the caste system and the State's enforcement of it. In the context of eighteenth century Maharashtra Fukazawa shows that the institution of caste and its development and diversification, far from continuing 'spontaneously' without any relation to the secular political power, was in fact bolstered by it. Fukazawa concludes that the State played an important part in suppressing the lower castes: it punished those who deviated from the traditional religio-social code of conduct, and enforced the distinctive codes of conduct to be observed by each caste. It also prevented the appropriation of codes to which the lower castes were not entitled.[12]

The Peshwai and its central bureaucracy sought to preserve the caste hierarchy in areas under its control. Caste distances were not only maintained but strengthened through the legal apparatus of the State. Sanctions were imposed by those who transgressed these injunctions. The State also ensured that the untouchables would continue to occupy the lowest rungs of the social and religious ladder. Fukazawa shows that there *was* a demand, even among the untouchables, for better treatment and that it was ultimately state power that suppressed such demands and kept them in the lowest position in society.[13]

From the point of view of this essay what is notable is that the Peshwai, with its notions of brahmanya and the rigid hierarchies of the caste system, could not but have a direct and crucial bearing on gender relations in eighteenth century Maharashtra. Among other things the brahmanya implied a strictly regulated code of conduct for women, differing to some extent according to caste but always *the index* in fixing ranking within the caste hierarchy. In Brahmanical patriarchy the relationship between caste and gender is crucial:[14] ultimately the degree to which the sexuality of women is controlled is the degree to which a caste group is regarded as maintaining purity of blood and thereby establishing its claims to be regarded as high.[15] And since caste disputes and contestations were, in the past (and continue to be), an important element in society, the relationship between control over female sexuality and the purity of blood, and thereby the claim to high status is, to a large extent, the key to understanding gender.

The sexuality of all women was closely monitored under the Peshwai although according to different norms for different castes. The brahmanya implied that questions about which women could be legitimate wives, which women could remarry, which women *must* remarry and *not* practice enforced widowhood such as the low castes, which women *must* practice it and never remarry, which women must have their heads tonsured, which women must be excommunicated for their lapses, *when* women must marry, and the appropriate rituals for legitimate marriage among the upper castes, were all objects of the regulation of the community, headed by the Brahmanas and then ultimately of the State's concern.[16] Most significantly the sexual 'offences' of women, especially wid-

ows, were punishable with imprisonment and uniquely with enslavement. Women lived under the continuous and combined
surveillance of the community and the State. Extending Fukazawa's
argument we might say that ultimately gender codes were *not*
spontaneous, not merely an arrangement of society — they were
extended, consolidated and reinforced by state power under the
Peshwas.

Elsewhere I have extensively documented examples of the State's
effective monitoring of gender codes, both actual and symbolic.[17]
I will focus here only on one aspect of women's attempt at non-
conformity and the State's effective suppression of it: the attempt
by widows to keep their hair. Resistance to the custom of enforced
tonsure was virtually impossible in the eighteenth century since
widows as propertyless, shelterless women lived in the custody of
kinsmen and within the larger social unit of the caste group into
which they were born. But it is significant that even if the immediate kinsmen of a widow made it possible for the widow to remain
untonsured the ultimate authority of the Brahmanical state in the
form of the Peshwai acted to uphold the Brahmanical gender
codes enforced by religious authorities.[18] To ensure the upholding of brahmanya in 1735 the government ordained rules for the
tonsure of widowed women along with codes of dress, food and
interaction with other women of the family.[19] Thus it is evident
that while the brahmanya of the Peshwai reserved the most privileged position for the Brahmanas it also expected the strictest
observance of caste and gender norms from them. The social
power of the community of Brahmanas, backed by the Peshwai,
was expressed through recourse to permanent excommunication:
Both were vigilant in punishing deviance through this repressive
mechanism which ensured social death for the resisters.[20]

To sum up the relationship between caste and gender during
the Peshwai, I have tried to show that the latter maintained the
status order with a pre-eminent position for the Brahmanas. It also
reiterated the structures of Brahmanical patriarchy because in a
very basic sense the pre-eminent status of the Brahmanas was
contingent upon the undiluted purity of its women. The Brahmanas
superior ritual and moral status entitled it to rule and to consolidate itself economically through dakshina, grants of land, and
other economic privileges cited earlier, apart from their hold over
administrative positions based on their reading and writing skills.

However, the Brahmanas entitlement to its privileged position was not always self-evident; in fact the moral and ritual superiority of the· Brahmanas needed to be physically demonstrated and perceived by the other castes as marking the Brahmanas off from themselves. It is in this context that the proclamation of the *Yadi dharmasthapanah* assumes importance.[21] Issued in 1735, within twenty years of the Peshwaship becoming hereditary (with power passing out of the hands of the Maratha rulers) and almost as soon as the new government had stabilised, it represented the public image of the Peshwai. It was a statement that the Peshwai was serious in its intent to 're-establish' the Dharma. And crucial to Dharma were rules and norms about Brahmana women, in particular pre-pubertal marriages, the maintenance of distinctions between married women and widows and the strict observance of ascetic widowhood, both visibly and actually. Only thus could the superior morality of the Brahmanas be established. In the final reckoning it was Brahmana women who in a large measure had to uphold the brahmanya of the Peshwai more than other categories of men and women.

### 2. Class formation, caste contestation and gender in the nineteenth century

The British takeover of Poona in 1818 marked a certain disruption in the structure of relations established during the Peshwai. The colonial intervention in western India created new patterns which require to be problematised, especially with reference to social relations. From the standpoint of gender, caste, and the State, certain questions are particularly relevant. How far did the hold of Brahmanism and Brahmanical patriarchy break, or seek to be reformulated, in the new political situation where the direct control of the Brahmanas upon the State (as in the Peshwai) gave way following the British takeover? How did other social groups react to such a situation? And finally in what way was gender shaped by, or a shaper of, some of these new social forces? These are some of the questions that we seek to explore in this section.

While numerous changes in the land tenure, administration, law and education accompanied the establishment of direct colonial rule in Maharashtra these unfolded gradually rather than dramatically over the nineteenth century. In fact, immediately after their takeover of power the British were not keen to appear to have caused a major disruption and the "new order of things" was sought to be cushioned. Furthermore the British administration in the Deccan proclaimed its intention to develop a system there which was in "harmony with Indian ways".[22] In practice this was expressed in the early years of colonial rule as a placation of the erstwhile ruling class, which in the Peshwa's territory had meant the Brahmanas. For example they continued the grant of dakshina, and retained the privileges of the holders of inams and jagirs. Since many of the great jagirdars and inamdars were Brahmanas, neither the religious nor secular power of the Brahmanas was radically altered, because even the district offices of the kamavisdars, occupied by Brahmanas, were retained.[23]

British 'concern' for 'oppressed' Indian women was expressed pragmatically in the early years of colonial rule in the Poona Deccan: all the subjects of the State had to be brought under the ambit of the British administration but this was done without ruffling the feathers of the Brahmanas and other elite groups. The handling of gender was therefore complex and cannot be seen only in issues like sati but through the everyday actions of the executive. One such instance was the recourse to traditional humiliation prescribed for adulterous widows in the Brahmanical texts, when the new collector of Poona ordered the blackening of the face and the parading of a Brahmana widow for committing adultery.[24]

Similarly the decision to uphold the authority of Panchayats in matters of dispute over castes, religion and marriage implied that women, whose sexuality was monitored by the caste, community, and male kin, continued to be governed by traditional laws; they were not immediately, and in all matters, provided with the 'protection' of the British courts.[25]

Despite the caution exercised by the British administration in the Poona Deccan and despite the evidence that in their handling of tradition, gender, and economic privileges, there was no major dilution of Brahmanical power by the colonial State, the end of the Peshwai was nevertheless perceived as an important moment by castes traditionally excluded from the privileged place occupied by the Brahmanas. That power was no longer *directly* in the hands of the Brahmanas, was quickly grasped by various castes and a spate of caste disputes, some of which had remained unresolved during the Peshwai, quickly surfaced.[26]

It soon became evident that the British would be willing to

permit the Brahmanas to excommunicate 'erring' members of their own caste who were willing to share Brahmana rituals with upwardly mobile castes but that they would not allow the coercive machinery of the State to be used by the Brahmanas to punish such castes. This 'neutral' stance, where they declined to ensure the compliance of other castes to Brahmana authority and an acceptance of their word in determining rank order, was the space into which non-Brahmana castes inserted themselves. Thus an intensification of caste contestations is discernible in nineteenth century western India, culminating in a frenetic move to have a higher status recorded by various castes during the censuses of 1891, 1901, and 1911.[27]

A crucial feature of the caste contestations whereby an individual caste group sought a higher rank for itself was that it was characterised by a double move made by the caste in defining itself: it had to resemble a higher caste and at the same time distance itself from the lower castes. The ideological parameters within which the contests occurred were important because gender was a basic element in the redefinition of caste identity. All castes seeking upward mobility argued their cases on the basis of entitlement to Vedic rituals and the claim that their womenfolk practised sacred widowhood and were barred from remarriage.[28] It was they purity of women that established the claim to high status. Thus all such caste movements, while using the break between Brahmanism and state power, and contesting their own existing ranking were working within the cultural hegemony of Brahmanism and therefore of Brahmanical patriarchy. Ideologically at least, despite British presence and the new socio-political order the cultural hegemony of Brahmanism remained, for the moment, more or less intact. What we need to explore is the manner in which other social forces were affecting western India and what bearing these had in contesting or reinforcing Brahmanical hegemony with special reference to caste and gender.

The establishment of the colonial state generated new social forces in western India leading to a process of class formation. The creation of new systems of administration, particularly a bureau-cracy, and a legal system based upon a distinctive method of recruitment to fill the lower rungs, opened up opportunities to particular segments of society in Maharashtra. This led to the emergence of a professional class. Entry into professions was

through an English education. Thus, the twin factors in the process of class formation were access to education and to the new
professions. Economic changes and urbanisation also provided
opportunities to certain sections in the formation of new classes.[29]
These processes were simultaneously open and closed. While
technically open to all castes, making it possible for mobility and
opportunity, these processes were unequally accessible to different castes and not infrequently virtually closed to the lowest among
them.[30]

The Brahmanas therefore continued to occupy a proportion of
professional positions far in excess of their numerical proportion
in the population as a whole — they were only four per cent of the
population in Maharashtra.[31] Far from the colonial state eroding
the social power of the Brahmanas it provided opportunities to
make up for their loss of direct political control by continuing to
exercise a hold on the administration; consequently they remained
the most influential social group in Maharashtra.

The concentration of educational opportunities and entry to
the civil services among the upper castes, especially the Brahmanas,
were important elements in social processes and class formation in
nineteenth century Maharashtra. Thus, although in formal
sociological terms, the concept of economic class and status group
are taken to be exclusive, in India, as Bayly has argued, class
formation was inextricably linked with caste and community
formation.[32] Further, because property structures were not radically disturbed, a broad congruence between caste and class was
sustained during the nineteenth century with pre-colonial elite
groups such as the Brahmanas and Prabhus feeding directly into
the new professional class.[33] Over the decades this burgeoning
class also reproduced itself, with children of government employees and professional men comprising the largest proportion of
students at the college level.[34]

This congruence between caste and class was a consequence of
the manner in which British policies (which were themselves
Janus-faced, both breaking down and able to work with traditional
social hierarchy) were devised, set in motion, and affected different strata of Indian society. Even as they struck a blow to the
intellectual monopoly of the Brahmanas by opening doors to all
classes and created an educated class comprising certain select
non-Brahmana castes, they also set off occupational, and therefore

some social, mobility as contended by Misra.[35] Because the opportunities provided by the British were both open and closed these new economic and social processes were generated without a radical re-altering of the relationship between caste and class.

The failure of the British to actually break the hold of Brahmanas upon society and the unfulfilled aspirations of the non-Brahmana cultivating castes as well as other 'low' castes became a central feature of the non-Brahmana contestation of social processes in the nineteenth century. The battle for democratic access to education was ably spearheaded by Jotirao Phule. Appearing before the Hunter Comission in 1884 Phule argued that the ignorance of the British government led it to support policies which strengthened the hold of the Brahmanas over the rest of society.[36] The diffusionist theory of education (whereby the British claimed that knowledge would filter down) had never worked because of the selfishness of the Brahmanas who used their advantageous position to monopolise the civil service and liberal professions. Finally, he argued that since the government drew the bulk of its revenue from a tax paid by the peasantry it was morally incumbent upon it to focus its attention on the non-Brahmana castes. Phule therefore demanded the introduction of compulsory primary education in the villages and special incentives to lower castes in institutions of higher learning.[37]

Jotirao Phule (1827-90) marks a definitive turning point in the history of caste contestations. He was the first non-Brahmana thinker in colonial India to reconceptualise caste by breaking the hegemonic control of Brahmanism. Unlike earlier caste contestations Phule rejected Sanskritisation becasuse he rejected Brahmana dominance and a hierarchical society.[38] Having broken the hold of Brahmanic ideology upon the cultural imagination of the lower castes he was able to mount a powerful critique of the caste system itself. The consequences for reconceptualising gender relations and launching a socio-political movement were thus vastly different from earlier caste contestations. Following his adoption of a conflict approach to social contradictions Phule founded the Satyashodhak Samaj to mobilise the oppressed non-Brahmanas and low castes in an attempt to emancipate them from the cultural and economic domination of the upper castes.[39] Further Phule also articulated a triadic relationship between the Brahmanas who had traditionally dominated the lower castes, the British government, and the lower castes themselves, who needed to extricate themselves from Brahmana domination. In this triad Phule regarded British power as the countervailing force against traditional Brahmanical dominance. It was viewed as providing the necessary space for the lower orders to tilt the balance of social forces in their favour.[40]

An analysis of social processes thus indicates that throughout the nineteenth century Brahmana power was simultaneously under challenge and being reassembled. In reassembling power and maintaining their social leadership, gender came to occupy a prominent position, first in defining the identity of a class and then, as the challenges and sense of crisis mounted, in defining the identity of the nation. Increasingly, a critique of Brahmanical patriarchy became difficult to mount. But here we anticipate. We must first describe the history, location and contradictions of the 'new Brahmanas' without which we cannot locate either Ramabai and her critique of Brahmanical patriarchy, nor her conversion to Christianity, nor the nature of the nationalist project as it was shaped by the Maharashtrian leadership which could not accomodate Ramabai within such a project.

*3. Class fractions, cultural identity and 'Hindu' womanhood: gender in the building of consent for a Hindu nationalism.*

The dominant feature of class formation in nineteenth century Maharashtra, in our view, is that it occurred in a contestatory situation. The upper castes in this region were thus subjected to the double pressure of changes generated by the colonial state through the administration, especially law, occupation, education and social life, as well as challenges from the lower castes who were seeking to use the colonial state against the traditional elite.[41] The stresses experienced by the Brahmanas through these developments affected the manner in which this traditional elite group sought to define itself in relation to the colonial rulers on the one hand, and to the common folk from which it had to distinguish itself on the other.

The general crisis of identity in a fluid and contestatory situation, and the distinctive way in which the new class in the process of formation responded to the crisis, led to an internal contestation within the class itself. The difficulties in meshing new economic and social relations, urbanisation and educational requirements with traditional rituals and practices, resulted in a certain ambiguity in the way the new class comprising the upper castes adapted themselves to the pressures.[42] This led to the formation of class segments, each sharing a similar material relationship but responding in contradictory ways to the changes under way. The class segments were marked by different self-definitions. They disagreed on their relationship to religion, tradition, the colonial state, and most significantly to gender, within what, it is necessary to emphasise, was a larger *shared* culture. As the century unfolded, the efforts to retain the social leadership and hegemony of the Brahmanas as the traditional elite was articulated through a factional struggle to shape the culture of the new Brahmana elite as well as the larger class it was feeding into, according to the different self-definitions; thereafter the nation itself was to be shaped in the image of this class.[43] The struggle between the two main class segments and the issues around which the identity of class and 'nation' coalesced is therefore important for our essay, and can be traced through the major conflicts over gender in nineteenth century in western India (which, as we have stated earlier, represented community, religion and nation). These were the widow remarriage controversy of 1869, Rakhmabai's refusal to accept the validity of a non consensual marriage and grant conjugal rights to her husband (1884–86), and the polarisation over the Age of Consent Bill (1890–91).

The widow remarriage controversy of the 1860s was the culmination of the first stage in the formation of class segments. Within the larger body of Brahmanas, a small section with access to English education and with membership of the emerging professional class represented the winds of change in the community. Sometimes characterised as the 'new Brahmanas' this section, which spearheaded a very modest critique of Hinduism,[44] represented the first evidence of the cultural and social crisis being experienced by the traditional elite. Focussing on the failure of Hindu society to meet the challenges thrown up by British rule they called for expanded horizons and for a revolution of traditional beliefs. Using the new print medium the early 'reformers', including Gopal Hari Deshmukh, advocated transformation through education and were strongly opposed to conversions. The theme of degeneration from an earlier pristine Hinduism which had been the work of the 'true' Brahmanas (unlike the superstitious and corrupt specimens in the present) figured in these writings and became a staple of all strands of middle class writing.[45]

By the 1860s the energies of this group, by now distinct from those who resisted change of any sort representing the orthodoxy, coalesced in the widow remarriage question. Concern over the problems of enforced widowhood went back to the Peshwai; by the middle of the nineteenth century some pamphlets had appeared and a couple of marriages had taken place without public hysteria.[46] This was before Vidyasagar's tract on the validity of widow remarriage appeared and the 1856 Act made legal the remarriage of a widow. The latter two events set off a storm in western India as the advocacy of widow remarriage was taken up seriously by a section of the educated elite. They set up a widow marriage association in 1866 and announced their intention to consider "the best means of *re-introducing* the practice of remarriage of females of the high caste community who have or may become widows and to advocate their cause on the '*authority of the Hindu Dharmashastra*'.[47] (emphasis added) From the outset the 'reformers' located themselves in tradition, in what they regarded as the 'real' tradition. Thus they did not concede, throughout the raging of the controversy, that they were in any way pushing a radical innovation—rather they claimed to be 'restoring the days of our past history'.[48] As the controversy proceeded the reformers privileged the Veda over Shastric text, but also pointed out that they were merely attacking 'specific social evils' and 'priestly despotism' while preserving the general authority of the Shastras.[49]

Using the new lines of communication in mobilising opinion, such as the newspaper, and also the newly available mofussil network of graduates who were spread out over a very wide area, an attempt was made to consolidate educated opinion through 'lecture tours'.[50] Combined with a recourse to tradition was also a strong dose of paternalism and humanistic concern to advocate "moderate" change, not of gender relations, in terms of structural inequalities, but rather a desire to alleviate some of the worst expressions of the oppressive practices enforced upon women. At the centre of this concern of the class segment was the child widow who for a section of the Brahmanas became a symbol of an oppressive culture evoking guilt and ambivalence about nineteenth century Brahmanism. This was clearly not in keeping with their self definition as a class entitled to leadership in society. An improvement in the status of the widow was therefore tied to a new self image of the educated upper castes and it is not surprising that the issue received the kind of attention that it captured from the reformers.

As the debate intensified the orthodox defenders of the status quo on religion, culture and gender norms prepared themselves to move from opposing the government on particular issues such as changes in the norms for disbursement of dakshina, or even the passing of the Widow Remarriage Act to combat their own caste fellows. For the orthodox, their violent defence of enforced widowhood was the culmination of a long period of disquiet beginning with British refusal to support the disciplinary power of the Brahmanas over other castes, their perception about the loss of respect that they had suffered in society, loss of their income from the dakshina and an anxiety about conversion and the general threat to the cultural uniqueness of their caste. In such a situation giving up a core of their belief — the much cherished ideal of sacred marriage for women, the strict control over female sexuality generally, and the enforcement of the non-sexuality of the widow — was tantamount to the loss of their identity as Brahmanas. What had distinguished the Brahmanas from the other castes traditionally was their exclusive right to certain ritual practices, their monopoly on learning (now theoretically, and to a certain extent in real terms, eroded) and the strictest of sexual codes for their women, topped by enforced widowhood.

The key to the strength of the resistance to widow remarriage (and thereafter to other gender issues in the nineteenth century) lay in the fact that the practice had traditionally represented a feature of lower caste morality and sexual practice; the championing of remarriage for the upper caste widow reversed traditional norms and advocated the adoption of a lower caste model to the highest and most ritually pure castes. We need to bear in mind that while the adoption of a high caste model by the lower castes had been an established feature of upward social mobility, the reverse was unheard of and not reconcilable with the framework of Brahmanic ideology. Furthermore, until the middle of the nineteenth century the Brahmanas had fiercely resisted attempts at 'Sanskritisation' by the lower castes. Now the very same pre-eminent caste was to adopt a custom that would bring them down to the level of those whom they despised as inferiors. Finally the intensification of caste contestations had generally increased the incidence of enforced widowhood and the high value placed on it. Such a situation of social flux exacerbated tensions which the widow remarriage issue played into. Gender and caste were inextricably linked in the orthodox Brahmana position on widow remarriage.[51]

A final point needs to be made about the widow remarriage controversy. The reform or resistance was about widows and yet strikingly no widow featured in these debates. Even the reformers had no women in their ranks. Thus, in an issue that crucially affected their lives, no women spoke, at least in any audible way.[52] It appears that upper caste women, the *objects* of reform, were tied up in larger social forces over which they had no control. Till the end of the century all over India among the higher castes only about 300 widows had been remarried.[53] The passion on both sides was out of all proportion to its real consequences; ideologically, however, it was a critical beginning to the battle over identity.

The polarisation of the elite over the widow remarriage issue had split them into two opposing groups comprising a small, articulate minority advocating modest change, and a much larger vociferous and coercive majority resisting what was perceived as an onslaught upon the unique identity of the Brahmanas. Thereafter, as a beleaguered minority, through the effective mobilisation and social ostracism of the conservative majority, the Brahmana reformers never again, *of their own accord*, centre-staged gender as an issue although they had to take stands when issues were forced upon them. Their isolation over the widow remarriage issue also led to the 'reformers' attempting to heal the breach within their community. One way was to turn the attention and energies of the community to non-divisive issues outside of religion and culture.

However, gender issues were not so easy to sweep under the carpet. The process of class formation, legal changes under the colonial state, education, urbanisation, and expansion of professions generated its own pressures not always easy to channelise or control. Gender was not an issue to bring into focus and then marginalise; it was located in the larger matrix of social processes. Contradictions inherent in these processes surfaced with a volatility and passion surpassing the widow remarriage issue in the

Rakhmabai case which flowed into the Age of Consent Bill of 1891.

By the last quarter of the nineteenth century women were being gradually drawn into the ambit of a new legal structure administered by the British-Indian courts.[54] As the quantum of legislation increased and the authority of the caste panchayats became dysfunctional or redundant in certain cases, women became subject to dual authority structures. Their everyday lives and many of their so called 'lapses' continued to be governed by the social power of the community, exercised through the caste panchayats but, at the same time, the new statutory laws also began to govern their lives, making them subjects of the colonial state in extraordinary situations. Both structures upheld the authority of the patriarchal family and its property forms even though the two were apparently dissimilar and at times in conflict with each other. The overlap between the two systems and their relationship to the larger entity of Hindu law also remained problematic and unresolved throughout the second half of the nineteenth century.

The case of *Dadaji vs. Rakhmabai* revolving around conjugality, law, and the State in the context of the middle class service gentry in an urban location, threw up various issues.[55]

Briefly summarised the case was as follows: Rakhmabai of the Sutar caste (which had lost its position under the Portuguese control over Bombay, been reduced to carpenters, but moved up again with opportunities under British rule), daughter of Jayantibai and the deceased Janardhan Pandurang, was married at the age of 11 to Dadaji (Dadaji however held that the marriage occurred when Rakhmabai was 13) who was related to her step-father. (On being widowed, Rakhmabai's mother was remarried to Dr. Sakharam Arjun according to acceptable norms among the Sutars.) For some time Dadaji, who was 20, resided with his in-laws and was being educated, but he moved out to his uncle's residence for reasons which were variously described by the contending parties. The marriage remained unconsummated during this period. In 1884 Dadaji moved the courts for restitution of conjugal rights when Rakhmabai refused to go to live with him. The case immediately captured the attention of the press since Rakhmabai indicated in writing to the court her unwillingness to live with Dadaji. Dadaji lost the case at the trial stage but won on appeal. Rakhmabai refused to accept the decision of the high court and the penal clause of imprisonment was thus applied. Finally a 'compromise' was worked out, with Dadaji relinquishing his claims upon his wife and Rakhmabai 'buying' her freedom for 2000 rupees, a substantial sum of money in the 1880s. She then set sail for England to train to be a doctor.[56] Before she left she promised her grandfather (her guardian) that she would not convert to Christianity.[57] She had earlier recognised that she would never be able to remarry. She returned to India after completing her medical training and served as a doctor in various districts of the Bombay presidency before she retired.[58] After her return Rakhmabai appears to have led a quiet and relatively unnoticed existence, retreating from the public gaze which had hysterically been transfixed upon her for almost a decade.

Central to the controversy that raged around Rakhmabai was the issue of the validity of the 'infant' non-consensual, 'Hindu' marriage, and its sacramental, rather than contractual, nature. Parties to the controversy were caught in a bind because neither the reformers nor the defenders of existing customs could directly address the non-consensual nature of the Hindu marriage. They took therefore to defining Hindu law and arguing over what was permissible and what was irreconcilable with it. For example, one argument that was advanced by a section of the reformers was that Hindu marriage was of course a sacrament but in order to become a sacrament it must be consented to. This implied that infant marriages were anomalous because they were inconsistent with the 'true' principles of Hindu law.[59]

Apart from a small section even among the reformers, for everyone else the Rakhmabai case generated unnamed fears. Consent and the pre-pubertal marriages of girls were contradictory. Yet pre-pubertal marriages were necessary according to the upper caste defenders of religious tradition, who argued that even the law of the land did not require consent and that the girl was not required to be a party to the contract—she was merely its subject.[60] The fact that Rakhmabai's marriage to Dadaji was unconsummated added to the anxiety about Rakhmabai's refusal to cohabit with him, especially because William Muir had suggested in the 1860s that the courts refuse to recognise unconsummated marriages.[61] If the courts had upheld Rakhmabai's refusal every unconsummated marriage could be struck down as null and void. It was this possibility that made the Rakhmabai case so traumatic. Other restitution cases initiated by the husband had come up before the courts, one going up to the Privy Council, but these had hardly caused a ripple.[62] Rakhmabai's case involved issues of infant marriage and a woman's refusal to permit a non-consensual consummation. It came at a time when public opinion on Hindu 'national' identity was fragile and could be easily disrupted, especially by women who did not conform to the defined norms of the class shaping such an identity; it was for these reasons that the case became so controversial.

Anxiety generated by a young wife's disavowal of her marital obligations were heightened by Rakhmabai's reasons for the disavowal: the incompatibility and unworthiness of her husband.[63] The fact that Rakhmabai was 'English' educated and a woman of substance clinched the fears of the Hindu middle class. Every Hindu bride could do what Rakhmabai did, drop the facade of 'willing surrender'[64] and refuse to conform to the ideological and material arrangements of nineteenth century 'Hindu' patriarchy.

Throughout the attack on Rakhmabai as a spoilt western educated woman who had disavowed her marital obligations but also the unique sacred traditions of Hindu womanhood, there was a play on the figure of Savitri and of Rakhmabai having turned her back on this powerful image. Since Dadaji was allegedly suffering from a lung disease the Savitri example was particularly evocative. The new woman, embodied by Rakhmabai, was refusing the chance to be immortal or to be a modern Savitri by ministering to her husband and trying to better his condition. As the press pointed out this would have provided an example which would be imitated all over India. It should be noted that the recourse to the Savitri model enabled men to skirt the real issue in the Rakhmabai case, that of *forced* consummation.

Although the public reacted with outrage to Rakhmabai's defiance the most influential criticism came from Tilak and his newspaper, the *Mahratta*. A conservative position on Hindu womanhood was central to his agenda of garnering support from the upper caste elite for a militant Hindu nationalism, and his first public foray in this venture was over Rakhmabai. Ably served by the contradictions in the personal lives and ideologies of the reformers, Tilak found the Rakhmabai case a good launching pad for his attack on the reformers' position on women in which education for them would have been the least controversial plank.

Tilak, however was opposed even to this and Rakhmabai's education and her unwillingness to accept an uneducated husband,
bandied about in the press but never made a part of the legal
argument, came in very handy in this onslaught. "It is believed that
education is supposed to expand and purify the mind but the
Rakhmabai case shows that God has so made the females that they
are quite unworthy of either liberty or enlightenment" wrote his
paper. The paper argued particularly against "English" education.[65]

The anxieties of the Hindu middle class and the isolation of the
'reformers' achieved by the militant stance of Tilak in the
Rakhmabai case were easily carried over to the Age of Consent
controversy whose central issues were an extension of those that
had featured in Rakhmabai's case: the rights of the girl-wife in a
non-consensual marriage.

The roots of the Age of Consent Bill can be traced back to the
major concerns of nineteenth century reformers on the 'status' of
women, particularly widows. Early marriage of girls came to be
regarded by a section of reformers as *the* reason for the large
number of child widows among the upper castes upon whom
enforced widowhood was applied. The linking together of infant
marriage and enforced widowhood in a book published by the
Parsi reformer, Behram Malabari, in 1884[66] became the starting
point of a debate on the need to advance the age of marriage for
girls in particular. The book was widely circulated to seek the
opinions of important public figures. Malabari, a journalist who
used his pen with passion, was a reformer who was very different
from even the most advanced Brahmana reformers of western
India.[67]

Through his descriptions of personal tragedies due to enforced
widowhood he appealed not only to the minds of the educated but
to the sentiments of all Indians. He also advanced a set of radical
measures to check infant marriages. These included punitive measures for young men who defaulted by not permitting them to take
university tests or recruitment and by using school textbooks to
describe the evils of early marriage. He wanted the government to
publicize their right to remarry to widows and to use its authority
to prevent excommunication, still an effective weapon in the
hands of the community.[68]

Clearly all this was too radical for the bulk of reformers, and much more for the defenders of existing customs. In fact when Malabari's *Notes* was published it got a lukewarm reception from all quarters including reformers and Governor-General Ripon's government. Both Ranade and Bhandarkar in Maharashtra felt that Malabari had exaggerated the evils of infant marriage and enforced widowhood; the government responded by advising caution and the need to proceed slowly. It was then argued that the Legislature should not enact new laws and place itself in direct antagonism to social opinion.[69] But gradually reformist opinion began to build up in broad support of Malabari's initiative, particularly after the grounds of the debate shifted away from legislating a minimum age for marriage to raising the age of consent in the Indian Penal Code[70] from 10 to 12 for girls for 'legitimate' sexual intercourse.

For the reformers the focus on the age of consummation rather than marriage was a way out of the impasse. It was considered to be a measure which was a reform from within the community rather than one forced upon them from the outside. But opposition, nevertheless, was virulent, especially in Bengal. The government's acceptance of the suggestion of the reformers, followed by the manner in which legislation was introduced, originated in very different motives from those of the reformers. The contradictions in the British position as well as the major issues that surfaced have been documented elsewhere.[71] From the point of view of this essay certain questions need to be highlighted as they have a bearing on the relationship between gender, 'nation', the colonial state and its consequences upon nationalism. The central question in the age of consent controversy was: when could a man legally have sexual access to his wife without it being deemed rape? This anomaly again rose out of Hindu custom which required early marriage for girls and was based on non-consensuality. There was a basic contradiction between English law on marriage and rape within it (which did not exist in England at that time), and such an application in India. In India, rape within marriage was a distinct possibility because the partners were not adults and the marriage was not consensual. Thus, because existing marriage practices were devalued by the Age of Consent Bill public attention was enormous.

The age of consent controversy was also the most publicly conducted debate on female sexuality that India has witnessed in recent times. Since support or opposition for legislating on fixing an age when a girl was considered 'fit' to have her marriage consummated was based on the likely occurrence of menstruation, the Indian woman's body was subjected to unprecedented attention.[72] 'Delicacy of speech' had to be thrown to the winds as men wrote about what they regarded as 'unspeakable' but nevertheless had to discuss.[73] When the debates on the issue of raising the age for marriage began a certain clinicality in tone was maintained but when the Phulmoni case hit the headlines and the government introduced legislation raising the age of consent from 10 to 12 for women, and regarded sexual intercourse before that age as rape even in the case of the husband, the tone of the discussions changed dramatically.

Phulmoni, a young girl aged 10, bled to death in 1890 following forcible intercourse by her 35 year old husband, Hari Maiti. The judge had ruled that the charge of rape was inapplicable because Phulmoni was 10 and the age of consent according to the 1871 law was fixed at 10. It was held that Hari Maiti's 'forcible' act leading to death was thus 'unintended' and an accident which may have been tragic but was nevertheless perfectly legal.[74] Riding the wave of moral revulsion, the government, which was looking for a 'pretext' immediately introduced legislation while 'Hari Maitism' quickly became an expression connoting male brutality.[75]

However not everyone shared the moral revulsion of a section of the reformers. Public reaction was decidedly aggressive and not merely because the legislation was ill conceived and messy in its application. Again what was at the heart of the controversy was the problem created by the non-consensual Hindu marriage, into which a restricted and statutorily defined notion of consent was being introduced. But the question that arises is: where exactly was this consent being located? Neither the State nor the community (resisting or approving the measure) were actually considering 'consent' as residing in the woman's decision to permit sexual access to her husband; instead it was the State which was consenting to providing the husband sexual access to his wife. This notion had no precedent in the past. Public hysteria, the argument of religion and culture in danger, or even the position of Tilak that an alien government had no right to decide on such matters,[76] had deeper implications than appear on the surface.

I have argued elsewhere and suggested here that female sexuality was closely guarded and subject to stringent control in the pre-

colonial period too. Brahmanical texts are explicit about the fact
that female sexuality (or even male sexuality but with less emphasis) is never a matter of choice or an individual's will but subject to
the collectivity of the caste or kin group. Marriages were therefore
organised to ensure caste purity and were in the hands of male kin.
Lapses were swiftly and sternly punished.[77] The State was closely
concerned with female sexuality which was monitored through
the community. However, both in the Brahmanical texts and
during the Peshwai the State aided and supported the authority of
the husband over his wife and reiterated the community's control
over female sexuality through the caste panchayats. At no point
had the State assumed authority over the wife directly, *superseding*
the authority of the husband and his kinsmen. The colonial state
had for the first time, through this legislation, assumed authority,
defined as protection, upon the child-wife, superseding the authority and 'rights' of the husband. The fundamental point about
the Tilakian resistance to the Bill was as much a statement that
female sexuality must remain a subject under caste and community control (not of course under women)[78] which the state, especially an alien state, must keep off and not erode.

It can be seen that the colonial state had thus shifted its ground
since the Rakhmabai case where we saw an interlocking of patriarchies despite the issue being one of non-consensual marriage.
Now there was an opposition of patriarchies; consent was not a
matter of the wife's choice but determined by the State which
sought in this way to protect the girl-wife, imposing the superior
morality of colonial patriarchy over that of indigeinous patriarchy.

The ideological position of an affronted, indigineous
(Brahmanical) patriarchy as articulated by the rational Tilak was
not of course stated openly but dressed up in emotive argument
regarding the sanctity of religion and custom which had also been
stressed in Bengal, where the affected custom itself had local
relevance.[79] For Hindu militants Hindu conjugality became the
essence of their religion and they defended it aggressively. It was
insisted that the British were about to commit a primal sin against
Hinduism by mounting an unprecedented attack on the last pure
space of a conquered people — the woman's body — by opening
it up to the possibility of defilement and gross violation.

What is significant is that the militants recognised that there
were harsh customs which might mean death for the Hindu woman,

but stated that such a discipline signified pride and glory for chaste women found only in Hindu society. At least in the case of Bengal, Tanika Sarkar shows that during the opposition to the Age of Consent Bill the Hindu woman's body became *the* site of struggle against an alien power and culture.[80]

The defence of community, custom and indigineous patriarchy against an alien power, regardless of its consequinces upon women, was successfully transplanted to and channelised by Tilak in Maharashtra. He had earlier defended Dadaji against Rakhmabai, now he exonerated Hari Maiti.[81] Phulmoni's death was not a reflection of a husband's brutality, something by which one might reformulate custom, but an unintended consequence of a very lawful custom. Since the non-consensual Hindu marriage was a sacrament nothing occurring within it could be deemed to be irregular, far less be regarded as illegitimate. For Tilak and other defenders of custom their considered position was that it was the husband and the traditional Hindu community who were to decide how to manage the sexuality of the wife; neither the State, nor the liberal reformers, nor even the women themselves had the right to do so.

On Tilak's militant stand the Age of Consent Bill was closely linked to his bid for leadership over the elite in Maharashtra. He had established during the concurrent Rakhmabai controversy that a conservative position on gender was more popular than a liberal reformist one. Gender issues had been deeply divisive but it was evident that the lines of division were unequal as going back to the widow remarriage issue, there was always a small articulate minority opposed by a large militant majority, usually less organised than the reformers. Now Tilak prepared to become the nodal point of inflamed opinion, planning his moves so well that he made himself acceptable to the orthodox. Towards this end he travelled to Allahabad, bathed in the Ganga and shaved off his moustache.[82]

Tilak's ability to sense the pulse of opinion, especially in Poona, captured the sense of alienation and economic and social crisis within the community which had grown in the last quarter of the nineteenth century. His militant championing of the orthodox view made him a key figure in the controversy over the Age of Consent Bill in western India. The culmination of the mobilisation by reformers and their confrontation with the conservatives was the disruption of the meeting organised by the reformers at the Kridabhavan in February 1891. A restive crowd of more than a 1,000 students, all now defending Hindu culture as symbolised by Hindu womanhood, and orthodox citizens broke into the hall, destroyed everything in sight and the meeting ended in a riot.[83] During the age of consent controversy Tilak secured support from diverse groups — religious leaders, student militant groups, and prominent Brahmanas in mofussil towns throughout the Deccan. He thus established himself as a key actor in Maharashtrian politics and through his popularity effectively marginalised the reformers as leaders of that society. And, even though the Age of Consent Bill became an Act with the reformers appearing to have gained their objective, it was Tilak who actually consolidated his position as the natural leader of the middle classes at the expense of the reformers. At the same time the old Shastris who had been active in the widow remarriage controversy were also sidelined, with important sections of the educated elite now espousing the orthodox position. Tilak thus politicised the issues of gender and religion. For the first time the Brahmana community had produced alternative leaders to the Shastris whose base of influence, though not divorced from traditional patterns, was independent of them.

Tilak's successful wresting of the initiative regarding the most intimate matters of high caste Hindu family and ritual tradition had ensured him success in his bid for leadership over the high caste/middle classes. Subsequently, Tilak built on the crucial gains from the age of consent controversy using communal unrest, the political mobilisation of the Hindus *as Hindus*, using the Ganapati festival, the cow protection movement, countering non-Brahmana mobilisation by taking over the symbol of Shivaji, and even breaking into working class organisations, to emerge as the undisputed leader with a 'mass' following in Maharashtra.[84] He conclusively undermined the position of the moderate hegemony of the Poona Sarvajanik Sabha and at the same time succeeded in shifting the stand of the Sabha regarding maintaining neutrality in religious matters in 1893. He finally took the organisation in 1895, forcing the moderate Gokhale to resign. The tussle for power over the Brahmana community was decisively resolved when Tilak carried this struggle onto the all-India platform and campaigned to change the location of the meeting of the national social conference which had spearheaded moves on social reform and held its meetings at the same premises as the Congress. Arguing that Poona was a conservative town and the linking of social reform with a Congress meeting would discourage the 'masses' (i.e. the Poona Brahmana elite) from participating in large numbers he manoeuvered so effectively that the reformers capitulated.[85] By the end of the nineteenth century the Poona Brahmana elite had crystallised its social position as the wresting of political power *without* a transformation of social or gender relations.

Thus, at the turn of the century, the Poona Brahmana elite, through its spokesman, Tilak, and with the press under its control, had, for the moment, suppressed caste and gender contestations, a suppression that was crucial for building consent for a particular kind of nationalism conflated with Hinduism. Issues of 'community' and gender were used, constructing both along a conservative axis. All those who did not accept the conservative position, such as the reformers, had in Tilak's opinion 'ceased to be Hindu' and 'were traitors to their country'.[86] Patriotism was henceforth to be defined by the conservatives. Claiming that the reformers had represented India as a nation of 'savages' during the age of consent controversy Tilak demanded that the reformers be excluded from 'our fellow countrymen' and form themselves into a separate nationality.[87] Thus Ramabai's controversial position in western India needs to be located in the context of defining the nation in terms of a narrowly exclusivist Brahmanical Hinduism.

## II

### Ramabai, Brahmanism and Brahmanical patriarchy

A close look at Ramabai's life and work reveals how unique it was in relation to the social location of the bulk of the Brahmana men of the nineteenth century. Born into a Chitpavan Brahmana family and thus capable of sharing in the social power of Brahmanas, Ramabai's father had, however, over the years begun to suffer the consequences of non-conformty. Brahmanical structures, as we have shown, were tightly organised and internally coherent; social and ritual power was available to its caste-fellows within that structure only if one accepted its basic premises and its contemporary practices. Ramabai's father's experiences with Brahmanism in western India both shaped her life and directly fed into it; the break with Brahmanism was therefore inevitable, and almost pre-determined, given the extraordinary nature of her father's life and the legacy she inherited.

Anant Shastri Dongre believed that women and Shudras had a right to learning and attempted to practice his beliefs in his own household by teaching Sanskrit to his young second wife, Lakshmibai, Ramabai's mother. While Lakshmibai proved an apt pupil Anant Shastri's action was regarded as 'heretical', and a confrontation with family and established Brahmanical authority quickly ensued. However, after a long drawn out debate about the scriptural sanction for women learning Sanskrit, when Anant Shastri provided an impressive amount of evidence from the Smritis and the epics, he succeeded in staving off excommunica-tion and became known as an 'orthodox reformer'. Later the family took to travelling around as *pauranikas*, public narrators of the Puranas, at temples or other sacred spots, and received gifts of food, clothes and flowers from their audience.[88]

It was during these travels as pauranikas, narrating stories from the Puranas but also performing worship at all the holy places across the country, that Ramabai's learning began. Since her father was by now too old to teach, Ramabai was taught Sanskrit by her mother[89] doubling the unconventionality of the venture. The difference in the early experiences of Ramabai from that of the 'new' Brahmanas is striking. Men like Ranade, Telang, and even Tilak went to school to avail of the new opportunities provided by English education. Their families invested in such an education because it was imperative to the pursuit of a career in the adminis-tration or the judiciary. In contrast Ramabai and her brother trained for no profession; unconventional though it was to teach a woman, Anant Shastri's family still carried on with the traditional ideals of the truly religious vocation prescribed for the Brahmanas — teaching, worship, and living off gifts.

For many years the Dongre family lived thus on the margins of society. In the normal course Ramabai would have had a very different life. The 'normal' householder compulsion of living within the tight grip of caste and kin had been consciously 're-nounced' because of its claustrophobic control over individuals, compelling them to be part of a system of oppressive practices.[90] In search of space for themselves the entire family tried to create an alternative existence by living away from the stranglehold of Brahmanical society. They managed to succeed only in part because even in their unusual existence caste norms had to be upheld, especially with regard to marriage. Ramabai's elder sister was married according to convention as a child; the marriage was tragic as the groom refused to abide by the arrangement agreed upon, of living as a member of Anant Shastri's family and devoting himself to learning.[91] Drawing upon this unfortunate experience Anant Shastri did not arrange a similar marriage for Ramabai. This was the most unique aspect of Ramabai's life — she remained unmarried far beyond the accepted limit for Brahmana girls. This would have been impossible had it not been for Anant Shastri's peripatetic existence. One can see in Ramabai's future life the same search for space, the need to cut away from oppressive practices and carve out a meaningful existence.

The alternative existence adopted by Ramabai's family also entailed great physical hardship. Ramabai's old father became too feeble to direct the reading of the Puranas by his children. Unfortunately the family was not equipped to do anything else and menial work was proscribed for Brahmanas. At the same time severe famine struck the Madras Presidency, in the area where the Dongre family was then residing. Like the rest of the poor they too wandered from place to place in search of sustenance. As the family was too proud to beg the strain was severe and soon Ramabai lost both her parents within a few months of each other.

Writing poignantly about the months when, as a young woman of 16, she was suddenly faced with the loss of both her parents, and later her elder sister, Ramabai also described the gradual erosion of faith in the traditional gods following the trauma:

> I cannot describe all the sufferings of that terrible time. My father, mother, and sister, all died of starvation within a few months of each other. My brother and I survived and wandered about, still visiting sacred places, bathing in rivers and worshipping the gods and goddesses in order to get our desire. We had fulfilled all the conditions in the sacred books and kept all the rules. . . For three years after the death of our parents and eldest sister we walked more than 4000 miles on foot without any sort of comfort. . . but the gods did not appear to us. After years of fruitless service we began to lose our faith. . . we still continued to keep the caste rules, worshipped the gods and studied sacred literature as usual. We wandered from the south to the north as far as Kashmir and then to the east (reaching) Calcutta in 1878.[92]

The visit to Calcutta proved to be momentous in a variety of ways. Ramabai and her brother met the intellectual elite, including Pandits and reformers and were welcomed and feted by them. These were the halcyon days of Ramabai's public life as she appeared as a godsend to the reformers,[93] providing them with a living embodiment of their perception of ancient Indian womanhood. To them Ramabai represented the recovery of the lost figures of Gargi and Maitreyi — a woman who was learned in Sanskrit at a time when women did not have learning of any kind and those who wished to learn still had to do so secretly. The euphoric reception she received also suggests that the second half of the nineteenth century was in some senses a historical conjuncture ripe for a Ramabai to appear. There was already a space for her, especially in Calcutta. Ramabai easily fitted into that space as ancient womanhood personified and captured the public gaze.[94]

In later years she recalled two landmarks of her Calcutta sojourn: she was asked to lecture on women, and was advised by the leading Brahmo reformer, Keshub Chandra Sen, to study the Vedas. Ramabai describes her encounter with Sen thus:

> K.C. Sen and his family showed great kindness to me and when parting he gave me a copy of one of the Vedas. He asked if I had studied the Vedas. I answered in the negative and said women were not fit to read the Vedas and were not allowed to do so. It would be breaking the rules of religion. . . . He could not but smile at my declaration of this Hindu doctrine. He said nothing in answer but advised me to study the Vedas and Upanishads. . . New thoughts were awakening in my heart. I questioned myself, why should I not study the Vedas and Vedanta? Soon I persuaded myself into the belief that it was not wrong for a woman to read the Vedas. So I began to first read the Upanishads, then the Vedanta and the Veda. I became more dissatisfied with myself.[95]

At the same time in order to lecture on the duties of women according to the Shastras, Ramabai had to first study the Shastras herself. The reading of the 'forbidden' texts had some unintended consequences. It is ironic, but characteristic, that male reformers let Ramabai into their charmed circle, pointed out to her their vision of high Hinduism, set an agenda for her in relation to uplifting other women, but did not conceive of a situation where Ramabai could go beyond it according to her own understanding. Ramabai's reading of the Dharmashastras led her to question the fundamental propositions of Brahmanic Hinduism.

Analysing the Dharmashastras for herself Ramabai became

deeply conscious of the contempt with which women of all castes and men of the lower caste were regarded. The rules did not permit Shudras to perform the same religious acts as the upper castes. Low caste untouchables must lead degraded lives and after repeated births in such conditions, after faithfully serving the high castes as their bondservants with *contentment*, they might be reborn into a higher caste and then gradually be 'uplifted'.[96] Struck by the common degradation of women and the low castes, on which the Shastras were unanimous, Ramabai's early Brahmanic socialisation was deeply shaken. It is worth noting that unlike Brahmana men, engaged in the reformist agenda, who researched the texts for ways to reconcile the Shastras with their project for reform and thus cast it as a revival of 'ancient' traditions, Ramabai found them irreconcilable with what she believed women must be entitled to by right—equality, dignity and self-realisation.

The travails of the wander years, followed by the failure of the family's collective search for salvation had been one aspect of Ramabai's trauma. Now followed the further erosion of a spirited young woman's faith in her traditional religion. Before she could recover or resolve her growing sense of alienation Ramabai suffered another severe blow: her brother Shrinivas also died following a sudden illness.

All alone in the world for the first time, homeless and without economic support, Ramabai accepted a marriage proposal from an acquaintance in Sylhet.[97] Bipin Behari Medhavi, a friend of her brother Shrinivas, was active in debates on the reform of caste and religious beliefs. He was of a different caste, a Shudra, and in accepting the proposal Ramabai chose to break decisively with tradition. By making a *pratiloma* marriage, she was defying Shastric injunctions which viewed such a marriage with horror. What is significant is that she did so consciously, even though there were other offers from fellow castemen. One such highly 'qualified' Brahmana suitor, a Sanskrit scholar but also a 'modernist' from Maharashtra, who was an officer in the Bombay Civil Service travelled to Assam to press his proposal.[98] From a contemporary account it is apparent that some Brahmana men, by virtue of their scholarship, regarded themselves as "fitting" partners for Ramabai with whom an intellectual kinship could be established while upholding caste norms. And yet unlike them Ramabai chose to cross the caste divide, describing it simply as "Having lost faith in the religion of my ancestors I married a Bengali gentleman of the Shudra caste."[99]

Ramabai and Bipin Behari were married according to the Civil Marriage Act as neither of them believed in traditional Hinduism. The marriage was subjected to much criticism and Bipin Behari was promptly excommunicated. Tragically, the marriage was brief as Bipin Behari died within two years and Ramabai was left alone once more, but this time with a baby to support.[100]

Ramabai's break with traditional codes now reached a decisive point. Her early life, unusual as it was with her late marriage had, however, been compensated by her learning; her image had thus been one that could be used in the nineteenth century reformist agenda. Her cross-caste marriage was unprecedented (most male reformers were still marrying very much within their caste) but it was intellectually 'acceptable' in the reformist circles of Bengal. With widowhood however Ramabai became a potentially dangerous figure. Her life was henceforth subjected to much greater surveillance by a public that was unused to seeing women except in the domestic space. Ramabai refused to stay confined — she refused also the traditional role for the widow, that of withdrawal from society. Instead, following widowhood, she turned once more to a 'public' career, this time with a focussed mission of serving the oppressed women of India. Her background, her life's choices, her personality and her career now catapulted her into the public gaze making her *the* most controversial Indian woman of her times.

On her part Ramabai began cautiously; like widows in Bengal she wore white and cropped her hair close. Left to fend for herself and her baby, without an income or property (her husband does not appear to have left Ramabai with any assets and is described as 'coming up the hard way' with Ramabai clearing off some of his debts) She decided to return to western India, the home of her ancestors.[101] The moderate reformers in the Prarthana Samaj like Ranade and Bhandarkar had invited her to come and promised to provide support for her.[102] Ramabai arrived in Poona in 1882 and worked with this group of reformers in their activities, setting up a chain of Arya Mahila Sabhas where a certain class of women could meet and discuss issues relating to the larger body of women.[103] She continued to narrate the Puranas, but this time to a new urban middle class audience and also to propagate the objectives of the

Arya Mahila Samaj.[104] She also appeared before the Hunter Commission on Education and made a fervent plea for the introduction of facilities for the education of women, with special training for them as teachers and doctors so that they could serve other women.[105] But the task with which she identified herself — the setting up of a widows' home for high caste Hindu widows, whose oppression was the subject of much rhetorical concern — made little progress. She had fitted into the reformer's agenda but as yet there was no substantial move on their part to set up the widows' home.

Ramabai's sense of social isolation was compounded by the absence of religious moorings. Her peculiar location as a woman, without any close kin in a male world of reformers 'intellectually' engaged in transforming Brahmanical Hinduism without addressing central questions, all well established in professions and surrounded, in the main, by docile and loving women, needs to be borne in mind. Ramabai's search for personal fulfilment as well as her struggle to understand, and conceptualise, women's oppression from her own position as a woman were vastly different from the motivations and world view of the men around her.

As a widow, Ramabai was also vulnerable in a way no man could ever be. Poona, as we have seen, was orthodox and could be vicious in its 'defence' of Brahmanic Hinduism. Except in the sheltered atmosphere of like-minded reformers Ramabai's public appearances, speaking on behalf of women, were too threatening and she was often shouted down by aggressive men.

The scorn in which Brahmana women held Ramabai and spoke about her would have also increased her sense of alienation from the dominant elite of Poona. This is graphically described by Ranade's wife (in her memoirs about her famous judge-husband) who herself was exhorted to be kind to the 'sorrowful' Ramabai. She records that other women in her family and neighbourhood regarded her as a wretched convert,[106] (long before she became a Christian).

Apart from the very presence of a widow in a public space what she said was also dangerous. The Arya Mahila Sabha was regarded as an institution set up to do away with the domination of men. Ramabai was reported as arguing that according to existing social practices women had to obey men, or be treated like slaves without being cared for at all. It was believed that the Pandita only ex-

horted women to free themselves from the tyranny of men at these
meetings in the Arya Mahila Sabhas, causing horror to the orthodox, both men and women.[107]

Thus even if Ramabai was a Brahmana woman herself she had
no 'community' , no social base and no real emotional bonds to
fall back upon. Ranade's wife describes how despite the approval
and support of her husband she was caught in a dilemma and, in
trying to seek the support of her female kin, reneged once in
public, on her association with Ramabai.[108] While Ranade could,
through his disapproval of his wife, force her to continue her
relationship with Ramabai, the fragility of such a relationship
would be no real consolation to Ramabai herself.

These experiences heightened Ramabai's vulnerability. Recalling her state of mind during this period Ramabai wrote:

> I was desperately in need of some religion. The Hindu religion held out
> no hope for me. The Brahmo religion was not a very definite one. For it
> is nothing but what a man makes for himself. He chooses and gathers
> whatever seems good to him from all religions known to him. . .The
> Brahmo religion has no other foundation than a man's own natural light
> and the sense of right or wrong which he possesses in common with all
> of mankind. It could not and did not satisfy me. . .[109]

What Ramabai appears to have been in need of was not some
abstract notion of god but a figure that she could express an
intense devotion to, one that could satisfy her both intellectually
*and* emotionally. Also Ramabai was a product of nineteenth century social forces; a widow who had a social agenda on widowhood.
Her need and search was therefore for a solution that could
simultaneously accommodate her social agenda as well as her
personal quest for religious fulfilment.

It was at this point that Ramabai first came across Christian
missionaries in any sustained way. Her own unfulfilled searches
had opened her up to influences outside those she had been
familiar with in her earlier years. At the same time her public
visibility, ever since she had appeared before the Hunter Commission, would have led to the Christian missionaries noticing her
seriously and they began to woo her as a potential catch.[110] Now in
Poona a missionary, Miss Hurford, taught her English and introduced her to the Bible in Marathi.

But the most crucial influence in the move to Christianity came
from someone who shared her own background, Nilkantha Goreh,

known after his conversion as Father Goreh. A Chitpavan Brahmana like Ramabai and a true seeker like her, Goreh had found personal fulfilment in Christ rather than ·in Christianity as it was institutionalised.[111] It was with Ramabai's reading of a book written by Goreh that she became 'intellectually' con-vinced of the truth of Christ,[112] but this was still in the future.

As suggested earlier, while in Poona (with its strong Brahmanical ambience) Ramabai's lifework had crystallised and come to focus on the need to provide practical support to battered and oppressed child widows. One such victim, a young widow of 12 who had been married at the age of five and been widowed a few days later, was brought to her in 1882. Regarded as the 'killer' of her husband she was thrown out by her in-laws. Ramabai took the young widow into her home and began to form a definitive idea of a widows' home. She wrote:

> As I looked on that little figure, my vague thoughts about doing something for my sisters in a similar condition began to shape. . . I began to place a plan for starting a home for Hindu widows before my countrymen and to ask for their help. For six months or more I tried my best to get help but could not. . .[113]

Disappointed thus in her 'countrymen' she decided to build up her own skills and make contact with people 'outside' the circle of her 'countrymen' for such a venture. In order to get a medical education as a preliminary step, she made up her mind to go to England 'if the way opened' for her.[114] Through contacts in the Church of England Mission in Poona she finally found an opening and in early 1883 she left for England. In order to raise money for her passage and possessing only intellecutal capital, she wrote and published the *Stri Dharma Niti*, a book about "morals" for women.[115] Dedicated to the memory of her deceased husband and in many ways a contrast to the *High Caste Hindu Woman*, which she wrote after her conversion, it represents, broadly, the reformist approach to Hindu womanhood, indicative of the close links she had had with the moderate Brahmana men with whom she had been associated. The writing and publication of the book to raise money, a practice she continued for some years, is also evidence of the uncertain economic location of Ramabai. She was probably one of the first women on record who wrote and lectured for a living in nineteenth century India.[116]

Accompanying Ramabai on her voyage to England were her

daughter, Manoramabai, then a child of three and Anandibai Bhagat, a friend. Upto the time she left, the competing pulls of the Prarthana Samajists and Christianity do not appear to have been resolved because she had publicly stated that she had no intention of becoming a Christian at Pandharpur in November/December 1882.[117] Anxious about her independence, Ramabai had also made sure before she left that she should not be beholden to the missionaries in England who were arranging her stay and education, by organising support for herself as a teacher of Marathi.[118]

However, Ramabai's visit to England was crucial in decisively resolving the tension she had been experiencing about religion in favour of Christianity. She was warmly welcomed by the sisters at Wangate where one of them, Sister Geraldine, became her spiritual mother. Thereafter she always referred to Sister Geraldine, as *Ajibai* or grandmother.[119]

The decisive move to Christianity appears to have followed Ramabai becoming aware of the 'rescue' work carried on by the sisters in London. She was moved particularly by her meeting with women who had once been inmates at the 'Rescue Home', an institution for 'fallen women' and who were now so 'completely changed', and so filled with love for Christ and compassion for 'suffering humanity', that these women had gone on to give their lives for the service of the sick and infirm. Through this exposure the service aspect of Christianity was revealed to Ramabai for the first time and she was drawn towards it.[120]

At this point in her life Ramabai was still in search of her 'mission' rather than the philosophical aspects of faith; what appealed to her were the practical aspects of a faith that drew people into action. Her attraction for Christianity in the initial stages was thus different from other high caste Brahmana men such as Goreh or even Waman Narayan Tilak who were drawn to Christianity on rational and philosophical grounds rather than any deep attraction for serving others. She was also struck by the fact that Christians, who were regarded by Hindus as outcastes, were attempting to do something for those "unfortunate women who were degraded in the eyes of society".

> I had never heard or seen anything of the kind done for this class of women by the Hindus in my country . . . The Hindu Shastras do not deal kindly with these women. The law of the Hindu commands that the king shall cause fallen women to be eaten by dogs in the outskirts of the town. They are considered the greatest sinners and not worthy of compassion.[121]

Adrift emotionally since the loss of her natal kin, and a religious seeker for as long as she could remember, she finally sought an anchor in Christ for her emotional and religious needs. Back home, however, there was a hysterical reaction to her conversion. Among those who reacted thus were Ramabai's erstwhile friends. The supposedly liberal press, in the hands of Brahmana men, swung from eulogising to damning her for her 'fickleness' which was peculiarly female.[122] The conservative Brahmanas were of course vituperative. Only Phule defended Ramabai arguing that, as a truly educated woman, she was bound to break with Brahmanic Hinduism because of its oppressive practices.[123] The impact of her conversion was to have far-reaching consequences for Ramabai's relationship with her people as she would soon discover.

Although the sisters at Wangate had been instrumental in Ramabai's visit to England and her conversion they were unable to help her with funds. There were also certain disagreements that she had with the Anglican Church which have been documented elsewhere.[124] The experiences may have impelled Ramabai to go to America in search of support. She was apparently the first public figure from India to solicit funds for setting up social institutions back home. (A few years later Vivekananda too would do the same using a very different strategy and for a very different agenda.) Ramabai appealed to American women as women, to help the oppressed widows of India. It was to publicise their miserable state that Ramabai wrote her best known work, *The High Caste Hindu Woman*. The book was widely sold; proceeds from its sale helped to repay the Wangate sisters for their support in England and set up a fund for the opening of a widows' home in India.[125] At the same time the book functioned to disseminate information about and focus on the plight of the high caste Hindu widow, and it resulted in the formation of the American Ramabai Association to provide funds for the opening and continued maintenance of a widows' home in India. When she finally set sail for India from San Francisco in 1888 she had completed the initial task of raising funds but was clearly nervous about the task yet to be undertaken. The road ahead, she wrote, "seemed dark, unknown, and so difficult",[126] that she felt almost as if she were going back to a strange people. It was not without reason because her actions continued to be independent and defiant, plunging her repeatedly into controversy.

Ramabai's visible achievements during the years she spent in America and the drive with which she proceeded to set up the home for widows, which· she titled Sharada Sadan, the home of learning, could not but impress the elite of Bombay and Poona. The disappointment and opposition expressed even by the reform party at her conversion melted, at least for the moment, since Ramabai had succeeded where others had not even seriously begun the process of setting up such an institution. Ramabai desired to open and run the widows' home with support from Brahmana men, some of whom she had worked within 1882-83, since the concept of such an institution was still somewhat unorthodox. In order to take off it required public support from at least a section of the communities from which the high caste widows were to be drawn. Sharada Sadan was inaugurated in March 1889 with Mrs. Kashibai Kanitkar presiding over the function. Characteristically, Ramabai's initiative was now hailed by the press as an indication that 'native' society was alive and vigorous. The 'race' that had produced her had nothing to despair proclaimed a journalist in the *Bombay Educational Record*.[127]

During the first three years following the setting up of Sharada Sadan in Bombay the number of the inmates gradually went up. Ramabai continued her role as a champion of women's issues and participated in the annual Congress meeting held in Bombay in December 1889. Speaking before an assembly of 2,000 delegates, including 10 women, at a time when the 'liberal' Ranade considered it undesirable that women should take part in politics, she pointedly drew the attention of the men to the way they had marginalised women. "It is not strange, my countrymen" she said "that my voice is small, for you have never given a woman the chance to make her voice strong".[128] A few days later she took a strong stand at the meeting of the Third National Social Conference on the humiliation of child widows. On the issue of introducing a regulation banning the tonsuring of widows Ramabai argued that women should be left to decide for themselves "freely" whether they wished to be tonsured. Recognising the agency of women she insisted that a widow must decide how she would live: if they wished to have their heads shaved they should be allowed to do so. But at the same time Ramabai made it very clear that although she had come across a great number of widows she had never yet met one who was *willing* to have her head shaved. Driving home her point she demanded to know from the men whether any of them would have their heads shaved on the death of their wives. Using the by now common arguments of the nationalists of their right to· free speech, about "which a great deal had been said in that very hall", she ended by demanding the same privilege for women. She concluded that on her part she was convinced that if Indian women were given the opportunity to decide for themselves they, like the women of Sparta, would then join their husbands in the defence of their people.[129]

Ramabai's understanding of patriarchy, her ready wit and quick repartee also came in extremely handy when faced by hostile men and women. When the age of consent controversy created a polarisation among the elite with the militant nationalists championing tradition, Ramabai drew the attention of the audience back to the real issues that confronted women. Women reformers such as Kashibai Kanitkar and Ramabai were charged with sacrificing family relations at a women's convention in Bombay. A woman participant demanded to know from Mrs. Kanitkar if she would like her son-in-law to be sued in a court for infringing the conditions laid down in the Bill. While Mrs. Kanitkar fumbled for a suitable reply Ramabai shot back, "Never mind the son in-law, his life is not worth more than that of the daughter".[130] Despite unsympathetic audiences Ramabai continued to throw in her weight over any issue that affected women even if she was shouted down. And in a characteristic reformulation she redefined loyalty and patriotism in terms of the worship of mothers rather than some tokenist display of loyalty to the "Queen".[131] And finally her pragmatic approach to social and national questions is revealed in her advocacy of Hindi as the most effective language for the nation.[132]

Significantly, Ramabai's attitude to the remarriage of widows was very different from that of the male reformers. It was merely one way of returning widowed women to society but not the only way. In her conception, widows were not merely sexual beings whose sexuality posed a threat to the social order as feared by most men. There were a number of ways by which widows could live as teachers, nurses, or workers. At Mukti Sadan in Kedgaon her girls did everything from weaving, dairying, cooking, gardening, running a printing press and even farming.[133] What she did insist upon was that all categories of women, including widows, be fully integrated into the social community in which no woman was regarded as inauspicious. When her first student, the child widow Godubai, was to be remarried to Dr. Karve a grand reception was attended by fifty or sixty widows who had organised the whole function.[134] By integrating widows into society Ramabai was reconceptualising widowhood and womanhood in a way that most male reformers could never conceive of doing.

In November 1890, a year after the Sadan was opened, Ramabai moved to Poona as Bombay was proving to be too expensive. Orthodox Poona maintained a more effective surveillance of the Sadan and soon a series of controversies arose about the impending, or actual, conversion of Brahmana widows in the institution. Brahmanical society in Poona became hysterical. Deep-seated fears about what an institution for widows, would do to Hindu society partly explained the lack of enthusiasm for setting up such an institution. The fact that it was headed by a Christian woman had added to the anxiety, but now the rumours about conversion gave a hysterical edge to the fears. That widows, the dregs of Hindu society, should have the audacity to seek conversion was unthinkable. This would imply a recognition of women's agency — a right to determine the course of their own lives which even the reformers were unwilling to grant to women but which Ramabai insisted upon. Further, such an assertion of choice was a rejection of the moral order of Brahmanism. It would also be an open statement by the widows that they found Brahmanical patriarchy unacceptable and it was for this reason they wished to make a break from it. The attack on Ramabai by Tilak and others was virulent because Ramabai was not only Christian but in charge of an institution housing young women away from the control of male kin. In recalling the controversy first over Ramabai's own conversion, and then the widows in Sharada Sadan, we need to note that other women like Lakshmibai Tilak followed their husband's example and converted did not arouse the same emotions. Their conversion was regarded as 'natural'. It was Ramabai and other widows who had decided *for themselves* who were dangerous, not women who pursued their husbands into another faith. The entire 'conversion' controversy brought to the fore the hypocrisy of upper caste Hindu society. While the conservative among them were not uncomfortable about the degradation and humiliation inherent to widowhood the reformers went along with the idea of an institution because it would provide a home for their social outcastes. But even they did not want an open recognition of the widows' abandonment of their ancestral faith since this was tantamount to a critique of Brahmanical patriarchal tradition within which they had comfortably accommodated their own agenda of reform.

The Board's limited agenda for widows and Ramabai's differences with it were summed up by her in this passage:

> We must never expect to give anything better then food and raiment, and teach a few letters to the girls. I had from the beginning intended in all sincerity to give my girls full religious freedom. I would not prevent them from reading the sacred books of their own religion, so too I did not mean to prevent them from reading the Bible if they wished to do so, fully understanding what they were doing. I would never have tried to deceive them not to induce minors to learn my religion against the wishes of their parents and guardians . . . but now as the case stands I shall be obliged to let the girls have full freedom regarding their ancestral religion and prevent them from reading the Bible even if they or the guardians wish me to let them know something about Christianity. Here my conscience smites me.[135]

Ramabai found out the hard way that along with American funds came conditions and control. The members of her Board who reacted sharply to her position that she had a right to practice her own faith on the premises without having to shut the doors against her girls were, in turn insecure about how the widows of their communities would react to religious ideas other than their own. At the core of the controversy was the question: who has custody of women? Can women be permitted to decide for themselves? Clearly the reaction over conversion indicates that men were not willing to give up their control over the women of their community even when they had little use for them otherwise.

The controversy regarding conversions finally ended with the reformers on the Board, including Ranade and Bhandarkar, resigning. For a while many high caste widows were withdrawn. But as long as there was no other institution to go to, widows from the upper caste who had no home had perforce to be sent to the Sharada Sadan. Ramabai describes how, even when rancorous attacks were being made against her and her institution, the othodox neighbours of a poor Brahmana widow who was being persecuted by her relatives and could no longer bear the sight of her misery pointed to the Sharada Sadan as *the* place for her to go to.[136]

The threat posed by Ramabai's institution, given her refusal to submit to an agenda set by middle class reformers, finally led to the setting up of a widows home in Hingne by D.K. Karve in 1896. Karve had married Godubai in 1891. Godubai had been Ramabai's first student in the Sharada Sadan and was among those who had shown an interest in Christianity. Karve made strategic use of the panic among the Brahmana community of Poona following the conversion controversy to set up his own institution (and push the cause of widow remarriage as well). As Karve recognised, 'from the orthodox point of view, even the remarriage of widows was not so objectionable as their conversion to Christianity.'[137]

Karve's institution was very cautiously administered and his work on widow remarriage was strictly separated from the institution he set up for widows. Its regulations were so framed that a widow of the school who remarried had to leave. Further the institution was open only to Brahmana widows unlike Ramabai's where women and widows of all castes could study and reside.[138] In Karve's institution Brahmana reformers finally found the perfect institutional answer to their project for young widows: a widows' home safely in the hands of a moderate, respectable Brahmana man — a marked contrast to that "disastrous" first experiment they had supported which had been an institution in the hands of a defiant widow herself.

Looking back at the controversy over the possible conversion of widows, how do we understand Ramabai's action? It has been suggested that with her conversion, particularly after the confrontation with the Board of Advisors, Ramabai ceased to influence her society.[139] This view is only partly tenable. It is possible that Ramabai could only have influenced Brahmanical society in a certain way if she had remained a Hindu widow. But the argument can also be turned around — how far could she have gone in her own life and in her conceptualisation of society and of women's place in it if she had remained a Hindu widow, contained within the agenda set by men of her caste and class? Ramabai had tried to work within certain norms even if she did not agree with them. For example, she made arrangements for the widows at Sharada Sadan to pursue their caste practices; cooking and living arrangements followed caste rules at all cost, even if they affected Ramabai personally.[140] But as the preceding account should indicate there were *real* constraints in an independent woman like her which made it difficult for Ramabai to work within structures of patriarchal authority.

Further, it is necessary for us to understand, *without prejudice*, that as a deeply religious woman with social concerns Ramabai's dissatisfaction with Hindu social practices led her to find fulfilment in Christianity. Thereafter she insisted also on the right of all, including the widows at Sharada Sadan, to have that same choice. While she believed in the higher value of Christianity and wished to proselytise she did not approve of intolerance or sectarianism. She continued to have very close relations with Godubai who had expressed an impulsive desire to become a Christian[141] but finally remained a Hindu. Many years later Godubai, who regarded Sharada Sadan as her 'mother's home' and returned to it periodically in the early years of her marriage, went on to incorporate a sense of social compassion in the practice of religion learning from Ramabai's example of "service to others".[142] Further, Ramabai clung to the principle of free will at all times despite the awareness that it would annoy those whose feelings she cherished as, for example, when she insisted that Manorama her daughter, decide for herself which particular sect of the Christian Church appealed to her.[143] Ramabai's position on religion was summed up as "neutrality in the Sharada Sadan in matters of religion along with liberty", and the right to exercise choice in matters of faith.[144]

If the break with Brahmanical/Hindu society came, it came consciously, but it was also inevitable given Ramabai's personality and the work she set out to do. Further it is also necessary to bear in mind that the years of controversy over the working of Sharada Sadan coincided with the struggle between various factions within the Poona elite reaching a high point of intensity. Tilak had used every issue of gender or religion to consolidate his base among the upper castes and had successfully wrenched leadership away from the moderate reformers. The marginalised reformers were caught on the horns of a dilemma. They broadly supported Ramabai's work but, in the face of the conservative assault upon them, did not wish to be marginalised further on the rights of widows to decide for themselves whether they wished to remain Hindus or adopt the religion of their beloved Ramabai. The break with Ramabai was inevitable given their own larger concerns of continuing to stake their claim for social leadership in Maharashtra against Brahmanas like Tilak. By the last decade of the nineteenth century the struggles of contending parties to define the social and national agenda had reached a flashpoint. The year of the controversy at Sharada Sadan also coincided with Vivekananda's address to the Chicago Parliament of Religions and his public denial in America of oppressive practices for widows in India.[145]

### Epilogue

It is because the 'nation' has come to be viewed, even by those who regard themselves as secular, in terms of a predominantly Hindu ethos that there has been a certain ambiguity about Ramabai's place in Indian society. If it were not so it would be apparent that neither her conversion to Christianity nor her use of funds from American supporters, nor even her acceptance of the colonial government's facilities for the education and welfare of women can make her a 'betrayer' of the nation. We have documented elsewhere Ramabai's conflict with the colonial government and her understanding of the manner in which colonial patriarchy interlocked with indigenous patriarchy to tyrannise women. We have also documented Ramabai's conflict with the Anglican church.[146] Her focus, at all times, was the *Indian* woman. As Phule argued, patriotism needed to be redefined: was it patriotic to oppress one's own people — the lower castes — while waxing eloquent about opposing the colonial government?[147] On our part we need to recognise that it is time to break down the false divide on loyalty to the nation created by those without real concern for its oppressed sections. It was not that Phule and Ramabai betrayed the nation, rather that they and their concerns were betrayed by nationalism.

### Notes

[1] Gabriele Dietrich, *Reflections on the Women's Movement; Religion, Economy and Development* (Delhi: Horizon Books, 1992), pp.21 ff.

[2] Flavia Agnes, who has been active in the women's movement in India from the Seventies onwards, raised the issue of the movement being 'officially' secular but in practice Hindu, in its cultural orientation at the conference of women activists held in Calicut in December 1990, and the Indian Association of Women's Studies Conference held in Calcutta in February 1991. She also suggested that while women from the minority communities had to break with their religious traditions to be regarded as 'secular' the break did not have to be so sharp in the case of women from a Hindu background.

[5] Padmini Sengupta, *Pandita Ramabai Saraswati: Her Life and Work* (Bombay: Asia Publishing House, 1970), 141 ff; 204.

[4] In popular parlance fundamentalism is often associated with those who regard particular religious traditions as having a sole claim to truth. In this sense Ramabai's belief in Christianity might be regarded as a fundamentalist view. However, if we consider a 'fundamentalist' position as a belief in a rigid, unchanging core as the essence of religion then Ramabai was far from being a fundamentalist. Ramabai's handling of religion was unorthodox, critical and highly individualistic. She accepted certain aspects of Christianity and dropped others according to personal, social and cultural criteria.

[5] *Mahratta*, 22 March 1891.

[6] The power of the Brahmanas has been aptly summed up thus: of the significant concentrations of power in society, namely the institutions of religion, the administration and the ownership of land, the Chitpavans virtually controlled all three. Their status in the scale of caste assured their supremacy over the institution of religion; their ties with the Peshwas secured for them a monopoly over the administration; and finally the ties of caste once again encouraged the Peshwas to create a landed aristocracy which was recruited from Brahmana families and in whose loyalty they could rely in all circumstances. Ravinder Kumar, *Western India in the Nineteenth Century: A Study in the Social History of Maharashtra* (London: Routledge and Kegan Paul, 1968), p.44.

[7] B.G. Gokhale, *Poona in the Eighteenth Century: An Urban History* (Delhi: Oxford University Press, 1988), pp.166 ff. Meera Kosambi, "Glory of Peshwa Pune" in *Economic and Political Weekly*, Vol.XXIV, No.5: 1989, p.248.

[8] Ravinder Kumar, Western India in the Nineteenth Century op. cit., p.39.

[9] Andre Wink, *Land and Sovereignty in India: Agrarian Society and Politics under the Eighteenth Century Maratha Swarajya* (Cambridge: Cambridge University Press, 1986), p.232.

[10] Thomas Duer Broghton, *Letters Written in a Mahratha Camp During the Year 1908* (London: John Murray, 1813), p. 76, cited in Rosalind O'Hanlon, *Caste, Conflict and Ideology* (Cambridge: Cambridge University Press, 1985), p. 17, n.5.

[11] Hiroshi Fukazawa, "State and Caste System (Jati) in the Eighteenth Century Maratha Kingdom", *Hitotsubashi Journal of Economics* Vol. IX, No.1: June 1968, pp. 32-44, (republished in Fukazawa, *The Medieval Deccan: Peasants, Social Systems and States, Sixteenth to Eighteenth Centuries* (Delhi: Oxford University Press, 1991).

[12] Ibid. pp. 41-42

[13] Ibid. p.43.

[14] Uma Chakravarti, "Conceptualising Brahmanical Patriarchy in Early India: Gender, Caste, Class and State", *Economic and Political Weekly* Vol. XXVIII, No.14, April 3: 1993, pp. 579-85.

[15] See for example the argument of the upwardly mobile Sonars in Wagle's account, regarding enforced widowhood and tonsure of widows to substantiate their claim to the status of Brahmanas and thus to the Vedokta. "A Dispute between the Pancal Devajna Sonars and the Brahmanas of the Pune. Regarding Social Rank and Ritual Privileges: A Caste Study of the British Administration of Jati Laws in Maharashtra, 1822-1825" in N.K. Wagle (ed.)

*Images of Maharashtra. A Regional Profile of India* (London: Curzon Press Limited, 1980), p. 131. Writing at the turn of the century Arthur Crawford refers to the Sonar's continuing resistance to accepting the status of Shudras (Arthur Crawford, *Our Troubles in the Poona Deccan* (Westminister: Archibald Constable and Company, 1897), p.210.

[16] V.S. Kadam, "The Institution of Marriage and Position of Women in Eighteenth Century Maharashtra", *Indian Economic and Social Historical Review*, Vol. XXV, No.3: July-September 1988, pp. 341-70, p.347.

[17] Uma Chakravarti, *Gender, Class and Nation: The Life and Times of Pandita Ramabai*, forthcoming.

[18] There are documented instances of widows who remained untonsured for certain periods of time with support from natal kinsmen, mainly fathers and brothers. However, the Brahmana community invariably brought excommunication orders from a religious head such as the Shankaracharya, as for example the case of a young man from Karhad who was banned from marrying till his untonsured widowed sister was tonsured. When the widow and her brother defied the ban they were excommunicated. *Marathyanchya Itihasachi Sadhane* Vol. 24, No. 31, undated, cited in Kadam, op. cit, p.356.

[19] Kadam, "The Institutions of Marriage" op. cit., p.355.

[20] Ibid. p. 356, Fukazawa, "State and Caste System", pp. 34 ff.

[21] Kadam, "The Institutions of Marriage", op. cit. pp. 343, 346-47, 349-55.

[22] Kenneth Ballhatchet, *Social Policy and Social Change in Western India: 1817-1830* (London: Oxford University Press, 1957), pp. 30-33.

[23] Ibid. pp. 73-87. Also see Laurence W. Preston, "The Authority of the State in Western India, 1818-1857", in N.K. Wagle, *City, Countryside and Society in Maharashtra* (Toronto: University of Toronto, 1988), pp. 77-95, p. 79.

[24] R. D. Choksey, *The Last Phase: Selections From the Deccan Commissioner's File (Peshwa Daftar) 1815-1818, With an Introductory Note on the British Diplomacy at the Court of the Peshwa* (Bombay: Phoenix Publications, 1948), pp. 223 ff.

[25] On the whole women were not an important element in the agenda of the colonial state in the early years of their rule in the Poona Deccan. In fact they were dispensible. This is starkly evident from the case of the murder of a young girl of 15 or 16 by Appa Desai the great Jagirdar of Nipani in 1825. For reasons of expediency the British decided not to intervene regarding the murder as a "minor irregularity". Further it was argued that since under the Peshwas the great Jagirdars had powers of life and death over their subjects there was no justification for the government to intervene. Ballhatchet, *Social Policy and Social Change*, op. cit., p. 210.

[26] Wagle has meticulously documented one of the earliest disputes between the Pancal Devajna Rathakaras or the Konkane Sonars and the Chitpavan Brahmanas of Poona which the British administration was required to arbitrate in 1822 and became a test case for the British position on caste disputes. N.K. Wagle.

[27] O'Hanlon, op. cit., pp. 24 ff; M.N. Srinivas, *Social Change in Modern India* (Bombay: Orient Longman, 1972), pp.96-100.

[28] Wagle, "A Dispute", pp. 130-31; Arthur Steele, *The Hindu Castes, Their Law, Religion and Customs* (Delhi, Mittal Publications (Reprint): 1986), pp. 363-64.

29  B.B. Misra, *The Indian Middle Classes: Their Growth in Modern Times* (London: Oxford University Press, 1961).

30  Education for example remained a highly restricted facility for the lower castes with government aided education monopolised by Brahmanas and some other upper castes such as Prabhus. As late as 1884 out of 109 students in the Deccan College 107 were Brahmanas. Brahmana domination in education gave them a lead over other castes in government service and the liberal professions such as law, teaching and journalism. Thus in 1887, 41.25 per cent of the deputy collectors, 75.5 per cent assistant deputy collectors and 71 per cent of the subordinate judges in the Bombay province were Brahmanas. Gail Omvedt, *Cultural Revolt in a Colonial Society: The Non-Brahman Movement in Western India: 1873 to 1930* (Bombay: Scientific Socialist Education Trust, 1976), p. 64. Ravinder Kumar, *Western India*, op. cit., p.283.

31  Gail Omvedt, *Cultural Revolt in a Colonial Society*, op. cit., p. 64.

32  C. A. Bayly, *Rulers, Townsmen and Bazaars : North Indian Society in the Age of British Expansion, 1770-1870* (Delhi: Oxford University Press, 1992), p. 481.

33  Christine Dobbin, *Urban Leadership in Western India: Politics and Communities in Bombay City, 1840-1885* (London: Oxford University Press, 1972), p.6.

34  Ibid, p.38.

35  Misra, *The Indian Middle Classes*, op. cit.

36  Ravinder Kumar, op. cit., pp.307-08.

37  Ibid.

38  Omvedt, op. cit., pp.100, 110; O'Hanlon, *Caste, Conflict and Ideology*, op. cit., pp. 306-07.

39  Omvedt, op. cit., p. 98, O'Hanlon, op. cit., p.230.

40  Uma Chakravarti, "Reconceptualising Gender: Phule, Brahmanism and Brahmanical Patriarchy, Occasional Paper, Nehru Memorial Museum and Library, 1994.

41  Richard Tucker, "The Early Setting of the Non-Brahmin Movement in Maharashtra", *The Indian Historical Review* Vol. VII, Nos.1-2 : 1981, pp.134-59. The contestations of castes in nineteenth century Maharashtra are the subject of Omvedt and O'Hanlon's books cited above.

42  D.K. Karve, *The New Brahmans: Five Maharashtrian Families* (Berkeley: University of California Press, 1963); Frank Conlon, *A Caste in a Changing World: The Chitrapur Saraswat Brahmans, 1700-1935* (Berkeley: University of California Press, 1977).

43  Uma Chakravarti, *Gender, Class and Nation.*

44  Karve, *The New Brahmans*, op. cit.; Ravinder Kumar, *Western India*, op. cit., pp.284 ff.

45  Ravinder Kumar, *Western India*, op. cit., pp. 264–97; O'Hanlon, *Caste Conflict, Ideology*, op. cit., 88-102.

46  Anon, *An Introduction to an Essay on the Second Marriage of Widows by a Learned Brahmin of Nagpore*, 1841 (MS) National Library, Calcutta.

47  *The Times of India Calender and Directory for 1869*, p. 304.

48  S. Natarajan, *A Century of Social Reform in India* (Bombay: Asia Publishing House, 1959), p.5.

49  Richard P. Tucker, "From Dharmashastra to Politics", *Indian Economic and Social History Review* Vol. VII, No.1: 1970, pp. 325-43, p. 336.

[50]  J.C. Masselos, *Towards Nationalism: Group Affiliations and the Politics of Public Association in Nineteenth Century Western India* (Bombay: Popular Prakashan, 1974), p. 90.

[51]  Uma Chakravarti, *Gender, Class and Nation.*

[52]  About half a century later, in 1910, some widows did speak about their miserable lives without referring to the question of widow remarriage. A group of young widows studying at Karve's school for widows in Poona wrote essays on widowhood which have found their way into the India Office Library in London. These provide a rare insight into how widows themselves perceived widowhood as distinct from how it was perceived by others. For an analysis of this material see Uma Chakravarti, "Social Pariahs and Domestic Drudges: Widowhood Among Nineteenth Century Poona Brahmanas", in *Social Scientist* 244-46, Sept-Nov 1993, pp.130-58.

[53]  C.Y. Chintamani, *Indian Social Reform*, II, p.133.

[54]  Lucy Caroll, "Law, Custom and Statutory Social Reform: The Hindu Widow's Remarriage Act of 1856", in J. Krishnamurthy (ed.) *Women in Colonial India: Essays on Survival, Work and the State*, (Delhi, Oxford University Press: 1989); Prem Chowdhry, "Customs in a Peasant Economy: Women in Colonial Haryana," in Kumkum Sangari and Sudesh Vaid, *Recasting Women, Essays in Indian Colonial History* (Delhi: Kali for Women, 1989), pp. 316 ff.

[55]  Uma Chakravarti, *Gender, Class and Nation.*

[56]  Ibid.

[57]  Phadke, *Women in Maharashtra* (Delhi: Maharashtra State Information Centre 1989,) pp. 27-29. This promise was probably extracted as a reaction to Ramabai's conversion to Christianity while she was residing in England.

[58]  Mohini Varde, *Dr. Rakhmabai, Ek Aurat* (Bombay: Popular Prakashan, 1982).

[59]  *Indian Spectator*, 20 March, 1887. The analysis of the Rakhmabai case in this essay is summarised from my extended discussion of the relationship between law and gender in *Gender, Class, and Nation.*

[60]  *Hindu Patriot*, 14 March 1887.

[61]  Dayanand Gidumal, *The Status of Women in India or Handbook for Hindu Social Reformers* (Bombay: 1889), p. 196.

[62]  *Indian Law Reporter*, Bombay Series, Vol.X pp. 301-13.

[63]  *Ibid.* Vol. IX, p. 531.

[64]  Tanika Sarkar, "The Hindu Wife and Hindu Nation: Domesticity and Nationalism in Nineteenth Century Bengal," in *Studies in History*, 8, 2, 1992, p. 233.

[65]  *Mahratta*, 10 April 1887.

[66]  B.M. Malabari, *Notes on Infant Marriage and Enforced Widowhood in India* (Bombay: Fort Publishers, 1887).

[67]  For example, he described his reaction to the sight of mistreated widows as something that "burnt themselves into my brains. It is not merely that I know the miseries of widowhood, not merely that I feel them, feel for and with the widow; I am the widow for the time being." *Famous Parsis: Biographical and Critical Sketches*, (Madras: Ist edition, 1930), p. 438, cited in Heimsath, *Indian Nationalism*, p. 151.

[68]  Heimsath, *Indian Nationalism*, p. 152.

[69]  Ibid. pp. 154-56.

70  V. N. Naik (ed.) *K.T. Telang, Selected Writing and Speeches* (Bombay: Gauda Saraswati Mitra Mandal, 1916), 1, p. 242.

71  Dagmar Engels, "The Age of Consent Act of 1891; Colonial Ideology in Bengal", *South Asia Research* Vol. III, No.2: November 1983; Tanika Sarkar, "A Rhetoric Against Age of Consent: Resisting Colonial Reason and Death of a Child Wife", *Economic and Political Weekly*, Vol. XXVII, No. 36, 1993, 99. 1869–78.

72  Uma Chakravarti, *Gender, Class, and Nation.*

73  Mahendra Lal Sircar to Chief Secretary to Government of Bengal on the Age of Consent Bill, reproduced in C.Y. Chintamani, *Indian Social Reform* IV, p. 254.

74  *Times*, 28 July 1890.

75  *Times*, 29 January 1891.

76  Richard I. Cashman, *The Myth of the Lokamanya*, (Berkeley: University of California Press, 1975), pp. 56 ff.

77  Uma Chakravarti, "Conceptualising Brahmanical Patriarchy in Early India", op, cit., pp. 583-85.

78  Only one person, Waman Narayan Bapat, participating in the debate on the Age of Consent controversy tried to relate consent to a woman's will. He suggested that the wife should, when she reached the age of twelve, convey her consent to a respectable Panch appointed by the government who should record such consent before the consummation of the marriage. Dayaram Gidumal, *Status of Women*, op. cit., p. 119.

79  Heimsath, *Indian Nationalism*, p. 169.

80  Tanika Sarkar, "The Hindu Wife and Hindu Nation," op. cit., pp. 223–29.

81  Stanley Wolpert, *Tilak and Gokhale: Revolution and Reform in the Making of Modern India* (Berkeley: University of California Press, 1962) pp. 37; pp. 52–55.

82  Life of Bal Gangadhar Tilak, Political History Sheet, 1897, p.5.; Political Despatches from Bombay, Political and Secret Department, 1899, Nos. 23-49, India Office Library; cited in Cashman, *The Myth of Lokamanya*, op, cit., p. 57.

83  *Times of India*, 27 February 1891; Cashman, *The Myth of Lokamanya*, op. cit., p. 58.

84  Cashman, *The Myth of Lokamanya*, op. cit., pp. 62 ff.

85  Wolpert, *Tilak and Gokhale*, op. cit., p. 70; Tucker, *Ranade and the Roots of Indian Nationalism* (Bombay: Popular Prakashan, 1977), pp. 277 ff; Gordon Johnson, "Chitpavan Brahmins and Politics in Western India in the Late Nineteenth and Early Twentieth Centuries" in Leach and Mukherjee, *Elites in South Asia*, p.111.

86  *Mahratta*, 15 March 1891.

87  *Mahratta*, 22 March 1891.

88  Pandita Ramabai, *A Testimony of our Inexhaustible Treasure* (Kedgaon, Pune: Ramabai Mukti Mission, 1907,) pp. 12-13.

89  Pandita Ramabai Saraswati, *The High Caste Hindu Woman* (Philadelphia: 1888), p. xi.

90  Pandita Ramabai, *Testimony*, op. cit., pp. 11-12.

91  Pandita Ramabai, *High Caste Hindu Woman*, op. cit., pp.62-63.

92  Pandita Ramabai, *Testimony*, op. cit., p.16.

[93]  B.C. Pal, *Memories of My Life and Times*, (Calcutta: Bipin Chandra Pal Institute, 1973) pp. 305-06.

[94]  Uma Chakravarti, "Whatever Happened to the Vedic Dasi: Orientalism, Nationalism, and a Script for the Past", in Kumkum Sangari and Sudesh Vaid, *Recasting Women*, p. 33.

[95]  Pandita Ramabai, *Testimony*, op. cit., p.22.

[96]  Ibid., p.20.

[97]  Ibid., p.22.

[98]  B.C. Pal, *Memories*, op. cit., pp. 306-07.

[99]  Pandita Ramabai, *Testimony*, op. cit., p. 22; Sister Geraldine, *The Letters and Correspondence of Pandita Ramabai* (Bombay: Maharashtra State Board for Literature and Culture, 1977), pp. 17-18.

[100]  Sister Geraldine, *Letters and Correspondence*, op. cit., p.18.

[101]  Ibid.

[102]  *Testimony*, op. cit., p.24.

[103]  Ramabai Ranade, *Amchya Ayushatil Kahi Athavani*, tr. as *Ranade: His Life's Reminiscences*, (Delhi: Publications Division, 1963) p.82-83: D.G. Vaidya "The Arya Mahila Samaj: Extracts from the History of the Prarthana Samaj" (Bombay: Prarthana Samaj), cited in Padmini Sengupta, *Pandita Ramabai Saraswati* (Bombay: Asia Publishing House, 1970), pp. 348-51.

[104]  Ramabai Ranade, *Reminiscences*, op. cit., p. 83; Sengupta *Pandita Ramabai*, op. cit., p.351.

[105]  *Education Commission, Bombay, Vol.II*, September 1882; Pandita Ramabai, *High Caste Hindu Woman*, op. cit., pp. xvi-xviii.

[106]  Ramabai Ranade, *Reminiscences*, op. cit., p. 82

[107]  Ibid., p. 83

[108]  Ibid., pp. 105–06.

[109]  Pandita Ramabai, *Testimony*, op. cit., pp. 37;

[110]  C.E. Gardner, *Life of Father Goreh* (London: Longman Green and Company, 1900), pp. 274–76.

[111]  Max Muller "My Indian Friends" in *Life and Letters of F. Max Muller*, edited by his wife (London: Green and Company, 1902), Vol.II, pp.47-65.

[112]  Pandita Ramabai, *Testimony*, op. cit.,p.26.

[113]  Mukti Prayer Bell (Kedgaon, Pune: Ramabai Mukti Mission, September 1907), cited in Macnicol, *Pandita Ramabai*, p.59.

[114]  Sister Geraldine, *Letters and Correspondence*, op. cit., p. 18; Pandita Ramabai, *Testimony* op. cit., p.24; Pandita Ramabai, *High Caste Hindu Woman* op. cit., p.xviii.

[115]  Pandita Ramabai, *Stri Dharma Niti* (Kedgaon, Pune, Ramabai Mukti Mission: 1966 (reprint). The government bought six hundred copies for distribution in schools. (*Letters and Correspondence*, p.18).

[116]  The *Subodh Patrika* (12 and 19 November 1882) reported the gift of purses at her public recital of the Puranas. The Cheltenham Ladies College Magazine reported in September 1884 that Pandita Ramabai's expenses had sometimes been defrayed by princes such as the Nawab of Junegarh (see Sengupta, *Pandita Ramabai Saraswati*, p. 98.)

[117]  Gardner, *Life of Father Goreh*, p.275.

118  Pandita Ramabai, *Letter to Sadashiv Pandurang*, 1883, cited in Sengupta, *Pandita Ramabai*, p.129.
119  Sister Geraldine, *Letters and Correspondence*, op. cit., p.24.
120  Pandita Ramabai, *Testimony*, op. cit., pp.25-26.
121  Ibid.
122  *Indu Prakash*, 11.6.1883.
123  *Sastar*, September 1885.
124  Uma Chakravarti, *Gender, Class and Nation.*
125  Pandita Ramabai, *High Caste Hindu Woman*, op. cit., pp., xxi-xxiv; Sister Geraldine, *Letters and Correspondence*. op. cit., pp. 181-82.
126  Sister Geraldine, *Letters and Correspondence*, op. cit., p.184.
127  *Indu Prakash* 11 and 18 March, 1889; *Bombay Educational Record* cited in Sengupta, *Pandita Ramabai* op. cit., p.184.
128  *Report of the Fifth National Congress*, p.155; Sengupta *Pandita Ramabai* op. cit., p.193.
129  *Times of India*, 30 December 1889.
130  Sengupta, *Pandita Ramabai* op. cit., p.206.
131  Ibid. p.207.
132  *Indu Prakash*, 6 May 1889.
133  See for example, Sister Geraldine, *Letters and Correspondence*, op. cit., p.392.
134  D.K. Karve, *Amta Vritta and Charitra* (Hingne Pune: Stri Shikshan Sansthan, 1958) p.117; also see Anandibai Karve, "Maze Purana" in D.D. Karve, *New Brahmans*, p.71.
135  Sister Geraldine, *Letters and Correspondence* , op. cit.,pp. 268-69
136  Ibid., pp. 275-77.
137  D.K. Karve, *Looking Back* (Poona: The Hindu Widows Association, 1939), pp. 60-61.
138  Sister Geraldine, *Letters and Correspondance*, op. cit., p. xxvi, n. 22.
139  N.C. Kelkar,*Lokamanya Tilak Yanche Charitra*, 3. Vols. Pune Vol. I pp. 319-31; tr. by D.V. Divekar, *Life and Times of Lokamanya Tilak* (Delhi: Anupama Publications, 1987 (Reprint) pp. 215-24, p.223.
140  Sister Geraldine, *Letters and Correspondence* , op. cit., p.249.
141  Ibid., pp. 246-47.
142  Anandibai Karve, "Maze Purana", op. cit., p.70.
143  Sister Geraldine, *Letters and Correspondence*, op. cit.,pp.196-97.
144  *Ibid.*, pp.264,310.
145  Marie Lousie Burke, *Swami Vivekananda in America: New Discoveries* (Calcutta: Advaita Ashrama,1966), p.567.
146  Uma Chakravarti, *Gender, Class and Nation.*
147  *Sastar* September 1885, reprinted in Y.D. Phadke, *Collected Works of Jotiba Phule* (Bombay: Pub. 1991), pp.345–62; O'Hanlon, *Caste, Conflict and Ideology*, p. 203.

# Institutions, Beliefs, Ideologies
## Widow immolation in contemporary Rajasthan

KUMKUM SANGARI
SUDESH VAID

Widow immolation is one of the most violent of patriarchal practices, distinct from other forms of patriarchal violence, first in the degree of consent it has received, and second in the supportive institutions and ideological formations that rationalise and idealise it. In fact the violence, the consent, and the complex of institutions and ideological formations are mutually interrelated. The event is mythologised precisely because of, and proportionate to, the intensity of violence inherent in it.

It is analytically useful to distinguish between two kinds of ideological formation — general ideologies and 'religious' belief in widow immolation as 'sati'. Although such beliefs are indeed transmuted ideologies, distinguishing between religious beliefs and other ideological formations helps to understand how events of widow immolation are locally structured by belief systems. It also helps to clarify and dismantle the popular ideological category called 'the faith of the masses'.

In this paper we have tried to use the term 'widow immolation' to designate the primary violence, and the word 'sati' to indicate those structures of belief and ideology that gain consent for widow immolation. In doing so, we have tried to distinguish our usage first from the religious aura of the word 'sati', second from the discrete set of cultural values separate from the event that contemporary ideologues claim 'sati' represents, and, finally, from the voyeuristic discourse that widow immolations have produced in colonial spectators and their contemporary progeny.

Events of widow immolation have emerged from caste, class and gender relations as well as from different kinds of sectional struggles for power (political, cultural, familial, community). However, each event is quite specific and produced through a disparate and variable set of factors; that is, each event is structured differently in different contexts. Except for the central fact of the immolation of the widow, events are not identical. However, their ideological representations function to homogenise them. These are formalised first at the site of the event and later through institutions, wider ideological formations and belief structures. The institutions, ideologies and beliefs that cluster around widow immolation serve to transform widow immolation into 'sati'. They function simultaneously as structures *representing consent* (of the woman, family, community) and *wresting consent* (from the same). As such they develop a causal, generative relation to the recurrence of widow immolation.

Changes either in class formation or in the intersecting histories of specific social groups interlock with changes both in the practice of widow immolation and in corollary institutions, ideologies and beliefs. Their interrelated histories, common constituents and functions produce several overlaps as well as internal differences. Contemporary institutions, ideologies and beliefs characterise widow immolation in differing ways through a set of centralising notions: the volition of the widow, the potency of *satt* (essence of purity) or *satitva* (virtue, chastity), and the assignment of suitable roles for family and community.

Institutions centred on widow immolation function as an organised site for the production and reproduction of ideologies and beliefs, and represent well-defined sectional interests. Institutionalisation works to normalise and canonise widow immolations, and situates them as part of a regional 'history' in the public memory; a widow immolation cannot cross over either into public, patriarchal discourses, or into belief systems without the assistance of institutions. The 'sati' temple which sacralises violence is the crucial intermediary between the event and the renewal of attendant ideologies and beliefs. Without the assistance of institutions, widow immolation could not perhaps be made to provide a locus either for the organisation of interests or for ideological and political mobilisation.

Beliefs and ideologies are mutually dependent and interpenetrative as well as discrete and internally differentiated. 'Religious' belief in widow immolation as 'sati' constitutes a specific kind of ideological formation, which because of its existential emphasis on pain, suffering, death, and their utopian dimensions, can draw on wider, more varied areas of social life for legitimacy.

Beliefs have a long cumulative history which carries the sediment of previous events and earlier representational structures; it is partly from their longer duration that they are able to efface the modalities of their constitution and appear to be more autonomous than they are (thereby enabling contemporary ideologies to encash them in various ways). Finally, those gender, caste and class differences or wider political processes to which beliefs have a specifiable relation repeatedly reconstitute beliefs within changing social formations; they can thus function, paradoxically, to temporarily enhance or renew the relative autonomy of beliefs.

Although ideological formations that function in the name of anything other than religious belief have a narrower time frame, they also have a specific history related to previous and present ruling groups, intra–class conflicts and political, economic conjunctures. They, too, enclose histories of contestation; but whereas this is fairly easily discernible in the terrain of general ideologies, the 'rules' for the changing symbolic constitution of the immolated widow within belief systems encode the histories of contestation in different and more obscure ways.

The maintenance and reconstitution of patriarchies is the material basis common to widow immolation, related institutions and ideological formations. Therefore domestic ideologies are central to this entire constellation. Here too, however, it is possible and ever necessary to make certain distinctions. (Or, to put it differently, remaking patriarchies is at once the common ground and the space for internal differentiation between ideologies and beliefs.) Beliefs carry patriarchal values and practices around widow immolation in the direction of prescription, ritual, salvation schemas, supernaturalism, sanctification and worship: that is, simultaneously towards forms of fixity and memorialisation and dispersal into different social and religious spheres. Ideologies, at least since the nineteenth century, have tended to bring such values into active relation with broader, contestatory formations that address concepts such as Hinduism, tradition, nation or Indian history; these situate widow immolation in relatively 'historical' frames and tend to affirm the family or traditions as units of social order whereas beliefs tend to affirm domestic ideologies by sacralising them. Because of the location of ideological formations in contemporary patriarchal practices and values, the 'sati' cannot exist at a purely symbolic or mythic level: the actual widow appears to be central to the pedagogy of both ideologies or beliefs. Indeed beliefs and ideologies can coexist in structural and historical relationship and use each other for self legitimation, as in the case of contemporary Rajasthan where local beliefs centre on miracles peformed through the agency of satt, while middle class ideologies produce high traditions.

Although formed in reponse to the same social realities, the perceptual modes, historical duration, forms of address and engagement of beliefs and ideologies with these realities is different. The particular interaction between specific patriarchies, events, ideologies and beliefs is one of the factors which acts to *resubstantiate* social belief in widow immolation as 'sati' at any given moment. The particular location of the patriarchies concerned in caste and class formations determines for which women 'sati' acts as a general ideology and for which women it can function as a material force. The theories of female subjectivity which attempt to separate and reify the voman's volition — that is to represent violence either as a product of female agency or as being anything than violence — are in fact, methodologically speaking, working on the same model as the ideological formations that strucuture the practice of widow immolation. Essential to both is the suppression of the materiality of the event and of the processes that inform the immolation.

The processes of the formation of instittutions, ideologies and beliefs, take place in relation to caste and class groups whose interests and involvement can be differentiated in a number of ways. But whereas events, and to a lesser extent, institutions and active worship are localised, ideologies spread across regional boundaries and have acquired a middle class, urban character. In this essay we propose to discuss one such history of contemporary renewal, composed of the recurrence of events, the construction of ideologies, the emergence of institutions and the constitution of belief in a specific conjuncture. The question of the women's volition is central to all of them and can be understood only in relation to them.

The essay attempts to elicit several interrelated dimensions of the localised phenomenon of widow immolation in the Shekhawati region of Rajasthan[1]. The paper is divided into three section. The section indroduces the Shekhawati region and then offers a detailed account of a widow immolation at Jhardli village in 1980 in order to locate its commonalities with other immolations in the area, including Deorala where Roop Kunwar was immolated in 1987. These commonalities include the role of rajput and other elites of the village; the role of the police and administration; the centrality of belief in satt which mediates between the social and the supernatural; and the local operation of institutional mechanisms and ideological structures. The second section describes the recent history, present location, and contradictory and collusive relationship of the group involved: brahmins, Rajputs and banias. It also examines the influence of the Rani Sati temple which commemorates the immolation of a bania widow and analyses the contemporary popular narratives generated around this 'medieval' event. Thhe third section discusses the overlaps and distinctions between regional and metropolitan ideological formation; and concludes with an analysis of the interrelated issues of popular belief and the question of consent.

### Shekhawati

Culturally the Shekhawati region includes the contiguous areas of Churu, Nagaur and Bikaner[2] but present day Shekhawati administratively consists of the districts of Jhunjhunu and Sikar in the Jaipur division of Rajasthan. Adjoining Jaipur district, they lie within fairly easy reach of both Delhi and the state capital, Jaipur. Traversed by the Aravalli hills, Shekhawat consists of two zones, one semi-arid and desert, the other relatively fertile and densely populated. Most of the immolations have taken place in the latter zone, stretching from Danta Ramgarh to Neem ka Thana. The districts of Jhunjhunu and Sikar, though administratively separate, are closely interconnected, physically through road and rail transport, culturally through their peoples and history. Jhunjhunu was an important trading centre even before the fifteenth century and a stronghold of the business community; Udaipurvati, in the same district, was a stronghold of the Shekhawat Rajputs. Both communities, as we will discuss later, have played a decisive role in the recurrent immolations. At present, while most of the actual widow immolations are taking place in Sikar district, the nearby town of Jhunjhunu with its Rani Sati Temple commemorating a medieval widow immolation, has become central to consolidating and propagating a cult around 'sati'.

The history of this region suggests that widow immolation was not widely practised in the past. The rajput chieftains of Shekhawat, part of the ruling Kacchwaha clan of Amber (Jaipur) managed to gain some local power only in the renewed struggles for political power prevailing in eighteenth century Rajasthan. Even then, however, they continued to be vassals of the Amber rulers who did not encourage widow immolation. In only a few instances were ranis (queens) and women of the zenana (attached to the royal household) immolated with the body of a deceased ruler. This is in sharp contrast to the rulers of Marwar (Jodhpur) and Mewar (Udaipur) who gave a wide legitimacy to widow immolation. In these states, the practice of burning some of the ranis and attendant women on the pyre of a deceased ruler became a virtually obligatory and institutionalised practice and was emulated even by minor chieftains.

Unlike them, the Amber rulers did not make the practice a recurrent royal event and one ruler in the eighteenth century even tried to abolish it altogether. During the colonial period, Jaipur was the first of the 18 states of the Rajputana Agency to abolish widow immolation and to make it a penal offence (1846). Significantly, leading Shekhawati chieftains gave their public assent to this abolition legislation.[3] Of the sporadic instances of widow immolation that regional records show occurred during the colonial period, only a few took place in Jaipur state. The overwhelming number were in Mewar and Marwar. There is both direct and indirect testimony to the absence of an active legacy of widow immolation. The decay and neglect of memorials for widows immolated during the medieval and colonial period indicate that the social or religious significance attached to the practice had become attenuated by the 1950s. Not even all rajput memorials have been accompanied by steady worship: it appears that the decline of ruling families has been accompanied by a decline in worship. The evidence we have gathered reveals ad hoc attempts beginning in the 1950s to piece together a set of beliefs and rituals which have now become part of the standardised 'plot' of widow immolation in the Shekhawati area.

## Jhardli

The specific constellation of social, religious and cultural meanings that are currently being attached to widow immolation can be seen in the case of Om Kunwar who was immolated in Jhardli village, Sikar district on 30 August, 1980. Jhardli, located seventy kilometres from Jaipur, is an extensive village with a metalled road leading to it, a post office, electricity, a high school and two new primary schools. Most of the population of about 10,000, consists of jat peasants, lower caste agricultural labourers and artisans. However, the village is socially dominated by Rajputs and banias (traders). The social structure continues to be caste based, but infringements and changes have begun to occur. For instance lower castes now build houses of brick or stone, which Rajputs had not permitted earlier. Due to lack of employment opportunities, large sections of both the high caste and low caste population gain their livelihood from urban areas and services — construction work in Delhi; trading in Jaipur, Delhi and Calcutta; employment in the police and the army.

On our first visit to Jhardli in 1981, we learnt from the villagers that they knew of no widow immolation except one which took place "about two hundred years ago". One small memorial with a story of adolescent love attached to it marks the place where an *unmarried* girl of the Gujjar caste is supposed to have immolated herself for an Ahir youth two centuries ago.[4] There is, however, little room for idealisation in the facts concerning the immolation of Om Kunwar, a 16 year old Shekhawat rajput girl. Her husband Ram Singh, aged 22, a truck driver in Bombay, had been suffering from tuberculosis. The *gauna* ceremony, marking the time when a bride begins to live with her husband,[5] had taken place six months before his death; the couple did not have much of a conjugal life together since Ram Singh was being treated in various hospitals outside the village. Shortly before his death Om Kunwar is said to have written to her brother describing the misery of her married life in her in-law's house.

The story, as told to us by those who were closely implicated in the event, began with the death of Ram Singh in a Jaipur hospital. His body was brought to the village by early afternoon. The funeral procession was already on its way to the cremation ground when Om Kunwar suddenly ordered that the body be brought back. She had decided to become a 'sati'. The sensational news quickly spread, a four foot high pyre was built with offerings of wood, etc., made by relatives and some of the villagers. Thousands watched the event with shouts of "*sati mata ki jai*" ("glory to mother sati"). The sarpanch (administrative head of the village) set out to inform the police at Thoi police station eight miles away, but needless to say the immolation had taken place by the time he returned at sunset with the police party. Some villagers said, however, that he was one of the *arthi* (funeral bier) bearers, so the veracity of his claim is by no means established. Cases were subsequently registered against six people for abettment to suicide. The ashes were guarded from both tantrics and lower castes for thirteen days by young armed rajput volunteers.[6] This was followed on the thirteenth day by the post-funeral *chundri* ceremony,[7] performed not as it customarily is with relatives and friends, but with great publicity and fanfare. Two hundred thousand people are reported to have converged on the village that day. A trust was formed to build a dharmashala (resthouse for pilgrims and travellers) and a commemorative temple, and soon after, donations began to come in.[8]

Like most Shekhawat Rajputs, Richpal Singh, the father-in-law of Om Kunwar, has a small landholding, a bare five bighas (regionally varied unit of land measurement) of unirrigated land which yields only one annual crop. Like other such small landholders, both he and his sons have taken to army service. Richpal, now retired, was in straitened circumstances. Tensions over financial matters are said to have occurred with the deceased Ram Singh. He had been adopted by a widowed paternal aunt married into the Richpal family and both were being supported for several years by Richpal Singh. The aunt, a child widow, had adopted Ram Singh in the hope of having a provider in her old age.

The immolation of Om Kunwar was represented as a 'voluntary' act. We should note at the outset that every successfully carried out immolation is *always* narrated as a story of pure volition on the part of the dead woman. Hence the specific nature of the 'volition' must be ascertained according to the particular exigencies of each case and should be seen in relation to determining social, cultural and religious factors existing in this region. In other words a discussion of the woman's agency must be related both to the situation and to ideologies. There are indications that Om was already subject to various kinds of pressure. She was in a state of acute emotional tension and had a hysterical fit ten days earlier. During her short stay in her in-law's house she had gauged the hardships of a widow's life visible in the postition of her mother-in-law. A local brahmin priest, Jamnalal Shastri, had already presided over an earlier immolation in the neighbouring village of Hathideh in 1978 and written a propagandistic booklet deifying the widow and eulogising that event as an example of the purifying force of *nari dharma* (moral and social obligation of a woman). It is not possible to ascertain the extent to which Om's immolation was premeditated by the priest and the family, and to what extent it was 'improvised' by them at the last minute; what is clear from their *contradictory* and *contradicted* accounts is that far from preventing it, they were central to the decision making process at every stage.

Many of the rites which could only have been performed with the assistance of the family and other people, were projected in local accounts as miracles. *Mehndi* or henna has to be ground into a paste,[9] trunks have to be unlocked and bridal clothes taken out. In Om's case some isolated instances of such assistance were privately acknowledged — her elder sister brought her ornaments to wear, gave the *pujari* (temple priest) 20 rupees to buy a chundri, which was then actualry provided by her *dharmapita*,[10] a tailor. However, such details are submerged in the broader, public story in which miracles are assembled into a seamless, virtually self-creating series of events: water turns into mehndi, trunks unlock themselves, Om's bridal attire rises to the top, Om leaps unassisted on to the tall pyre, the fire lights by itself. The projection of mundane events as miracles has a dual function: it becomes a means of concealing and denying individual assistance and community responsibility (miracles by definition are 'unperformed'), and the miracles become the evidence of the presence of satt.

These miracles and satt are complicit and mutually reinforcing and it is difficult to ascertain which comes first. However, possession of a widow by satt is a prerequisite for being 'eligible' for immola-tion. Kappu Kunwar, Om's sister-in-law, described satt as a trance-like state in which the woman behaves as one possessed: in this state, the woman's interest in material life ceases, she is now in direct communication with god. What is remarkable is the unques-tioning co-existence of Kappu's description with her own memory that Om had behaved in a similar manner ten days earlier when her husband was still alive. At that time her behaviour was seen and treated as a demonic possession; but later, when Om became widowed, the same behaviour was seen as evidence of her possession by satt. The notion of satt appears to be flexible enough to incorporate and redefine any extreme emotional state. The chief arbiter of whether Om Kanwar was possessed by satt seems to have been the priest, Jamnalal Shastri. He asked Om Kunwar to reveal her satt and allegedly *his own* hands started to burn. Shastri also undertook to interpret her gestures, for example, he told us that Om had raised her arms above her head in the posture of one who had given herself up to god. (Om Kunwar's brother was said to have doubted Shastri's diagnostic powers.)

Since a woman who is possessed by satt is believed to have special powers to bless and curse, fear of her curse becomes a useful explanation for not crossing 'her will' or preventing her immolation: all decisions are henceforth ascribed to the woman. Satt is also supposed to endow her with the power of prophecy, the power to cure diseases and exorcise evil spirits, and the ability to will the pyre to light itself. The family recounted the blessings Om bestowed on them while the priest described her blessings to the village and her promise to grant boons to her devotees. The blessings conveniently absolve family, priest and village of all blame — they function as a reassuring sign of the widow's good will and their own good intentions in obeying her behest, i.e. carrying through the immolation. The statements of the pujari of the present temple dedicated to Om, as well as of Shastri, were in keeping with this rationale. The pujari maintained that Om told *him* to perform the last rites. Thus, obtaining the coveted position of the salaried pujari of the temple became the alleged outcome of the widow's *own* wish. Shastri and other's professed to have asked Om, once she was on the pyre, "*ab aapka kya hukum hai?*" ("what is your command now?"), and claimed merely to have obeyed her orders. Even in their own account, however, Om did not answer any of the questions related to prophecy and disease that were put to her before she was on the pyre; nor had anyone in the village either been cured or had their wish granted.

As for the pyre that lights itself, family and villagers admitted privately that this fire was lit with matches by a school-going nephew.[11] The myth of the self-lighting pyre was sought to be maintained, however, by other narratives — that of the headmaster, for example — which claimed that the fire went out after half an hour and *then* relit itself. And, according to Shastri, when the fire went out Om took an *agarbatti* (incense stick) from the pujari, waved it over the pyre and the flames re-appeared. Doubts had been and were still being expressed by some villagers as well as visitors to the village about whether this was a 'genuine sati' since a match had been used. Further, a harijan (low caste) woman told us that other witnesses reported Om pleading, "Don't light the pyre!"

The satt supposedly makes the woman immune to the fire and enables her to sit composedly on the burning pyre. The absence of pain proclaims the presence of superhuman power, signals the transformation of woman into goddess: ironically, the ultimate and incontrovertible proof of satt can be had only when the woman is actually burning. In Jhardli, the idealised versions (headmaster's, priest's, shoemaker's ) emphasise Om Kunwar's calm expression, composed behaviour, unmoving body as proof of her immunity to the fire. Movements which could not be ignored were rationalised: Om's swaying to and fro and saying she was in pain, and her pushing away of the brambles which were being thrown on the pyre in the attempt to relight it, were all explained as the pulling away of her satt by an evil *dakait* — a low caste worshipper of the god Shani (Saturn). The relatively less idealised versions were provided by a harijan family, who claimed to have seen signs of her pain and noted her efforts to move, which were impeded by the arrangement of the logs and by the throwing of brambles on her. In their perception the brambles were deliberately thrown to prevent her from running away — it seems she was throwing off the brambles even as onlookers kept piling them back on. The narrators of these less idealised versions did not doubt the validity of satt as a concept, they only doubted its presence in this particular case.

The whole question of 'voluntary' widow immolation hinges on the *local* acceptance of the presence of satt. Satt structures the interrelated, mutually generative factors of community participation in widow immolation as well as its wider perception. As is evident from the immolation of Om Kunwar, if even a theoretical space exists for the exercise of a woman's volition it would be restricted to a stage in the proceedings *before* the proclamation of satt. Once a woman is proclaimed to be possessed by satt, an inexorable logic is set into motion and she has barely any scope to protest, to change 'her' mind or even to grasp the full implications of 'her' decision, assuming that she ever made such a decision. Once proclaimed, satt only creates a space for the woman's consent not for her resistance — for not only does the declaration of satt itself depend on others who can *attest* to the miracles, it opens the way for wider community participation.

The transformation from an inauspicious widow to a goddess begins with the utterance of the word satt, long before the actual burning. As soon as this virtual transformation has taken place, the coercive pressure of the crowd's collective will to witness the 'actual' moment of transformation — namely the burning — shapes the event. For the woman, satt only provides the space for reflecting or accepting the will of others; she is swept on the wave of the gathered community's 'religious' feeling, compelled to die according to the dictates of satt. Satt makes the public burning of the woman possible by obliterating the horror of the act. Any visible evidence that she is struggling against immolation is itself construed as a struggle within her, between her satt and whatever is supposedly antagonistic to satt around her. Because her unwillingness to be burned is *seen* as an expression of the influence of elements antagonistic to her satt, it can be censored from the meaning, the experience and later the dominant narratives of the event. Crucially the concept of satt submerges the material and social bases of the event and gives a sense of religious euphoria to the mass witnessing of the immolation. At every stage, belief in satt becomes the religious equivalent of physical force.

Through the conception of satt the entire event of widow immolation is construed as an epiphany of divine intervention projecting its victim as the embodiment of *shakti* or divine feminine power. The power of satt is created in inverse proportion to and reinforced by the low status of women as well as by patriarchal ideologies. Without the prescriptive ideal of a *pativrata* or a devoted self-sacrificing wife the notion of satt would lose much of its potency. Significantly, local accounts of satt implicitly acknowledge its relation both to the social position of widows and to the patriarchal perception of widowhood as a continuation of wifeliness, particularly for the upper castes. The reasons given by local women as to why *only* widowed women are possessed by satt, embodied this acknowledgement either as an experience of victimisation (Om's widowed mother-in-law felt that god chooses as vehicles of satt those widows who have no one to care for them) or as an expression of mild cynicism (a harijan woman said that satt possessed women and not men because men can remarry). Local men placed satt as an expression of female virtue that is either innate or socially inculcated. While the headmaster said women in general have greater spirituality and fortitude, hence they, not men are the vehicles of satt, the priest ascribed it to the good, correct *samskara*[12] of the woman. The belief in satt functions to elevate what would otherwise be seen either as ritualised murder or as 'suicide' into a supremely holy act of wifely devotion.

The value which accrues from satt obtains both at the ideological and material levels. Traditionally widow immolation increased the honour and prestige of the family and clan. In Jhardli this has benefitted mainly the village which has become a sacred and well-publicised place. The power axis of the village — its panchayat,[13] priesthood, traders and the literati — seems to be in a better position to exploit the event than the family. Richpal Singh in fact complained that he had been denied his 'rightful' place in the temple trust (with its attendant advantages) because his political affiliations differed from those of the panchayat. The temple trust, consisting of eleven men, had amassed one hundred thousand rupees in donations within a few months. The village has profited from increased transport facilities, trade, inflow of money, avenues for the employment of labourers. These benefits evidently had been foreseen to some extent. Some deliberation had gone into the choice of a site that could become a pilgrimage place. In recounting the event, the local headmaster represented Om's ability to lead the funeral procession to an appropriate site as another proof of her special power; but other accounts, including Shastri's own, indicate that she was in fact *led* to the site by Shastri and others: she walked *behind* the bier carrying her husband's corpse. They chose this site instead of the usual *shamshaan* (cremation ground), for its accessibility from the main road linking it to Jaipur; its proximity to the older Ahir-Gujjar 'sati' site, and its suitability as an undisputed, unclaimed property. The eye to publicity was evident in the unavailing effort to procure a camera to commemorate the event.

On our second visit to Jhardli in 1986 we found that, as the villagers had anticipated, legal action had petered out. The case against the culprits had been dropped after a year for "want of witnesses". The village still had the same bania sarpanch. We also found some gain for the family; the temple established as a collaborative and profitable institution functioning along the joint axis of class power and caste grouping, complete with idealised and ideological representations of the event; as well as visible and invisible reinforcement of a patriarchal model for women. The gains for Richpal's family were petty and personal. A small memorial shrine had been set up within their modest dwelling. A set of bridal clothes, purporting to be Om Kunwar's, were on display, while a sword and sheath, emblematic of rajput valour, were newly hooked on the wall. We learned that Richpal and his brother no longer cultivated their small landholding themselves; the land was now leased to sharecroppers. This was a step up since it is considered to be beneath a Rajput's dignity to touch a plough. The large marble commemorative temple which had been built, and financed by both Marwari businessmen and Rajputs, represented a broader-based institutionalisation of the event. A marble statue of Om Kunwar on the pyre with the body of her husband in her lap had been ceremonially installed in 1983, graced by the presence of Sawai Bhawani Singh, the ex-maharaja of Jaipur. The composition of the temple committee was exclusively male and upper caste. However, the majority of the pilgrims were rajput women arriving in chartered buses to the temple, and donations came from towns and cities, not from the village itself, indicating in part the organised though invisible spread of 'sati' as an ideology. This same upper caste patriarchal model embodied in the temple and its activities was being visibly reinforced among lower castes. The old memorial of the Ahir-Gujjar 'sati' was freshly painted, a boundary wall had been built to mark the site of the 'proper' temple which was to be constructed by the caste groups in question. This temple was now positioned to face Om Kunwar's.

Scenes of the 'glory' of a rajput Rajasthan were painted on the walls of the temple dedicated to Om: Padmini of Chittor leading women to *jauhar*[14] and Rana Pratap with his famous horse. This was in keeping with wall paintings in other contemporary rajput temples which primarily draw not on local Shekhawati or Jaipur based legends or history, but on the glorified past of a 'Hindupat' Mewar, aligning widow immolation to previous rajput and nationalist constructs.[15] Also painted on the walls was a woman on a pyre with the rays of the sun miraculously lighting the flames, alongside various gods and goddesses from the Hindu pantheon.

Two propaganda booklets soliciting donations, one introduced by a local rajput lawyer, Raghubir Singh Rathor, and the other by Jamnalal Shastri, were available.[16] These printed booklets, containing prose and verse, biographical narratives and devotional songs, seek to *finalise* the formulaic public story of Om's immolation. However, they find it difficult to synchronize Om's volition with community sanction. Significant deviations and discrepancies — from the verbal accounts, from each other, as well as within each booklet — remain. In *Mahasati*, introduced by Rathor, Om is said to be publicly planning immolation long before her husband dies. This prior announcement is intended to accentuate Om's will, but contradictorily it enlarges the space for family and community participation. Shastri's cautious effort to blur his personal involvement is apparent in his introduction to the *Bhajanmala* where it is not Om but the community which has 'premonitions'! In Shastri's account, well *before* the funeral procession left, at a point when all Om had purportedly done was to put a coconut on the corpse and say "Hari Om", people were already whispering, "*Sati hone ka mahaul dekh*" ("See, this is the scenario for being a sati"). When Om called back the procession a crowd of thousands is said to have already gathered to praise her. Elsewhere, however, the *Bhajanmala* claims the procession was called back not by Om herself but by local children.

Though the details vary, the two booklets work within a similar ideological framework, situating the immolation in a structure of different levels and forms of consent. Both place Om in traditions of patriotic Hindu nationalism and in the line of the heroic jauhars and widow immolations of Rajasthan including the Shekhawati region. Both seek to revive pativrata behaviour as a familial ideal in order to counter the decline of nari dharma and the evils of westernisation; and both describe Om as a *roop* (manifestation) of the goddess Durga; both establish Om's satt as miraculous, thereby rendering legal intervention irrelevant if not sacreligious. Both build up the absence of pain: in *Mahasati* Om delivers an *updesh* (edifying speech) as she burns while in *Bhajanmala* she chants as she burns. Both depict a happy, elated and worshipful community; *Bhajanmala* establishes the community's approval or participation at every stage. Both contain lengthy accounts of the dissuasion of Om by family and village elders. None of these dissuasions express doubt about widow immolation as an event or about 'sati' as an ideology, only about Om's capacity and *will* to become a 'sati'. Indeed in both narratives, the dissuasions are a formal stage in the process of asking Om to prove her satt through miracles *before* the family and villagers concerned can 'permit' immolation. In sum, both booklets try to *disperse* the responsibility of individuals into the sanction of the community or crowd, as well as *concentrate* agency for the immolation in Om Kunwar.

### Deorala

Like Jhardli, Deorala, where Roop Kunwar was immolated on 4 September 1987, is a village dominated by Shekhawat Rajputs. With a population of 13,000 it is located only 30 minutes off the main Delhi-Jaipur highway. Deorala falls under the same police jurisdiction as Jhardli and Hathideh. During her eight months of marriage, Roop had lived for less than a month with her husband and in-laws. When preparations for her immolation began, according to some witnesses, she ran and hid but was dragged back; she was surrounded by armed guards on the way to the funeral, and her struggle to escape when the pyre was lit was prevented by these guards as well as by the logs and coconuts piled on her. Eyewitness accounts attest to her struggle, her shouts for help and her abnormal physical condition at every stage of the 'event'.[17]

The 'plot' or public account of the Deorala case replays what is by now an established formula for immolating a woman and representing it as 'sati'; it reveals a family resemblance to the public acounts of Om Kunwar's immolation as well as those of other widow immolations in the region, and runs as follows. The husband's death occurs after a long illness and is usually anticipated. The widow proves her eligibility by dressing unaided in her bridal finery, and by mysteriously producing henna marks on her palms and on the walls of her house. She asks her family to inform as many people as possible, leads the procession, personally chooses a site near the entrance of the village, instructs the 'ignorant' family pundit in the correct rites. It is impossible to prevent her because of the power of her satt (in this case evinced by the scorching heat of Roop's body attested to by an aunt)[18] and for fear of her curse. The senior male members and/or her father-in-law are inexplicably called away at the time, or as in the case of Roop's father-in-law, conveniently fall unconscious for three hours. The village patwari (revenue and land records official) or sarpanch is either missing or on his way to the police station, which he never reaches in time. The funeral rites are performed with undue haste, nevertheless several thousand people gather to watch. The movement of hastening crowds remains invisible to the police or, if they notice it, they do not have a sufficient police force to intervene. The hapless woman always leaps unaided onto a four or five foot high pyre and commands a minor relative (in Roop's case the 15-year old brother-in-law) to light it. Soon after, when perfunctory police proceedings begin, the child criminal is either transformed into a miraculous ray of sunlight or a whiff of incense that lights the pyre. Sometimes the igniter is eliminated altogether and, in retrospect, the pyre is said to have lit itself (here in response to Roop's raised hands). In either case the woman suffers no pain as she burns. By a strange collective amnesia the event, though photographed by a few and seen by thousands, is witnessed by no one. However, it is instantly commodified and converted into petty cash and large donations. The woman's life is recast as a hagiography, with eager help from her natal family, representing her as being pious or possessing satt from her childhood. (In this case Roop was established as a pious devotee of Rani Sati.) A temple commemorating successful murder is constructed.

This was the 'plot' of the Jhardli and Deorala immolations as well as the dozen others we have investigated. Everywhere, the onus for orchestrating the entire event is everywhere put on the widow. All verification is made to rest on the unavailable testimony of the dead woman. Every detail of the event is selected to disguise premeditation and to make the helpers and colluders invisible. Their invisibility is then represented as a divine miracle. In reality, of course, divine miracle is legal alibi. Not only is the crime consciously structured in *full knowledge* of the prohibitory law, it is also assembled around the *inability* of existing law to deal with community crimes, to take cognisance of and contend with patriarchal ideologies or to recognise and act on the nexus between religion and patriarchal ideologies. The political will to enforce even the existing law has been conspicuously absent.

Most of the immolated women in this region have been married into relatively 'impoverished' families. Roop Kanwar's Jaipur-based natal family seems to have been exceptionally affluent;[19] her in-laws were not. Her father, among those Rajputs who have gone into business, owns a transport agency. Her father-in-law holds an M.A. degree and teaches Hindi at the Khejroli secondary school. His brother is a city dweller (Jodhpur) while his nephew is studying medicine. Both sides of the family, whether in business or in education, have taken a leading role in glorifying her immolation as a 'sati'. The village itself has eight schools, a literacy rate of 70 per cent, electricity, radio and TV. Soon after the event, the village literati analysed news reports of the crime, disseminated printed pamphlets, composed eulogistic songs and poems; local headmasters and teachers took pride in the event and attested its 'miraculous' nature. In Jhardli, too, the school headmaster (a kayasth by caste) felt honoured to be the first to put a chundri on the fourth day, while a schoolteacher had assisted in the rites. A large number of Rajputs from Deorala, as from many other villages in the area, join the army. Significantly, the village that undertook to celebrate the Deorala immolation in a *mela* (fair) on 29 September 1987, in defiance of government orders, was Mawda Kalan. A widow was immolated here on 11 October 1975, and subsequently deified; half the Rajputs (who constitute about 90 per cent of the total population) in this highly literate village are employed in the armed forces. Similarly, relatives of other immolated widows — the father in Madhav-ka-Vas (24 March 1954), the deceased husband in Surpura (25 February 1975) and the father-in-law and brother-in-law in Jhardli — were employed in the army.

The persons involved form an amorphous group, difficult to define sharply in class terms. Not being either cultivating farmers, large landholders or agricultural labour, they are at once structurally peripheral to the local agricultural economy and integrated into urban orbits through trade, education or the armed services. Most of them have petty landholdings but their primary occupations are non-agrarian. Due to their upper caste status and their integration in the professions, the bureaucracy and the wider economy, they form an influential social stratum and are able to call on the local police and administration, many of whose members belong to the same set of families and economic stratum. Again, as an important section of the rural electorate they also attract political patronage.[20] Further, regional and community ties give them access to the more privileged classes in the cities. Almost every contemporary temple has influential patrons and donors:

ex-maharajas, politicians, and most important, industrialists and traders.[21] Without their financial support, not a single 'sati' temple would either have been built or be able to sustain its propagandistic function. Significantly, it is the successful immolation of a widow, which pulls the village out of mundane anonymity and elicits both social support and financial patronage from sections of the middle and upper classes in urban and metropolitan areas.

## II

### Brahmins and Rajputs

The village elite who orchestrate the event on site are clearly connected to and represent a wide and interlocking set of forces. The most central of these are sections of the brahmin, rajput and bania communities, who otherwise constitute a minority of the population. They have differential histories, internal class contradictions, as well as interlocking roles in the formation of supportive ideologies and disseminating institutions (temples, schools, melas, committees, societies).

Historically, the brahmins as priests, and the *bhats* and *charans* as genealogists, bards and eulogisers attached to courts, were important social groups in rajput kingdoms. Apart from their roles in the political domain, they were important in the social sphere and in family life. They regulated and maintained clan and caste superiority, arranged matrimonial alliances and played a determining role in the lives of women, particularly among the Rajputs.[22] They also assisted in the production of the ideology of rajput male *veerta* (martial valour), with all its prescriptive implications for rajput women — especially in the patriarchal practices and supportive ideologies of jauhar and widow immolation.

The contemporary role of brahmins, although less visible than that of Rajputs and banias is also important — whether as involved individuals, as part of local religious organisations, as forming regional networks that 'influence' and instigate events or as functionaries presiding over commemmorative temples. For instance, the so-called 'living sati' (her immolation was prevented in 1985) at Devipura, a few kilometres from Deorala, had asked for instructions from her guru at the Triveni temple located near the village. A guru from the same temple was associated with the immolation at Hathideh and the priest who officiated at Jhardli had links both with the Hathideh family and the Triveni temple. Since at least the mid-1980s local brahmin networks have tied up with other religious and educational institutions (*peeths, maths*) or, increasingly, with militant Hindu organisations for *prachar* (propaganda), *yagna* (ritual to make offerings to gods and purify the environment) and other forms of ideological reinforcement.

The brahmins, however, form an ancillary social group to both the rajputs and the banias. By the late nineteenth century widow immolation had almost ceased among the rajput ruling class and reported incidents are very rare within Rajasthan as a whole. But although this period was marked by the virtual cessation of widow immolation as a social practice, at a symbolic and ideological level it garnered fresh reinforcement, and acquired new shapes. Assertions of the 'exceptional' nature of the history of Hindu Rajputs as a 'race' and cultural group in part revolved around the immolation of their women. This construct was partly encouraged by British valorisation of Rajputs as one of the 'martial races'. Such cultural valorisation coincided not only with the kshatriya (warrior caste) self-image of Rajputs but, ironically, was coincident with rajput submission to British paramountcy. This submission, which ensured for the aristocracy a continuation of their position as a ruling class in Rajasthan, simultaneously enabled a mythical aura to be created around 'martial qualities'. A symbolic cohesion, which glossed over internal occupational, economic and cultural stratification among Rajputs, came to be maintained as group 'identity'. In part this colonial construct was a product of the romanticisation of Rajputs by Colonel Tod who incorporated the already idealised charan narratives of jauhar and widow immolation into the *Annals and Antiquities of Rajputana* (1829). The emblematic figures of these tales — the martial rajput and his consort, the brave rajputni — with their attendant ideologies, were re-used by sections of the emergent middle classes and became a staple of their cultural Hindu nationalism from the late nineteenth century (especially in Bengal) to the present. In this process the historical specificities of both jauhar and widow immolation were repressed and both practices became exemplars of willed self-sacrifice.[23] The defence, by sections of the nationalist intelligentsia, of widow immolation as symbolic of the cultural and spiritual glory of 'Indian womanhood', is part of a long history, takes many involuted shapes and has differing ideological locales that we cannot trace here. In its broad contours it produced a constellation of meanings which fuse a notion of 'sati' as volition with nationalist aspirations and with a specific idea of the nation. 'Sati' comes to signify an inviolable womanhood comprising ideal wifeliness, heroic death and ascetic self-sacrifice — grafting a set of patriarchal ideals onto nationalist aspirations.

Soon after Independence, nationalist reconstitution of rajput legend and history became potent ideological weapons within Rajasthan for another set of reasons and within an altered social configuration. At this time, a connection was frequently made between the mutually supportive nature of rajput cultural authority and rajput political power, in which the former, centred largely on male heroism and its female counterparts, was held to be the *basis* for both right to property and right to rule. The defence of rajput patriarchy became one basis for the defence of patrimony. The political articulation of this appeared in an agitation opposing land reforms that took place during the Fifties in the wake of the Rajasthan Land Reform and Resumption of Jagirs Act (1952, amended 1954). Initially the agitation was led by the Kshatriya Mahasabha, an organisation comprising ex-rulers and big *jagirdars* and the mass of petty landholders.[24] Their defence of the *jagirdari* system of land entitlement, which had been in use since Mughal times, was based on, among other things, a claim to its extreme antiquity (it was said to date back to "the dawn of civilization" and to the Vedas) and on the claim that jagirs had been acquired in return for "unparalleled heroism and sacrifice. . .in devotion to the cause of the Ruler, Country and Religion". Finally members of the Kshatriya Mahasabha claimed to be a class of hereditary landholders with a historical record of and potential for leadership in rural India — a class with martial traditions now in the service of the defence forces. Upholding the right of private property they condemned land reforms as "partial communism", and claimed that such economic discrimination against "one class of income" amounted to cultural discrimination against "one race or religion or language".[25]

Later, the petty landholders formed their own organisation, the Bhuswami Sangh, to carry on the agitation when the princes and big landowners withdrew in 1954, after arriving at a favourable settlement with the government. The epicentre of the Bhuswami

Sangh agitation was Udaipurvati, the bastion of the Shekhawat rajputs. The Bhuswami Sangh like its parent organisation, also mediated its opposition to land reform through a powerful cultural ideology combining rajput 'identity' with militant Hinduism. A contributory factor in promoting this ideology was its support by the Rashtriya Swayamsewak Sangh (RSS) which had become active in Shekhawati during the forties. One supporter of the Bhuswami Sangh explicitly conflates Indian, Hindu and kshatriya history identifying them with a nationalist defence of *"bhartiya sanskriti"* (Indian culture) which always had and must continue to rest on caste stratification and inegalitarian social relations![26]

The Bhuswami Sangh represented not only the existing class contradictions within the rajput community, but also specifically, the emergence of a middle class, with links both to modern professions and agrarian society. The majority of Shekhawat rajputs were and are petty landholders or *bhumias*,[27] needing to supplement their income from non-agrarian sources. Some have taken to business and academic professions, but from the mid-nineteenth, century onward, when the Shekhawati Brigade was formed, they have joined the army and police in large numbers. This service has helped them maintain a sense of their 'martial' tradition as a 'kshatriya' caste group. The leadership of the Bhuswami Sangh was drawn from the bhumias and jagirdars who in 1947 had formed the Ram Rajya Parishad, a militant Hindu organisation closely associated with several religious leaders.[28] This urban middle class leadership was able to mobilise small landholders in massive numbers in the 1950s to fight with "religious dedication in the defence of ancient rights to the soil. . .in the name of a kshatriya's religiously sanctioned claim to power and state and society." The leaders exhorted tens of thousands of lathi wielding, saffron clad rajputs to remember that their "ancestors" had fought for "dharma" and "their wives had committed jauhar."[29] The higher ranks of upper class rajputs had betrayed them. On themselves, therefore, rested the responsibility to preserve rajput tradition. Thus the ideology of the erstwhile rajput ruling class was, militantly propagated under transformed conditions, to defend the economic and social interests of small proprietors.

Although the agitation was finally called off in 1958, the claims to tradition and the heritage of Rana Pratap, Mewar and Chittor — consisting of the heroic rajput man defending the motherland while the heroic rajput woman committed jauhar or 'sati' — accrued a special strength from the militancy of the movement. Female immolation was vociferously regrounded in a kshatriya *parampara* or grand tradition, described as resting on the material basis of the jagirdari system (linked to clan ownership), political power and martial violence.[30] Though belied by the long history of rajput alliances with the Mughals and the British, the eulogistic representation of widow and mass female immolation as patriotic acts in defence of Hindu religion and custom aligned itself with certain nationalist tendencies and drew its emotional resonance from them. Significantly however, these were now directed against an indigenous, not a colonial, government. At one level the ideologies of the Kshatriya Mahasabha, and more sharply, of the Bhuswami Sangh represent their respective self-perception and consciousness as classes. At another level — even as the land reforms affected the class-divided rajput community differentially — a certain cohesiveness was nevertheless achieved regarding patriarchal ideologies. These ideologies of the Kshatriya Mahasabha and Bhuswami Sangh, linking 'cultural' revitalisation to a hoped-for rajput return to political power,[31] have played a part in activating social sanction for widow immolation as an exemplum of female *veerta* or heroism.

The grounds on which ideological cohesion was sought by the rajputs in the 1950s, apart from the broad assistance it received from and rendered to militant Hindu forces, was also crucial in the local self-definition of 'rajput' versus other castes at a time when the cultural power of rajputs coexisted in contradictory fashion with economic and political decline. Yet, significantly, a supporter of the Bhuswami Sangh, acknowledging class distinctions among rajputs, argues that Hindu power must now be sought on a class basis while retaining caste distinctions and community identity.[32] In mobilising rajputs in defence of the Deorala culprits, the present (Sati) Dharma Raksha Samiti (SDRS) draws on this legacy. The same class fraction that constituted the Bhuswami Sangh now leads pro-'sati' agitations and stages rallies reminiscent of the Bhuswami Sangh rallies of the 1950s.[33] Its ideological position on widow immolation both draws on and constitutes a development from the 1950s. Significantly, the ideologies produced in that decade have been in live interaction with the recurrent widow immolations carried out with impunity in this area for the past 35 years, starting with the immolation of young Taradevi in Madhav-ka-Vas in 1954 right uptil the Deorala incident.

The ideological formation as it has now crystallised is marked by the attempt of pro-'sati' rajputs to broaden the social base of support for widow immolation. This is in striking contrast to the attempt in earlier periods of rajput hegemony to preserve it as a 'privilege' of rajput women. There is a history of contestation of the 'privilege' to carry out widow immolation by other upper castes (and in isolated instances by a few lower castes) in the erstwhile rajput principalities. Nevertheless, it continued to be claimed as a special mark of rajput blood and rank. Now however, rajputs are attempting to elicit ideological support from a broad range of upper and lower castes. Regional, religious and patriarchal commonalities are invoked to give other castes groups a stake in the eroding cultural hegemony of the rajputs. In this attempt, patriarchal norms governing women are being widened and redistributed by bestowing upon widow immolation a central position, in simultaneous relation to rajput history and caste identity on the one hand, and to the purported essence of a homogenised Hinduism on the other. This can be seen in the pamphlets distributed and in the speeches at rallies organised by pro-'sati' groups and organisations in the wake of nationwide protests at the Deorala immolation and the new legislative prohibition of widow immolation and its worship (Commission of Sati Prevention Act, 1987).

In "Hinduon se Apeel", as in the speeches delivered at the 8 October 1987 rally in Jaipur,[34] widow immolation is made to represent a Hinduism whose patriarchal content cuts across caste and class. The pamphlet makes a simultaneous bid to create a regional identity and an overarching Hinduism: forced widow immolation is acknowledged as a crime, but voluntary widow immolation is said to have the sanction both of the Shastras in general and of their *own* local traditions in Rajasthan in particular. The pamphlet asserts that the present government, worse than the Muslim or the British, is the antagonist of a generalised Hindu dharma and of the constitutional right of freedom to worship. The men and women who dare worship Roop Kanwar are described as valiant *virs* and *virangans*. The sanctioning power of rajput tradition is claimed on two distinct grounds. First, identifying widow immolation with jauhar, they claim its practice in Rajasthan as superior to its counterpart in nineteenth century Bengal on the illusory grounds that widow immolation in Rajasthan was always voluntary and therefore was too noble to be banned. Second, since rajputs are claimed to be both a martial race and historic defenders of Hindu dharma, the legislation is construed as a direct challenge to which they must collectively respond. Widow immolation is used simultaneously as a locus for community cohesion and for universal 'appeal', for the pamphlet claims, the 'sati' 'tradition' is the property of many different non-rajput castes. This attempt to universalise the practice and ideology of widow immolation was also represented by the presence of various non-rajput speakers at the Jaipur rally.[35] Similarly, the statement of Devi Singh Mandawa, President of the Rajasthan Kshatriya Mahasangh, represents 'sati' as not merely the heritage of rajputs but also of brahmins, oswals, mahajans, menas, sunars, malis and nais.[36] These social groups probably have little sustained interest in maintaining rajput cultural hegemony in actual practice; any cohesion across caste/ class lines becomes precarious in the face of the rajputs assidous efforts to maintain caste distinctions in most areas of social life ranging from worship at temples, to use of village well and marriage arrangements. However, such alliances serve the double ideological purpose of keeping women in place and reinforcing a Hindu militancy that can generate greater consensus; moreover they often benefit the particular individuals and groups who take a leading role in mobilising them.

The indigenism of the SDRS pamphlet and the speeches at the rally is displayed in their abusive attacks on irreligious and westernised individuals, especially women — *azad kism ki auraten* (free/immoral women) — who are characterised as opponents of Hindu dharma. A sharp opposition, both regional and ideological, is constructed between the sexual immorality and independence of such women and the *patibhakti* (dutiful worship of the husband) demonstrated in widow immolation. Finally, all women of Rajasthan are upheld as exemplary: unmarried girls are virtuous, wives are faithful, never seek divorce, and widows do not remarry.

However, the social degradation of the widow is the patriarchal substratum of the ideologies of female valour and 'sati'. Economically dependent, most rural rajput women live in such strict seclusion that they are not permitted daily outdoor tasks such as fetching water or gathering fuel, let alone taking up remunerative employment. Unlike women from the majority groups, the jats and lower castes, rajput widows are not permitted to remarry. They are expected to be maintained by their in-laws and are deemed to have only a moral right to the deceased husband's share of property. Even if the in-laws abide by their responsibility to maintain her, the widow's life, stripped of the protection and status accorded by a husband, is often miserable. If treated badly by her in-laws a widow may return to her parents; but after their death she can expect little from her natal family. Often a widow adopts a male child to provide for her when he grows up. Widows must still remove all symbols of marital status, give up jewellery, suffer dietary restrictions, and wear only certain colours and fabrics. Although the severity of social opprobrium has decreased, even now a woman is required to sit for fifteen days in a corner on the death of her husband; and because widows are considered inauspicious, their movements are restricted to certain times of the day. The actual situation of the majority of contemporary rajput women is in inverse relation to the idealising myths created on their behalf.

## Banias

The colluding role of a section of the corporate business sector consisting of leading industrialists, entrepreneurs and traders hailing from the Shekhawat area has been crucial to the recurrence of widow immolation in the region. One group, chiefly of Agarwals and their subcastes, either resident or migrant from the area, is actively engaged in propagating 'sati' worship.

The enterprising bania community of this area (as of other parts of Rajasthan), collectively known as marwaris, has continuously migrated to other places and prospered. For instance, out of the 101 top business houses in India at present, 27 are of Shekhawati origin.[37] The local traders are 'poor' compared to their urban counterparts. It is the latter, along with metropolitan business houses, that provide a strong financial base for 'sati' worship. Through such financing, worship has been extensively institutionalised in recent decades within the region and to a lesser extent, in different parts of the country. Institutional modes, centred around newly built temples, have widened the spatial reach and diversified the channels for propagating ideologies and beliefs in widow immolation as 'sati' through ritual ceremonies, annual religious fairs, welfare activities, the induction of print, audio and visual media.

The Shekhawat Agarwal business community has more difficulty than the bhumia rajputs in negotiating its past history to claim the cultural symbols of the former ruling classes. There were some instances of widow immolation in this community during the medieval period but these may simply have been symptoms of proximity to rajput life-styles and a kshatriya ethos. For leading *sahukars* and *mahajans* (bankers, moneylenders and traders) were usually close to the court, and as financiers and administrators, they received various honorific titles from rajput rulers. Some of them maintained a princely style of living with armed retainers who guarded their goods on caravan routes. There are also some scattered instances of their participation in battles. Alternately, widow immolations among some bania families may have been early manifestations of a desire to appropriate rajput patriarchal practices and acquire higher cultural status.

The formation of a regional network, which has figured prominently in the support of 'sati' in the past few decades, dates back to medieval times. As traders, bankers, financiers and moneylenders, they were encouraged by local chieftains and village thakurs (landlords) to establish commercial centres within their territory. Among such centres were Sikar, Ramgarh, Lakshmangarh, Fatehpur, Nawalgarh and Jhunjhunu.[38] Despite large scale migration to the cities, the trading community continues to have a substantial presence in these towns and the adjoining villages.

The colonial period, often termed the 'golden age' of the banias, gave a tremendous boost to the fortunes of both impecunious banias and rich mahajans, and it saw the formation of a community network that now encompasses large parts of India. With the opening of the Delhi-Calcutta railway route in 1860, thousands of Agarwals from this region spread along the Gangetic belt to Assam, Bengal, Orissa, and farther east into Burma and South East Asia. Calcutta became the headquarters of marwari capital amassed through cotton, jute, oil seeds, opium trade as well as banking and speculation.[39] To a lesser extent, fortunes were also made in Bombay. From these fortunes huge havelis (mansions), with their now famous wall paintings (some of which commemorate widow immolation) were constructed in the home villages of the entrepreneurs.[40] This widespread network has determined both the mode of institutionalisation and the proliferation of 'sati' temples in several parts of the country and abroad (Singapore, Hong Kong). The period of marwari expansion was also the period of their sectional involvement in nationalist versions of pan-Hinduism of the one hand and on the other in *goraksha* (cow protection) movements in the 1890s and 1910s, and in engineering Hindu-Muslim riots in urban Bengal in the 1920s. Also around the 1870s they began to take a growing interest in tracing their own genealogy and origins, an activity that represents the contradictory face of expansion — the search for community solidarity and cultural authority.

Post-Independence policies provided further opportunities for expansion to Shekhawati businessmen. Families such as the Jhunjhunwalas, the Poddars, the Khaitans, now head leading industrial houses. Although these industrialists and businessmen no longer have the local economic interests they had in colonial times, they maintain their cultural and religious links with the Shekhawati area; one form this has taken in the past four decades has been the construction of huge 'sati' temples. The wide network of small traders, especially from northern, central and eastern India, has joined the representatives of metropolitan business concerns in their support for 'sati' by making donations, setting up local temples, propaganda and annual pilgrimages to Jhunjhunu and other 'sati' temples in Rajasthan. Here we will confine our discussion to the Rani Sati temple in Jhunjhunu, the largest and most influential of bania temples dedicated to Aggarwal woman said to be immolated in medieval times.

*Rani Sati Temple*

The contemporary institutionalisation of 'sati' worship by the bania community has three major aspects: the re-formation of beliefs and ideologies through contemporary narratives about medieval immolations and their dissemination in various forms; the relation between the ideologies produced and contemporary immolations; and the collusive material and ideological interaction between banias and rajputs.

The history of Rani Sati temple indicates that the participation of marwaris in a nationalist construction of 'sati' with its accompanying patriarchal values and Hindu chauvinism, began quite early but acquired a substantial shape in this region only after Independence. The commemoration of Narayani Devi, hitherto worshipped as a *kuldevi* or family goddess within the privacy of Agarwal homes, was converted into public worship sustained by massive amounts of money. The original shrines were small *mundhs* (memorials) in a forest at some distance from Jhunjhunu town which later expanded. According to the Census of India (1961) an annual mela, a temple managing committee and plans for minor expansion were all introduced in 1912. The main gate was completed in 1936 but the *mundhs* were not converted into temples until 1956 — two years after the immolation of a rajput widow in Madhav-ka-Vas in this region. The Rani Sati temple trust is privately controlled by Shekhawati Aggarwals settled in Bombay and Calcutta, and the 105 'sati' temples the Rani Sati Sarva Sangha has supervised in building all over India, consolidate a formidable network of donors within the trading-manufacturing community. While the present shape of the temple dated to 1960 (Census), the temple has continued to expand.[41] No longer a family deity of the Jalans, Rani Sati is now worshipped by many castes. Years of propaganda in the form of cultural programmes, commemorative and eulogistic meetings (Census) have paid dividends. Ostensibly a philanthropic venture, the adjacent Rani Sati Girls Primary School was established with 175 students in 1961. According to local accounts, hardly anyone came to temple in the 1950s; with the establishment of the school, students could be and were made to line up for daily homage at the temple — an activity suspended only after the Deorala incident.

The historical veracity of the legend of Narayani Devi, alias Rani Sati, is difficult to prove. The two dates given for her immolation — 1295 and 1595 — do not match either with the history of Jhunjhunu or with the number of generations of Jalans descended from her. What is significant here is not only the claim to historical veracity but also the ostentatious concern with historical legitimisation through alleged facts, research and evidence displayed by the official annual journal of the Rani Sati Sarva Sangh. This concern stems partly from the attempt to manufacture long genealogies to compete with those of rajput families and to emulate the rajput worship of *shakti* (divine female energy). More important, it reflects a need to institutionalise worship not merely of 'sati' as an embodiment of shakti — the defensive bania claim — but rather of a real immolated woman as 'sati'.

The ideology of the prachar and legends has much in common with that of rajput temples. More significantly it reproduces the same configuration — a compound of domestic ideology for women, voluntaristic versions of the event centred on satt and a relocation of family and community responsibility — which makes immolations possible. A large quantity of supportive narrative literature has been directly produced by the temple trust in Jhunjhunu and in its branch in Delhi and much more has been sold in the temple precincts, and distributed at public meetings arranged by the trust or its subsidiaries, in the past two decades.

These biographical narratives of Narayani Devi substantially negotiate the legal and social contours of contemporary immolations and their representations, a problematic that could scarcely have been carried over from the medieval period, i.e. presenting the woman's agency as orchestrating the event, the problem of the witness being an interested even culpable participant in immolation yet without whom the miraculous nature of the event cannot be established, the difficulty of squaring widow immolation as a product of the woman's own volition with the necessarily public and participatory nature of the funeral, and finally, the need to cite, establish and generate consent and belief as a basis of institutionalised worship of widow immolation as 'sati'.

The basic narrative of Narayani Devi is as follows. After the death of Narayani's husband in battle, the servant Rana, the lone survivor, gathers wood from the jungle and builds the pyre, She puts her husband's body in her lap, sits on the pyre, and then instructs him that she is henceforth to be called Rani Sati, and that in the temples dedicated to her there will be no *murti* (idol) but only a *trishul* (trident, weapon of Shiva).

However, there are essentially two versions of this story as well as several variations of each version in both prose and verse which contain different emphases. In the more common version, Narayani's life resembles the hagiography of contemporary immolated widows and the event is more or less 'spontaneous'. In the other, semi-mythicised version, reflecting kshatriya aspirations, Narayani is an avatar (incarnation) of Uttara (Abhimanyu's widow in the Mahabharata who is not permitted concremation because she is pregnant), and Narayani's immolation is predestined, being a boon granted to Uttara by the god Krishna.

Although neither version is fully mythical, the first version, unsupported by the predestination or semi-mythical paraphernalia of the Uttara version, is not only more involved in establishing a context for historical veracity but also with addressing the agency of those — family, servant — involved in the immolation. Both versions, however, are engaged though differently, in the struggle to free from responsibility those involved in the immolation.

In the semi-mythicised Uttara version Narayani is determined to be 'sati' from her childhood; she and her parents know through Krishna, who has had the event planned to the last detail from centuries, that soon after she marries, her husband will be killed[42] Krishna, disguised as a religious mendicant or *sadhu* (accompanied by his similarly disguised consorts, Radha and Rukmini) here functions as a surrogate brahmin and so provides a divine precedent for similar contemporary intermediaries! Krishna is an arbiter of Narayani's satt i.e. he tests her will and determination to be 'sati'. The job of dissuading her falls to him and to her mother. However, the dissuasion functions only to confirm or establish Narayani's agency and simultaneously constitute Narayani (as yet unmarried) as the spokesperson of patriarchal values that seem to emanate from her.[43] In one of the two variations of the Uttara version, once Narayani proves her determination, her mother shifts from weeping and scolding to joy, and later at the wedding, addressing her daughter as '*amar suhagin*' ('one who is eternally married'), bids her be a dutiful wife and to bring glory to both families.[44] The consent of the natal family to Narayani's future immolation being established, the celebration of the wedding becomes simultaneously a celebration of 'sati'. The Uttara versions thus not only spread satt across the whole of Narayani's life but are studded with miracles: the infant Narayani lights a fire magically, joins the severed head and body of her husband's corpse, stops the sun at ten past six so that wood for the pyre can be gathered, causes a well to dig itself in order to rectify the absence of water, and speaks while burning. The semi-mythicised Uttara versions acknowledge family and other participation more openly since they are able to displace individual and family responsibility onto predestination. Of course, Rana, who collects wood and builds the pyre, asks for and is given instructions in all versions. However, in one of the Uttara versions, he is not only represented as a loyal, feudal retainer of Narayani's marital family, but Narayani elevates him to the status of being Abhimanyu's charioteer and servant in every birth. She even changes her name so that he will be worshipped before or with her.[45]

The non-mythicised versions contain no scenes of family dissuastion and only one contains a miracle—Narayani restores a wounded Rana to health so that he can assist her.[46] The immolation is represented as a spontaneously improvised incident for which the only preparation is the pious childhood of Narayani, thereby reducing the space for family or community participation. In these accounts satt is confined to the time of battle and burning. In most, Narayani is made to declare, either after the pyre is alight or when she reappears after her death, that she is obeying her wifely duty and going with her husband of her own free will.[47] In one of the non-mythicised variations, where Rana is a bystander, Narayani discovers him worshipfully singing her praise before she has declared her decision to be a 'sati'; here, not only is Rana described as fortunate but participation in immolation is equated with worship and devotion so the man who actuates immolation is sanctified as a blessed witness. While Rana ecstatically watches the pyre, the gods rain flowers on it.[48] The trauma-free happiness of the 'witnesses' establishes the very mode of 'seeing' an immolation.

Thus the narratives of both the semi-mythicised Uttara version and the non-mythicised version, without acknowledging it, revolve around the contradiction between female volition and community participation, which they manage to displace but do not resolve. In attempting to do so, however, they reveal their own social agency in mediating the contradiction between 'spontaneity' and premeditation of contemporary widow immolation. The social agency of these narratives is also evident in the elements they share with actual immolations as well as with subsequent accounts and visual depiction of these immolations. These common elements involved are either replicated or remodulated by the narratives of Narayani Devi which are indelibly marked and shaped by the history of past and contemporary immolations. These narratives thus provide a mediating middle ground between the violence of actual immolations and the euphemisms of subsequent worship. We will take up only a few significant aspects that are common to most of the Narayani Devi biographical narratives.

The representation of Narayani Devi consciously establishes a continuum between a domestic ideology of husband worship and wifely fidelity for women, popular beliefs, a kshatriya version of nationalist notions of female heroism, transformational myths of satt and specific ways of institutionalising worship. These are especially significant because the banias have claimed, after the legal ban on the glorification of widow immolation in 1897, that their versions of satt, 'sati' and shakti are unconnected to widow immolation. Yet all of the narratives function equally as description of and prescription for patriarchal obedience; in all of them Narayani is taught her duty by her natal family, while in one narrative Narayani herself prescribes patriarchal conduct for her family.[49] The annual journal of the Rani Sati Mandir unequivocally states that the highest ideal for a Hindu wife is to maintain her contract with her husband upon his death which is what Narayani fulfils when, in obedience to her pativrata dharma, she burns on the pyre.[50] This high ideal cannot be achieved by all women but only by exceptional women such as Narayani Devi. Therefore her worship cannot be confined to the family alone. In this way the journal prepares a basis both for inclusion and exclusion of non-banias. Narayani is claimed as a *kuldevi*, a gooddess for a bania subcaste, while for all others she can be a universal *muradi* goddess, that is a granter of boons.

Satt as a rational for belief and the representation of the woman herself orchestrating the event are replicated in all versions. In most biographical narratives[51] the pyre is lit by her own *tej* (inner heat) or by supernatural shakti. In one variation, the servant is eliminated; Narayani herself prepares a pyre on the battlefield sits on it, taking her husband's body in her lap. She then prays to the fire god to turn them into ashes and the fire breaks out by itself.[52] As soon as the fire is extinguished, she appears in the form of a trishul-bearing shakti or Durga to the servant Rana and instructs him to carry her ashes to Jhunjhunu. She saves her husband's soul, becomes a protectoress of her kul (lineage) and lights the undying flames of satt.[53] In this variation, the other meaning of the word satt eternal truth — is intended. However, this truth or purity only comes into existence and becomes available through her immolation. Consequently its separate or general philosophical meaning becomes, in practice, both subsidiary to and inseparable from widow immolation.

Similarly, the visual depictions encash the same set of beliefs centred on satt which underwrote the immolations at Jhardli and

Deorala. Picture prints that show Narayani Devi as a woman on a burning pyre holding her husband on her lap have been selling rapidly outside the temple. The cover of a book of devotional songs shows a lighted pyre with a trishul planted on it while poised above is a woman receiving blessing and power from Krishna.[54] The forty feet long *jhanki* (sequential tableaux) in the temple enclosure depicting Narayani Devi's life and death, had an explicit, gimmicky transformation scene. The figure of a woman holding her husband's head in her lap, bobs up and down burning in red crepe-paper flames worked by a hidden mechanical device and a fan. As the figure subsides into the flames, goddess arises behind her with a trishul in one hand and a revolving *chakra* (halo) around her head.[55] As we were watching, a peasant woman exclaimed "*dekho satt kaise hota hai*" ("see, this is how satt happens"). The next two tableaux show the reception of Narayani Devi in heaven and her subsequent deification in Jhunjhunu with the help of a detailed model of the temple including the shrines of twelve women of the same lineage who were subsequently immolated. What the banias attempt to obfuscate is that the entire meaning of both the trishul as a symbol and shakti as a concept rests on the material fact of the immolation of a widow.

The significance of this reiterated narrative is enormous. Without the support of this story, Narayani Devi can neither earn her title of 'sati' or gain such status with her devotees. The meaning of the word 'sati' in this context derives from the story of her immolation and it has had this fixed connotation over the years. In all the narratives, the worship is instituted by the marital family, and not only the immolation itself but the entire modality of worship — site of temple, nature of worship, the kind of goddess she will be and the rewards for worshipping her — is presented in a woman's voice. The immolated widow becomes the voice of social sanction and provides a composite justification for the temple as an institution, even to the point of herself explaining the time lag between her immolation and the institutionalisation of worship. As in accounts of contemporary events, the widow *herself* seeks deification and publicity, but whereas the participation of crowds in the actual event is seen to exalt the immolation, here it is more the participation of crowds in temple worship that justifies and exalts immolation. The temple becomes the chief end-product of immolation.[56] The stress falls on darshan (sight of divinity) or paying homage by visiting her temples, i.e. not just on individual belief but on structures which reflect and solicit belief and crystallise it into public worship.

In addition to 'voluntary' immolation dictated by the woman and the self-lighting pyre, other similarities between the bania's defence of widow immolation and that by the perpetrators in Jhardli or Deorala also emerge from this literature. Both use ancient and medieval episodes to defend contemporary episodes of widow immolation, and both claim that opposition to the glorification of widow immolation past and present is anti-Hindu and anti-national. In *Sati Parampara, ki Jvalant Jyoti Shikhayen* by Ram Chander Vir,[57] not only does the introduction explicitly approve of 'voluntary' widow immolation, but a large number of widow immolations, both contemporary and historical (of which Rani Sati is one), are minutely described. Eighteen of the twenty contemporary immolations described in Vir's book have occurred in Rajasthan, and all but three of these occurred in the Shekhawati area. Not only is the proportion of historical to contemporary half and half, but past episodes serve only to legitimise the contemporary re-emergency of widow immolation in the area. Further, Rani Sati is placed at the head of coherent 'tradition' of which the contemporary incidents are but a continuation. Thus despite Vir's disavowal of supporting the practice of widow immolation, and being concerned only with the 'pure'and purifying ideology of 'sati', the two mesh at every level.

*Further bania and rajput convergence*

In their legends the banias have appropriated the rajput ideology of veerta, particularly female veerta. The explicit axis of assimilation is of course Durga and her trishul, more covertly it is a nationalist paradigm of the brave, self-sacrificing woman or virangana (a surrogate for all Hindus),[58] who dies in an actual or symbolic confrontation with Muslims. Most written versions of the narrative, insert veerta into domestic ideology. Narayani is projected as a virangana who engages in battle herself after her husband has died fighting the soldiers of a Muslim ruler. Her heroism is represented as a product of wifely devotion or satt;[59] in some variations she is shown fighting with a combination of *vir ras* (heroic passion) and *satt ka tej* (strength of satt).[60] In other versions 'sati' and virangana are conflated "*sati roop se shatru sanhaare*" (she killed her enemies with the power of her manifest form as 'sati').[61] Narayani's heroism displayed *after* the death of her husband and *prior* to her immolation is bounded on either side. Contained, it does not present a challenge to patriarchal norms. The 'sati' produces the virangana who also carries traces of Hindu nationalism. Narayani's contemporaries are represented as a "Hindu *jati*" *(race)* protecting their dharma by maintaining the pativrata tradition.[62] In one variation Narayani even fights the nawab (Muslim governor) herself; the nawab who is now elevated to shah (ruler), threatens her chastity and she kills him.[63] *Amar Virangana*, written after the recent anti-'sati' legislation to disapprove legal charges of glorification, recasts the devoted wife more emphatically as the heroic warrior of a quasi-nationalist parable, without obliterating her wifeliness. The story does this by first purposively omitting the description of the servant building the pyre, and second by omitting the pyre itself in the accompanying illustration. Narayani is shown sitting in midair holding her husband in her lap with a blank, empty space underneath; the narrative proceeds to describe the self-lighting fire and her transformation into trishul-bearing shakti who appears to the servant and instructs him to carry the ashes. An invoked tradition is clearly a tradition in-the-making.

The trishul, Shiva's weapon, also carried by Durga as shakti, has now become an insignia of 'sati' in bania temples. Not only does it carry resonances of Durga worship in Bengal with Narayani being compared to "*Calcutta ki Kali*" [64] but, as used by banias, the trishul also attempts to approximate the murti used by rajputs. It is made to represent a married woman, young and distinctly bridal in appearance: eyes are painted on while the bindi (vermilion mark), nathni (nose ring) and red chundri draped below or behind the insignia of the trishul, all indicate marital status .

The changing symbologies of 'sati' worship have a wider significance. At one level, the present cult is assimilative, and has marauded many existing modes of worship for its symbols. Further, if marwaris have capitalized on rajput culture and innovatively merged 'sati' with shakti, recent rajput and other temples have also begun to share the symbol. All recent temples have adopted the trishul as an appendage to the murti of a woman sitting on a pyre and holding her husband on her lap. Here too, in imitation of the marwari temples, 'sati' and shakti are coalescing. In the Kotdi temple, the altar virtually replicates the Rani Sati trishul. The temple office had a large framed print which represented Savitri, immolated two decades ago, as Durga astride a lion, carrying a trishul similar to the Rani Sati insignia. At the bottom corner was another such trishul along with wood, a small flame and the words *"jyoti prakat"* (flame manifesting itself) in reference to the self-lighting pyre. The site of Roop Kunwar's immolation in Deorala was also marked by a trishul with a red chundri draped over it to resemble the figure of a woman.

The present iconography of 'sati' in the area, the feminised trishul, embodies the convergence of several ideological currents and interest groups: assertions of a 'glorious' rajput community identity, aspirations to kshatriya status by the business community, militant Hindu revivalism (where the trishul is frequently used as a symbol of an aggressive Hinduism),[65] and the attempt to retain hegemonic control by the upper castes. Separately and together, they all fuel a reassertion of patriarchal norms for women. Some marwaris may be appropriating the 'heroic' medieval narratives of rajput culture, and some rajputs may now be vocally defending contemporary widow immolation, but the supporting ideology of both is directed towards binding women within a restrictive domesticity which can interlock with an aggressive Hinduism. In this sense they reinforce each other.

The marwari enterprise is interacting with contemporary widow immolations in a variety of other ways. Individuals from the community have been donors and participants at most incidents and members of this community frequently serve as treasurers and/or members of the committees formed to raise commemorative temples after a widow immolation has taken place.[66] The palatial Kotdi temple memorialising the immolation of Savitri, a widow from a sonar (a lower artisan caste) family, in April 1973, has been built principally through donations from Calcutta and Bombay businessmen. A photograph of a jhanki bearing procession lauding Savitri in Calcutta was displayed on the temple office wall. Reciprocally, booklets glorifying the Kotdi immolation have been sold in the Rani Sati temple precincts at Jhunjhunu. Family members and other persons from villages where immolations have occurred in the past 15 years have visited and been inspired by the Rani Sati temple. At least four bania widows, all belonging to relatively poor families in the community, were propelled into immolation in the late 1970s in this region.[67] The Jhunjhunu temple is the model for the Kotdi and Jhardli temples. Recent 'sati' temples imitate its modes of public worship, its organisation, means of prachar, and its performance of mahayagyas (large scale yagyas). Pilgrims to the Jhunjhunu temple invariably go to nearby Kotdi on the way and perceive little difference between the commoration of medieval and contemporary widow immolation, or between the legend and the reality. The visual, symbolic and ideological overlap renders the time gap between the two indeterminate. In fact contemporary cases of widow immolation are swiftly being recast as legend, their dates are already blurred in popular recall. It is no coincidence that most contemporary incidents of widow immolation have taken place within a small radius of the Jhunjhunu temple.

All three groups — brahmin, rajput, bania — are anxious to manage the entry of women into a changing society in which the situation of women is also changing. The ideologies interact with events and operate differentially depending on a range of factors such as class, urbanisation, caste and affluence. The rajputs' ideological propagation has resulted in the immolation of many rajput women; the banias' ideological propagation has resulted in the immolation of relatively few women from their own community; but given their wider networks, economic power and support for enshrining immolated women of other castes, they have been far more influential. Like the rajputs the banias, too, are interested in a cross class/caste ideology.

These two groups have specific relations of collusion at several levels as well as a wide complicity in the scale of values. At other levels, they retain a distance from each other. Each group worships its own immolated widows, and banias publicly deny that they support rajput immolations. At local levels, rajputs express resentment at the success of bania 'satis', cast doubt on their 'authenticity', claim that the government has 'favoured' the Jhunjhunu temple above their own and retain different interests as a community. However, the inclusion of Jhunjhunu into the 'sati' canon by the 8 October 1987 SDRS pamphlet, constitutes a thinly veiled appeal for marwari bania support and in fact, recognises their complicity.

In some indirect ways bania organisations have come out in defence of contemporary rajput immolations with the help of

intermediary priests. The Aitihasik Sati Mandir Bachao Committee, formed by banias in defense of the Rani Sati temple, issued a
pamphlet by Dharmendraji Maharaj. This pamphlet claimed, on
the evidence of Maharaj Ram Chander Vir, that there have been
no contemporary cases of instigated or forced immolation — they
are all products of purity, wifely love and female volition.[68] The
contents of the book by Ram Chander Vir have been described
already. Interestingly, Vir has been a participant in at least one
local immolation. On his own admission, he was imprisoned for
three months for abetting a widow immolation near Virat Nagar in
Rajasthan several years ago. While Dharmendra, who conducted a
Bhagwad Gita recitation for Roop Kanwar's death anniversary in
defiance of the government ban, has been part of the vicious anti-
Muslim campaign on the Babri Masjid versus Ram Janam Bhoomi
issue,[69] and was a chief speaker at the thinly attended Aitihasik
Mandir Bachao Committee meeting in Delhi in 1989.

At a practical level, the legislative ban on glorification has, for
the time being, led to an increased confluence of interests. Significantly, the Burrabazaar area of Calcutta, a business locality dominated by traders from Shekhawati and other areas of Rajasthan was
the scene of pro-'sati' demonstrations following the legislative ban
on the glorification of widow immolation after the Deorala incident.[70] The committee formed in Jhunjhunu to defend the continuation of the mela and worship of Rani Sati has been in open
conference with a similar committee formed in Deorala to defend
and expand the worship of Roop Kanwar.[71] The Deorala committee has openly acknowledged that its future plans for building a
temple and its legal strategy depend upon the success of the
Jhunjhunu case now pending in the Supreme Court. The Deorala
committee tacitly acknowledge the Rani Sati temple as a major
ideologue of the area and recognises the practical need for such a
centralising ideology in order to institutionalise worship.

### The metropolitan ideologies

With the strong protests following the Deorala event initiated by
the courageous action of Jaipur-based women activists, widow
immolation has become a controversial issue involving increased
subterfuge and obfuscation by its covert and explicit defenders. As
the legislation affects both the perpetrators of the Deorala immolation and the trustees of the Rani Sati temple, their petitions and

counter petitions at the Rajasthan High Court and the Supreme Court represent the alignment of sections of urban rajputs, banias and allied upper castes with those involved in widow immolation or its glorification at the mofussil (small town) centres. These ideologies emanating at the sites of immolation and glorification overlap or align with metropolitan ideologies producing an overarching ideological formation cutting across regional boundaries. This functions as a counter to urban-centred protest by liberal, left and democratic sections and organisations, including the feminist.

The first overlap is a consensus around the concept of 'authentic' or 'voluntary sati'.[72] There are, however, gradations and differences in the way volition is constituted. As we have pointed out, at the local village level, the widow's volition is its own opposite since it is embedded in belief in the agency of a supernatural power. For the urban supporter, volition usually rests on the liberal notion of rational choice. Here the notion of agency rests centrally on the woman herself, while in the former it is subsumed under divine agency. This transference of volition and agency to the woman makes the immolation simultaneously deplorable and admirable: deplorable because it is a sign of the miserable social status of the widow, but nevertheless admirable as representing courage to undergo 'self-immolation.' For conservative ideologues, the concept of volition is traversed by structured notions of cultural identity. They construct the immolation as a symbolic event which has the power to hold together all that seems to be in danger of falling apart: the extended family, female obedience to patriarchal norms, sectional group identities, Hindu tradition, Indian spirituality and the nation itself. Further, by representing 'sati' as definitionally opposed to modernity, westernisation and materialism, defending it is construed as combatting the colonial legacy.[73]

The second ideological overlap occurs in the arguments centring on concept versus practice. When the practice of widow immolation is, tactically or otherwise, considered, 'sati' is defended as a glorious civilisational concept or even philosophy: the Idea is maintained as a purified realm.[74] But can the 'idea' of 'sati' be isolated from the changing variables of custom, belief, practice? Are these separate compartments in the social lives of people? Do they not interact ? As it turns out metropolitan ideologues themselves confront this difficulty.

This is evident in their recurring anxiety over the 'true' meaning of the word 'sati'. There is an active debate on whether 'sati' is simply a good wife, or an immolated widow or the divine·female principle of shakti. Each of these terms has a complex social history, but all three meanings are compressed in the present social meaning of 'sati' as it inheres in incidents of immolation, modes of worship and domestic ideologies. Ironically therefore, to uphold any single meaning does not serve the desired ideological purpose and becomes a self-contradicting enterprise. The anxiety to preserve the three meanings as separate comes from several directions. It comes, of course, from those who wish to resist legal action on the charge of glorifying 'sati'.[75] It comes also from those who are interested in maintaining unviolated enclaves of tradition, heroism, asceticism or abstract self-sacrifice and in preserving the concept—alternately named 'satitva' and 'sati'—as sacrosanct while condemning the practice.[76] It is impossible, however, to separate the concept from the practice by intellectual fiat since the practice itself gives substance and social legitimacy to the concept.[77] Finally, the concept being primarily patriarchal, even the compartmentalisation of the meaning of 'sati' continues to use immolation prescriptively i.e., to define what a woman should be. Paradoxically, those insisting on a separation of meanings are in fact deeply implicated not only in the conflation of these meanings, but also in the patriarchal ideology that such a conflation represents.[78]

The third aspect, common to both local and metropolitan ideologues is a domestic ideology centred on the good wife as upholding familial ideals, with its implicit or explicit regulation of female sexuality. The patriarchal family is upheld as an ideal unity of complementary gender roles and as the prime practitioner of tradition, thereby evading the issue of family involvement in immolation.[79] The regulatory potentials of the ideology rests on representing widow immolation as an exceptional or stray event, not as a custom; otherwise, most widows would burn. This 'stray' event is then neatly aligned with a grand tradition or parampara that in turn is composed of a series of such exceptional events![80] The argument that it is a stray event is based on the statistically lower incidence of widow immolation as compared to dowry deaths. In this way, beginning with the SDRS, an attempt has been made to delink widow immolation from other forms of violence and crimes against women. This manoeuvre is based on the recognition that as the most public and publicised of crimes, widow immolation has enormous normative and symbolic value—is indeed more serviceable as an exceptional event.

Fourth, local and metropolitan ideologies are based on a common historiographic model which refines the distinction between custom and incident, and localises the distinction between voluntary and coerced widow immolation. Epidemics of widow immolation, as opposed to incidents, are said to be the product of either cataclysmic social transitions or foreign rule — Muslim or British. The onus is put, in a typically communal historiography, on 'external' elements. Bengal under the British is a hotbed of coerced immolations, while Rajasthan is proved to be (now and/or in the past) the sanctified home of voluntary ones.[81] Both claims are based on a species of anti-colonialim which makes a violent patriarchal practice the gift of an invader, and then uses this as a rationale to defend a terrible and recurrent abuse of women. The idealisation of immolations in Rajasthan remains possible because, unlike Bengal, the violence involved was not demystified by a reform movement in the colonial period.

Finally, the sections of the intelligentsia engaged in constructing pro-'sati' ideologies claim to be defending authentic Indian traditions — especially the culture, tradition and faith of the worshippers in Rajasthan. These traditions are seen as existing from time immemorial within Rajasthan where a religious world view has miraculously remained intact; they give a new lease of life to the static, self-validating sociological model of tradition versus modernity.[82] There is a direct investment here in an indigenist, populist notion of 'Bharat' and her tradition-led masses which can function profitably to maintain India as a backward enclave and as a cultural spectacle favored by neo-colonialism. The worshipful community is perceived as an undifferentiated mass that is inert in all but its faith. While this faith is represented as centred on 'sati' as a concept and on voluntary widow immolation, it is at the same time disconnected from the actual events of immolations and from supportive institutions. The worshipful community in these accounts seems to have little volition regarding the immolation of the widow. This is not surprising, since like local worshippers, metropolitan ideologues also set out to erase the fact that widow immolation is a community crime. Evidently such populist idealisation of the faith of the masses is quite selective because it obliterates from past and present historical memory not only those vast numbers of Indian people who have *never* practised widow immolations, but also those who did *not* and still do not share its assumptions.[83]

*Popular beliefs and the question of consent*

As we have seen, not only are assumptions of the mystique of rural backwardness or of an isolated village community in the grip of immemorial custom or indeed any argument resting on the 'belief of the masses', ideological in character, but local institutions and metropolitan ideologies obscure the constitutive and generative relation of ideologies (including their own) to belief. They create a receptive environment for those beliefs.

There can be no originary moment in the constitution of faith — it is a specific process which interacts with and is activated by forces within a particular social formation and with specifiable patriarchies. Belief is socially constructed; it is at once freshly constituted and has pre-existing or pre-structured constituents which can be re-attached to familiar and new objects. If faith was not labile, new cults would never emerge. Though existing constituents are remodelled or re-attached, faith in 'sati' is also constituted by the immolation, or as in this region, by a series of successive immolations rapidly institutionalised and commodified. Pre-existing symbols, existing and evolving structures of feeling, and modes of belief, enter into new relations with each other.

There are crucial questions of faith and consent which need detailed and rigorous examination. In this section we will only look once again at some of the issues we have already raised, the re-activation of faith in widow immolation and the various forms of consent to it, in the light of those new relationships which enable a reformulation of its pre-existing constituents as pure 'continuity'

To some extent faith in 'sati' has been kept alive by nationalist and rajput patrimonial ideologies which have maintained the concept of 'sati'. Private family worship of immolated women, mainly rajput and bania, has also played a part. However, contemporary institutions reconstitute these elements and represent 'sati' as a sign of unbroken continuity by eliding the new elements within the old. All institutions represent 'sati' as a sign of continuity — of wifely virtue, of tradition and of belief. Belief, whether rajput, bania or popular, is thereby represented as pre-existing. For it would be a contradiction in terms to take credit for authoring a goddess. So despite indisputable evidence of the contemporary expansion and reconstitution of worship, the goddess is represented as one in a continuing series of such objects of worship.

Belief is inextricable from the social processes that generate it; it has no autonomous origin; but once articulated in rituals and institutions it acquires an aura of autonomy much greater than other ideological formations have. And in this case the aura of autonomy from the material realm is partly generated by the very forces which play a determining role in the practice of contemporary widow immolation. Marwari finance is one element that generates an 'autonomous' realm for the parampara of 'sati' in the region. The divine miracle, among other things, also makes for an eminently commodifiable event. Belief in 'sati' is partly fostered by the spectacular and systemic commodification of the event. The best evidence for this, pointed to earlier, are the neglected, scantily worshipped 'sati' memorial stones which lie adjacent to some of the temples of recently immolated widows. Villagers often do not even remember the legends of small dilapidated 'sati' memorials which lie close to home and they flock in large numbers to the recently built huge, ostentatious marble temples. Without the glamour, recognition and institutionalisation of a palatial temple the meaning of immolation would neither circulate nor gather 'value'. The big temples legitimise the event, fix it visibly in public consciousness and memory, poplarise worship. They give the final stamp of 'religion' to the event. The huge sums of money spent in construction and acquired through donations appear like proofs of faith and belief. Faith and profit appear to run parallel to each other, intersect, depend on each other.

The circulation of reified values allied to the persuasive vocabulary of popular culture transforms the institutional mode of address. Commodification catches the gimmickiness of popular, especially cinematic, culture. All the pictorial representations of immolated widows, including the jhanki in the Rani Sati temple, depict the instantaneous deification of the woman. The neon and kitsch of the Rani Sati and other bania temples do not visually represent the authority of timeless tradition, rather they represent the authority of flashy technologisation.

To some extent, the effectivity of 'sati' as a universalising ideology depends both on the syncretic nature of belief and of popular modes of worship, which enable it to touch the lives of different people in various ways. Significant overlaps also exist with a wide range of other forms of worship. The connections of 'sati' worship with a popular composite culture are mainly limited to the belief in the new 'sati' goddess as muraad (boon) giver which overlaps with the already syncretic pir traditions in Rajasthan. Votive offerings at the tomb of a pir, usually a holy Muslim man, are made by people of all communities. Syncretisation from various Hindu customs and traditions include innumerable private and public rituals: festivals like Gangaur and Teej which are structured around acquiring or preserving women's *suhaag* (marital status), and other rituals performed on occasions such as birth and marriage, overlap in content, method and assumptions with those now built around 'sati' worship. Both Gangaur and Teej are popular Rajasthani festivals in honour of Parvati, the consort of Shiva; they are observed by unmarried girls to obtain a good husband and by married women to preserve marital happiness.

We would, however, like to stress the problematic nature of syncretism both as a general concept as well as in 'sati' worship. As a concept, the positive connotations of liberal pluralism which syncretism acquired during the nationalist period (especially in the struggle against communalism) tend to obscure its transactional aspects. Further, the much applauded internal flexibility or adaptability of Hinduism acquires another meaning in the matter of widow immolation. Here, an intra-Hindu syncretism functions, through specific transactions, to normalise 'sati' worship by drawing it into active relation with other adjacent modes of worship. For example, the narratives and devotional literature about the Jhardli immolation (like those that surround other contemporary immolations as well as Narayani Devi of Jhunjhunu) place the widow in traditions of puranic Hinduism, ascetic renunciation, yog, bhakti,[84] Durga worship, local gurus, recent cults (e.g., Santoshi Ma) and simultaneously into a composite regional and national tradition comprising Mirabai, Padmini, Lakshmibai, thereby amalgamating bhakti with anti-Muslim and anti-British sentiments. Such syncretism functions on a variety of fronts — drawing on generally acceptable pantheons, new and old, Shaivite and Vaishnavite — to fit 'sati' worship into generalised worship, easing cross-caste participation. In both rajput and bania temples, the use of popular bhajans, (devotional songs), some of them specially adapted to 'sati' worship, as well as 'sati' bhajans based on Bombay film songs and marriage or *bidai* songs (the latter sorrowfully bid farewell to the departing new bride), relates the 'sati' worship to a customary sphere and inserts it into popular culture. The syncretism draws into its ambit even those traditions which are indifferent or hostile to widow immolation. For instance the incorporation of Mirabai as emblematic of ascetism or renunciation and thereby an ancestress in the 'sati' tradition, obliterates the sharp opposition that Mirabai's corpus contains to widow immolation and to some other patriarchal practices. The overlaps with other forms of worship cannot therefore be interpreted in a formalist language which ignores their contextual and substantive nature.

In the assimilation of 'sati' into other forms of worship, not only does 'sati' worship *retain* its ideological character, the ideology of 'sati' actually *facilitates* certain forms of affiliation. Those modes of worship which exist in dispersed form and are related to structuring the lives of women and obtaining their consent to patriarchal values, have come to be concentrated in 'sati' worship. Whatever be the similarity with adjacent modes of worship (and the domestic ideologies inhering in them) the 'sati' goddess is singular, because unlike any other goddess she never transcends the violent event or narrative which gives her birth and assigns her a specific, exemplary female role. For instance, there are overlaps between worship at the new medieval 'sati' temples and Durga worship both in symbols and in rituals. However, as we have shown, the perception and meanings of this worship continue to be contextually determined, and depend on the immolation of a woman. All the villages in this area where widows have been immolated in recent decades are known as 'sati dhams' (abodes of 'sati', places of worship) — widow immolation is the fulcrum around which other meanings or connotations of 'sati' revolve. The identity of the dead woman is certainly reinforced by her affiliation to Durga but the fact that she only acquires this affiliation from having been immolated remains at the forefront of common perception. Further, socially sanctioned symbolic modes for women — shakti, motherhood, ascetcism inspired by devotion to (future) husband — cluster around Durga, simplifying if not assisting the affiliation of 'sati' to Durga. In short, of the neighbouring modes of worship that are synthesised in 'sati' worship, many are specifically grounded in the everyday maintenance of patriarchies — in a form in which many women themselves consent to their own oppression. It is this consent to 'everyday' religious forms of patriarchal legitimisation which opens the way and eases the consent to the exceptional form of such legitimisation that 'sati' represents.

Belief in 'sati' can transform everyday consent to patriarchy into a menacing form of social agency during an immolation, ranging from more or less passive forms of involvement to active perpetration. The double nature of an event of widow immolation seems on the surface to compartmentalise perpetration from belief: the actual event which is premeditated and conspiratorial seems to split off from consent and faith, which operate along diverse lines differentiated by caste, gender, closeness to and distance from event. However, the division that this seems to imply between perpetrators and colluders is, as we discussed in our account of Jhardli, difficult to maintain with any rigidity. The division inhabits much popular perception too, partly because it complements the division of a pure Hinduism from its corrupted versions, which prevails in contemporary liberal positions opposing communalism; this tends to obstruct critical examination of Hindu traditions and practices as a whole.

At the local level there are no simple demarcations between so- called participants and believers, given the fact that the event itself, after the declaration of satt, is structured by mass participation. The *active* pressure of the witnessing crowd shapes the event; indeed, the desire to witness is itself coercive. The crowd represents a closure of alternative options for the woman, it approves, supplements and finalises the machination of families, priests etc. The widow's immolation becomes a public spectacle, the property of persons of all ages and social groups. The line between perpetration and belief can be thin — perpetration itself both rests on and creates a substratum of belief. The relation between faith and coercion comes up repeatedly in the case of the family, of the witnessing crowd, or of a village.[85] The belief in miracles which is empowering for the crowd and allows them to witness the event, is a form of coercion, sanctioning their active and passive participation in an immolation. Reciprocally, coercion, both physical or ideological, plays a part in re-constituting faith. Hence it is difficult to neatly compartmentalise the faith of those who perpetrate the crime self-servingly from those who watch it done, and those who later worship.[86]

The social character of divine intervention can be seen from the nature and function of miracles. The 'primary' miracle is of a woman turning into a goddess. The 'subsidiary' miracles establish the *prerequisites* for and *authenticate* the primary miracle, and at the same time they *structure* the event around its illegality.[87] What is striking in these is the adaptability of faith — not its traditional character or purity. A criminal mystification — the self-lighting pyre — forms a substratum of popular belief. The fact that divine intervention is said to take place at the precise moment when somebody is *about to* light the pyre says something about agency and belief. Those who have participated as perpetrators and collaborators, *know* that it is a crime even if they continue to *believe* in its religious character. We know, too, from the frequent presence of armed guards at immolations, that reliance on supernatural powers is limited. It is difficult in the circumstances to make a mystique of faith or to hold as infallible a faith which supports a crime, and rests in large part on structures of belief which directly conceal the facts of the crime.

People do not simply lie or tell the truth about the event. They often see what they expect to see, since individual, narrative and institutionalised agencies authorised to interpret 'religious experience' who guide the act of seeing, already exist. In some sense, then, faith precedes sight and enters into a dialectic of expectation and re-interpretation. And yet even this powerful process cannot produce a 'final' version of the event. The ideal plot is overlaid on the real one which in fact constantly slips out at interviews — admissions of human agency compete with the intervention of divine agency. Even local perception of the widow reveals its own inconsistencies: she seems to vacillate between being human and superhuman. She is seen as a heroic woman because she can *bear* the pain of the fire as well as be believed to be immune to the pain of burning because of her satt and goddesshood. Finally, as far as the apparent split between participation and belief is concerned, structures of belief exist simultaneously with structures of use and exploitation, faith is inseparable from instrumentality.

It is worth emphasising that the idealised miracle-laden 'plot' suffers a major breakdown in the case of prevented immolations. In Devipura, where the police prevented the immolation of Jaswant

Kunwar in April 1985, verbal interviews and the commemorative booklet contain not only relatively direct admission of the agency of relatives, family and community but, most significantly, there is not a single miracle. The help of Jaswant's sister-in-law and other persons is acknowledged. Even the crowd is represented differently. A newspaper report describes the crowd as being aggressive, angry and infuriated, and the booklet, in a departure from the norm, describes the crowd around the pyre as fearful and worshipful, and, after police intervention, as disappointed, saddened and frightened.[88] The joyful crowd then is an effect of successful immolations. Although the explicit theme of the booklet is the autonomy of religion from law, its own description of the attempted immolation is shorn of all religious markers — except the woman's devoutness. Significantly, the disappointed sons of Jaswant attributed to the police the same role that tantrics and evil dakaits were given at Jhardli: they accused the police of destroying their mother's satt.[89]

This brings us to another important mechanism of belief in widow immolaion as 'sati'. In both Jhardli and Devipura, opposition to widow immolation — whether material or ideological — is construed as threat and danger to satt. Whereas in Jhardli the so-called threat posed by tantrics and dakaits provided a reason for guarding the pyre and acted to maintain the facade of Om's volition, in Devipura, the snatching of satt by the police provides a rationale for an unsuccessful immolation that allows belief structures to remain intact. In both cases we can discern a mechanism by which forms of social opposition to widow immolation, past and present, are transformed and appropriated by or incorporated into structures of belief. This not only forecloses (for many) ideological contest, but functions to erase the *history* of these very forms of social opposition. However, the history of such opposition becomes the hidden history of structures of belief themselves insofar as they have condensed and transformed histories of earlier opposition into their own assimilative mechanisms.

As an aspect of belief, popular consent involves consent both to the supernatural and to the social values implicit in the belief. In this sense consent works through consensus as in the matter of satt. Though satt is activated by an impending immolation, it depends on a prior substantive belief that what is being witnessed is a deification, and that the viewer embodies the beneficence by watching. As we have shown, satt translates and sublimates actual social agency — of those involved in invoking satt, family, villagers, other women — into something external or beyond control. Satt is manufactured and gains consent partly because it first elides human participation, then 'benevolently' re-inducts the participants who can express the pride of participation without feeling the guilt of collusion.

Consent can also work through contradiction: satt gains consent partly because it acts as a system of *exclusion*. As a principle of selection satt also guarantees that *not* every woman will be possessed. So, by virtue of its exceptional character, it gains consent in the form of religious belief from other women. The very concept of satt is infused with domestic ideology albeit in the ironic form of exceptionalism. The exceptional character of satt works to maintain patriarchal ideology — the exceptional event is made to do ideological work in the everyday sphere. The satt that gains consent at once legitimates the patriarchal and the supernatural, and more especially, the former through the latter. Since women themselves are often invested in these patriarchal structures, as for example through the ideology of *suhaag*, social structures of voluntary and enforced consent to everyday patriarchal practices can be drawn into public consent.

There are wider social parameters to the relation between patriarchies and beliefs. Patriarchal values not only gain consent for the event, rather the need to reformulate them in part informs the modalities of both the rajput defence of their patrimony and bania assertion in the cultural realm through the expansion of 'sati' temples. One mode of reformulating patriarchies is precisely to locate them in a configuration of religious event, community history and popular belief. Then in turn patriarchal values themselves become a sanctioned mode of building a wider social consensus — one not confined to these communities — which can then play a part in the constitution of militant Hinduism through other issues.

What is the object of popular consent? It is consent for the patriarchal subjugation of women within wider ideologies of permanence and change. What is sought to be preserved is what is seen to be changing: monogamous fidelity, the woman inside the domestic role, the woman as the preserve of 'truth' and 'tradition', the arena on which to defend personal religion against the law.

The universalising definition of the pativrata is not mechanically tied to a caste or class, but to what *may* be a class consciousness shared by those who do not physically belong to it. The pativrata woman is being defined against women who work (in the Shekhawati area, women in agricultural labour), non-Hindu women (only Hindu women can be 'sati'), the popular caricature of the westernised woman (the model that urban banias have to contend with), women in marriage arrangements other than monogamy (most likely to belong to lower caste groups), widows who may seek remarriage, divorced and unmarried women, educated women who may seek employment, urban feminists, and any women who challenge their given role. It is to these women and the complex, changing forces which they appear to embody that the consent to widow immolation, together with attendant ideologies and beliefs, is addressed. Clearly this address goes beyond any single social group or class though it may originate in them. The domestic jurisdiction of pativrata dharma enlarges into a powerful patriarchal discourse which performs a range of functions in the public domain which are not restricted to either women or widow immolation. It is discourse that marks within itself both contestation and the changes to which it is addressed. As far as women are concerned it is a discourse which challenges the notion of the woman as a citizen, i.e., in the consciousness of democratic rights and individual abilities, in the right to choice, and in the right to an identity not governed by religious denomination.

The internalisation of ideologies and beliefs produced by the event is thus related to a wider social process and not confined to the narrower stakes in the practice of widow immolation or to the patriarchies of the specific groups involved. However, once internalised, these ideologies and beliefs become a part of the objective forces and structures which can produce further widow immolations or carry over into other forms of violence against women. For these reasons we need to explore the wide range of relationships between patriarchies, the systemic violence which inheres in them, the consent they need to generate and contemporary processes of social change.

## Notes

[1]  Stray cases of widow immolation have occurred in Uttar Pradesh, Madhya Pradesh and Maharashtra, but the largest number have taken place in

Rajasthan — no less than 28 of an estimated total of 40 in the past four decades.

The primary material on widow immolation in this area was collected in investigative visits to Rajasthan between March 1981 and October 1988. For earlier essays based on fieldwork see K. Sangari and S. Vaid, "Sati in Modern India: A Report", *Economic and Political Weekly*, 16:31 (1 August 1981), pp. 1284-88; Sangari and Vaid, "The Politics of Widow Immolation", *Imprint* (October 1987), pp.27-31; and Sudesh Vaid, "Politics of Widow Immolation", *Seminar*, no.342 (February 1988), pp. 20-23. An earlier version of the present essay appeared in *Economic and Political Weekly* 26:17 (27 April 1991).

2   According to colonial records, Shekhawati was the largest *nizamat* (an administrative district) covering 4,200 square miles, bounded by the Rathor states of Bikaner and Jodhpur, and by Patiala, Loharu and Jaipur (*The Imperial Gazetteer of India* (Oxford: Clarendon, 1908, vol.22, pp.268-70).

3   Sutherland to H.H.Greathead, 18 August 1846, RAO, f.43, Gen 11 1846, National Archives of India (hereafter NAI); Ludlow to Sutherland, ibid., NAI. See also R.K. Saxsena, *Social Reform: Infanticide and Sati* (Delhi: Trimurti, 1975), pp.127-31 and V.N. Dutta, *Sati: Widow Burning in India* (Delhi: Manohar, 1988).

4   In this region the Ahir and Gujjar castes are cultivators.

5   This ceremony involves taking a bride to her husband's house, where she takes residence for the first time, and the marriage is consummated, and may take place several years after the wedding ceremony.

6   *Tantras* are teaching occult rituals for the worship of deities to gain superhuman power. Tantrics are followers of the tantra, an anti-brahminical, shakti worshipping religious sect who have at times opposed widow immolation. In Jhardli, the ashes were believed literally to *contain* the satt which had earlier possessed the women; and since the ashes had the ability to *confer* their power, they were guarded to ensure that no tantric could steal or misuse them. We were also told that the living 'sati' of Jodhpur could not become a 'sati' because a sunar (person from a lower artisan caste) robbed her of her satt by throwing a blue veil over her. This colour was said to have 'Muslim' associations in the district.

7   A chundri is a length of tie-and-dye cloth used to cover the head on festive occasions and in marriage rituals, and is never worn by a widow.

8   A businessman donated 30,000 rupees towards the dharamshala and another built a well costing 40,000 rupees.

9   A rajput widow customarily leaves mehndi hand prints on a wall of the house prior to immolation.

10   A dharmapita or 'godfather' is adopted for brides, in certain exigencies, from the village of her husband's family. He performs ritual functions in lieu of her own father.

11   A minor cannot be prosecuted for abetment to murder under present criminal law.

12   Samskara is literally, that which purifies; here it refers to the history of conduct and the formative influences which mould a person in this life as well as previous lives.

13   A panchayat here is a statutory village council under the Rajasthan Panchayat

Act but it can also refer to non-official, caste or community-based councils.

[14] A jauhar was a mass immolation of women, sometimes along with male servitors, in the context of imminent defeat in battle.

[15] The term Hindupat means committed to Hindu ideals and faith and itself reflects a retrospective hinduisation of medieval rajput history.

[16] Kunwar Narayan Singh, *Mahasati Om Kunwar, Jhardli, Sikar*, intro. Raghubir Singh Rathor (Jhardli: Mahasati Om Kunwar Trust, n.d); Surendratt Diwakar, *Mahasati Om Kunwar Ma Bhajanmala*, intro. Jamnalal Shastri, 3rd edition (Jhardli: Shri Satimata Samiti Trust, 1982).

[17] See *Trial by Fire: A Report on Roop Kanwar's Death* by the Women and Media Committee, Bombay Union of Journalists (Bombay: Bombay Union of Journalists, 1987).

[18] And also by the Shankaracharya of Puri who was not present but who claimed in an interview that Roop's father-in-law was trying to save her by holding her back but "there was a lightning effect from her body and he was thrown back." (*Sunday Observer* 20 September 1987).

[19] Roop's dowry is reported to have consisted of 25-40 *tolas* of gold, fixed deposits worth 30,000 rupees, a television, a radio, fans, a refrigerator and some furniture. Her father donated one lakh rupees to her temple in Deorala, and the expensive chundri ceremony was performed by her Jaipur-based brother.

[20] Among the politicians who vociferously supported the right to worship and glorify the immolation in Deorala were: Kalyan Singh Kalvi (State Janata Party President), Om Prakash Gupta (Bharatiya Janata Party), Hukum Singh (BJP), Jai Singh (Lok Dal) and Chan Singh Pradhan (Lok Dal).

[21] As in the case of earlier immolations in the region, the Deorala committee was instantly assured financial support by an official representative of an industrial group (*Times of India*, 17 September 1987).

[22] See K.L. Qanungo, *Studies in Rajput History* (Delhi: S. Chand, 1969).

[23] See for example, Romesh C. Dutt, *Pratap Singh: The Last of the Rajputs: A Tale of Rajput Courage and Chivalry* (Allahabad: Kitabistan, 1943).

[24] A jagir was a territorial assignment for land revenue purposes, and grantees had to provide military and other feudal services; jagirs were also granted in recognition for administrative service, and granted without military and tax obligations for charitable and religious purposes. A jagirdar is the holder of a jagir while the jagirdari system refers to the system instituted during the Mughal period under which such assignments were made.

[25] Memorandum submitted to the Rajasthan-Madhya Bharat Jagir Committee by the Special Organisation of Rajasthan and Madhya Bharat Jagirdars (18 November, 1949, Jaipur). See also *Report of the Rajasthan Madhya Bharat Jagir Enquiry Committee* (Delhi: Govt. of India, 1949); *Report on Rajasthan Jagirdari Abolition* (Jaipur: Govt. of Rajasthan, 1953); Deol Singh, *Land Reforms in Rajasthan: A Report of a Survey* (Delhi: Govt. of India, 1964).

[26] See Ayuwan Singh, *Rajput aur Bhavishya*, 2nd edition, (Jaipur: Ayuwan Singh Smriti Sansthan, 1981).

[27] A bhumia is a landholder under the *bhumichara* tenure system; bhumias claim that land held under this system was, unlike the jagir, personal heredi-

## Institutions, Beliefs, Ideologies    293

tary property. For a history of bhumias and jagirdars see Dilbagh Singh, *The State, Landlords and Peasants: Rajasthan in the 18th Century* (Delhi: Manohar, 1990), pp. 42-50, 144-57.

[28]   K.L.Kamal, *Party Politics in an Indian State* (Delhi: S. Chand, n.d.), pp. 76-79.

[29]   Suzanne Rudolph and Lloyd Rudolph, *Essays on Rajputana: Reflections on History, Culture and Administration* (Delhi: Concept, 1984) pp. 60-61. A lathi is a wooden staff; dharma refers to a combination of duty, righteousness, faith and religion.

[30]   See Singh, *Rajput our Bhavishya.*

[31]   Ibid.

[32]   Ibid.

[33]   The richer Rajputs now also have business interests and a public school education. For instance, the convenor of the SDRS, Narendra Singh Rajawat, is in the leather export business.

[34]   "Hinduon Se Apeel", a pamphlet attributed to the SDRS and written to mobilise Hindus in 'traditional attire' for the 8 October 1987 pro-'sati' rally in Jaipur; transcript of speeches made at the same event. In these speeches the RSS, BJP and Vishwa Hindu Parishad were upheld as political organisations symphathetic to their cause.

[35]   The speakers included representatives of other communities — meena, gujjar, dholi, kayasth and brahmin as well as a token Muslim. Some were representatives of organisations like Akhil Bharatiya Hindu Mahasabha, Akhil Bharatiya Gujjar Mahasabha, Chittor Jauhar Samiti, Bharatvarshiya Dharma Sangha, and the Math of the Shankaracharya of Puri.

[36]   *Hindustan,* 26 September 1987. Devi Singh Mandawa, a member of the Rajput Sabha, active in organising pro-'sati' rallies, the author of a history of the rise of Shekhawati power, takes pride in the land reform agitations of the Bhuswami Sangh.

[37]   D.K.Taknet, *Industrial Entrepreneurship of Shekhawati Marwaris,* (Jaipur: Taknet, 1986), p.103. Apart from heading large industrial houses, migrants from Shekhawati have developed numerous smaller-sized businessess and firms. By 1940, 156 firms belonged to Agarwals from this region alone (pp. 179-211).

[38]   Taknet, *Entrepreneurship,* pp. 36-37; Thomas Timberg, *Marwaris: From Traders to Industrialists* (Delhi: Vikas, 1978), pp. 111-12.

[39]   By 1900, 280 out of the 444 family firms from Shekhawati were located in Calcutta (Timberg, *Marwaris,* pp. 116-17).

[40]   See Francis Wacziarg's and Aman Nath's introduction to their *Rajasthan: The Walls of Shekhawati* (Delhi: Vikas, 1982).

[41]   In 1986 a new section to the temple and a 51 kilogram gold *kalash* (cupola) were added, and by 1988 it had acquired more land.

[42]   Ramdev Sharma, *Shri Rani Sati Mangal (Byavala)* (Jhunjhunu: Satyanarayan Goenka, 15 August 1986); Ramakant Sharma, *Shri Narayani Charitmanas* (Varanasi: Nand Kishore Jhunjhunwala, n.d. [sold in the Delhi Rani Sati temple, 1987], hereafter referred to as *Narayani Charitmanas (1).*

[43]   *Mangal; Narayani Charitmanas (1).*

[44]   Ibid.

[45] Ibid.

[46] *Shri Rani Sati Charitamrit: Pramanit Jivan Charitra evam Stutian* (Jhunjhunu: Shri Rani Sati Mandir, n.d. [sold 1988]).

[47] *Charitamrit; Amar Virangana Shri Rani Sati Ji* (Jhunjhunu: Rani Sati Mandir, n.d. [sold 1988]).

[48] Verse narrative in Gopigram Joshi, *Shri Rani Sati Ji Chalisa* (Jhunjhunu: Om Printers, n.d.). See also *Shri Rani Bhajan Pushpmala* (Delhi: Shri Rani Sati Sarva Sangha, n.d. [sold 1987]), and hereafter referred to as *Pushp Mala (1)*.

[49] *Charitamrit.*

[50] *Shri Rani Sati Mandir, Varshil Karya Vivran,* 1983-84. Pativrata dharma is the code of obligations for a devoted wife.

[51] *Shree Rani Sati Bhajan Pushpmala* (Delhi:1985), distributed by the Rani Sati temple at Jogibara, Delhi and hereafter referred to as *Pushpmala (2); Shri Rani Sati Charit Manas: Pramanit Jivan Charitra evam Stutian* (Jhunjhunu: Shri Rani Satiji Mandir, n.d. [sold 1988]); Ramakant Sharma, *Shree Narayani Charit Manas* (Bombay: Shri Rani Sati Ji Mandal: 15 August 1986), hereafter referred to as *Narayani Charitmanas (2);* Vijay Laxmi Aggarwal, "Jhunjhunu Mela", *Kulpali* (Delhi: 1984), pp. 11-13; *Charitamrit; Chalisa.*

[52] Kailash Jatia, "Shree Rani Sati Ji is Our Ancestor. We Worship Her as Our Family Goddess". This pamphlet was distributed at a public meeting organised in Delhi on 6 March 1988 by *Kulpali,* a weekly magazine brought out by the Rani Sati temple in Jogibara, Delhi, which is an organ of the Delhi and Jhunjhunu trusts.

[53] *Narayani Charitmanas (2).*

[54] *Pushpmala (2).*

[55] The chakra here carries the resonance of the disc, a weapon of Vishnu and his incarnations.

[56] *Mangal; Amar Virangana; Charitamrit; Chalisa; Pushpmala (1).*

[57] Mahatma Ram Chander Vir, *Sati Parampara ki Jvalant Jyoti Shikhayen* (Virat Nagar, Rajasthan: Panchkhand Peeth, 1986) with an Introduction by Acharya Shri Dharmendra. Distributed at the meeting called by *Kulpali* in 1988.

[58] For a discussion of the overlaps between the virangana, Durga and the "truthful, just" woman capable of self-sacrifice in other North Indian narrative traditions see Kathryn Hansen, "The Virangana in North Indian History", *Economic and Political Weekly* vol 23, no 18 (30 April 1988), pp. WS 28-29.

[59] *Mangal ; Amar Virangana.*

[60] *Narayani Charitmanas (1).*

[61] Verse narrative in *Chalisa.*

[62] *Charitamrit.*

[63] *Narayani Charitmanas (1).*

[64] *Chalisa ; Charitamrit.*

[65] In this context it is significant that *Amar Virangana* carried a picture of a map of India that shows a goddess carrying a trishul in the centre, and also that recently a section of the Marwari community has been actively supporting the Vishwa Hindu Parishad.

[66] Some Aggarwals set up a reception pandal (tent) for Rajputs in Deorala, defying the ban on the chundri ceremony (*Indian Express,* 11 September 1987). The treasurer of the Jhardli temple belongs to this community.

67 One of these was in Hathideh, adjoining Jhardli, and the immolation of two of these women was prevented. When one of the women whose immolation was prevented at Depolia, Chirana, was brought to the Jhunjhunu police station by the police, she reportedly said that she too wanted the glory of Rani Sati.

68 Dharmendra Ji Maharaj, *Hinduon ki Divya Sati Parampara evam Vartman Sandarbh*, distributed at a meeting called by *Kulpali* in Delhi on 6 March 1988, (Calcutta: Aitihasik Mandir Bachao Committee, n.d.).

69 *Times of India*, 10 September 1989. At the time this revised essay goes to press, Babri Masjid has been destroyed by the combined action of the BJP, VHP and RSS, leading to widespread violence mostly against Muslims in the country.

70 *Times of India*, 12 November 1987.

71 *Indian Express*, 30 August 1989.

72 *Rajasthan Patrika* 20 September 1987; SDRS pamphlet and transcript of speeches, ibid., and as reported in *Indian Express*, 30 September 1987; *Rashtradoot* 6 September 1987; Ashis Nandy, "The Sociology of Sati", *Indian Express* 5 October 1987; Om Prakash Gupta (BJP) in *Trial by Fire*. For an earlier analysis of some of these tendencies see Kumkum Sangari, "Perpetuating the Myth", *Seminar* no. 342 (February 1988).

73 SDRS pamphlet and speeches; Nandy, "The Sociology of Sati"; Banwari, "Nar-nari Sambandh", *Jansatta*, 29 September to 1 October 1987.

74 Speeches at a meeting organised by the Aitihasik Mandir Bachao Committee in Delhi, 1989; Ashis Nandy, "The Human Factor", *The Illustrated Weekly of India*, 17 January 1988,pp. 20-23.

75 This position is to be found in the publications of the Rani Sati Sarva Sangha, the speeches of the Aitihasik Mandir Bachao Committee, the *Kulpali* editorial (1987), and the pamphlet entitled *Kulpali Saptahik dwara 6 March 1988 FICCI Sabhaghar mein ek 'Sati Nivaran Vidheyak Sambhavnae' Vishay par Ayojit Summelan mein Vicharniya Mudde*.

76 For example, Banwari, "Nar-nari"; Nandy, "The Human Factor".

77 Thus Nandy is reduced to locating "the authenticity of the idea behind sati" in mythological times or in "historical times read mythologically" and gives the example of medieval Rajasthan! ("The Human Factor", p.22).

78 The *contrast* between the legal defence by the Rani Sati Temple Trust in the Supreme Court, based on the claim of only worshipping shakti in the form of Durga, and the actual activities of the Rani Sati Sarva Sangha and the Aitihasik Mandir Bachao Committee, does not need reiteration.

79 SDRS pamphlets and speeches; Banwari, "Nar-nari".

80 Acharya Dharmendra, speech at Aitihasik Mandir Bachao meeting, ibid; SDRS pamphlet and speeches; Banwari, "Nar-nari"; Nandy, "The Human Factor" and "The Sociology of Sati".

81 Statement of Rajawat, SDRS convenor in *Trial by Fire*; Acharya Shri Dharmendra, "Hinduon ki Divya Sati Parampar Vir, Sati Parampara, Jvalant Jyoti Shikhayan*; Nandy, "The Sociology" and "The Human Factor".

82 Editorial, *Jansatta*, 18 September 1987; *Rajasthan Patrika*, 18 Sept. 1987. In "The Human Factor" Nandy assures his readers that the natural moral discrimination of villagers ensures that they will only worship authentic 'sati's.

[83]  Interviews with women from Rajasthan, mostly working women, reveal that
many are aware of the factors which come together in a widow immolation:
the control and oppression of women within the family; the inculcation of
certain patriarchal beliefs in women themselves; the dependent status of
widows which determines the *family's* actions; the self-interest of priests and
members of the village; and the commercialisation of religion. The women
interviewed recognise the fact that pro-'sati' attitudes are anti-women, that
religious cults can be fabricated, and show various degrees of scepticism,
though not entire disbelief, about the miraculous powers of satt. Among
lower caste men and women there was some indifference towards both the
worship and the ideology centred on widow immolation. (This is based both
on our interviews and on Kavita, Shobha, Shobhita and Sharda, "Rural
Women Speak", *Seminar,* (no.342, February 1988, pp. 40-44).

[84]  Yog is a school of philosophy emphasising rigorous control of the body to
enable concentration on transcendental reality; bhakti is a form of
unmediated, personalised worship associated with specific individuals and
movements.

[85]  The rajputs of Mawda Kalan, whom one could represent as attached to
'tradition', neither preserve nor worship the ruins of a small 'sati' memorial
adjoining the village. They have however, built a marble temple for a widow
immolated in the mid-1970s. They organise melas, go to Jhunjhunu, are
raising donations to construct a dharmashala, and came out in vociferous
support of the immolation in Deorala. Are these 'traditional' villagers?

[86]  A small Aggarwal trader admitted to lighting the pyre to burn his own mother
(Hathideh, 1977) but claimed in the next breath that there were witnesses
who stated the fire lit by itself. If this man did not have faith in some of the
empowering myths of 'sati' he could hardly have set about burning his own
mother. And if witnesses did not have some kind of 'faith' they could not
have claimed that the fire lit itself even as they watched the son light it.

[87]  These subsidiary miracles can be subdivided into five groups: the first group
establishes the eligibility of the woman. These miracles are usually banal,
such as the woman raising her arms above her head, or a woman telling her
son that his missing watch is in the pocket of his shirt. The second group
establishes more direct alibis which erase signs of participation. The third
group distances the guilt of the event — the woman appears in a dream to
the family and tells them she has suffered no pain in the fire, or it is said that
her nylon sari does not burn first but along with the woman, thus making the
fire untrue to its 'nature'. The fourth group explains why the family did not
prevent immolation — proofs of the widow's ability to curse, the fact that she
cannot be touched because her body burns with satt. The fifth group are
deterrents to police or legal action — the tyres of the police jeep puncture,
making it impossible for them to arrive in time to prevent immolation, or the
son of the police commissioner falls ill until the family is released.

[88]  *Times of India,* 7 April 1985; *Mahamahim Mahasati Jaswant Kunwar Chandrawat*
(No publisher or date, sold at the temple in Devipura in 1987).

[89]  *Times of India,* 7 April 1985.

# Notes on Contributors

**Sonia Nishat Amin** is Associate Professor in History at Dhaka University. She is involved with the women's and cultural movements in Bangladesh. A forthcoming book, *The World of Muslim Women in Colonial Bengal: 1876–1939* (E.J.Brill, Leiden and New York) discusses the emergence of the modern gentlewoman or *bhadramahila* in colonial Bengal.

**Paola Bacchetta** holds a DEA (MPhil) from the IEDES in Sociology, a Maitrise (MA) in Political Science and Law, a Licence in Political Science and Law, and a BA in International Relations. She has published widely in France and the USA on racism and sexism and on French feminism. At present, she teaches Sociology at Sarah Lawrence College, New York.

**Jasodhara Bagchi** is Professor of English and Director of Women's Studies, Jadavpur University. An activist in the Indian Women's Movement, she has edited *Indian Women: Myth and Reality* (1995).

**Kamla Bhasin** has been active in the area of women and development for the last twenty years. She has written extensively on participatory training in development; on women; on sustainable development; and is the author of numerous activist songs and non-sexist books for children. She is co-editor of *Against All Odds: Essays on Women, Religion and Development from India and Pakistan* (Isis International, Manila and Kali for Women, Delhi: 1994).

**Uma Chakravarti** teaches History at Miranda House College for Women, University of Delhi. She is the author of *The Social Dimensions of Early Buddhism* (1987) and has co-authored *The Delhi Riots: Three Days in the Life of a Nation* (1987). She is currently editing a collection of writings by Pandita Ramabai.

**Malathi de Alwis** is presently a doctoral candidate in the Department of Anthropology at the University of Chicago. Her commitment to feminist politics both in Sri Lanka and the USA has led her to research and write on issues of mobilisation and agency in the context of nationalism and militarism.

**Neloufer de Mel** teaches English at the University of Colombo, Sri Lanka. She wrote her doctoral dissertation at the University of Kent, Canterbury, on the plays of Wole Soyinka and Derek Walcott, and has written on nationalism and the Sinhala theatre, Sri Lankan drama in English and women's writing. She is editor of *Options*, a quarterly on Sri Lankan women's issues.

**Kumari Jayawardena** was Associate Professor in Political Science at the University of Colombo, Sri Lanka. At present she is involved in a Gender History project at the Social Scientists' Association while teaching in the Women's Studies Programme at University of Colombo. She is author of *Feminism and Nationalism in the Third World* (Zed Books) and *The White Woman's Other Burden* (Routledge).

**Kalpana Kannabiran** is a feminist, sociologist and activist. She was an active member of the Stree Shakti Sanghatana, Hyderabad, 1979–85. She has co-edited, in Telegu, a book-length report on the Anti-Liquor Struggle in Andhra Pradesh, as well as a volume of essays on feminist politics. She is currently with Asmita Resource Centre for Women, Hyderabad.

**Ritu Menon** is co-founder of Kali for Women (Delhi). She has written and published widely on women and media, women and violence and women and fundamentalism, and is working with Kamla Bhasin on an oral history of women's experiences of the Partition of India. They have both co-edited *Against All Odds: Essays on Women, Religion and Development from India and Pakistan* (Isis International, Manila and Kali for Women, Delhi: 1994).

**Shahnaz Rouse** is Professor of Sociology at Sarah Lawrence College, New York. She has written and published widely on women, the State and fundamentalism in' Islamic societies and is currently working on Muslim women's writings in Egypt, Pakistan and India.

**Kumkum Sangari** teaches at Delhi University and is active in the Women's and democratic rights movements. She has written and published widely on a range of subjects and is the author of *Politics of the Possible: Literature, Gender History* (forthcoming).

**Sudesh Vaid** teaches literature at Indraprastha College for Women, University of Delhi. She has co-edited a collection of essays entitled *Women and Culture* (Bombay: 1985), and one entitled *Recasting Women: Essays in Colonial History* (Kali for Women, Delhi: 1989). She is active in women's and civil liberties movements in India, as well as in the PUDR.